CREATING MENTAL ILLNESS

D0817225

CREATING MENTAL ILLNESS

Allan V. Horwitz

THE UNIVERSITY OF CHICAGO PRESS
CHICAGO AND LONDON

The University of Chicago Press, Chicago 60637
The University of Chicago Press, Ltd., London
© 2002 by The University of Chicago
Paperback edition 2003
All rights reserved. Published 2002.
Printed in the United States of America

20 19 18 17 16 15 14 13 12 11   6 7 8 9 10

ISBN-13: 978-0-226-35381-4 (cloth)
ISBN-10: 0-226-35381-8 (cloth)
ISBN-13: 978-0-226-35382-1 (paper)
ISBN-10: 0-226-35382-6 (paper)

Library of Congress Cataloging-in-Publication
Data
Horwitz, Allan V.
    Creating mental illness / Allan V. Horwitz.
        p.   cm.
    Includes bibliographical references (p.) and
                                                index.
    ISBN 0-226-35381-8 (cloth : alk.paper)
    1. Psychiatry—Philosophy. 2. Psychiatry—
History—20th century. 3. Deviant behavior—
                        Labeling theory. I. Title.
RC437.5 .H674 2002
616.89′001—dc21   2001027897

For my daughters—Becky, Jessica, and Stephanie

Contents

Preface

Although I did not realize it at the time, the idea for this book came to me more than twenty-five years ago, when I was doing the research for my dissertation about patterns of help-seeking among people who sought outpatient psychiatric treatment at a community mental health center. My interviews with them, as well as their official records, documented numerous problems that included social isolation, extramarital affairs, marital dissolutions, financial difficulties, drinking problems, and persistent interpersonal conflicts with spouses, children, and parents. Regardless of whether their social difficulties led to their psychological problems or their mental conditions were responsible for their life circumstances, these people had serious problems with their lives. In retrospect, what seems remarkable about these data is the insignificant role psychiatric diagnoses played in characterizing the kinds of difficulties this group faced. Indeed, many charts recorded no diagnosis at all and those that did usually mentioned a diagnosis only in passing.

From the vantage point of the early 1970s, it was impossible to predict that the general disturbances of living that troubled these outpatients would soon metamorphose into the specific psychiatric diseases that afflict the clients of mental health professionals today. In the contemporary mental health professions, the search for the correct diagnosis—panic disorder, major depression, social phobia, generalized anxiety disorder, somatization, various personality disorders, and the like—is of paramount concern. Likewise, community studies of psychological disturbance have gone from emphasizing very general and diffuse conditions to focusing on discrete diagnoses that parallel the disease entities of the mental health professions. Within a brief period, both the conditions of the clients of mental health professionals and the subject matter of the disciplines concerned with studying mental health and illness had changed almost beyond recognition. Presentations of mental illnesses in newspapers, magazines, television, radio, and film also have come to emphasize not only that people suffer from distinct mental disorders but also that science has "proven" that their conditions are real diseases.

I became interested in understanding how general psychological problems that had been closely connected with social situations were transformed into disease conditions. My search led me to study the history behind this transformation, the internal developments within psychiatry that generated it, and the broader changes in the social and economic environment that sustained it. I found that neither conventional accounts of the psychiatric profession nor sociological accounts grounded in labeling theory, which emphasized scientific advances in knowledge or the oppressive practices of mental health professionals, respectively, could adequately explain this cognitive revolution. Psychiatric accounts seemed insufficient because the "diseases" they took for granted seemed to be social constructions that emerged in a particular historical era rather than characterizations of a natural underlying state. However, labeling theory also seemed inadequate because clients, mental health professionals, and the culture at large seemed to participate in a shared culture that believed in the reality of these mental diseases. Although I became far more of a social constructionist than I ever anticipated during the writing of this book, I have also tried to sustain the position that there is a natural reality behind mental disorders that social explanations must take into account.

This book is a product of the auspicious environment in which it was written. The Institute of Health, Health Care Policy, and Aging Research at Rutgers University, directed by the remarkable David Mechanic, has been an exceptional place in which to work. David himself has not only provided me time and resources for writing this book but also has served as a mentor, friend, and model of scholarship. In addition, he read an earlier draft of the entire manuscript and responded with his usual generosity, insight, and tolerance for diverse points of view. The Institute encompasses an extraordinary interdisciplinary group of scholars in the mental health field, all of whom have had major influences on my research. In particular, Gerry Grob has taught me how to view mental illness through a historical lens, and Jerry Wakefield has provided a philosophically informed conception. My fellow sociologists and friends, Ellen Idler and Sarah Rosenfield, have also made essential contributions to my work, as have the anthropologist Peter Guarnaccia and the psychologist Jamie Walkup. Each made perceptive suggestions about earlier drafts of particular chapters of the book and, I am sure, would make numerous additional suggestions in the final manuscript.

Over the past twenty years I have also been fortunate to co-direct with David Mechanic the NIMH-sponsored Rutgers Postdoctoral Program in Mental Health Systems Research. The seminar associated with this program has brought to Rutgers many of the best scholars in the mental health field, whose research has considerably influenced the arguments in this book. They include, among many others, Joan Brumberg, Peter Conrad, Stanley Jackson, Stuart Kirk, Arthur Kleinman, Bruce Link, Elizabeth Lunbeck, Mark Micale, Leonard Pearlin, Thomas Scheff, Sharon Schwartz, and Edward Shorter. None, of course, are responsible for the uses to which I have put their work.

Another source of inspiration for this book stems from the Culture and Cognition group in the Rutgers Department of Sociology. The brilliant Eviatar Zerubavel and the other faculty and graduate students associated with this group have substantially shaped my thinking about the sociology of mental illness in recent years.

A number of people connected with the University of Chicago Press also made invaluable contributions in bringing this book to fruition. I am grateful to my editor, Doug Mitchell, and to his assistant, Robert Devens, for their assistance at every stage of bringing this book to publication and to Evan Young for his exceptional editing. Two anonymous reviewers also made many excellent suggestions that have greatly strengthened the manuscript.

Finally, my daughters, to whom this book is dedicated, have made the whole enterprise worthwhile.

Introduction

THE PROLIFERATION OF MENTAL ILLNESSES

[handwritten margin note: psychwent through a revolution]

Every society, regardless of time or place, has considered some of its members to be mentally ill. For most of human history, mental illness was identified with madness and labels of mental illness were reserved for extreme states of bizarre, inappropriate, and withdrawn behavior.[1] When specialized asylums arose to treat the mentally ill at the end of the seventeenth century in Europe and the beginning of the nineteenth century in the United States, they managed a small number of very serious mental conditions.[2] The leading psychiatric classifier of the late nineteenth century, Emil Kraepelin, formalized only two major diagnostic categories: dementia praecox, which we know as schizophrenia; and depression, including bipolar disorder (Kraepelin 1896). Historically, labels of mental illness were reserved for people whose behavior was extremely strange, incomprehensible, and disruptive.

At the turn of the nineteenth century, Sigmund Freud revolutionized thinking about the nature of mental illness. Freud's theory of psychoanalysis, and the more general system of dynamic psychiatry that stemmed from it, expanded the field to take in a broad range of neurotic conditions rather than the small number of psychotic conditions that asylum psychiatry emphasized.[3] Dynamic psychiatry found common sources for both neurotic and normal traits in the persisting unconscious influences of repressed childhood emotions and experiences. This blurred the boundary between ordinary and pathological conditions, greatly expanding the range of behaviors the mental health professions might treat.

In contrast to asylum psychiatrists, who tended to identify and treat distinct conditions such as schizophrenia and bipolar disorder, dynamic practitioners paid little attention to particular diagnoses. Dynamic theories posited that neuroses were continuous with normal behavior, not categorical illnesses distinct from normality. For these practitioners, overt symptoms were chameleon-like disguises for a few fundamental underlying causal mechanisms. Their focus was not on manifest symptoms but instead on the deep intrapsychic causes of a broad range of problematic conditions. Because of the fuzzy boundary between normality and pathology, dynamic psychiatry came to treat a wide variety of neuroses and problems in living.[4]

The publication of the *Diagnostic and Statistical Manual* (DSM-III) in 1980 marked a second revolution in thinking about mental illness. The promulgators of the DSM-III overthrew the broad, continuous, and vague concepts of dynamic psychiatry and reclaimed the categorical illnesses of asylum psychiatry.[5] They imported a medicalized framework organized around specific disease entities to formulate the basic nature, causes, and treatment of disturbed behaviors.[6] The fundamental premise of the DSM-III was that different clusters of symptoms indicated distinct underlying diseases such as schizophrenia, depression, panic disorder, or substance abuse.[7] I call the model of mental illness developed in the DSM-III "diagnostic psychiatry" because all of the major functions of the mental health professions—formulating the causes of, treatments for, and policies about mental illness—follow from the classification of mental illnesses into discrete diagnostic entities.

Diagnostic psychiatry claims to inherit the legacy of asylum psychiatry, but there is a crucial difference between the two. Asylum psychiatry considered only psychotic disorders, particularly schizophrenia, bipolar, and other psychoses, as distinct mental diseases. Diagnostic psychiatry, in contrast, encompasses a huge and diverse number of behavioral and psychological conditions. Indeed, although diagnostic psychiatry repudiates thoroughly the dynamic system it replaced, the range of conditions that it classifies actually have far more in common with the subject matter of dynamic psychiatry than with that of asylum psychiatry. Diagnostic psychiatry reclassified as specific diseases the huge realm of human behavior that dynamic psychiatry had already successfully defined as pathological.

The most recent version of the DSM, the DSM-IV (scheduled to become the DSM-V in 2002), now classifies nearly four hundred distinct mental disorders. It includes conditions such as schizophrenia that have universally been considered to be mental diseases. Because it uses symptoms to classify disorders, it also categorizes an enormous diversity of human emotions, conduct, and relationships as distinct pathological entities. The hundreds of diagnostic categories of the DSM are a heterogeneous collection that include, among many others, people who hallucinate, become distressed after the failure of a romantic relationship, drink too much, eat too little, or behave badly in classrooms.[8] For example, major depressions encompass unhappiness and clinical depression alike; generalized anxiety disorders include the fearful as well as people who have crippling anxieties; social phobias afflict both the shy and those who cannot function because of their fears. People with sexual problems with their partners have sexual dysfunctional disorders. Children and, increasingly, adults who have trouble keeping their minds on things have attention deficit disorders.[9]

Not only do these conditions cover a wide variety of behaviors; they also presumably afflict huge numbers of people. About a fifth of the population of the United States are seen as suffering from a mental disorder each year and about half from at least one disorder at some point in their lives.[10] The Surgeon General's Report on Mental Health, for example, states that fifty million Americans develop mental disorders each year (USDHHS 1999).

The classification of symptoms into discrete disease entities is perhaps the most essential component of diagnostic psychiatry because precise diagnostic schemes presumably distinguish particular conditions from one another in ways that matter for their etiology, prognosis, and treatment. Although diagnostic psychiatry is officially agnostic about the variety of factors that lead people to develop mental diseases, the medicalized system of classification it uses emphasizes underlying organic pathologies (see Andreasen 1984; Guze 1989; Kandel 1998). Biological models seek the primary causes of mental diseases in genetic and biochemical factors and so locate the pathological qualities of psychological conditions in the physical properties of brains, not in the symbolic systems of minds. In particular, many types of mental disorders are claimed to stem from chemical imbalances that drug treatments can restore to normal levels. Although many mental health professionals continue to locate the origins of psychological problems in disturbed childhood relationships with parents, the study of the biological foundations of discrete mental disorders has gained unquestioned primacy in the profession of psychiatry.[11]

Another aspect of the medicalized model of mental illness in the DSM lies in how these disorders can best be treated. Because mental illnesses are seen as diseases, sufferers are encouraged to seek help from professional specialists.[12] Psychiatrists and other mental health professionals are the socially recognized experts in classifying and treating these disorders. Some of these specialists employ an array of psychotherapies to understand how symptoms reflect the biographies of their clients. More commonly, however, the assumption of diagnostic psychiatry that mental illnesses stem from disorders of the brain leads to a search for ways of changing neuro-chemistry. The use of various psychopharmacological agents now dominates the psychiatric profession (Luhrmann 2000).

Treatments for mental illnesses are no longer directed at a small number of seriously ill persons. Instead, they are aimed at the many millions of people who presumably have some mental disorder. In the quarter-century between 1970 and 1995, the number of mental health professionals quadrupled (see Center for Mental Health Services 1996, 1998). Each year about 15 percent of the adult population of the United States seeks some type of professional treatment for mental health or addiction problems (Regier et al. 1993). Pervasive educational and advertising campaigns urge those sufferers who are not yet in treatment to recognize that they have genuine disorders that should be relieved through medication and therapy.[13] Pharmaceutical companies, as well as mental health professionals, have seen an explosive increase in demand for their products. In the decade between 1985 and 1994 alone, the number of prescriptions for psychotropic medications soared from about 33 million to about 46 million.[14] The brand names of medications such as Prozac have become as generic as "kleenex" or "xerox"; three of the seven most prescribed drugs of any sort are antidepressants.[15]

A broad range of mental health professionals now treat mental illnesses not only in specialized practices but also in many social institutions including schools, courts, and corporations.[16] Media portrayals too frame an extensive variety of psychological problems, not just a small number of serious conditions, as discrete disorders. On television and in print both famous and ordinary people discuss their experiences with depression, recovered memory syndrome, anorexia and bulimia, and substance use disorders, among many others. The culture of mental health that not so long ago was the province of a relatively small group of intellectuals and bohemians is now the everyday reality of daytime talk shows, television series, popular magazines for girls and women (and sometimes men), and virtually all advice columnists.

A huge cultural transformation in the construction of mental illness has occurred in a relatively short time. The broad array of mental illnesses at the beginning of the twenty-first century has little resemblance to older stereotypes of madness that persisted throughout most of human history. Categorical classifications of distinct mental illnesses are far more extensive and more diverse than those found in asylum psychiatry. Neither do the discrete, categorical diseases that are firmly embedded in discourse about mental illness share many similarities with the broad neurotic conditions based on unconscious mechanisms that dynamic psychiatry emphasized for most of the twentieth century. The extensive use of disease categories for a wide variety of human behaviors is unique in human history; most of the many mental illnesses that are now taken for granted as objective natural entities are recent creations.] → Categorization became social constructions

MENTAL ILLNESSES AS DISEASES

The proliferation of mental illnesses illustrates the spread of a medicalized disease framework to encompass many sorts of problematic psychological conditions (Conrad and Schneider 1992). Psychiatric researchers and clinicians, as well as much of the public, now view mental illnesses as biomedical diseases of the brain that are comparable to other physical illnesses. Because the brain is viewed as part of the physical world it is seen as subject to laws of cause and effect rather than to cultural frameworks of motives, actions, meanings, and responsibilities that are applied to social objects. The symptoms of brain-based diseases can be abstracted from their individual and social contexts and studied as things that have distinct causes, courses, and responses.

The psychiatric profession does not view the disease categories in the DSM as one possible way of viewing mental illnesses. Instead, mental health professionals regard the diseases defined in the DSM as natural entities, not arbitrary constructions (see, for example, Clinton and Hyman 1999; Leshner 1999; USDHHS 1999). Diseases presumably exist in nature, regardless of the social meanings attached to them. For example, cancers are cells that grow uncontrollably, hyperthyroidism stems from an overactive thyroid gland, and asthmatic conditions reflect narrowed air passages. The fact that different social groups might define these conditions in various ways is irrelevant: regardless of time and place, the essential nature of a disease is the same wherever it arises. Likewise, the disordered thought processes that mark schizophrenia, the mood swings that are signs of bipolar disorders, or the crippling compulsions in obsessive-compulsive disorders are indicators of underlying natural mental diseases. The disease categories of the DSM are not just one particular way of viewing mental illness among other possibilities; instead they are lenses that reflect the assumed objective reality of these conditions.

For its advocates, the model of mental illness in diagnostic psychiatry is not just different from, but better than the earlier dynamic model because the scientific methods it employs are equated with objectivity, truth, and reason (see, for example, Kendler 1990; Sabshin 1990; Kandel 1999). Because the mental illnesses the DSM classifies are seen as physical entities, they can be precisely measured, quantified, and compared across individuals. Just as the natural sciences produce ever greater knowledge of the material world over time, the conceptualization of mental illnesses as disease entities is perceived to lead to cumulative understanding of them. The disease entities of diagnostic psychiatry represent progress over the discredited unconscious mechanisms of dynamic psychiatry they replaced. Indeed, psychoanalysis is now likely to be seen as a temporary hiatus in the constant progress psychiatry has made since the last century in understanding abnormal behavior.[17] Diagnostic psychiatry has transformed psychiatry from an ideological to a scientific discipline (Sabshin 1990; Leshner 1999).

The disease model of mental illness entails moral claims as well as ways of classifying and studying these phenomena. If mental illnesses are diseases, then mentally ill people should be treated in certain ways. People who suffer from the diseases of schizophrenia, depression, substance abuse, or any other disorder in the DSM ought to be helped, not stigmatized or punished. The view of mental illness as a disease presumably leads not only to growing scientific knowledge but also to a more enlightened view of how mentally ill people ought to be treated.

MENTAL ILLNESSES AS SOCIAL CONSTRUCTIONS

In contrast to the disease model, the social constructionist view sees systems of knowledge as reflections of culturally specific processes.[18] The central assumption of the constructionist tradition is that mental illnesses are inseparable from the cultural models that define them as such. Social constructionist studies assume that taken-for-granted categorizations do not simply reproduce the natural reality of mental symptoms; they are socially contingent systems that develop and change with social circumstances.[19]

For constructionists, mental illnesses do not arise in nature but are constituted by social systems of meaning. The defining characteristics of mental illnesses reside in the cultural rules that define what is normal or abnormal. Terms such as "inappropriate," "dysfunctional," "irrational," or "unreasonable" that are used to define various mental illnesses do not refer to aspects of natural entities themselves, but are cultural definitions placed on behaviors that in other times and places may seem normal, functional, rational, and reasonable. Depending on the cultural and historical setting, symptoms now regarded as mental illnesses have in the past been regarded as signs of religious afflictions, sins, or lack of self-control, among many other possibilities.

The view of mental illnesses as social constructions has a long history in sociology. The origins of this view are found in Durkheim's *The Rules of Sociological Method* (Durkheim 1966 [1895]).[20] In this work (unlike in his better known *Suicide*), Durkheim views all sorts of deviant behaviors as violations of social rules. Crime—and, by implication, mental illness—has no reality apart from the cultural rules that define its existence. What activities groups consider as criminal depends on value systems that define and apply rules of appropriate and inappropriate conduct. The "same" behavior manifested in different circumstances can be defined in various ways depending on the system of classification applied by the particular group. Durkheim's seminal contribution was to move the object of sociological analysis from the behavior of individuals to cultural systems of meaning that define various sorts of behaviors.

The first specific application of Durkheim's approach to the study of mental illness was Ruth Benedict's "Anthropology and the Abnormal" (Benedict 1934). Benedict questioned the validity of Western definitions of normality and abnormality. She asserted that the sorts of behaviors Western psychiatry defines as abnormal—such as paranoia, seizures, trances, and the like—are often considered normal in other cultures. Among the Shasta Indians in California or the native people of Siberia, for example, seizures are viewed not as dreaded illnesses but as signs of special connections to supernatural powers that single out people for authority and leadership.[21] In ancient Greece, homosexuality was presented as a major means to a good life rather than as an abnormality. Among the Dobuans of Melanesia, a constant fear of poisoning that runs through life is seen as normal rather than paranoiac behavior. Conversely, behaviors that are normalized and even rewarded in our culture would be considered abnormal in other cultures. The Dobuans, for example, would regard a person who is always cheerful, happy, and outgoing as crazy. Normality thus resides in culturally approved conventions, not in universal psychological standards of appropriate functioning. For Benedict and for the anthropologists who followed her, "all our local conventions of moral behavior and of immoral are without absolute validity" (Benedict 1934, 79).

The hugely popular writings of the French philosopher Michel Foucault extended the Durkheimian vision into the history of mental illness in Western civilization (see especially Foucault 1965 and 1973). Like Benedict, Foucault viewed madness as a property of cultural categories rather than of individual symptoms. What makes the mentally ill mad is not anything they do but how their cultures categorize their behaviors. These categories are not constant but change according to the dominant modes of thinking in each time period. For Foucault, mental illness did not exist until the seventeenth century, when the madman replaced the leper as the signifier of threat and disorder in Europe. He asserted that before then madness was linked with wisdom and insight, and since then it has been associated with alien forces that must be controlled by reason or by chains.

In 1966 Thomas Scheff brought the social constructionist viewpoint on mental illness into American sociology in his study, *Being Mentally Ill* (Scheff 1966). Scheff defines what are more typically called "psychiatric symptoms" as "residual rule-breaking." Residual rule-breaking refers to norm-violating behaviors that lack explicit cultural labels; "mental illness" is thus a category observers use to explain rule-violating behavior they cannot explain by any other culturally recognizable category. For Scheff, psychiatric symptoms are violations of residual rules rather than intrapsychic disturbances of individuals; it is only possible to recognize symptoms through the cultural categories that classify what sort of phenomenon they are.[22]

Conrad and Schneider place the growing use of disease models for mental illnesses within a broader twentieth-century trend to "medicalize" many sorts of behaviors (Conrad and Schneider 1992; see also Conrad 1992, Brown 1995). Medicalization means that problems are considered to be discrete diseases that professionals discover, name, and treat. It also means that psychiatrists and other mental health professionals become the culturally legitimated agents with the greatest authority to deal with conditions that in the past would have been seen as crime, deviance, disruption, sin, or bad habits. Scull's studies of psychiatric legitimacy in the nineteenth century and Kirk and Kutchins's research on the construction of the DSM-III broadly illustrate how the successful efforts of mental health professionals to gain authority led to the medicalized definition and management of mental illness (Scull 1979; Scull, MacKenzie, and Herevey 1996; Kirk and Kutchins 1982). Other studies examine how particular categories of possible mental illnesses such as posttraumatic stress disorder have gained recognition as "official" illnesses while others, such as homosexuality or premenstrual syndrome, have failed to do so.[23]

Social constructionists have made important contributions in demonstrating the limits of disease perspectives about mental illness. Nevertheless, the constructionist view also has a number of limitations. Social constructionists do not deal with the issue of whether or not a biological condition underlies illnesses that are constructed in various ways.[24] For them, disease models are as much the product of social and historical circumstances, specific group interests, and particular cultural belief systems as is any other way of characterizing mental illness (Fleck 1979 [1935]). Biological explanations that define mental illnesses as brain diseases legitimize particular constructions of social reality that have great credence in contemporary Western societies. Attributing psychiatric symptoms to depleted levels of serotonin, for example, has no more inherent validity as a cultural explanation than attributing them to unconscious forces or to demonic possession. The view of mental illnesses as diseases is not better than alternative views; it is simply one among many possible views. This assertion, however, has some serious limitations for the study of these phenomena.

1a) One problem with constructionist views is that they beg the question of *what* is being constructed in divergent views of mental illness. Pure constructionist premises preclude the possibility of defining mental illnesses in ways that are independent of any particular social context. If all behaviors are constituted by their social classifications, none have meaning outside of the culture-bound rules that define them. Yet, phenomena such as the distorted thought processes of schizophrenia, massive and continual alcohol consumption, or depleted levels of serotonin can have consequences regardless of the social definitions placed on them (Murphy 1976). Biological dysfunctions can create inherent constraints that limit social variations in constructions of mental symptoms.

1b) Another problem of pure constructionist perspectives lies in their inability to develop standards for comparing divergent views of mental illness. When mental illnesses are defined solely through culturally specific definitions, no grounds exist for establishing a concept of mental illness that transcends different contexts. Yet, comparison is only possible if something constant serves as a point of reference to observe meaningful variation.[25] For example, the claim that depression takes on fundamentally different forms in Western and non-Western cultures is only coherent if some underlying standard of what constitutes depression is available to classify both forms as variants of a common underlying category.

The lack of a valid concept of mental disorder that is not reducible to particular cultural categories also precludes the possibility of critiquing any particular view of mental disorder. Only standards of judgment that stand outside a particular paradigm can say that one model is more or less adequate than any other. Paradoxically, while constructionists are generally among the most strident critics of the psychiatric profession, the premise that mental illness is whatever is considered as such in a particular cultural context provides no logical grounds for claiming that any view of mental illness is either better or worse than any other (Hacking 1999).[26] For example, a constructionist has no justification for replacing a view of homosexuality as a mental illness with a view that regards it as an expression of a lifestyle. Nor do constructionists have more warrant for calling schizophrenics mentally ill than for applying the same designation to the political dissidents who shared their hospital wards in the former Soviet Union. A pure constructionist perspective has no extra-cultural criteria for developing a valid concept of mental illness and therefore cannot judge the adequacy of any classification of mental symptoms.[27]

Not only can an adequate concept of mental disorder serve as a standard for cross-cultural comparisons and for critiques of the practices of the mental health professions; it can also distinguish conditions that ought to be called "mental disorders" from those that ought not. Both disease and constructionist models usually lump all conditions without distinction into a single overall category of mental disorder. The DSM defines all of the many particular conditions it classifies as mental diseases without seriously considering the fundamental differences among them.[28] Likewise, constructionist critics often make sweeping claims about "mental illness," ignoring both the wide variety of conditions this term encompasses and the features that distinguish them from non-disordered behaviors (see, for example, Szasz 1961). Diagnostic psychiatry and its constructionist critics alike often fail to distinguish serious from less harmful conditions, expectable unhappiness from uncaused depression, or addictions from culturally normative substance use. One considers all, the other none, of these conditions as mental disorders. In contrast, the use of an adequate concept of mental disorder can serve to separate the various sorts of problematic psychological conditions that both views now lump together.

THE USEFULNESS OF
DIAGNOSTIC CLASSIFICATIONS

Diagnostic psychiatry uses symptoms to classify various discrete psychiatric disorders. It assumes that each cluster of symptoms indicates a distinct underlying disease and, conversely, that each underlying disease becomes manifest through dissimilar symptomatic presentations. The classifications of distinct mental disorders that are the basis of diagnostic psychiatry are useful when they meet two broad criteria: (1) that each constellation of symptoms is actually a valid mental disorder; and (2) that using manifest symptoms to distinguish different diseases aids in establishing distinct causes, prognoses, and treatments for each condition.

What Is a Valid Mental Disorder? Mental disorders are not found in nature; like all concepts, they are human constructions. The appropriate question to ask about a problematic condition is not whether it is "really" a mental disorder, but what advantages stem from viewing it as such. A concept of mental disorder is necessary for a variety of reasons: to assess the adequacy of different models of mental illnesses, to compare disorders across cultures, to critique mental health practices, and to distinguish from among all conditions now seen as mental illnesses those that are valid disorders and those that are not. The concept of mental disorder does have a legitimate domain beyond arbitrary social judgments. I will use Wakefield's definition that a valid mental disorder exists when some internal psychological system is unable to function as it is designed to function and when this dysfunction is defined as inappropriate in a particular social context (see especially Wakefield 1992a, 1992b, and 1993).

Wakefield's definition has both a universal and a culturally specific component; I will explicate these in more detail in chapter 1. One necessary aspect of a mental disorder is that something must be wrong with the internal functioning of a person. Mental disorders arise when psychological systems of motivation, memory, cognition, arousal, attachment, and the like are not able adequately to carry out the functions they are designed to perform. These functions are not social constructions but properties of the human species that have arisen through natural selection (Wakefield 1999a). People with internal dysfunctions have some psychological system that is incapable of performing within normal limits. Only symptoms that reflect internal dysfunctions, which are universal qualities of the human species, can be mental disorders.

It is, however, impossible to define mental disorders solely through universal standards of psychological functioning because these standards inherently involve the use of terms such as "inappropriate," "unreasonable," "excessive," and "normal," whose meaning stems from the norms of particular cultures and not from natural processes. Hallucinations, for example, are indicators of schizophrenic disorders only when they are defined as inappropriate styles of thought. Symptoms of profound sadness and immobilization are only signs of depression when they are disproportionate to the situation in which they occur. Likewise, the symptoms of panic attacks such as pounding heart, trembling, dizziness, and feelings of losing control are not intrinsic indicators of mental disorders except when they emerge in situations where they are not expectable. The terms "inappropriate," "disproportionate," and "expectable," however, are cultural judgments, not natural processes. Cultural values, which are relative rather than universal, therefore must play a part in our determining when a psychological system is functioning in an appropriate or inappropriate way (Kleinman 1988). Mental disorders always have culturally specific as well as universal components: mental disorders are internal dysfunctions that a particular culture defines as inappropriate.

The concept of mental disorders as socially inappropriate psychological dysfunctions indicates both the legitimate use of definitions of mental disorder and the limits that should be put on these definitions. On the one hand, people whose disturbed behavior stems from internal dysfunctions, when these dysfunctions are also socially defined as inappropriate, have mental disorders. On the other hand, people whose symptoms fluctuate with the emergence and dissipation of stressful social circumstances are psychologically normal: they do not have internal dysfunctions and so should not be defined as suffering from a mental disorder. Likewise, people can violate social norms for many reasons besides having internal dysfunctions. Viewing mental disorders as arising from socially inappropriate internal dysfunctions can show how the contemporary mental health professions overstate both the types of mental disorders and the number of people who presumably suffer from these disorders.

When Are Distinct Diagnoses Useful?   Because various conditions meet the criteria for valid mental disorders does not necessarily indicate that symptom-based diagnostic classifications are the most useful way to study them. Symptom-based diagnoses are appropriate when symptoms serve as indicators of underlying disorders and when distinguishing between different disorders helps to delineate distinct causes, prognoses, and treatments for each one. Diagnostic classifications based on discrete disease entities are not equally useful for all of the conditions the DSM defines but are more or less helpful depending on the type of condition they classify. A few of the many entities in the current classification scheme of diagnostic psychiatry are both valid mental disorders and specific diseases. Others are valid mental disorders whose symptoms are culturally structured manifestations of general vulnerabilities rather than indicators of specific underlying

— which disorders can actually be seen as mental diseases. Finally, many conditions now seen as mental illnesses are neither valid forms of mental disorder nor disease entities.

The premises of diagnostic psychiatry best fit disorders such as schizophrenia, bipolar disorder, and other psychoses. These disorders seem to be clear dysfunctions of mechanisms that regulate perception, thinking, communication, and other psychological processes. In addition, although psychotic disorders, like all phenomena, are named, classified, and treated according to the social categories in which they are placed, the formal structures of their symptoms are similar regardless of the social context in which they arise (Wing 1978).[29] The particular content of these disorders may differ—schizophrenics in New Guinea will not have delusions that the CIA has implanted electrodes in their brains nor will those in Tel Aviv think that voodoo spirits possess them—but the underlying structure of psychotic symptoms will be comparable across time and space.[30] Therefore, the symptoms of these disorders can be seen as indicators of underlying disease entities. Distinguishing different psychotic disorders such as schizophrenia or bipolar disorder also indicates distinct causes, prognoses, and treatments for each disorder.[31] While it is therefore useful to view psychotic disorders as discrete entities whose symptoms indicate underlying disease conditions, these diseases make up only a small proportion of conditions among the approximately four hundred entities of diagnostic psychiatry.[32]

these are psychotic disorders or mental illnesses that do not change

Beyond the psychoses, the premises of diagnostic psychiatry do not fit most of the conditions it classifies. Diagnostic models are problematic for studying various nonpsychotic conditions. On the one hand, persistent depressions, crippling compulsions, inexplicable anxiety, or self-starvation appear to indicate clearly dysfunctional and socially inappropriate psychological mechanisms and so are valid mental disorders. On the other hand, depression, anxiety, somatoform disorders, and psychosexual dysfunctions do not fit the categorical frameworks of diagnostic psychiatry because their symptoms are not specific indicators of discrete underlying diseases. Instead, the symptoms of many of the most common mental disorders vary from time to time and from place to place in ways that are socially structured to fit predominant cultural models of illness representations. For example, eating disorders that flourish among young women at the turn of the twentieth century were rarely found in earlier periods. Conversely, the dramatic physical symptoms of hysterics at the end of the nineteenth century are virtually nonexistent at present. Instead, they now arise in quite different forms such as chronic fatigue syndrome, fibromyalgia, Lyme disease, or multiple chemical sensitivity.[33]

_Ex:_

The symptoms of these disorders might be better viewed as culturally structured forms that reflect more general underlying vulnerabilities rather than as specific underlying diseases. While the vulnerability that leads to the symptoms of the most common neurotic disorders might often stem from psychological or biological factors, cultural factors often explain the particular forms that nonpsychotic disorders assume.[34] Therefore, although many of the nonpsychotic conditions in the DSM are valid mental disorders, their symptoms are often products of particular cultural contexts rather than invariant reflections of disease entities. In addition, nonpsychotic disorders are more likely to have common than distinct causes, prognoses, and treatments, so that distinguishing distinct entities from one another is rarely a useful endeavor.

The categories of diagnostic psychiatry fit even more poorly with the distress that arises because of stressful social conditions. The basic assumption of the diagnostic framework is that the presence of enough particular symptoms, regardless of their cause, indicates an underlying disease. This assumption is especially problematic when psychological and psychosomatic symptoms are products of taxing social environments. People who become depressed and anxious or who develop psychophysiological symptoms when they struggle with stressful life events, difficulties in interpersonal relationships, uncertain futures, bad jobs, and limited resources, react in *appropriate* ways to their environments; they do not have internal dysfunctions and so are not mentally disordered if their symptoms disappear when their social circumstances change. The classification system of diagnostic psychiatry mistakenly equates expectable responses to stressful conditions with mental disorders.

The sorts of symptoms that arise from stressful social conditions are not valid forms of mental disorder. In addition, they are not usefully defined as specific disease entities. It is unlikely that the stressful consequences of social arrangements are etiologically specific for particular mental disorders.[35] The psychological consequences of stressful circumstances are not distinct measures of particular disorders but overlap many various diagnoses. These consequences are typically generalized and nonspecific manifestations of distress including depression, anxiety, and psychophysiological symptoms (Cassell 1974; 1976). They are also typically continuous rather than discrete (Mirowsky and Ross 1989a). There are, therefore, no sharp demarcations between people under stress and those who are not. Distress that emerges from social conditions is neither a mental disorder nor a distinct disease condition.

Finally, diagnostic psychiatry mistakenly categorizes many forms of social deviance as mental disorder (Wakefield 1996). People who persistently suffer negative effects from repeated substance use, compulsively pursue activities that are not in their self-interest, or are unable to refrain from engaging in socially disvalued activities may have mental disorders when their conduct both stems from an internal dysfunction and is socially defined as inappropriate. Often, however, drinking heavily, persistently using the wrong kind of drug, or offending the wrong type of person are types of deviant social behaviors: violations of social norms that define standards of proper behavior (Toby 1998). Only socially disvalued conditions that are also products of internal dysfunctions should be classified as mental disorders. In addition, cultural forces strongly structure the manifestations of deviance, and so medicalized models that assume overt symptoms are indicators of underlying disease conditions are rarely appropriate for the study of these phenomena (Cullen 1983).

but having a mental illness can lead to such behaviors

The view that mental illnesses are genuine disease entities is thus often misleading. Diagnostic models handicap rather than aid us in understanding both distress that emerges from social conditions and deviant behavior that does not result from internal dysfunctions.[36] The categorical classifications of diagnostic psychiatry also obscure how overt symptoms can reflect cultural rather than disease processes. A consequence of categorizing a broad scope of behavior as "mental disorders" has been our considering much ordinary social behavior as pathological and overestimating the prevalence of mental disorder. Many of the conditions encompassed by the diagnoses in the DSM are neither mental disorders nor discrete disease entities; instead they reflect expectable reactions to stressful conditions, culturally patterned forms of deviant behavior, and general human unhappiness and dissatisfaction. Only a small number of serious mental disorders are both internal dysfunctions and categorical diseases.

How does society affect individual

main point!

The terminology I use in the chapters that follow illustrates these distinctions. *Mental diseases* are conditions where symptoms indicate underlying internal dysfunctions, are distinct from other disease conditions, and have certain universal features. *Mental disorders* include all mental diseases as well as psychological dysfunctions whose overt symptoms are shaped by cultural as well as natural processes. Finally, *mental illnesses* refer to whatever conditions a particular social group defines as such. In contrast to the concepts of "mental disease" and "mental disorder," which have valid and invalid applications, the concept of "mental illness" refers to the actual labeling processes in any group and so cannot be true or false.

The emergence and persistence of an overly expansive disease model of mental illness was not accidental or arbitrary. The widespread creation of distinct mental diseases developed in specific historical circumstances and because of the interests of specific social groups. The disease conditions in diagnostic psychiatry were created because they provide a far better fit than dynamic conditions did with the socioeconomic environment of the mental health professions in the last decades of the twentieth century. By the time the DSM-III was developed in 1980, thinking of mental illnesses as discrete disease entities rather than blurry unconscious mechanisms offered mental health professionals many social, economic, and political advantages.[37] In addition, applying disease frameworks to a wide variety of behaviors and to a large number of people benefited a number of specific social groups including not only clinicians but also research scientists, advocacy groups, and pharmaceutical companies, among others. The disease entities of diagnostic psychiatry arose because they were useful for the social practices of various groups, not because they provided a more accurate way of viewing mental disorders.

The demonstration that a system of discrete mental illnesses emerged because of social and contextual factors, however, does not necessarily indicate that the knowledge claims that stem from these classifications are false (Conrad 1992; Aronowitz 1998). Concepts of mental disease and mental disorder are contingent upon, but not reducible to, social factors. The socially constructed disease frameworks of diagnostic psychiatry are far better suited to some of the conditions it categorizes than to others.

main point about psychoses {

PLAN OF THE BOOK

The starting point for the general critique of diagnostic psychiatry offered in this book is a definition of the valid range of mental disorders. Chapter 1 goes on to develop a conception of mental disorders as socially inappropriate psychological dysfunctions. Its major theme is that a valid definition of mental disorder should be narrow and should not encompass many of the presumed mental disorders of diagnostic psychiatry, especially appropriate reactions to stressful social conditions and many culturally patterned forms of deviant behavior.

Chapter 2 shows how the rise of dynamic psychiatry in the twentieth century transformed "mental illness" from a very limited number of conditions to a huge and heterogeneous class of behaviors that were continuous with normality. Freud developed a theory of dynamic psychiatry that joined neurotic and normal behavior in a single framework. Diagnoses and classifications of particular psychiatric conditions were largely irrelevant in this theoretical system. This view became the basis for a cultural understanding of psychological functioning that was widely embraced in the United States. In the 1970s, however, an antagonistic group of psychiatrists gained control of the profession and rejected the premises of dynamic psychiatry due to its limitations vis-à-vis research, treatment, and professional prestige.

Chapter 3 illustrates how diagnostic psychiatry emerged as a form of psychiatric thought radically different from dynamic psychiatry. Although it replaced the continua of dynamic psychiatry with discrete disease categories, diagnostic psychiatry nevertheless embraced the vast realm of behaviors that dynamic psychiatry had already successfully defined as forms of mental pathology. The DSM-III did not so much overthrow dynamic psychiatry as reclassify the expansive range of dynamic behaviors into specific diagnostic entities. Cultural, political, and economic factors, not scientific progress, underlie the triumph of diagnostic psychiatry and the current "scientific" classification of mental illness entities.

Chapter 4 describes how the discrete clinical entities of the DSM expanded beyond clinical practice to become the basis of community studies that presumably show the pervasiveness of untreated cases of mental disorder. The prevalence estimates of mental disorder that stem from these studies, however, are products of the symptom-based classification system that generates them, not of the actual presence of so many people with mental disorders in the community. A number of specific groups, however, have major stakes in asserting that untreated mental disorders are widespread.

The remaining chapters evaluate the adequacy of diagnostic psychiatry for understanding the classifications, causes, and treatments of mental disorders. The fifth chapter develops the view that the symptoms of many mental disorders do not stem from discrete underlying disease entities, but instead reflect culturally appropriate illness displays. People develop symptoms that are congruent with appropriate patterning of illness representations in their culture, that fit their major identity categories, and that are fashionable in the mental health and medical professions. That symptoms are products of cultural forces, however, does not preclude the possibility that they are also manifestations of legitimate mental disorders.

The sixth chapter considers the prevailing view of diagnostic psychiatry that locates the causes of mental disorders in genes and in other properties of the brain. Assertions that mental disorders have genetic foundations fit some disorders better than others. Even when these assertions are credible, however, they are generally overstated. Chapter 7 discusses the influence of social factors on distress. It postulates that social phenomena such as acute and chronic stressors, the strength and quality of social ties, and the degree of dominance and subordination in relationships are primary reasons for the emergence of symptoms of distress, which diagnostic psychiatry mistakenly classifies as mental disorders.

The penultimate chapter examines the two major forms of treatment diagnostic psychiatry combines—drug therapy and psychotherapy. Considerable evidence indicates that drug treatments are often beneficial, but that their benefits arise in ways that undermine, rather than support, the principles of diagnostic psychiatry. Likewise, there is little evidence that the psychotherapies work in disorder-specific ways. In general, distinguishing discrete disorders is not related to the provision of distinct forms of treatment. The concluding chapter summarizes some of the major issues the earlier chapters raise and speculates about factors that might serve to stabilize or to undermine the diagnostic system in the future.

This book will not satisfy sociologists who view all mental disorders as purely social constructions. Nor will the book satisfy proponents of diagnostic psychiatry who believe that their classifications of mental disorders reflect disease conditions. Those who claim that mental disorders have no reality apart from their cultural definitions have a difficult time dealing with the inherent constraints psychological dysfunctions impose on social categorizations. These dysfunctions create natural limits for interpretation whenever and wherever they appear. Similarly, those who believe that mental disorders are objective facts that are reflected by the diagnostic categories in the DSM cannot explain the consequential implications of social conceptions for the definition, course, and treatment of these disorders and the historically contingent nature of many current mental illnesses. Social factors explain why medicalized disease models have become the dominant framework for viewing mental illness in a particular place and at a particular time. These models have an appropriate role in the classification system of the contemporary mental health professions but this role is far smaller than the one that they currently play.

Chapter One
A CONCEPT OF MENTAL DISORDER

Any adequate definition of mental disorder must be *valid.* A valid definition provides an answer to the question "what is a mental disorder?" It includes conditions that may productively be considered types of mental disorders and excludes those that may not, and so defines the boundaries of mental disorder. In particular, it distinguishes mental disorders from normality and from deviant behavior. Although a valid definition of mental disorder defines the appropriate subject matter for the field of mental health and illness, few studies focus on issues of validity. Instead, there have been two contrasting approaches toward definitions of mental disorder.

Most sociologists and anthropologists reject the possibility of developing a general concept of mental disorder that would be valid across social groups. They view mental disorders as culturally specific phenomena; mental illness is whatever a particular group defines as such. For example, Benedict (1934) claims that the Siberians assign people who hallucinate valued religious roles, presumably showing the culturally relative nature of schizophrenia.[1] Foucault, as well, states that madness is a culturally specific category that developed only after the leprosariums closed at the end of the Middle Ages in Europe (Foucault 1965). In this relativist view, the great diversity of social definitions of mental illness precludes the possibility of a concept that transcends particular social contexts.

In contrast to the relativist view, research psychiatrists, epidemiologists, and clinicians simply accept as mental disorders whatever conditions the DSM lists.[2] They do not ask how these conditions came to be regarded as mental disorders. Instead, researchers strive to develop reliable measures of particular diagnostic entities without questioning whether the conditions they measure are valid disorders or not. Likewise, mental health professionals often obsess over the question of what particular disorders their patients have but take for granted that these entities are mental disorders (Spitzer 1999). Yet, in the absence of a well-defined and conceptually adequate definition of mental disorder, there is no reason to accept that any particular group of symptoms represents a valid form of mental disorder.

Despite the mental health community's relative inattention to issues of validity, it is more fundamental to attain validity than reliability (Kleinman 1988; Wakefield 1992a; Kirk and Kutchins 1992). Conditions that are reliably measured are not mental disorders unless they meet criteria of validity. Because diagnostic psychiatry has little concern for validity, it indiscriminately combines conditions that have defensible claims to be mental disorders with conditions that reflect the expectable consequences of stressful social circumstances and with norm-breaking, but not disordered, behaviors. Current conceptions of mental illness include far more behaviors than a valid definition of disorder warrants. The consequences of this are that rates of presumed mental illness are elevated to artificially high levels, nondisordered people are treated as if they are disordered, social behaviors are defined as individual pathologies, and the mental health system overemphasizes the treatment of problems of living at the expense of serious mental disorders.

No concept, especially one as controversial as mental disorder, is universally true or false. Rather, any particular concept of mental disorder is more or less useful for various purposes (Brodbeck 1968). One central sociological task is to distinguish between mental disorders and normal reactions to social stressors. There is nothing wrong with people who respond to stressful environments, situations, and relationships with depression, anxiety, and other signs of distress. Their reactions are normal, not abnormal, responses to their environments. Another essential distinction is between mental disorders and social deviance. Deviations from social norms arise not only because of internal pathologies but also because of many other reasons including conflicting cultural norms, conformity to the standards of subcultures, or a lack of adequate social control (see, for example, Merton 1938; Sellin 1938; Hirschi 1969). An adequate concept will only label deviance that arises from internal dysfunctions as mental disorder. This chapter develops a definition that limits mental disorder to symptoms that result from psychological pathologies, thus distinguishing mental disorder from expectable responses to stressful environments and from social deviance.

A good place to begin the consideration of validity is with the definition of mental disorder found in the official diagnostic manual of the American Psychiatric Association, the *Diagnostic and Statistical Manual, Version IV* (DSM-IV). This definition is nearly hidden in three paragraphs of the prefatory material to a 900-page manual. It is framed with an apology that states it is "a reductionistic anachronism of mind/body dualism," that it persists "because we have not found an appropriate substitute," and that it is included "because it is as useful as any other available definition" (APA 1994, xxi). Hardly a ringing endorsement, this passage perhaps reveals why there is no further discussion or application of the concept to the nearly 400 disorders that follow in the manual. Indeed, many of the actual definitions of particular conditions in the DSM do not meet the criteria delineated in the concept of mental disorder. The major problem with the DSM concept of mental disorder is the failure of the manual to apply it to the many particular conditions it defines.

The DSM defines mental disorder as follows:

> In DSM-IV, each of the mental disorders is conceptualized as a clinically significant behavioral or psychological syndrome or pattern that occurs in an individual and that is associated with present distress (e.g., a painful symptom) or disability (i.e. impairment in one or more important areas of functioning) or with a significantly increased risk of suffering death, pain, disability, or an important loss of freedom. In addition, this syndrome or pattern must not be merely an expectable and culturally sanctioned response to a particular event, for example, the death of a loved one. Whatever its original cause, it must currently be considered a manifestation of a behavioral, psychological, or biological dysfunction in the individual. Neither deviant behavior (e.g. political, religious, or sexual) nor conflicts that are primarily between the individual and society are mental disorders unless the deviance or conflict is a symptom of a dysfunction in the individual, as described above. (APA 1994, xxi–xxii)

This definition has three critical aspects: mental disorders are internal dysfunctions, mental disorders are not expectable responses to particular events, and mental disorders must be distinguished from deviant behavior.

The philosopher Jerome Wakefield has developed the most useful elaboration and critique of the DSM definition of mental disorder.[3] Wakefield argues that when the conceptual redundancy, inconsistency, and confusion of the DSM definition is eliminated, it can be reformulated more simply as stating that mental disorders are harmful internal dysfunctions. In Wakefield's reformulation, there are two essential components of valid mental disorders: they are internal dysfunctions, and they have harmful consequences for individuals as defined by sociocultural standards. A mental "disorder exists when the failure of a person's internal mechanisms to perform their functions as designed by nature impinges harmfully on the person's well-being as defined by social values and meanings" (Wakefield 1992a: 373). I use Wakefield's definition, although I believe that "socially inappropriate" more adequately captures the social aspects of mental disorder than the notion of "harm."

Wakefield's concept addresses the central problem a valid definition of mental disorder must overcome: how to reconcile cultural particularism with biological universalism (Fabrega 1992). A valid definition has two components, which take into account the universal and the cultural aspects of mental disorder, respectively. Internal dysfunctions, which are universal, are necessary components of mental disorders. The universal component of mental disorders implies that similar failures of functioning in internal mechanisms would be mental dysfunctions regardless of the particular social context in which they occur. This aspect of mental disorder produces natural constraints around which culturally specific definitions vary. Although internal dysfunctions are necessary components of mental disorders, they are never sufficient components. Only internal dysfunctions that are also defined as socially inappropriate are mental disorders.

The Universal Component of Mental Disorders   Mental disorders are dysfunctions of some internal psychological mechanism.[4] A mental disorder exists when psychological systems of cognition, thinking, perception, motivation, emotion, memory, or language are unable to function appropriately. These functions are very general and universal properties of the human species: perceptual apparatuses are designed to convey accurate information about the environment, fear responses allow people to avoid danger, language allows for communication, and so on. In this sense, they are components of human nature shared in all times and places. The essential aspect of an internal dysfunction is that some psychological system is unable to work as it has been designed to work by the processes of natural selection (Wakefield 1999a). Internal dysfunctions are necessary components of mental disorders—if nothing is wrong with people's internal functioning, they are not mentally disordered.

An internal dysfunction exists only when an internal mechanism is *unable* to perform its natural function, not when it simply doesn't perform this function (Wakefield 1992b, Klein 1999). For example, unlike the self-starvation of modern anorexics, the fasting of holy women in medieval Italy was not a mental disorder because there was nothing wrong with their psychological functioning.[5] Their failure to eat reflects an individual choice, not a dysfunctional internal mechanism. Likewise, people who have internal dysfunctions that preclude them from having sexual orgasms are distinct from those who are not orgasmic because they choose to be celibate, have bad interpersonal relationships, or engage in sex for monetary compensation. It is not the failure to have orgasms but the *inability* of sexually dysfunctional people to be orgasmic that distinguishes them from monks, people in troubled relationships, or sex workers. Similarly, all nondisordered people have the capacity to use language appropriately: the difficulties in communication that are products of autism are mental disorders, while the intentional silence of members of some religious orders is not.

Using the criterion of dysfunction to define mental disorders implies that the presence of symptoms alone is never sufficient to indicate a mental disorder: only symptoms that stem from internal dysfunctions reflect disorders. The same symptoms that might result from internal dysfunctions in other contexts might be normal reactions to stressful environments. This is why bereaved people do not suffer from the mental disorder of depression. People are *naturally* depressed after the death of an intimate; there is nothing wrong with their affective mechanisms. Likewise, fear mechanisms are designed to enable people to detect danger. Intense symptoms of anxiety that arise among soldiers who are about to enter combat are not products of an internal dysfunction but are rational responses to external circumstances. The identical symptoms may indicate an anxiety disorder when they do not reflect a proportionate response to environmental dangers. Mental disorders must be distinguished from deviant behavior as well as from expectable responses to stressful environments. Heavy drinking need not indicate alcoholism, nor is career criminality equivalent to antisocial personality disorder. These would only be mental disorders if it were clear that they stemmed from internal dysfunctions that render alcoholics or sociopaths unable to control their conduct.[6]

That all mental disorders involve internal dysfunctions does not imply that all mental disorders must have internal causes. The DSM appropriately states that the causes of an internal dysfunction need not themselves be internal: "Whatever its original cause, (this syndrome or pattern) must currently be considered a manifestation of a behavioral, psychological, or biological dysfunction in the individual" (APA 1994, xxi–xxii). Psychological dysfunctions exist when some internal system of cognition, memory, linguistic ability, motivation, aggression, or perception is unable to perform properly. Social as well as biological or psychological factors might be responsible for causing these dysfunctions. The presence of dysfunctional internal mechanisms, not particular kinds of causes of the dysfunctions, determines whether a mental disorder exists or not.

The dysfunctional aspect of mental disorders parallels the dysfunctions of bodily mechanisms that define physical disorders; in principle, the determination of adequate mental functioning is very similar to that of adequate physical functioning (see Lewis 1953; Klein 1978). In practice, however, there is generally consensus on the appropriate functions of physical systems: the eyes should accurately convey visual information, the ears should hear only sounds that are present in the environment, the heart should circulate blood, the digestive system should absorb nutrients and discard wastes, and so on.[7] There is far less consensus on, and far less knowledge about, what constitutes appropriately functioning systems of cognition, emotion, reasoning, motivation, and the like. This lack of consensus insures that the boundaries between "appropriate" and "inappropriate" functioning will often be very fuzzy (Lilienfeld and Marino 1995).

The Culturally Relative Component of Mental Disorders The dysfunction criterion used to define mental disorders is analogous to definitions of physical diseases that are dysfunctions of bodily organs. The second criterion, however, distinguishes definitions of mental illnesses from definitions of physical illnesses: cultural values and meanings are necessary components of any valid definition of mental disorder.[8] While all mental disorders involve failures of internal functions, only internal dysfunctions that are also socially defined as inappropriate qualify as mental disorders (Wakefield 1992a, 384). In contrast to the notion of internal dysfunction, which refers to universal properties of human organisms, the notion of inappropriateness arises from social definitions applied in particular contexts. Cultural standards of normality are integral parts of a valid definition of mental disorder.

All definitions of mental disorder must contain culturally specific components. The DSM, for example, uses terms such as "inappropriate," "bizarre," "unexpectable," and "maladaptive" when defining the disorders of major depression, schizophrenia, panic disorder, and alcohol intoxication, respectively (APA 1994, 237, 275, 402, 197). Such terms have no universal referents but are only meaningful within given social and cultural contexts. For example, cultural definitions are necessary aspects of decisions about whether or not hallucinations are signs of dysfunctional perceptual processes. Bereaved Native Americans often hallucinate visions of their dead spouses and talk to them (Kleinman 1987). Such hallucinations are not mental disorders in this context because they are culturally appropriate ways of reacting to grief. Likewise, cultural values always enter into judgments over whether reactions to stressors are proportionate or disproportionate. The DSM, for example, considers a diagnosis of major depression after bereavement appropriate when symptoms persist for longer than two months. In Mediterranean societies, however, widows traditionally have been expected to grieve for periods of time that would be considered excessive by American standards (Kramer 1993). Grief of comparable intensity and duration might be a mental disorder in the United States but not in Greece. Comparably, a fear of snakes might be appropriate where snakes are plentiful but indicative of a phobia in an urban area; and fear of crime in a city might be adaptive while the same fear in a secure vacation resort area might be inappropriate (Simpson 1996).

Standards of appropriateness are not universal properties of the human species but culturally specific norms that regulate roles and situations. Social expectations of appropriate behavior must always play a part in determining whether behaviors indicate psychological dysfunctions, expectable reactions to social circumstances, or social deviance. Erving Goffman notes: "The delusions of a private can be the rights of a general; the obscene invitations of a man to a strange girl can be the spicy endearments of a husband to his wife; the wariness of a paranoid is the warranted practice of thousands of undercover agents" (Goffman 1971, 356). The implication of Goffman's statement is not that deluded privates, sexual predators, or paranoids do not exist. The private who thinks he has the rights of a general can legitimately be viewed as disordered. Whether intense suspicion is a sign of paranoia cannot be judged by symptoms alone, but only in light of the appropriateness of suspicious behavior in terms of the social roles and situations of the parties involved (Lemert 1962). Because judgments of appropriateness, rationality, proportionality, and the like are intrinsically connected to culturally defined normative systems, valid definitions of mental disorder always involve the use of social values.

That conceptions of mental disorder must have a social component does not vitiate the possibility of a universal definition of mental illness. For example, the Yoruba tribesmen of Nigeria sometimes carry special boxes as protection against witchcraft and claim that these boxes contain their souls (Coulter 1973, 146). While this is considered appropriate behavior among the Yoruba, an American who made the same claim could have a mental disorder. Likewise, a member of mainstream American culture—unlike a Navaho—who hallucinates the presence of a dead spouse, perceives him to be real, and talks to him is not acting in a socially appropriate fashion. That the specific behaviors called "mentally ill" in different cultures vary does not mean that the definition of mental disorder is culture-bound in the same way. The meaning of mental disorder as socially inappropriate psychological dysfunction is universal; it is the particular behaviors to which this definition applies that are culture-bound (Horwitz 1982a, 22; Wakefield 1994; compare Kirmayer 1994).

The value component of the appropriateness criterion in definitions of mental disorders insures that all disorders will have blurry rather than distinct boundaries. Most people would agree that the sudden and unexpected collapse of a longstanding marriage would naturally lead the victimized spouse to become depressed, but what about the loss of a month-long relationship? Would the death of a beloved dog be grounds for bereavement? When is heavy drinking hedonistic and when a sign of an internal dysfunction? At what point does suspicion that one's spouse is having an affair cross over into paranoia? Such judgments are rarely clear-cut because definitions of psychological dysfunctions must contain a value component that defines what is comprehensible or incomprehensible, rational or irrational, compulsive or chosen, expectable or unexpectable in particular situations.

Valid definitions of mental disorder thus contain both a universal quality that refers to internal dysfunctions and a culturally specific quality that defines what conditions are inappropriate in particular contexts (Wakefield 1992a). One implication of this definition is that no behavior can be defined as a disorder that is not also socially defined as inappropriate. For example, many Yemenese make daily use of a cocaine derivative, qat. Their culture does not consider the continual use of this drug to be inappropriate and so it would not indicate a mental disorder (Kennedy 1987). In contrast, daily use of cocaine in the contemporary United States is generally regarded as improper and so would be considered a mental disorder—that is, when it is also the product of an internal dysfunction.

Another implication of this definition, however, is that the inappropriateness of a behavior is not sufficient to indicate the existence of a mental disorder. For a mental disorder to exist requires not only inappropriateness as defined by social norms but also an internal dysfunction that transcends the social context. This means that many socially inappropriate behaviors are labeled mental disorders erroneously in that they do not stem from internal dysfunctions. In various times and places, slaves who run away, women who have orgasms, or children who masturbate have been defined as mentally disordered (Wakefield 1992a, 386). Each of these diagnoses was wrong because runaway slaves, orgasmic women, or masturbating children did not have malfunctioning internal systems. Only a definition of mental disorder that includes a universal, culture-free component has the capacity to say that some indigenous definitions of disorder are incorrect. Mental disorders reflect the combination of universal internal dysfunctions and contextual social values.

The quality of social inappropriateness distinguishes mental disorders from physical disorders, which usually can be defined through bodily dysfunctions alone, without consideration of their social aspects.[9] This intrinsically contextual nature of mental disorders insures that their definitions will never approach the consensual nature of most physical disorders. Conversely, the socially inappropriate aspect of mental disorders links them to forms of social deviance, which do not involve internal dysfunctions but which can generally be defined solely by the violation of social standards of appropriateness. Mental disorders thus stand at the intersection of physical disorders and social deviance: their distinctiveness from both physical illness and social deviance is that they necessarily involve *both* dysfunctions and inappropriateness.

Mental Disorders Are Not Adaptations to Stressful Environments   A valid definition of mental disorder delineates not only the necessary components of mental disorder, but also what conditions are *not* signs of mental disorders. In particular, mental disorders should be distinguished from the expectable psychological consequences of stressful social conditions. A mental illness only exists when some internal system cannot function appropriately. The DSM definition recognizes this quality of mental disorder when it asserts that "a syndrome or pattern must not be merely an expectable and culturally sanctioned response to a particular event, for example, the death of a loved one" (APA 1994, xxi). The DSM definition of disorder appropriately indicates that people whose mental symptoms are expectable products of social situations are not disordered because they are responding as expected to stressful situations.

But this same logic also suggests that the symptoms of children who act out in abusive environments, of jilted lovers who get depressed, or of laid off workers who drink too much are not disorders. Likewise, persistent feelings of hopelessness and helplessness among people whose lives are marked by chronic deprivation are not internal dysfunctions. In each of these cases, there is nothing wrong with any internal mechanism; people are responding normally to stressful environments. Only depression in the absence of loss, fear in the absence of danger, or elation in the absence of reward indicate internal dysfunctions and so might indicate mental disorders (Klein 1978).

Internal dysfunctions only exist when symptoms are not appropriate responses to given social situations. Panic, for example, can often be functional in the presence of real danger. What makes panic attacks mental disorders is not their occurrence but their emergence in the absence of dangerous situations that would explain them. Panic attacks only indicate mental disorder when they "come from out of the blue" (Goodwin and Guze 1996; Nesse 1987). Conversely, when in extreme situations such as wartime combat "soldiers trembled and jerked, vomited, whimpered like children, coughed from fear, or relieved themselves involuntarily" (Schaffer 1991, 160), these symptoms of extreme anxiety do not indicate mental disorders because they are normal psychological responses to extremely stressful social situations. —▷ How?

Symptoms of depression are the most common outcome of stressful social arrangements. Therefore, depression provides a particularly important example of the need to distinguish symptoms that are appropriate responses to social circumstances from those that cannot be attributed to a cause that would naturally produce them. In Western cultures, the core symptoms of depression include deep sadness, hopelessness, aversion to food, sleeplessness, irritability, restlessness, fearfulness, and fatigue.[10] These symptoms in themselves never necessarily indicate a mental disorder; they are often universal human experiences that result from unpleasant situations.

Throughout Western history, discussions of depression distinguish expectable symptoms that arise from social losses from extreme states of sadness *without cause* and only link the latter to mental disorder (Jackson 1986, 315). The theme of "without cause" is reiterated over and over in historical discussions of depression. For example, a sixteenth-century English physician stated: "Melancholy . . . is a kind of mental alienation in which imagination and judgment are so perverted that *without any cause* the victims become very sad and fearful" (Jackson 1986, 91). In his classic work, *The Anatomy of Melancholy*, first published in 1621, Robert Burton defined melancholy as "a kind of dotage without a fever, having for his ordinary companions fear and sadness, *without any apparent occasion*" (Burton 1948 [1621], 331; see also MacDonald 1981). Later, in the most popular psychiatric text of the late nineteenth century, Krafft-Ebing defined melancholia as "painful emotional depression, which has no external, or an insufficient external, cause, and general inhibition of the mental activities, which may be entirely arrested" (Krafft-Ebing 1904, xiii). The experience of a contemporary American sociologist also illustrates this aspect of depression: "I thought for sure that my depression was rooted in these situational demands and that once I got tenure it would go away. I was promoted in 1977 and found that the depression actually deepened" (Karp 1996, 6). Only depressions that persist after their presumed cause has ended indicate that something internal is wrong rather than that people are responding normally to stressful conditions. *= How Long does it have to presist for?*

"Without cause" does not mean uncaused, for throughout history depression has been attributed to physical or psychological causes such as black bile, disturbances in the circulation of blood, or depletion of energy (Jackson 1986). Rather, it means that the symptoms of depression are not associated with the sorts of events that would *appropriately* lead to sadness such as bereavement, rejection in love, economic failure, and the like. Hence, depressions whose symptoms begin before a seemingly precipitating event may indicate a psychological dysfunction (Goodwin and Guze 1996, 14). Indeed, that depression is "without cause" implies that symptoms of depression "with cause" would *not* be considered signs of a mental disorder. Symptoms of depression have historically been regarded as mental disorders only when they represent internal dysfunctions, not when they are seen as natural and expectable reactions to stressful circumstances. The same is true with many common mental symptom such as generalized anxiety, panic, or substance abuse.

how so? *1st it's Not normal anymoe* *I have anxiety disorder especially GAD has No specific cause or event*

⌐ what about those that dly have a tendency but never hadit unheared

Social Factors as Causes of Internal Dysfunctions If mental disorders are not expectable responses to stressful social circumstances, is it ever possible for social factors to be causes of mental disorders? Social factors can cause internal dysfunctions when symptoms lose their link to an external precipitant and persist independently of their initial cause. As Wakefield says:

> The critical distinction that needs to be drawn is between those situations in which an environmental stress causes a breakdown of an internal

mechanism such that the breakdown becomes independent of the original stress versus a natural response that is initiated and maintained directly by the ongoing stress and that would subside if the stress disappeared. (Wakefield 1992b, 238)

People whose symptoms initially stem from social causes but persist long after the conditions that gave rise to them have disappeared—unlike children who behave normally when their parents stop fighting, rejected lovers who are no longer depressed once they find new partners, or unemployed people who stop drinking excessively after they find new jobs—may have internal dysfunctions.

Posttraumatic stress disorder (PTSD) provides an example of how environmental causes can lead to dysfunctional psychological mechanisms. Experience of a traumatic event often leads to symptoms including pervasive anxiety, nightmares, and a constant reliving of the intensely frightening occasion. For example, the terror of actual or expected combat may give rise to the hysterical symptoms of soldiers who develop paralyzed limbs or become unable to speak (Showalter 1985).[11] The distinction between soldiers in combat who suffer extreme, but normal, symptoms of anxiety and those with comparable symptoms who develop mental diseases is that the symptoms of the former will abate without treatment once they are removed from the anxiety-provoking situation. Likewise, rape victims often become agoraphobic, feel terrified in ordinary situations, and develop numerous symptoms of depression and anxiety (Burgess and Holstrum 1974). Unlike people who do not venture out of their houses in unsafe situations, rape victims may stay inside because their internal defense mechanisms no longer work appropriately. Such symptoms would expectably diminish over time. If they do not, however, environmental causes have led to dysfunctional fear mechanisms and the person may have the disorder PTSD. In these cases symptoms are products of social events, but are nevertheless internal dysfunctions because normal fear responses cease to function in the way they are designed to function (Wakefield 1992b).

One distinction between symptoms that are appropriate responses to stressful environments and those that are internal dysfunctions is whether they are of disproportionate *severity*. For example, symptoms that emerge following situations that would expectedly produce depression might go beyond sadness to indicate anguish, terror, desolation, and extreme suffering (Jackson 1986, 133). Grief over the death of a loved one that leads to immobilization, hallucinations, delusions, and other severe symptoms would cross the line from expectable sadness to internal dysfunction. Thus, Jackson notes that in the late sixteenth and early seventeenth centuries in England, "instances of grieving or sadness occasioned by the loss of loved ones (sadness 'with cause') were often considered akin to melancholy without being thought to be indicative of that disease, but if they acquired 'unusual intensity or duration,' they might well be considered examples of melancholy the disease" (Jackson 1986, 107). Likewise, symptoms of anxiety, guilt, grief, loneliness, boredom, fatigue, and so on that can be adaptive in many circumstances can indicate internal dysfunctions when they become severe or incapacitating.

Duration is a second characteristic that distinguishes expectable distress from symptoms that represent internal dysfunctions. Symptoms that persist after they would expectably have disappeared can indicate mental disorders. For example, people who have recently experienced a marital dissolution and as a result must change jobs, residences, and patterns of social relationships will expectably be depressed. If the depression remains well beyond the persistence of the stressors that gave rise to the initial symptoms, however, this can indicate that expectable consequences of social stressors have become internal dysfunctions.

Internal dysfunctions thus either arise in the absence of any stressor that would expectably produce them or persist with greater than normal severity and for a longer than expectable time after the initial stressor has disappeared. Depression that lingers after a divorced person enters a new relationship, problematic drinking that continues once an unemployed person finds a new job, or anxiety that persists after tenure is granted are not proportionate reactions to social situations. Disproportion can only be defined according to social judgments of the normal range of responses to various stressors in particular contexts. Whether symptoms represent internal dysfunctions or proportionate reactions to stressors thus depends both on the presence of an internal dysfunction and on social judgments of the proportionality between the stressor and the severity and duration of the resulting distress.

Mental Disorders Are Distinct from Social Deviance The DSM definition recognizes the need to distinguish mental disorders not only from expectable distress but also from deviant behaviors: "Neither deviant behavior (e.g. political, religious, or sexual) nor conflicts that are primarily between the individual and society are mental disorders unless the deviance or conflict is a symptom of a dysfunction in the individual, as described above"

30 · 31

(APA 1994, xxii). Although the DSM does not define deviant behavior, its general principle is that violations of social norms are only mental disorders when they are products of internal dysfunctions. The concept of deviance is extraordinarily broad, encompassing behaviors that violate the normative standards of appropriate and inappropriate behavior of some group (see for example Parsons 1951; Gibbs 1981; Black 1976; Horwitz 1990) Depending upon who is making the judgment, deviance might include adolescents who smoke marijuana, college students who engage in binge drinking, children who disrupt classrooms, or people who regularly steal goods.

Social groups universally distinguish norm-breaking behaviors that arise because offenders violate social standards from those that stem from some internal dysfunction (Horwitz 1982a, chap. 2). For example, Talmudic scholars in ancient Israel noted the fundamentally internal nature of mental illness that distinguishes it from deviant behavior:

> (one scholar) proposed that a person who wandered about alone at night, who spent the night in a cemetery, or who tore his garments and destroyed what was given to him might be considered deranged—if such behavior appeared irrational. However, it was pointed out that otherwise normal persons could also behave in this way, e.g. one who spent the night in a cemetery might have done so to practice magic, or that another who tore his clothes might have done so in a fit of anger, or because he was a cynic philosopher exhibiting his contempt for material things. (Rosen 1968, 67)

Aristotle too noted that when a strange behavior such as cannibalism occurs as part of a social pattern, as among savages, it is not a form of mental disorder; when it occurs in settings where there is no plausible social reason available, however, as when a man kills and eats his mother, the individual is mentally disturbed (Aristotle, cited in Rosen 1968, 174). And there is nothing wrong with the internal functioning of survivors of a plane crash in a remote area who engage in cannibalism; they act comprehensibly in a desperate social context and so do not have mental disorders (e.g., Read 1992).

East African tribesmen also clearly distinguish between murders that arise from internal dysfunctions and those that stem from "appropriate," although deviant, motivational systems for murder:

> There is one essential feature of African psychosis. Respondent after respondent qualifies his description of a psychotic behavior by saying

"without reason." That is, murder as such is not psychotic—only murder *without some good reason is psychotic*. The same thing is true of every other behavior cited. (Edgerton 1966, 419; italics in original)

This group also clearly recognizes the distinction between deviance and mental disorder:

Eating feces, collecting trash, living in the bush, going naked, and all the other behaviors, are not necessarily psychotic. Each behavior can occur in exceptional circumstances, such as in ceremonies, or as the result of injury or illness, etc., without any suggestion of psychosis. (Edgerton 1966, 419)

Socially deviant actions in themselves—whether murder, collecting trash, or going naked—are not signs of mental disorder. Only deviant actions that arise because of the internal failure of a psychological mechanism are mental disorders.

An example from Ernest Hemingway's *A Moveable Feast* that contrasts the alcohol problems of the author F. Scott Fitzgerald with normal alcohol use also indicates the need to distinguish putative deviance from internal dysfunctions:

In Europe then we thought of wine as something as healthy and normal as food and also as a great giver of happiness and well being and delight. Drinking wine was . . . as natural as eating and to me as necessary, and I would not have thought of eating a meal without drinking either wine or cider or beer. I loved all wines . . . and it had never occurred to me that sharing a few bottles of fairly light, dry, white Macon could cause chemical changes in Scott that would turn him into a fool. (Hemingway 1964, 166–67)

Here, Hemingway notes that heavy alcohol consumption is often normative. He recognizes, however, that for certain people such as F. Scott Fitzgerald excessive alcohol consumption is an internal dysfunction that possibly arises because of biochemical reasons. For Hemingway alcohol use that indicates an internal dysfunction *contrasts with* normal heavy drinking. Calling both heavy, but normative, consumption of alcohol and alcohol use that reflects an internal dysfunction "mental disorders" combines two distinct types of behaviors. Not symptoms themselves but only symptoms that stem from internal dysfunctions should be considered signs of mental disorder.

There are many ways to engage in socially inappropriate behaviors. Nonconformity in itself does not indicate a mental disorder unless some internal mechanism renders an individual unable to conform to social norms. Many people use the wrong kinds of drugs, drink too much, lie, have sex without regard to consequences, and otherwise act in ways that violate normative standards. Most of them do not have internal dysfunctions (see for example Kennedy 1987; Klein 1978; Fingarette 1988; Alarcon 1995; Black 1983; Toby 1998). People who commit crimes that provide higher payoffs than conventional behaviors do not have "anti-social personalities"; more often they are acting rationally within their circumstances. Psychoactive drug use that occurs as part of religious ceremonies is socially sanctioned, not pathological. The heavy use of alcohol has been associated with ritual and celebratory occasions since ancient times.[12] Most members of college fraternities, street gangs, or religious orders who drink too much, fight too often, or refrain from sexual activity do not have disorders of "alcohol abuse," "anti-social personality disorder," or "sexual dysfunction," respectively.

The DSM definition of mental disorder explicitly recognizes this need to distinguish social deviance from mental disorders and to consider only symptoms that represent "dysfunctions in an individual" as signs of disorder (APA 1994, xxii). In fact, however, the symptom-based definitions of categorical disorders such as alcohol and drug abuse and dependence, oppositional defiant disorder, attention deficit disorder, and the like in the DSM ignore the heterogeneous nature of social deviance and consider *all* possible symptoms signs of mental disorder. Wakefield's analysis of conduct disorder exemplifies the ways the DSM, despite its definition, conflates mental disorder and social deviance (Wakefield 1994). According to the DSM, mental health professionals should diagnose conduct disorder in children when over a twelve-month period they display symptoms involving aggression, property destruction, deceitfulness, theft, and violation of social rules. The three best criteria for distinguishing this disorder are stealing, running away from home, and lying. Hence, clinicians who apply the criteria without exercising any discretion would diagnose an adolescent girl who attempts to avoid an abusive stepfather through lying, staying out past curfew, and leaving home as disordered. Likewise, in the absence of discretion, they would consider that a normal adolescent boy who responds to peer pressure to shoplift, lies to his parents about it, then runs away from home after he is punished has a mental disorder.

Swearing, arguing with adults, disobedience, and the like can indicate

What are these internal dysfunctions / mechanisms?

Who are these [handwritten, left margin]

culturally normative ways of asserting identity. Many children who meet symptomatic criteria for conduct disorder do not have internal dysfunctions but instead respond to social circumstances in ways that annoy their parents, teachers, and other adult authorities. Only symptoms that result from the failure of some internal mechanism to function appropriately are indications of mental disorders. [Otherwise, the rebellious, the troubled, the unhappy, or the foolish would all be lumped together with the truly disordered] (Wakefield 1992b).

may be a way to stop misbehav— [handwritten, right margin]

What distinguishes internal dysfunctions from immoral or idiosyncratic behavior, bad character traits, personal inadequacies, or bad judgment? A mental disorder indicates that something is wrong with the *capacity* of an internal mechanism to perform as it is designed to perform, not that an individual has made poor choices in how to behave. This incapacity renders an individual unable to conform to social rules and so their impairment is involuntary (Klein 1999). Deviant behaviors are not mental disorders unless they stem from some dysfunction of an internal psychological mechanism. The distinction between mental disorders and deviant behavior is the distinction between people who *can't* conform and those who *won't* conform (Wakefield 1997b). People with valid antisocial personality disorders, for example, would lack the capacity to feel guilt or remorse for their actions. A valid definition of mental disorder does not encompass deviant behaviors unless they are also internal dysfunctions.

How is it possible to know whether a particular behavior results from an internal dysfunction or from an individual choice? Social value judgments underlie this distinction. For example, adults who are only sexually aroused by young children may suffer from the disorder of pedophilia because normal mechanisms of sexual arousal among adults are directed at other adults and not at young children (Spitzer 1999). Adults who sexually molest young children, however, are generally treated as having criminal responsibility for their behaviors because of the extreme social abhorrence of child molestation. The distinction between people who can't function appropriately and those who won't function appropriately is far more a moral value judgment than a judgment based on psychiatric knowledge.

CONCLUSION

[Mental disorders are internal dysfunctions that sociocultural standards define as inappropriate] According to this definition, all mental disorders have a universal component that indicates some internal mechanism of thought, cognition, feeling, motivation, memory, or the like is not functioning as it is designed to function (Wakefield 1992b). In addition, however, mental disorders are inescapably tied to social values. Only internal dysfunctions that are also viewed as socioculturally inappropriate are mental disorders.

This definition links mental disorders both to physical disorders, which are primarily distinguished through their dysfunctional quality, and to social deviance, which is defined by its socially inappropriate nature. Yet it also distinguishes mental disorders from physical disorders, because social definitions are not necessary components of most bodily dysfunctions, and from social deviance, which need not involve any internal dysfunction. Mental disorders uniquely involve *both* internal dysfunctions and social definitions of inappropriateness.

How far does the valid range of mental disorders extend? Historically, this category has been very narrow. Dysfunctional perceptual mechanisms that lead people to hear voices that are not present or to see objects that are not visible, when no social system of rules accounts for the sounds or visions, have universally been considered to be mental disorders. Likewise, symptoms that represent unprovoked sadness or sadness disproportionate in intensity and duration to its context commonly indicate affective disorders. In addition to schizophrenia, bipolar disorder, and major endogenous depression, severe phobias, obsessions and compulsions, panic disorders, somatization disorders, eating disorders, alcoholism, and drug dependence all can be signs of internal dysfunctions. Although social values necessarily define what sounds are appropriate to hear and what sights are appropriate to see, what is reasonable fear and what is unreasonable paranoia, what is cleanliness and what is compulsion, or what are reasonable levels of alcohol and drug consumption, dysfunctional internal mechanisms are present in all mental disorders.

Even these conditions are only mental disorders when they are not expectable consequences of social arrangements and when they persist to an irrational degree as defined by the norms of a particular culture. Although, as chapter 5 emphasizes, these disorders rarely fit the categorical measurement model of diagnostic psychiatry, they are valid forms of mental disorder. In each case, however, it is necessary to distinguish symptoms that are expectable consequences of social arrangements from those that represent psychological dysfunctions.

Mental disorders are thus socially inappropriate psychological dysfunctions, which either emerge independently of social stressors or persist with disproportionate severity and duration after the stressors that gave rise to them have disappeared. Although this definition is compatible with the definition of mental disorder in the DSM-IV, it is very different from the actual use of the concept of mental disorder both in this manual and in psychiatric research. Contrary to its definition of mental disorder, a basic principle in the DSM definitions of particular disorders is to avoid inferences about the causes of symptoms (Goodwin and Guze 1996, 9). Yet, the presence of particular symptoms is *never* sufficient for a diagnosis of a mental disorder without consideration of the causes and contexts of these symptoms. People whose lovers have left them, who are in dead-end jobs with no future prospects, or who are unable to pay their bills develop the same symptoms of depression, anxiety, or substance abuse as those whose symptoms emerge in the absence of external stressors or "out of the blue." Although their symptom profiles are the same, only the latter group would be mentally ill because their moods, cognitions, and perceptions are not appropriate responses to their situations.

The failure to consider whether or not the most common symptoms of psychiatric disorders are actually harmful internal dysfunctions is the single most serious flaw in current psychiatric thinking (Wakefield 1996). An important implication of the concept of mental disorder as socially inappropriate internal dysfunction is that a large proportion of behaviors that are currently regarded as mental illnesses are normal consequences of stressful social arrangements or forms of social deviance. Contrary to its general definition of mental disorder, the DSM and much research that follows from it consider *all* symptoms, whether internal or not, expectable or not, deviant or not, as signs of disorder. The result is that contemporary psychiatry and psychiatric epidemiology considerably overestimate the amount of mental disorder (e.g., Robins et al. 1984; Kessler et al. 1994; Regier et al. 1998).[13]

How and why has such an expansive use of mental illness labels emerged? The reasons for the proliferation of mental illnesses lie in the historical development of the psychiatric profession over the course of the twentieth century and in the useful social functions such expansive definitions perform for a number of different groups. The next two chapters trace the historical developments that have led to the current broad use of the concept of mental illness.

Chapter Two

THE EXPANSION OF MENTAL ILLNESSES
IN DYNAMIC PSYCHIATRY

At the beginning of the twenty-first century, the ascendancy of diagnostic psychiatry is almost unquestioned. The many heterogeneous entities that it studies, whether schizophrenia, major depression, panic disorder, substance abuse and dependence, or attention deficit disorder, are accepted as "real" disorders. Yet, most of the disorders that form the core of psychiatric thought, research, and practice are, paradoxically, relatively new entities. At the beginning of the twentieth century, mental illnesses were limited to a small number of very serious disorders. Until recently, discrete disease entities had a minor role in psychiatry and allied mental health professions.

The classification of a large and heterogeneous group of conditions as "mental illnesses" emerged from a particular historical context. This chapter outlines the dynamic system of psychiatric thought that preceded the development of the diagnostic view of mental illness that now dominates the mental health arena. It shows how dynamic psychiatry changed mental illness from a restricted concept, limited to a small number of categories, to an expansive range of conditions. Dynamic psychiatry, however, viewed mental pathologies as nonspecific reflections of unconscious mechanisms, not as discrete symptom-based diseases. During the 1970s, the vague neuroses of dynamic psychiatry were reconceptualized as the specific diseases that are now foundational for diagnostic psychiatry. This chapter and the one that follows show the historical circumstances that led classifications of mental illnesses to expand to encompass a vast and heterogeneous range of human conditions.

THE ORIGINS OF PSYCHIATRIC CLASSIFICATION

Until the twentieth century, mental illness was equated with madness. The label of mental illness was mainly reserved for people who seemed to be "out of their minds," "lunatic," "mad," and "crazy" or for people whose deep depressions did not arise out of any recognizable social cause (see Rosen 1968; Grob 1973; Scull 1979; Tomes 1984; Jackson 1986; Eldridge 1996; Shorter 1997). The professional ancestors of psychiatrists, the alienists of the nineteenth century, treated only a narrow segment of serious mental disorders (Shorter 1992, 1997). The classifications of mental illnesses developed at this time were very simple and were limited to the categories of imbecility and insanity. When the profession of psychiatry emerged in the early nineteenth century, it dealt with a small number of highly bizarre and disruptive behaviors (Rothman 1971).

Before the emergence of dynamic psychiatry, mental illness was virtually identified with psychotic behaviors. The leading psychiatric classifier of the late nineteenth century, Emil Kraepelin, emphasized only two major types of mental disorders: affective psychoses, including bipolar as well as unipolar depression; and dementia praecox, now known as schizophrenia (Kraepelin 1896). When the first official psychiatric nosology was published in the United States in 1918, it comprised twenty-two categories, twenty-one of which referred to various forms of psychoses; the remaining category was reserved for all patients who were not psychotic (Grob 1991b). Psychiatrists viewed the behaviors enumerated in this classification system as discontinuous entities, each with distinct symptoms, courses, causes, and treatments.

An emphasis on the biological underpinnings of this small number of severe conditions characterized psychiatry in the nineteenth century (see Shorter 1997; Scull, MacKenzie and Herevey 1996; Grob 1973). During this period, psychiatrists believed that symptoms of mental illness arose out of disordered brains. The most influential biological psychiatrist of the time, Wilhelm Griesinger, stated this most starkly in his dictum that mental disorders were brain diseases (Griesinger 1845; see also Shorter 1997, 76). Symptoms of these disorders were seen as surface manifestations of underlying morbid states of the brain and the nervous system.

At the end of the nineteenth century, when dynamic psychiatry emerged, psychiatrists treated a small number of well-known disorders. Other categories, such as "nerves," "neurasthenia," "lovesickness," or "hysteria," were few in number, nonspecific, and expansive (Shorter 1992). Most people who sought help for these disorders would see general medical practitioners who did not identify with the psychiatric profession. These practitioners used cures that emphasized somatic techniques including rest, diet, and electricity. Wealthier sufferers often saw specialized practitioners such as spa doctors or nerve doctors who avoided any connection with madness (Shorter 1994; Caplan 1998). Outside of medicine, people might discuss unhappiness, dissatisfaction, interpersonal conflict, and life crises with the clergy. No cultural category defined as illnesses the general feelings of angst or maladjustment patients came to display in later decades (see Abbott 1988, chap. 10). Psychiatric classifications were reserved for the sorts of conditions that required hospitalization.

The fact that people did not use psychiatric categories as interpretations of personal troubles and did not seek help from psychiatric professionals does not mean that people did not experience distress. Rather, it indicates that distressed people used other culturally shaped modes, especially forms of physical illness or of spiritual crises, to define their conditions. Psychiatric practice was limited to the treatment of seriously disturbed institutionalized patients; outpatient psychiatry barely existed. Members of the psychiatric profession treated the most severe and disruptive forms of disorder, almost always in institutional settings. No mental health profession was associated with the treatment of nonpsychotic forms of mental disorder.

Until the end of the nineteenth century, it was culturally impossible for sufferers from any but the most severe mental disorders to formulate their problems in psychiatric terms. Over the course of the twentieth century, this limited classification of mental illness changed beyond recognition.

THE RISE OF DYNAMIC PSYCHIATRY

The most influential student of mental disorder in the twentieth century, Sigmund Freud, published his first major work, *The Interpretation of Dreams*, in 1900.¹ At this time, psychiatry was an asylum-based discipline that treated the most serious cases of mental disorder through somatic therapies. By the time of Freud's death in 1939, the most basic ways of thinking about mental disorder had been transformed. When the diagnostic counterrevolution against dynamic psychiatry emerged in the 1970s, Freudian thought had completely altered the landscape of psychiatry. Several aspects of the dynamic view of mental disorder are critical for understanding the subsequent transformation of dynamic into diagnostic psychiatry. These include an expansion of the scope of psychiatry to include an enormous range of symptoms and behaviors, the redefinition of the basic motivations behind human behavior, the development of a lay subculture devoted to the tenets of dynamic psychiatry, and the relocation of psychiatric practice from the asylum to the office.

Dynamic psychiatry laid the foundation for the sprawling mass of troubling behaviors that diagnostic psychiatry would later formulate as distinct disease entities. The language dynamic psychiatry created spread far beyond the psychoses and neuroses to explain a wide array of problematic psychological and behavioral conditions. Mental health professionals became culturally recognized arbiters not only of serious mental disorders but also of personal problems, unhappiness, and deviant behavior. Diagnostic psychiatry did not invent therapeutic culture—it inherited that culture from its dynamic predecessor.

they became authorized knowers.

The Classification of Symptoms   Dynamic psychiatry revolutionized the classification of psychiatric symptoms. The basic principle of dynamic classification was to link neurotic with normal behavior and to classify both as variants of common developmental processes. This endeavor blurred the distinction between the normal and the neurotic but kept the distinction between the psychotic and all other behaviors. The result was to narrow the gap between neurotic and normal behavior while maintaining the distinctions between psychotic conditions and both neuroses and normality. This categorization allowed mental health professionals to treat a vastly expanded realm of patients in outpatient practices and to neglect the problems of institutionalized mental patients.

For Freud neuroses stemmed from universal childhood experiences; the differences separating normal from abnormal behavior were only matters of degree, not of kind. Dynamic psychiatry was built on viewing the origin of neuroses in universal psychological processes such as infants sucking at their mother's breasts, unresolved oedipal complexes, toilet-training practices, and parental giving and withholding of love and hostility. Ordinary experiences in childhood such as masturbation, for example, might be precursors to a variety of adult addictions such as smoking, drug addiction, or compulsive gambling (Freud 1989 [1924]).

Just as Freud normalized pathology, he also showed how ordinary behavior stemmed from the same roots as the pathological. Freud provided a general psychology to understand all human behavior, not just neurotic behavior. The highest virtues, as well as the worst perversions, stemmed from the same instinctual basis. The genesis of sexual perversions and great scientific and artistic achievements alike was found in the different ways people repressed common forms of sexual energy found among all children (Freud 1960 [1924]). Repression of normal sexual development might lead in one case to sexual perversion, but in another case to great artistic achievement.

The central works of Freud's early career, *The Interpretation of Dreams* and *Psychopathology of Everyday Life*, focused on examples based on non-clinical cases (Freud 1958 [1900], 1960 [1914]). The mechanisms that underlie dreams or slips of the tongue among presumably normal people were analogous to the mechanisms that underlie symptoms of neuroses among neurotics. Dynamic psychiatry used the same techniques to uncover the unconscious meanings expressed in fairy tales, jokes, dreams, or neurotic symptoms. The major works of the last part of Freud's career, *Civilization and Its Discontents* and *The Future of an Illusion*, applied dynamic theories to major social institutions (Freud 1930, 1928). The use of common explanations for normal as well as for pathological behaviors thoroughly blurred the boundary between normality and abnormality and linked both normal and neurotic behaviors to the same principles of human development. The joining of neurotic with normal behavior served at the same time to make pathological, nonpsychotic behavior ordinary and to pathologize ordinary, everyday behavior (Roazen 1992).

The new classificatory system fundamentally changed the relationship between mental illness and normality. When mental illnesses were limited to psychotic behaviors, they were readily distinguished from normality. Psychoses differ qualitatively, not just quantitatively, from normal behavior. In contrast to psychotic disorders, there are only gradients of neuroses. Neurotic behaviors were conceived as continuous with normal behaviors, the two blurring indistinctly into each other (Grob 1991a; Hale 1995). The conditions at the core of dynamic psychiatry, such as sexual perversions, hysteria, obsessions, compulsions, phobias, and anxiety, were viewed not as forms of illness but as exaggerations of normal behavioral functions. For example, on one end of a personality continuum was the rigidity of the obsessive-compulsive, which shaded into the well-organized normal individual. On the other end of this continuum was the disorganization of the hysterical personality (Fenichel 1995 [1945]). The assumption of a near universality of psychopathology made the abnormal less strange and at the same time heightened the strangeness of the normal.

Dynamic psychiatry came to encompass both neurotic and seemingly normal behavior. What place do psychotic mental illnesses have when neurotic symptoms are lumped with normal behaviors? The extensive attempts of analysts to break down the boundaries between neuroses and normality contrasted with their great ambivalence over whether psychoses and neuroses were continuous or discontinuous. Although analysts did not always follow his advice, Freud counseled his followers against treating psychotics.

"I am skeptical," he wrote, "about the effectiveness of analysis for the therapy of psychoses" (quoted in Roazen 1992, 142). The ambition of analysis to create a theory of all human behaviors inevitably led practitioners to attempts to explain psychoses. Yet, according to the major textbook of psychoanalysis, the mechanisms underlying schizophrenia were different from neurotic mechanisms and were difficult to integrate into the body of analytic knowledge (Fenichel 1995 [1945], 443). The essence of psychoanalytic classification was to abolish the boundary between neurosis and normality, not the boundary between psychosis and all other behavior. Although analysts hoped someday to encompass all behaviors, including psychosis, within the same general theory, their focus clearly lay on neurotic and normal behavior, and not on psychotic behavior.

The Interpretation of Symptoms Another revolutionary aspect of dynamic psychiatry was its reconceptualization of the nature of mental symptoms. Before the development of dynamic psychiatry, psychotic conditions located in the brain virtually exhausted the realm of mental disorders. For asylum psychiatry symptoms of psychiatric disorders were direct indicators of underlying brain diseases (Grob 1973; Scull, MacKenzie, and Herevey 1996). In a disease, the same constellation of overt symptoms in different people is likely to indicate the same underlying disease process.

When Freud began to construct his theories, psychological explanations were not well-established ways of interpreting mental symptoms. Although earlier theories, particularly magnetism, emphasized the importance of the unconscious mind, Freud was the first psychologist to develop a comprehensive theory and technique of psychotherapy that focused on interior mental processes (Ellenberger 1970). Before Freud, people generally used physical idioms to interpret nervousness, anxiety, paralyzed limbs, or sexual problems and they sought help from medical professionals. Others consulted with religious authorities and developed spiritual interpretations to interpret sadness, dissatisfaction, and general problems of living (Abbott 1988; Caplan 1998).

Freud and his followers redefined these spiritual or somatic problems with no demonstrable physical cause as symbolic expressions of psychological conflicts rather than as disorders of the body or spirit (e.g., Freud 1917, 1964 [1933]; Alexander 1948). In this view, symptoms only became meaningful as symbolic reflections of personal biographies. Symptoms did not directly indicate underlying diseases but arose from a complicated interplay between unconscious dynamics and processes of repression. Their meaning

[handwritten marginalia: Conven assignment]

[handwritten at bottom: also related to movie — because we can only go by what ppl tell us.]

42 · 43

only became clear after sufferers engaged in intensive and extensive explorations of their most intimate thoughts and feelings with therapists in an effort to understand how their symptoms stemmed from their personal histories.[2]

The psychodynamic view formulated psychological symptoms as completely distinct from symptoms with clear physical causes. In particular, dynamic psychiatry radically altered the relationship between overt symptoms and the underlying diseases they indicated. Symptoms became symbolic expressions of the mind and, in particular, those aspects of the mind that were not accessible to consciousness. There was no longer a direct link between symptoms and diseases, and the same symptom could take on entirely different significance for different people. "The hysterical symptom," as Freud wrote, "does not carry (any particular) meaning with it, but the meaning is lent to it, soldered to it, as it were; and in every instance the meaning can be a different one, according to the nature of the suppressed thoughts which are struggling for expression" (Freud 1963 [1905], 57). Particular biographical contexts that vary from person to person, not a connection to an underlying disease entity, accounted for the meaning of symptoms.

Because symptoms had no direct relationship to underlying diseases, the causal processes that produced symptoms rather than the nature of symptoms themselves determined the type of neuroses people had. Sexual and aggressive instincts, in particular, provided the particular focus of analysis. In a sweeping statement, Freud proclaimed: "I can only repeat over and over again—for I never find it otherwise—that sexuality is the key to the problem of the psychoneuroses and the neuroses in general" (Freud 1963 [1905], 136). Sexual instincts, unlike other instincts such as hunger or thirst that display themselves directly, are highly changeable and become manifest in many different forms (Fenichel 1995 [1945], 194). The repression of deviant sexual urges, for example, might lead in one case to hysterical symptoms but in another case to an obsessive-compulsive disorder. The critical focus of dynamic attention became the general mechanisms that could produce a variety of outward manifestations in particular cases. For example, understanding the mechanism of reaction formation that presumably led phobics to wish for what they feared was of much greater importance than understanding the particular phobic symptoms. Central to the treatment of a boy who displaced a fear of his father onto horses, therefore, was an analysis of the displacement, not of the horse phobia (Freud 1924 [1909]).

The particular etiological claims of dynamic psychiatry are not important for the purposes of this work. What is important is that in the dynamic view symptoms were never *direct indicators* of underlying disorders; instead they were *symbolic expressions* of conflicts that involved the entire personality. Symptoms in themselves were not important because similar symptoms can represent many different underlying disturbances. Indeed, diametrically opposite symptom patterns, such as intense fear or intense attachment, could stem from a common etiology and so might indicate the same type of disorder. In fact, overt symptoms inevitably *masked* the underlying conflict that gave rise to them. "The theory of repression," Freud claimed, "is the cornerstone on which the whole structure of psychoanalysis rests" (Freud 1924, 16). The physical symptoms of hysterics, for example, might express secret and repressed wishes that could not be expressed directly. What appeared on the surface were transformations of socially unacceptable unconscious drives and instincts that had been reformulated into more acceptable forms. Overt symptoms thus did not reveal diseases but disguised underlying conflicts that could not be expressed directly or even consciously recognized.

For dynamic psychiatry, symptoms represented chameleon-like expressions of underlying unconscious conflicts. Just as the same symptoms could represent different disorders, any underlying disorder could manifest itself in many different overt guises. The particular symptoms of anorexia, chronic fatigue, sleep disturbance, or hypochondria were not given much importance in the dynamic view because common mechanisms might underlie these various symptoms. Depending on many contingencies of personal biography and social context, the same underlying conflict might result in hysterical symptoms, phobias, or obsessions, among many other possibilities. Because the manifestations of underlying conflicts included physical as well as psychological symptoms, the distinction between physical and psychological disorders was virtually impossible to delineate and maintain. Indeed, the most prevalent symptoms of neurosis—dyspepsia, headaches, insomnia, neuralgia, fatigue, and the like—were also common indicators of many physical disorders. Only deep, extensive, and intensive exploration of the individual personality could indicate the true meaning of any symptomatic presentation.

> classification
as diff.

When symptoms indicate underlying diseases they can be used in fairly straightforward ways to create diagnostic systems. Patients who display given collections of symptoms are expected to have distinct conditions with common etiology, course over time, and response to particular treatments. Thus, a pock is an indicator of smallpox or persistent wheezing can be a sign of asthma. When, however, symptoms are symbols that have highly

we were specifically ask why particular mental disorders occur with particular systems

able meanings depending on their particular context and underlying dy-
ics, they cannot be used to construct a well-defined diagnostic system.
In dynamic psychiatry, symptoms at best only provided clues to what disorder might underlie them. Freud's view of the symptoms of one of his famous
hysterics is typical: "we should understand just as much or just as little of
the whole business if the result of the trauma had been symptoms quite
other than *tussis nervosa* (nervous cough), aphonia, depression, and *taedium
vitae* (boredom)" (Freud 1963 [1905], 42).

When the various shapes taken by underlying conflicts were so numerous and amorphous, it was neither possible nor desirable to develop elaborate symptom-based classifications. Overt symptoms were actually an obstacle to accurate dynamic classifications because they only represented the
most socially acceptable ways of manifesting unconscious conflicts. Because
the same symptoms could indicate different disorders or the same disorders
could become manifest through different symptoms, a highly elaborated
diagnostic system was not useful in dynamic psychiatry (Hale 1995). Dynamic classifications came to be based instead on very general etiological
schemes.

Psychiatric practice in the first part of the twentieth century did not put
too much stake in particular diagnostic categories and so the classificatory
vagueness of dynamic psychiatry was not a problem at that time. The first
official manual of the American Psychiatric Association, the DSM-I (1952),
reflected views of dynamic psychiatrists, especially of Adolf Meyer, the
most prominent American psychiatrist of the first half of the twentieth
century (Grob 1991b). Specific diagnostic entities had a limited role in the
DSM-I and its successor, the DSM-II (1968). These manuals conceived of
symptoms as reflections of broad underlying dynamic conditions or as reactions to difficult life problems, and they made little effort to provide any
elaborate classification scheme. When, however, the culture of medicine
changed to demand well-defined disease entities, the intellectual inability
of dynamic psychiatry to produce specific diagnoses came to be felt as a
crippling defect.

The Development of Psychotherapeutic Culture   The intellectual system of
dynamic thinking about the nature, causes, and treatment of mental disorders does not in itself explain the success of dynamic psychiatry in a particular historical period. Systems of thought generally become credible and are
institutionalized because they fit the needs of specific social groups. The
success of dynamic psychiatry was due to the development and growth of

a lay culture that accepted dynamic explanations (Grob 1991a; Kadushin 1969; Hale 1995; Herman 1995). In contrast, many psychiatric treatments can be imposed on involuntary populations, regardless of whether these groups share the basic assumptions of practitioners of these treatments. The coercion of the asylum, the changes a medication produces in the brain, or a psychosurgical operation require neither the consent nor the willing participation of subjects in order to be successful. Far more than previous responses to mental illness, such as asylum psychiatry, medication treatment, or medical care, the nature of dynamic psychiatry required that its audience *believe* in its tenets. Dynamic therapies could only work when clients and therapists cooperated in exploring how symptoms represented personality dynamics and so they required a clientele who accepted the tenets of its conceptual system and who felt they could benefit from this kind of treatment (Frank and Frank 1991; Horwitz 1982a, chap. 8). How did a clientele of this nature emerge?

Dynamic explanations posited that symptoms were symbolic manifestations that only became meaningful in the context of the personal history of the individual. Dynamic treatment strove to uncover the intrapsychic conflicts that lay beneath manifest symptoms. The most essential aspect of treatment in dynamic psychiatry, therefore, was to turn individuals inward toward a consideration of their biographies. The focus of analysis was the total personality and life experiences of the person that provided the context for the interpretation of symptoms. Dynamic treatments emphasized techniques, especially dream analysis, that helped patients gain access to their unconscious processes and that focused on the recovery of childhood memories and repressed sexual and aggressive thoughts. Feelings that rose to the surface in analysis were connected to underlying unconscious experiences. In the therapeutic process, patients learned to overcome the various defense mechanisms and resistances they used to avoid recognizing the true reasons why their symptoms developed. These reasons were assumed to lie in forgotten experiences of childhood and especially in childhood sexuality. Meaningful and lasting change only occurred when patients and their analysts hit upon the correct symbolic interpretation of unwanted behaviors.

Dynamic therapy thus turned patients away from the public arena to examine themselves and their personal emotions. Indeed, dynamic psychiatry interpreted the public spheres of politics, religion, and culture themselves in terms of inner psychological dynamics and early family experiences (Freud 1928, 1930). The view of the individual found in dynamic psychiatry was not of a person integrated into a network of encompassing social and cultural ties but of someone constantly in conflict with social and cultural demands. Human nature was inherently and permanently unsocial. Freudianism inculcated "skepticism about all ideologies except those of private life" (Rieff 1961, 278).

The practice of dynamic psychiatry thus required patients who were willing to reveal their innermost feelings, thoughts, and memories to their therapists. Therefore, dynamic psychiatry could only succeed when its clients believed that its tenets provided a compelling explanation for their problems. The spread of dynamic psychiatry presupposed a culture of patients who spoke the language of analysis and who were eager to engage with their therapists in the symbolic interpretation of symptoms. There was, therefore, an elective affinity between a system that interpreted overt symptoms as symbolic manifestations of personal biographies and people whose own lives were not enmeshed in strong groups or powerful collective systems of meaning.

Dynamic psychiatry initially enjoyed particular success among intellectuals and people with unconventional lifestyles. Meaningful existence for such persons stemmed from individual experiences rather than from strong ties to traditional groups. Therapies that found the ultimate meanings of life within the most interior recesses of the personality would resonate with the values and activities of such individuals. People in these categories were already knowledgeable and informed about the premises of dynamic psychiatry and so presented the problems of sexuality, anxiety, interpersonal relationships, and depression that dynamic theory considered important (Abbott 1988). Analysis was a resounding cultural success in a particular time and place because it addressed the needs of this particular clientele (Kadushin 1969; Lunbeck 1994).

The initial appeal of dynamic psychiatry was to those who rejected conventional morality, especially conventional sexual morality. Its tenets appeared to maximize personal freedom and to reject traditional cultural systems of belief and behavior. Analysis was associated with attempts to overcome a repressive society that stymied genuine expression of basic instincts. Hence, artists, writers, bohemians, and intellectuals who were associated with rebellion against mainstream society were the first enthusiasts of dynamic psychiatry (Hale 1995).

Jews, in particular, were attracted to dynamic psychiatry (Shorter 1997). Psychoanalysis was developed in Vienna, an urban center of European culture at the turn of the twentieth century and possibly the most cosmopolitan city of the time. Many Viennese Jews were not far removed from the psychological upheaval that stemmed from movement from shtetl life in small towns or in rural areas to the cosmopolitan life of a major urban center. While some Viennese Jews retained the strong ties to the community typical of traditional Jewish culture, many others had become assimilated into the wider cosmopolitan culture of the city (Ellenberger 1970; Janik and Toulmin 1973; Decker 1991; Walkup 1986). Freud's own father was a freethinker who raised his children in a secular atmosphere. As Rieff notes, Freud's religion was "not of the Jew integrated into his own community but of the 'infidel Jew' standing on the edge of an alien culture and perpetually arrayed against it" (Rieff 1961, 283). The progenitor of dynamic psychiatry was, in his own life, an urban intellectual alienated from the culture of his forefathers and a member of a marginal ethnic group. Such a man was well-suited to develop a system of thought based on the dual notions of the repressiveness of conventional social ties and the inner exploration of the individual psyche. It is not surprising that it "was above all among the middle-class Jews of Berlin, Budapest, and Vienna that psychoanalysis proved such a hit" (Shorter 1997, 183).

With the rise of Hitler and the approach of the Holocaust in the 1930s, many of the founders of dynamic psychiatry fled to the United States. In the United States Jews have always been vastly overrepresented as clients of dynamic psychiatry. Although only about one percent of the U.S. population is Jewish, Jews have made up about half the clients of dynamic therapists since the 1920s (Kadushin 1969; Rogow 1970; Marx and Spray 1972). Indeed, a national survey in 1976 found that more than half of Jewish respondents had entered psychotherapy at some point in their life, a rate far higher than for any other group (Veroff, Kulka, and Douvan 1981).

Dynamic psychiatry came to form the basis of a cultural view of troubling conditions of all sorts. The artists, intellectuals, writers, educators, bohemians, Jews, and others who were attracted to the symbolic system of analysis found in it a worldview, not only a system of therapy. For these groups, the language of dynamic psychiatry became a widely recognized, well-understood, and prestigious basis for interpreting personal troubles. The primary clients of psychotherapists during the decades of the predominance of dynamic psychiatry in the first two-thirds of the twentieth century were college-educated middle- and upper-middle-class professionals and intellectuals whose culture centered on verbal and symbolic skills and was congruent with the introspective and psychological norms of the mental health professions (Horwitz 1982a, chaps. 3–4; 1987). The clients of dynamic psychotherapists were disproportionately white, Jewish, intellectual, highly educated, and wealthy and were very rarely members of lower-SES groups or of disadvantaged ethnic groups (Hollingshead and Redlich 1958; Goldberg and Huxley 1980; Redlich and Kellert 1978). Kadushin, for example, found that typical clients of outpatient psychiatric care in New York City during the late 1950s went to plays, concerts, museums, and art galleries, and worked in occupations that stressed the artistic and the psychological, such as the health professions, teaching, the arts, and communications (Kadushin 1969).

The nature of dynamic psychiatry explains its affinity with disaffiliated intellectuals and nonreligious Jews. Analytic explanations focused on symbols derived from personal experience, not from collective experiences in the group.[4] Individuals who lacked strong collective bonds and who were marginal to mainstream society were especially drawn to therapies that emphasized self-exploration and self-awareness rather than conformity to the normative order of groups. Likewise, intellectuals liberated from traditional groups were attracted to interpretive systems that emphasized how true meaning was hidden from the conscious mind and how knowledge was acquired only by exploring private and obscure layers of the self that led to the unconscious. Their social context led such people to mistrust public communication and to embrace a system that found the real self only after therapy stripped away the social self.

The Extension of the Abnormal　The lumping of neurotic with normal behaviors and the splitting of both from psychoses had major consequences for psychiatric practice as well as for theory. Before the emergence of dynamic psychiatry, the practice of psychiatry was indistinguishable from the treatment of psychosis within institutional settings. Neurologists, internists, nonspecialized physicians, or clergy, rather than psychiatrists, treated people who displayed what came to be viewed as neurotic symptoms. Indeed, no classified realm of phenomena outside of the asylum existed for psychiatry to treat. "To survive as a discipline," observes Edward Shorter, "psychiatry had to break free of insanity and of organicist assumptions about the nature of nervous disease" (Shorter 1997, 144; see also Abbott 1988).

The new dynamic classificatory scheme provided a solution to this dilemma. It allowed psychiatrists to leave the asylum and to extend their practices to a new range of clients and symptoms (Lunbeck 1994). The reclassification of symptoms also enabled psychiatrists to neglect the treatment of the seriously mentally ill and to turn their attention to the people with neurotic conditions. It also allowed their clients to distinguish their suffering from madness and from the stigma of a label of madness.

After 1920 the practices of psychiatrists began to shift from the asylum to the office. The number of American psychiatrists in private practice rose from 8 percent in 1917, to 38 percent in 1941, to 66 percent by 1970 (Shorter 1997, 160). By the beginning of World War II, dynamic psychiatrists far outnumbered asylum psychiatrists and had captured the intellectual leadership of the psychiatric profession. The role of dynamically oriented psychiatrists in World War II reinforced psychiatry's institutional role and prestige. During the war, these psychiatrists played central roles in screening draftees for mental disorders, in developing the view of combat neuroses as normal adaptations to stressful environments, and in treating soldiers with these conditions (Grob 1990). After World War II, the dominance of dynamic psychiatry in American academic psychiatry was almost complete and most chairs of psychiatric departments were drawn from the ranks of this group. By the 1950s, the image of dynamic psychiatry had shifted from one identified with radical currents in art, morality, and politics to one integrated into mainstream institutions. In a period of roughly fifty years, dynamic psychiatry had transformed the landscape of psychiatric thought and practice (Grob 1991a).[5]

Not only the institutional location of dynamic psychiatry but also the sorts of conditions it treated broadened over the first half of the twentieth century. Dynamic psychiatry originally studied and treated conditions such as obsessions, compulsions, phobias, frigidity, and anxiety disorders, collectively called the "neuroses."[6] But the principle that the boundary between neurotic and normal behavior was fluid and that mental disorders were continuous with normality naturally led to a great expansion beyond these particular conditions.

Over the first half of the twentieth century, dynamic psychiatry created a language through which troubled people could interpret and seek relief for a wide variety of their problems. It broadened its focus from the neuroses to more generalized maladaptive patterns of behavior and character and the even more nebulous and far broader realm of personal problems. During the era in which dynamic theories dominated the mental health professions, its clients came to be people who were dissatisfied with themselves, their relationships, their careers, and their lives in general. They had poor marriages, troubled children, failed ambitions, general nervousness and diffuse anxiety, and general discontent with their lives. Psychiatry was trans-

'd from a discipline concerned with insanity to one concerned with lity.[7]

Further, the territory of dynamic psychiatry expanded beyond neuroses and personal problems into the containment of deviant behavior. The mental hygiene movement, which was founded in 1910, extended mental health principles into schools, juvenile courts, child guidance clinics, and educational programs (Danziger 1990). Its central premise, adopted from dynamic psychiatry, was that childhood conflicts formed the basis for problematic behaviors in adulthood. These conflicts could be prevented through the early intervention of mental health professionals, social workers, and teachers versed in dynamic premises (Davis 1938).[8]

The jurisdiction of the mental health professions expanded into the treatment of many forms of deviant behavior (Hale 1995). During the 1930s, the mental hygiene movement came to pervade the "new criminology" that viewed crime, delinquency, and addiction as problems that should be subject to therapy rather than to punishment. It became the basis of therapeutic programs dealing with juvenile delinquents, adult criminals, alcoholics, drug addicts, and other troublesome persons. Unlike the clients of outpatient therapists, who were immersed in a culture of therapy, this population did not voluntarily seek dynamic treatment; they had no choice but to enter programs that were intended to change their deviant behaviors.

Dynamic psychiatry thus expanded from the treatment of neurotic conditions to the involuntary treatment of a variety of deviant and criminal behaviors. By the 1950s dynamic psychiatry had also entered conventional culture, albeit in ways that watered down its criticism of social institutions and its emphasis on sexual instincts. Accounts of psychoanalysis in the popular press and movies in this period were highly favorable. During the period of its greatest influence from the late 1940s through the mid-1960s, psychiatrists were portrayed as wise, humane, and effective and their patients as ordinary people beset by common symptoms (Hale 1995).

Although the subsequent diagnostic counterrevolution in psychiatry displaced most of the dynamic legacy, it never abandoned the vast expansion of conditions encompassed within dynamic psychiatry. Indeed, an essential feature of contemporary psychiatry—the broad range of phenomena it now treats—is a direct legacy from its now thoroughly repudiated predecessor. As Lunbeck notes:

> the sources of psychiatry's widely noted dominance lie neither in its long-overdue embrace of science, as those writing from within the disci-

pline have argued, nor in its enduring commitment to social control, as many critics of psychiatry have proposed, but here, in psychiatrists' delineation of a realm of everyday concerns—sex, marriage, womanhood, and manhood; work, ambition, worldly failure, habits, desires, inclinations—as properly psychiatric. (Lunbeck 1994, 47)[10]

Dynamic psychiatry transformed the jurisdiction of the mental health professions from people with serious mental illnesses to those with problems in their everyday lives.

The great professional achievement of dynamic psychiatry was to create a new and nearly boundless field of practice for psychiatry outside of an institutional context. Its success, however, came at the expense of the institutionalized mentally ill who had formerly constituted the core of psychiatric practice. By 1957, only 17 percent of the members of the American Psychiatric Association had any affiliation with a mental institution (Grob 1991a; see also Murray 1979). Most clients of psychiatrists now had problems that had nothing in common with the bizarreness and disconnection experienced by the seriously mentally ill. The potential domain of psychiatric classification was now all of human behavior. "The optimum conditions for (psychoanalysis) exist where it is not needed—i.e., among the healthy," Freud once wrote (Roazen 1992, 160). Psychiatric therapy had become a means of understanding the self and of adjusting to social demands more than a treatment for specific mental disorders.

Dynamic thought became widely institutionalized and dominated thinking about mental disorder until the 1970s. Freud's cultural status during the period of the ascendancy of dynamic psychiatry was most succinctly stated by the poet W. H. Auden (1991):

> To us he is no more a person
> Now but a whole climate of opinion.

The rapid collapse of dynamic psychiatry from its dominant cultural position was due to a changing scientific, political, and economic environment that compelled psychiatry to redefine its subject matter as specific disease entities.

move from Symbols/meaning → disease formation with symptoms/classification!

CONCLUSION

Before Freud, a rigid boundary existed between the insane and others. Freud transformed this boundary by creating a new class of neurotic behaviors and linking it with normal rather than with psychotic behaviors. The dynamic system of categorization was fluid with fuzzy boundaries between neurosis and normality. The mode of explanation found in dynamic thinking, which promoted a deep understanding of unconscious motivations underlying behavior, was attractive to an intellectually prominent clientele. Psychoanalysis and related dynamic systems became central modes of understanding not only in psychotherapy but also in literature, the arts, and popular culture.

Between the mid-1960s and the mid-1980s the fortunes of dynamic psychiatry declined rapidly and a totally new system of diagnostically based psychiatry suddenly emerged. Beginning in the early 1960s, the percentage of psychiatrists and clinical psychologists identifying with dynamic psychiatry began to fall (Grob 1991a; Hale 1995).[11] By the beginning of the twenty-first century, virtually no dynamic practitioners head departments of psychiatry, many of which no longer even teach courses based on dynamic principles. While dynamic psychiatry remains popular among some nonpsychiatric mental health professionals, few psychiatrists now identify themselves with therapeutic schools guided by dynamic tenets (Hale 1995, 302). The emergence of diagnostic psychiatry was not a gradual and piecemeal evolution, but a total reorientation of the discipline over a short period of time. The transformation of psychiatric thinking was less the result of new knowledge than an epistemological revolution that focused a new mental lens on the same set of psychological conditions. The subject matter of psychiatry, which had been blurry continua produced by vague underlying psychic mechanisms, suddenly became sharply delineated disease entities. Indeed, at the beginning of the twenty-first century, dynamic thinking is commonly viewed as an embarrassing lapse in the continuous progress of scientific psychiatry (Shorter 1997).

The next chapter considers the reasons behind the fall of dynamic psychiatry and its replacement by a radically different system of psychiatric thought. No single reason accounts for the fall of dynamic psychiatry, but changes both in professional norms and in the external cultural, political, and economic environments of psychiatry were contributing factors (Hale 1995, chap. 20; Michels and Marzuk 1993; Shorter 1997). Dynamic thinking came to be incompatible with legitimate models of disease in medicine, the need to be accountable to third-party payers, the requirement of pharmaceutical companies to have diseases for their products to treat, and changes in the politics of mental health. In addition, the dynamic view of personal problems was incompatible with the cultural climate that emerged in the

1960s. The demise of dynamic psychiatry did not result from the demonstration that its premises were false. Rather, these premises were no longer useful in a changed medical, social, cultural, political, and economic environment. The social context of psychiatry demanded a total transformation of thinking if psychiatry was to survive as a medical discipline.

Diagnosis had, at best, a minor role in dynamic psychiatry. A diagnosis might emerge after a long period in therapy but was hardly ever a starting point of treatment (Pichot 1997). The insignificance of diagnosis in dynamic psychiatry follows from the premise that overt symptoms disguise a far more complex reality. The same symptoms might indicate different basic causal mechanisms and different symptoms might represent the same underlying mechanism. Symptoms in themselves were of limited importance for dynamic psychiatrists, whose major endeavor was to search for the basic psychic processes that accounted for various conditions.

In the 1970s, psychiatry imported the diagnostic model from medicine to replace the dynamic model. In a remarkably short time, psychiatry shed one intellectual paradigm and adopted an entirely new system of classification. In sharp contrast to the limited role of diagnosis in dynamic psychiatry, in clinical medicine diagnosis is "the keystone of medical practice and clinical research" (Goodwin and Guze 1996). Psychiatry reorganized itself from a discipline where diagnosis played a marginal role to one where it became the basis of the specialty. The diagnostic model did not arise arbitrarily or randomly. Its success resulted from its ability to meet changing demands both in the internal culture and in the external social, economic, and political environments of the psychiatric profession. Underlying this success was the classification of the subject matter of the psychiatric profession into discrete disease entities.

In many respects, the adoption of the diagnostic model in the official manual of the psychiatric profession, the DSM-III, in 1980 provides a textbook case of Thomas Kuhn's model of scientific revolution. For Kuhn, scientific styles of thought, or paradigms, are rooted in the social practices of scientific communities (Kuhn 1970; see also Fleck 1979 [1935]). These communities dictate certain assumptions about the nature, causes, and control of the discipline's subject matter and reject alternative ways of thinking. New paradigms are not built upon old ones to accumulate toward closer approximations of truth; rather, successive paradigms are fundamentally incommensurate ways of viewing the world. In Kuhn's view, a transformation from one thought community to another rarely arises out of the development of new knowledge; instead, such change is only undertaken in order to resolve a state of crisis in the previously dominant paradigm. The new model gains acceptance not so much because it more accurately characterizes the natural world as because it is better able to justify the social practices of the relevant discipline.

Although the adequacy of Kuhn's model for explaining scientific change in general has been widely debated, it provides a good explanation for the rapid discrediting of dynamic psychiatry and the ascendancy of diagnostic psychiatry in the last decades of the twentieth century.[1] Indeed, in many ways the thoroughgoing crisis in psychiatry that began in the 1960s, accelerated during the 1970s, and was resolved in the 1980s exemplifies Kuhn's model of scientific change. In dynamic psychiatry, pathological conditions such as anxiety, hysteria, sexual perversions, and character disorders were not sharply defined entities but indeterminate manifestations of underlying unconscious mechanisms (Freud 1960 [1924], 1964 [1933]). Dynamic clinicians sought the causes of psychological disturbances in repressed intrapsychic experiences and the cures for these disturbances in treatments that explored the deepest recesses of each person's biography. This model was suitable when the mental health professions did not require a rationalized, quantitative system of thought about mental illnesses. Once professional, economic, and organizational circumstances changed, however, the glaring weaknesses of the dynamic system became apparent.

The replacement of the vague, opaque, and continuous unconscious mechanisms of the dynamic system by the incommensurate precisely defined, symptom-based disease entities of the diagnostic system was not gradual—it was a total transformation of the system of psychiatric thought over a short period of time (Wilson 1993; Kirk and Kutchins 1992; McCarthy and Gerring 1994). In contrast to the dynamic model, diagnostic psychiatry defines diseases through the presence of overt symptoms, regardless of the causes of these symptoms. It regards diseases as natural entities that exist in the body and that generate the particular symptoms a person displays. These diseases became the object of scientific claims that can be made in isolation from the personalities and social contexts in which they arise, an abstraction that would be unthinkable in the dynamic model (e.g., Sabshin 1990; Maxmen 1985; Kendler 1990). The diagnostic model also seeks the primary causes of disorder in disturbed brains rather than in dysfunctional childhoods and moves the treatment of disorders from intrapsychic explorations to searches for the best medication to relieve symptoms. The premises of diagnostic psychiatry about the basic nature, causes, and treatments of mental illness are incompatible with those of the dynamic system it replaced. This chapter traces the decline of the dynamic model and its replacement with the incommensurate system of diagnostic psychiatry.

THE DECLINE OF DYNAMIC PSYCHIATRY

A Changed Medical Culture   The dominance of dynamic psychiatry in the United States in the half century between 1920 and 1970 was tied not only to its expansive definition of psychological disorder but also to its fierce identification with the profession of medicine. Freud himself saw no reason for psychoanalysis to be limited to medically trained physicians and, indeed, was often antagonistic to the medical profession (Freud 1927; see Roazen 1992). In the United States, however, dynamic psychiatrists justified their system of knowledge and protected themselves from competition from social workers and psychologists through their status as physicians. The close identification of dynamic psychiatry with medicine in the United States that was responsible for raising the field's prestige in the first half of the twentieth century was also in large part responsible for its decline and fall in the last three decades of the century (Hale 1995; Starr 1982).

In the United States, psychoanalysts had staked their professional legitimacy and professional monopoly on their medical background. When dynamic psychiatry emerged in the early twentieth century, its central method—the case history—was a standard and respectable part of the intellectual culture and practice of medicine (Starr 1982; Abbott 1988; Grob 1991a; Hale 1995; Porter 1995). The core works of psychoanalysis, which consisted of ingenious interpretations of particular case histories, were typical of medical research at the time. By the 1960s, however, the norms guiding medical research dismissed case studies as anecdotal and unscientific. Medicine had adopted far different methods more congruent with classical conceptions of science, which are predicated on disease entities that can be precisely defined and subjected to scientific analysis. The use of large statistical studies, control groups, and double-blind placebo trials of medication had become the normative standard in medical research (see especially Starr 1982; Abbott 1988; Porter 1995). American analysts who had used their status as physicians to ward off nonmedical competitors were now judged by the changed standards of a medical profession upon which they depended to justify their professional legitimacy. Within the biomedical paradigm, psychiatrists were in no better position to practice successful psychotherapy than the many competitors who had entered the lucrative and growing psychotherapeutic marketplace.

The changing norms of medicine hoisted dynamic psychiatrists by their own petard. These norms had come to emphasize statistical knowledge over clinical intuition, the study of groups over individual cases, and demonstrations of efficacy according to standard scientific methods over claims of insight. The centrality of nonmeasurable symbolic entities in dynamic psychiatry was antithetical to medical practice, which could now only embrace disorders that were defined as categorical entities. The diffuse and inclusive concept of disorder found in dynamic psychiatry was not congruent with the precise classificatory schemes that came to dominate medical culture (see Faust and Miner 1986; Wilson 1993). "Legitimate" disorders have discrete boundaries, are linked to specific underlying etiologies, and can be treated through physical means. The vague continua of analytic disorders had none of these features. In fact the symbolic, verbal, private, and interior essence of dynamic psychiatry was in many ways the opposite of the direct, objective, public, and overt emphasis of classical scientific methods. The new norms of biomedicine could no longer encompass the claim that dynamic psychiatry was a branch of medicine.

Advocates of biomedical psychiatry questioned not only the validity of the core concepts of dynamic psychiatry but also its ability to measure the entities it studied. A number of studies indicated that measurement of even the most basic types of mental disorder was uncertain. In particular, studies that compared the identification of schizophrenia and bipolar disorders between the United States and the United Kingdom indicated wide variations in how experienced psychiatrists identified these disorders in the two countries (Kendell, Cooper, and Gourlay 1971; Cooper et al. 1972). For example, after viewing videotapes of two English and American patients, 85 percent and 69 percent of American psychiatrists made diagnoses of schizophrenia compared to only 7 percent and 2 percent of British psychiatrists. In contrast, British psychiatrists were far more likely than their American counterparts to diagnose manic-depression. This should not have been surprising—the basic intellectual premises of dynamic psychiatry were not compatible with precise systems of measurement.

Even more fundamentally, dynamic psychiatry was ridiculed for failing to meet even the most elementary tenets of science. A basic principle of scientific method is that scientific statements must be falsifiable (see especially Popper 1959). Yet, how could anyone be shown *not* to have an Oedipal complex when protestations that one had no such desires were taken as evidence of resistance to admitting its presence (Hale 1995)? Freud, for example, interpreted his patients' refusal to accept his interpretations of their symptoms as confirmations of his theory of repression (Freud 1963 [1905]). Key concepts of dynamic psychiatry, especially the unconscious, were inherently not subject to measurement; others, such as the ego, id, and superego, were too vague to be operationalized. Psychodynamic therapy, moreover, could provide no specific outcomes that would demonstrate its effectiveness. An apocryphal statement is apt in this regard: "Psychotherapy is an undefined technique applied to unspecified problems with unpredictable outcome. For this technique we recommend rigorous training" (quoted in Grob 1991a, 127).

Untestability and nonfalsifiability in themselves do not disqualify disciplines from being perceived as scientific. For example, the concept of rationality in classical economics is no more refutable than the basic concepts of dynamic psychiatry. The reason dynamic psychiatry was discredited as nonscientific was that it had linked itself so thoroughly with the culture and institutions of medicine. The legitimacy of dynamic psychiatry depended on conformity to the norms of biomedicine, which had substantially changed since the early part of the twentieth century. The ideal, if not the practice, of medicine demanded measurement systems in which symptoms were direct indicators of underlying disease entities, precise classification systems, and clear criteria of therapeutic effectiveness. Yet, the basic dynamic principles that illnesses were continuous rather than discrete, that symptoms were symbols rather than indicators, and that therapy required deep intrapsychic reflection, not just overt change in symptoms, were fundamentally at odds with the new scientific norms of medicine.

By the 1970s, dynamic psychiatry lacked not only scientific credibility, but also the ability to maintain the professional dominance of psychiatrists in the mental health marketplace. Dynamic clinicians had been so successful in applying psychiatric definitions to personal problems that there was a greater demand for therapy than psychiatrists were able to supply (Abbott 1988). Competing disciplines including clinical psychology, social work, and counseling emerged, all loosely based around the intellectual principles of dynamic psychiatry. Psychiatrists protected their claims against other mental health professions based on their unique status as physicians and on the medical knowledge they possessed. This created a dilemma for dynamic psychiatrists. Medical training seemed irrelevant for the understanding of the central dynamic processes of repression, childhood sexuality, and symbolic interpretation of symptoms. Indeed, in dynamic psychiatry the body and the brain were irrelevant except as patients symbolized them. There was nothing explicitly *psychiatric* about dynamic psychiatry; nonmedical and medical professionals alike were equally able to learn and to practice it.

In the climate that emerged in the 1970s and that had become dominant by the 1990s, only biomedical-oriented psychiatry could advance the prestige and legitimacy of psychiatric practice. A biomedical model presumes that psychiatric disorders are brain diseases similar to diseases of other bodily organs. Mental disorders such as depression are distinct entities analogous to cardiac dysfunctions or liver failures (Luhrmann 2000). A model premised on discrete disease entities provided the only intellectually respectable scheme for biologically and scientifically oriented psychiatrists. Jurisdiction over categorical diseases was a prerequisite for the entry of psychiatry into the new prestige system of biomedicine. If psychiatry was to survive as a medical discipline, it had no choice but to conform to the intellectual norms of the medical profession. To maintain their professional standing, psychiatrists had to reject an intellectual model that both diminished their standing within the medical profession and offered no protection against nonmedical professionals (Hale 1995).

Deinstitutionalization of Mental Patients   Another factor that served to undermine the dynamic model was brought about by the deinstitutionalization of the mental health system. Until the 1950s there had been two separate systems of mental health services (see especially Grob 1991a). The public mental health system managed the most seriously disturbed individuals in large, residential, and custodial institutions. Most residents of these facilities were poor, isolated, and socially marginal people who suffered from very serious and debilitating mental conditions. Dynamic psychiatry had, at best, a small role in public mental institutions. In contrast, dynamic clinicians had established themselves in outpatient practices that catered to urban, cosmopolitan intellectuals favorably disposed toward lengthy and expensive treatments grounded in psychoanalysis (Hale 1995). They were not well suited to treat most of the conditions of patients in public mental institutions, such as schizophrenia, degenerative brain disorders, and serious alcoholism.

Beginning about 1955 and accelerating during the 1960s and 1970s, a revolution in mental health services resulted in the widespread exodus of persons with serious mental illness from public mental institutions. The average number of residents in public mental hospitals began to decline in 1955 from a peak of 550,000 to 370,000 in 1969; by 1994 only about 80,000 remained in these institutions (Center for Mental Health Services 1996; 1998, 146). Taking into account growing population size, the reduction in the number of state hospital residents is even more dramatic: rates fell from 405 per 100,000 persons in 1950 to 351 in 1960 and to 213 in 1970 (Kramer 1977). The movement of persons with serious mental illness out of hospitals forced policy makers to try to devise alternative ways of meeting their many needs (Mechanic 1999; see also Dowdall 1996). People with serious mental illnesses typically require housing, food, job training, income, social skills, social support, and management of problem behaviors. Public mental institutions had provided these residential, social, and behavioral services in a single, controlled setting. Once seriously ill persons left these institutions, tremendous problems arose in replicating these services in community settings (Mechanic and Rochefort 1992; see also Horwitz and Mullis 1998).

Dynamic psychiatry, which focused on providing intensive and expensive psychotherapy to an elite group of clients, had no answers to how persons with serious mental illness could be treated in community settings. These treatments had to combine social services and medication, neither of which were major parts of dynamic practice. The focus of the dynamic model on the exploration of intrapsychic processes was largely inappropriate to the issues policy makers faced when persons with serious mental illnesses began to enter the community. Dynamic psychiatry was irrelevant to efforts to solve the social problems deinstitutionalization had created.

Cultural Delegitimation   Not only was dynamic psychiatry unable to meet the needs of newly deinstitutionalized mental patients; it was also becoming increasingly anachronistic within the changed culture that arose in the United States during the 1960s. While psychiatrists were celebrated in American culture during the 1940s, 1950s, and early 1960s, an influential antipsychiatry movement developed in the mid-1960s. At this time, critics of the field were regarded not as marginal eccentrics but as major figures in an intellectually prominent counterculture. Best-selling books by Thomas Szasz, R. D. Laing, Ken Kesey, and Erving Goffman all mocked the pretensions of psychiatry (Szasz 1961; Laing 1960; Kesey 1962; Goffman 1961). Worse, they questioned the validity of the subject matter of psychiatry itself. Szasz's central work, *The Myth of Mental Illness* (1961), raised the issue of whether psychiatry's subject matter, mental illness, existed at all. Szasz likened psychiatrists to ministers at best and to jailers at worst and considered their medical pretensions to be a sham. He claimed that psychiatric concepts of health and disease were pseudoscientific masks for value judgments of good and bad behavior. Not only Szasz, whose politics identified him with the libertarian Right, but also critics on the ascendant Left, derided psychiatry's aspirations to be a legitimate science (Halleck 1971; Liefer 1969; Chesler 1972). For them, psychiatric practice involved adjusting people to a repressive status quo. The dominant cultural narratives about mental illness in this period, such as the book and film *One Flew Over the Cuckoo's Nest*, Goffman's *Asylums*, or Rosenhan's "On Being Sane in Insane Places," depicted mental patients as sane victims of oppressive psychiatrists.[2] The influential psychiatrist R. D. Laing, for example, portrayed schizophrenics as people who possessed special insights into reality but who were persecuted by their pathological families and communities (Laing 1967).

The culture of dynamic psychiatry had come full circle from its embrace by radical critics of conventional social institutions. Far from being part of the solution to repressive social institutions, dynamic psychiatry itself was viewed as an institution that upheld conformity and stifled dissent. A plethora of alternatives arose including existential therapy, Gestalt therapy, self-actualization, client-centered therapy, encounter groups, psychodrama, and many others (see, for example, Perls 1964; Back 1973; Bart 1974). The dominance of the dynamic paradigm was unraveling as many alternative therapeutic cultures arose during the 1960s.

The culture that came to prominence in the late 1960s made dynamic psychiatry anachronistic in another way. When dynamic psychiatry first emerged, it was associated with a rebellion against repressive social norms, especially repressive sexual norms (Hale 1995; Shorter 1997). By the end of the 1960s, sexual practices bore little resemblance to the sexual strictures that had tormented Freud's patients. The availability of contraception and opportunities for premarital and extramarital sex were far greater than during the time when Freud developed his theories. The dynamic emphasis on repression of sexual instincts would have little resonance for people who were far freer to act upon their sexual desires. Dynamic psychiatry lost not only its bohemian, but also its Jewish roots. By the 1960s, Jews who had formerly embraced dynamic thinking because of their social marginality had become far more assimilated into mainstream culture (Shorter 1997, 182–89). The social basis for the culture of dynamic psychiatry that had been rooted in freethinking intellectuals and Jews was disintegrating as the mainstream culture absorbed these groups and as the ideas behind dynamic psychiatry became more conventional.

THE ORIGINS OF DIAGNOSTIC PSYCHIATRY

As Kuhn postulated, the most profound crises in scientific thought arise when the core concepts of a discipline are attacked (Kuhn 1970). This situation describes the situation in psychiatry as it entered the 1970s. The basic premises of the dynamic model no longer met either the standards of biomedicine or the needs of its lay clientele. In addition, the unconscious processes at the core of dynamic thought had become unsuitable for the economic and political environments of the psychiatric profession of the time. Only a radically different model could resolve the profound crisis of psychiatry.

The psychiatric profession did have an alternative to the dynamic paradigm. During the period when dynamic psychiatry was dominant, the Department of Psychiatry at Washington University in St. Louis had been isolated from the psychoanalytic mainstream of American psychiatry and was an outpost of medically minded thinking. Led by two prominent psychiatrists—Eli Robins and Samuel Guze—the Washington University group emphasized the importance of using well-defined, specific criteria as the basis for diagnostic decisions. In 1972 John Feighner, then a resident in the department, codified and published these diagnostic criteria in what came to be called the "Feighner criteria" (Feighner et al. 1972; see also Robins 1986). Building on the traditional diagnostic emphasis in this department, these criteria categorized the symptoms of fourteen different and presumably distinct categories of mental disorder.

The Feighner criteria rested on several assumptions. Most fundamentally, they assumed that psychiatry was a branch of medicine based on scientific principles, on diagnosis and classification, and on statistical methods. In this model, the major prerequisite of a scientific discipline was to order phenomena into discrete disease entities. The Washington University school is often called "neo-Kraepelian" because of its emphasis on classifying, categorizing, and describing discrete disease entities through their overt symptomatic manifestations and consequent prognoses (Klerman 1977; Goodwin and Guze 1996; Baldessarini 2000). These entities must be directly observed, not inferred from nonobservable mechanisms such as the unconscious. The emphasis on observable phenomena presumably ensured that the resulting classification system would be factual and objective. Careful observation of overt symptoms was the most important aspect of classification because the other goals of a diagnostic system—etiology, prognosis, and treatment—followed from accurate classification.

The Feighner criteria were also based on a classical Baconian model of classification, where scientific laws emerge from closely observed facts (Robins and Helzer 1986; Klerman 1977).[3] An ideal system of classification is mutually exclusive; no entity overlaps with another entity within the same system. Different disorders consist of co-occurring symptoms whose presence is not coincidental. Each disease entity is presumed to be distinct from other disease entities, not a point along a continuum of disorder. The association between the symptoms within one entity should be maximal and that between symptoms of different entities minimal. The indications of obsessive-compulsive disorders, for example, will differ from those of phobias, and these differences will be consequential for prognosis, etiology, and treatment. Thus, in this biomedical model of scientific psychiatry, mental disorders are discrete natural entities equivalent to disorders of the body (Robins and Helzer 1986).

The conceptualization of anxiety provides a good example of the divergence of dynamic and diagnostic psychiatry. For dynamic psychiatrists, anxiety was often the core phenomenon underlying all forms of neuroses. It was a very broad and universal aspect of human experience that stemmed from conflicts between unconscious desires and external frustrations. Furthermore, it lay behind *all* forms of neuroses, so was not associated with any particular disease (Fenichel 1995 [1945]).

In contrast to the dynamic view, the Feighner criteria for anxiety neurosis rested entirely on manifest symptoms. A diagnosis of an anxiety disorder required a specified number of overt symptoms that indicated the presence of the disorder. For example, at least four symptoms from among dyspepsia, palpitations, chest pain or discomfort, choking or smothering sensation, dizziness, and paresthesias (tactile disorders) must be present during the majority of anxiety attacks. At least six of these attacks, separated by at least a week from each other, are required for a diagnosis. Symptoms cannot result from physical exertion, a life-threatening situation, or a medical condition. Anxiety was transformed in this way from a very general concept underlying all sorts of manifest symptoms into a discrete, quantifiable disorder based on overt symptoms (Feighner et al. 1972).

The emphasis on manifest symptoms in the Feighner criteria led to a focus on the reliability of psychiatric diagnosis (Spitzer et al. 1967; Spitzer and Fleiss 1974; see especially Kirk and Kutchins 1992). Reliability means have they done observations since??

that different observers of the same case will provide the same diagnosis. One of the presumed major problems of the DSM-II, which was based on the principles of dynamic psychiatry, was that the users of its loose diagnostic scheme might make different diagnoses of the same case. A scientific psychiatry could not be based on categories that would not yield the same results in different hands. In order for the field to be scientific, appropriately trained members must apply the same definition and rules to observable phenomena, resulting in a system with measurably high reliability. Each disorder should be a meaningful entity with similar cause, course over time, and response to treatment. The demonstration that a psychiatric system of classification could be reliable became central to the effort to establish the biomedical credentials of psychiatry (Kirk and Kutchins 1992).

Once distinct disorders are reliably differentiated, diagnostic psychiatrists then search for the causes of the disorders. The logic of the classification system of diagnostic psychiatry does not dictate any particular set of causes for disorders. What is critical is that differential diagnoses help specify the causes of different diagnostic entities. Somatization might be rooted in traumatic childhood experiences, while panic disorders may stem from irregular functions of neurochemical systems. In fact, however, there is a strong presumption that different psychiatric illnesses ultimately reflect different biochemical states of the brain and that these physiological states are more powerful influences on mental diseases than psychological or social influences. Because "real" disorders are physiological, diagnostic psychiatry anticipates that natural causes will eventually be found for those disorders that lack a current biological status (Klerman 1977). Although the basic causes of disorders may presumably be found within the structure of the brain, there is no reason why psychological or social causes might not also play a role in their development and course. — *play huge role!*

The final aspect of diagnostic psychiatry lies in the treatment of disorder. Medications that alter brain chemistry provide the most efficient means of changing symptoms. Different disorders should be alleviated or cured through distinct sorts of manipulations. Lithium may be the treatment of choice for bipolar disorders and phenothiazine for schizophrenia (Klerman 1989). Every aspect of the Feighner criteria—grounding classification in overt symptoms, looking for distinct etiologies for different conditions, and expecting specific treatments to work for different disorders—completely diverged from the model of dynamic psychiatry.

The Feighner criteria, in marked contrast to the subsequent DSM-III, were based on a small number of diagnoses. The original criteria included

(marginalia, left column top): who that use if we don't will this criteria?

(marginalia, left column middle): this is bullshit what about anxiety, mental disorders develop from trauma? —Just not a mental switch

(marginalia, left column bottom): No/all mental disorders had this only five cases

only fourteen entities. The most recent edition of a major psychiatric text based on the Feighner criteria contains only eleven diagnostic entities (Goodwin and Guze 1996). Although these criteria provided no definition of "mental disorder" that justified the validity of the classification system, they did not lay claim to the entire territory of human behavior encompassed in dynamic psychiatry. The limited range of psychiatric diagnoses the Feighner criteria included were in certain respects an improvement over the boundless phenomena of dynamic psychiatry. Indeed, this model is a useful way of thinking about the classical entities of psychiatry, the psychoses, where symptoms indicate distinct underlying diseases. The Washington University group could not have envisioned that their highly delimited classification scheme would metastasize into the huge domain of pathology in the DSM-III.

THE DSM-III

The Role of Researchers   The evolution of psychiatric diagnoses is typically presented as a cumulative process of growing knowledge about the nature of the various mental illnesses. The portrayal of the DSM in the Surgeon General's Report on Mental Health is illustrative:

> The standard manual used for diagnosis of mental disorders in the United States is the *Diagnostic and Statistical Manual of Mental Disorders*. Most recently revised in 1994, this manual now is in its fourth edition. The first edition was published in 1952 by the American Psychiatric Association; subsequent revisions, which were made on the basis of field trials, analysis of data sets, and systematic reviews of the research literature, have sought to gain greater objectivity, diagnostic precision, and reliability. (USDHHS 1999, 44)

In this view, the current system of psychiatric classification builds on its predecessors to create a system of ever more adequate, precise, and scientifically based categories of mental illness.

In fact, the DSM-III and subsequent DSM-III-R and DSM-IV were radical departures from the earlier versions of the manual. The premises of dynamic psychiatry loosely underlay the DSM-I and DSM-II (Grob 1991b; Wilson 1993). These manuals provided short descriptions of disorders and emphasized the underlying psychic mechanisms that presumably led to pathology. The drafters of the DSM-II explicitly rejected the notion that mental disorders were fixed disease entities (Skodol 2000). In contrast, the DSM-III emphasized categories of illness rather than blurry boundaries between normal and abnormal behavior, dichotomies rather than dimensions, overt symptoms rather than underlying etiological mechanisms, and static manifestations of symptoms rather than their dynamic unfolding.[4] In each respect, it totally transformed thinking in psychiatry. In contrast to the claims of the Surgeon General's Report, the revolution in psychiatric classification in the DSM-III was not a product of any new scientific findings. Instead, political, social, and economic considerations led to the new classification scheme (see especially Kirk and Kutchins 1992).

The Feighner criteria provided the intellectual framework for the DSM-III. In 1974 the American Psychiatric Association appointed Robert Spitzer head of the task force charged with revising the psychodynamically based DSM-II. Spitzer was a leader of research-oriented psychiatrists who needed to work with carefully defined conditions that would not vary across research sites. This small but powerful group could not use the vague and often idiosyncratic processes of dynamic psychiatry to develop a psychiatry grounded in classical scientific principles. Spitzer had the power to choose the members of this task force, a third of whom consisted of psychiatrists trained at Washington University. Most of the others, especially Spitzer himself, Gerald Klerman, and Donald Klein, were close collaborators with the Washington University group (Blashfield 1982). They considered themselves "Neo-Kraepelians" because they believed the careful classification of manifest symptoms was the most essential defining criterion of psychiatric disorders. In addition, like Kraepelin, they considered each psychiatric disorder as discontinuous with the others. Symptoms, causes, courses, and treatments were all seen as disorder-specific, not generally shared. This view placed them in fundamental opposition to the continuous and nonspecific view of mental disorder found in dynamic psychiatry. Their intellectual roots lay in St. Louis, not in Vienna, and their intellectual forefather was Kraepelin, not Freud (Spitzer and Williams 1987; Spitzer, Williams, and Skodal 1980; Bayer and Spitzer 1985).

The goals of the DSM-III Task Force and of the Feighner group, however, were very different. The Washington University group was made up of research psychiatrists, who formed a small, albeit highly prestigious, part of the profession. Their goal was to create entities solely and explicitly for research purposes. Spitzer's mandate as head of the Task Force was far more ambitious: to create a diagnostic system that would serve the purposes not only of the relatively small psychiatric research community, but also of the vast and expanding ranks of mental health professionals in clinical practice.

Research psychiatrists study a limited number of well-established illness entities. For them, the achievement of a reliable system of measurement was a primary goal (Kirk and Kutchins 1992). Reliability was a particular problem for research-oriented psychiatrists; it was of little interest to clinicians concerned with particularities of the individuals they treat. Researchers needed a system that would allow them to aggregate like cases, employ statistical procedures, and generalize beyond any particular research site. For research purposes, it was essential that what was called, for example, "schizophrenia" in one research site was comparable to a case or conception of schizophrenia at a different site. This liberated cases from their particular contexts and created uniform and universal constitutive elements out of the messiness of actual clinical symptoms. As Kirk and Kutchins emphasize, a focus on reliability became a key justification in the development of a symptom-based classification in the DSM-III (Kirk and Kutchins 1992; see also Faust and Miner 1986, Millon 1983). •

The focus on the reliability of diagnoses provided the perfect intellectual tool to justify the new categorical system. The demonstration that different observers could agree on whether a particular cluster of symptoms indicated a particular mental disorder allowed the proponents of diagnostic psychiatry to contrast their reliable system with the older DSM-I and –II. The discrete, categorical entities of the DSM-III could thus be favorably compared with the vague, unmeasurable mechanisms of dynamic psychiatry. The emphasis on the measurement of overt symptoms also allowed diagnostic psychiatry to appear more scientific, regardless of whether these symptoms actually fit a categorical model. Finally, defining symptom-based entities made these entities seem as if they were real. The focus on reliability provided the justification for psychiatry to claim it was scientific without having to demonstrate why any of the classified entities ought to be considered instances of mental disorder.

The fact that the symptoms of schizophrenia and bipolar depression seemed to indicate distinct underlying disorders, to point to a certain set of causes, and to mandate different treatments led these disorders to become the models for other diagnostic categories (Robins and Guze 1970).[5] Although the psychoses had been central to Kraepelin's diagnostic scheme at the beginning of the century, dynamic psychiatry had displaced them to a more marginal status. The Feighner criteria and resulting DSM returned the psychotic disorders to their status as prototypes of the usefulness of categorical thinking in psychiatry. In the DSM-III classifications modeled after the discrete symptoms of the psychoses became the basis for categorizing a vastly extended range of diagnoses.

The Role of Clinicians   In one sense the DSM-III was a revolutionary document that researchers and their allies in government and professional organizations created (Kirk and Kutchins 1992). However, the largest constituency for the DSM-III was not the research community, whom the Washington University psychiatrists and their allies represented, but the thousands of clinicians whose practices depended on patients who had embraced the expansion of psychiatry into everyday life. The vast majority of the users of the new diagnostic manual would be clinicians whose interests were very different from those of research psychiatrists. The DSM Task Force had to create a new intellectual system that would not only establish psychiatry's position as a scientifically oriented research discipline but would also satisfy the bulk of working mental health professionals. It had to find some way to fuse the divergent interests of researchers and clinicians (Frances et al. 1990).

Clinicians had little concern with the issues of reliability that preoccupied researchers. How a condition is defined in other settings has little relevance to practicing therapists, who must establish rapport with particular patients (Spitzer 1991; Nelson-Gray 1991). The therapeutic encounter need not rely on standardized categories. In contrast to the carefully defined entities that research psychiatrists study, clinicians treat patients who have a broad range of ill-defined problems. Indeed, the highly structured interviews that increase reliability would by their very nature have little relevance for the actual practices of mental health professionals (Persons 1991).

The major concern of clinicians was to maintain their client base, regardless of the degree of precision of particular diagnoses. By the time the Task Force was developing the DSM-III in the 1970s, dynamic psychiatry had successfully spread the idea in prominent segments of the culture that personal problems ought to be defined as psychiatric problems. The clients of clinicians were primarily troubled upper-middle- and middle-class people who wanted help with their personal and social problems (Abbott 1988; Hale 1995). The dynamic revolution had been so successful that when troubles arose, these people invoked the language and the imagery of dynamic psychiatry and viewed mental health professionals as the purveyors of social support, consolation during crises, and relief from loneliness.

Studies of therapeutic clients in the 1960s and 1970s indicated the extent to which psychotherapy had become a tool for the resolution of numerous problems of living. Kadushin's study of three psychiatric clinics in New York City was illustrative of this research. It indicated that the most prevalent presenting complaints were problems with social relationships, particularly conflicts with spouses, children, and co-workers. Other prominent problems included diffuse feelings of unhappiness, general uneasiness and anxiety, value conflicts, and somatic problems. Kadushin's attempt to cluster these problems accurately characterized the nature of psychiatric clients in general at this time: "The empirically derived clustering here presented covers a wide range of problems; indeed it is one way of grouping all of life" (Kadushin 1969, 103).

One large portion of the clientele of mental health professionals, then, were participants in psychodynamic culture. Another large group of professionals worked not with the voluntary participants in analytic culture, but with children who had problems in school, delinquents, criminals, addicts, alcoholics, and others who had run into trouble (Davis 1938; Lunbeck 1994). Their clientele typically entered treatment involuntarily, through the intervention of social control agents or of their family members. The developers of the DSM-III also had to take into account the interests of professionals who counseled, treated, and medicated in these coercive settings.

The philosophy of Spitzer and his colleagues insured that the DSM-III would maintain all the conditions inherited from dynamic psychiatry as categorical diagnoses:

> Because the DSM-III classification is intended for the entire profession . . . the Task Force has chosen to be inclusive rather than exclusive. . . . If there is general agreement among clinicians, who would be expected to encounter the condition, that there are a significant number of patients who have it and that its identification is important in the clinical work, it is included in the classification. (Spitzer, Sheehy, and Endicott 1977; see also Wilson 1993)

In other words, the grounds for inclusion of the conditions found in the DSM-III, and perpetuated in the DSM-III-R and DSM-IV, did not stem from either theory or research but from the need to maintain the existing clientele of mental health professionals.

Whatever problems the culture of dynamic psychiatry had already created became, *de facto*, the discrete disorders of diagnostic psychiatry. As two of the major figures behind the development of diagnostic psychiatry, Lee Robins and John Helzer, state: "The two (diagnostic) systems in greatest use today, ICD-9 and DSM-III, have as their goal complete coverage of the population of persons who present to psychiatrists" (Robins and Helzer 1986, 426). Contrary to the common view that the DSM-III expanded the range of pathology the mental health professions should treat, in fact it simply recategorized as discrete diagnostic entities the wide range of problems that dynamic psychiatry had already pathologized.

From Personal Problems to Discrete Diagnoses   To satisfy its clinical constituency, the DSM Task Force had to be inclusive, rather than exclusive, in its diagnostic categories and had to encompass the various conditions that clinicians were treating.[6] Spitzer (1991, 294) stated: "The Task Force recognized, correctly I believe, that limiting DSM-III to only those categories that had been fully validated by empirical studies would be at the least a serious obstacle to the widespread use of the manual by mental health professionals." No diagnostic revolution could succeed that abandoned the established clientele of working clinicians.

The framers of the DSM took the problems that dynamic psychiatry had so successfully defined as psychological disturbances and reformulated them in the language of categorical illnesses. The many categories of the DSM-III thus originated in the self-definitions of psychotherapeutic clients, who were themselves the products of the culture of dynamic psychiatry. The new diagnostic system not only had to invent categorical diseases to maintain a claim as a medical specialty and to satisfy researchers; it also had to invent *many* disease categories to maintain the allegiance of working clinicians. While perceived scientific exigencies dictated the adaptation of a categorical system, demands from mental health professionals and their clients necessitated a large categorical system that would include all behaviors clinicians encountered in their practices.

If the categorical diagnostic logic of the Feighner criteria was to be the basis of the new DSM-III, there was no political choice but to apply it to the entire range of problems that the membership of the American Psychiatric Association was already treating. Problems of ordinary life such as dealing with troublesome children and spouses, poor marriages, frustrations in careers, personal identity crises, and general unhappiness had to be reconceptualized as discrete forms of individual pathology. Likewise, the deviant behaviors treated in dynamic programs had to be transformed into disease entities that could be properly formulated and treated within the diagnostic framework of the DSM-III.

The transformation of vague neuroses and general problems of living into discrete diagnostic categories was accomplished in several ways. The first was simply to create enough categories to encompass the conditions that clinicians were currently treating. The reclassification of the neuroses through their overt symptoms into anxiety, obsessive-compulsive, somatization disorders, and the like did not satisfy psychoanalysts, but it also did not eliminate any symptom clusters from the diagnostic manual (see Bayer and Spitzer 1985). Other diagnoses, such as Major Depression, were so broad that they would encompass virtually any person who had experienced a recent crisis of any sort; dysthymia could characterize many others with long-term but low-grade symptoms (APA 1980). The later addition of adjustment disorder, including unspecified adjustment disorder, to the manual could encompass virtually any problem at all (APA 1994, 623–27).[7]

Most of the major diagnostic categories also featured residual categories such as anxiety disorder "not otherwise specified," attention deficit/hyperactivity "not otherwise specified," communication disorder "not otherwise specified," and the like. Criteria also captured the disorders of clinicians with specialized clienteles such as sufferers of multiple personality disorder (renamed dissociative identity disorder in later versions of the DSM), eating disorders, or sexual problems. Those who treated deviants found checklists of criteria for many substance use disorders and antisocial behaviors. The classifiers did not develop new problems; instead, they reorganized and systematized the culture of dynamic psychiatry into discrete and categorical disorders.[8]

A second way the DSM ensured that the entire realm of clients already in treatment would obtain a discrete diagnosis was by adapting a purportedly atheoretical strategy that focused on observable symptoms, regardless of the cause of these symptoms (Rogler 1997). Through discarding etiology as a means of classification, the DSM could encompass the conditions treated by all competing schools of psychopathology. The need to achieve professional consensus, rather than any scientific knowledge or empirical research, lay behind the decision to classify symptoms without regard to etiology (Eysenck, Wakefield, and Friedman 1983; Pichot 1997). The DSM-III stated: "The major justification for the . . . approach . . . is that the inclusion of etiological theories would be an obstacle to use of the manual by clinicians of varying theoretical orientations" (APA 1980, 7). To this end, DSM-III discarded terms such as "neuroses" that contained etiological inferences (Bayer and Spitzer 1985).

When symptoms were classified without regard to their causes or to whether they indicated a mental illness, there was no limit on the sorts of conditions that could enter the new diagnostic manual. Chronic dissatisfaction with life could be renamed "dysthymia"; the distress arising from problems with spouses or lovers could be called "major depression"; the disturbances of troublesome children could be renamed as conduct, personality, or attention deficit disorders. A symptom-based approach had the dual advantages of providing a seemingly objective and factual basis for diagnosis and of including any entity that mental health professionals currently treated.

A third way that the DSM-III facilitated growth in the number of diagnoses was through focusing on the technical issue of reliability, rather than on issues of validity (Kirk and Kutchins 1992). An emphasis on reliability is a useful tool in developing a large categorical system because, in the absence of a valid definition of mental disorder, there is no limit to the number of discrete conditions researchers and clinicians can develop. If a professional wants to argue, for example, that there is an entity called "compulsive television watching" she can easily come up with specific criteria—at least five hours per day, at least six days a week, limits outside activities, friends and family comment on the behavior, etc.—and train observers to measure the disorder in a consistent way.[9] The high reliability would be meaningless, however, without a demonstration that compulsive television watching is a *mental disorder*.

The initial impetus behind the conceptual scheme of the DSM thus lay in the intellectual framework most congenial to research psychiatrists. It allowed psychiatry to justify itself as a medical specialty through the only model that was able to provide medical legitimacy. This framework was then extended to cover the problems clinicians saw in their practices. The politics of mental health professionals had a major role in generating a broad categorical system. The application of this system to the broad range of problems of psychiatric clients was not a triumph of science over ideology, but rather a use of the ideology of science to justify current social practices.

Changing Reimbursement Systems Require Categories The aspirations and interests of researchers to be part of a respectable medical specialty that treats diseases and that has a reliable system of measurement were prominent reasons for the emergence of a categorical system. The changing economic basis of psychiatric practice was another factor that promoted a categorical model of illness. While research psychiatrists needed categories to apply conventional scientific methods, clinicians often needed them to obtain reimbursement for their services.

In the first half of the twentieth century most clients of dynamic psychiatry paid for therapy as an out-of-pocket expense. Payment was a transaction between the client and the therapist and so required no accountability to third parties. The growing demand for psychotherapy, coupled with the

dart board truth?!

(term used to say trust we could as if the world as it is

created by social forces we as a society belief the category as real!

prosperity of the 1960s, led many medical insurance plans to include therapy as a partially reimbursable expense. By the 1960s, insurance paid for about one quarter of outpatient treatment. During the 1970s, along with a rising rate of insurance reimbursement, the federal Medicaid program became a major source of payment for therapy (Mechanic 1999). The economic basis of the therapeutic relationship was no longer solely between therapists and their patients; it had come to involve private and public third-party payers.

Payment through insurance brought not only a lucrative source of funding but also a demand for greater accountability to external economic forces (Wilson 1993). The rise of third-party payers contributed to pressures to impose a categorical, rather than a continuous, model of illness. The continua and symbolic mechanisms of dynamic psychiatry did not fit an insurance logic that demanded discrete categories representing particular conditions. Continua were not reimbursable. Nor were vague disorders where symptoms might represent one thing in one person and another thing in another person compatible with an insurance logic. In contrast, the discrete disease entities of the biomedical model provided guides to reimbursement and to efficient data collection strategies.

Third-party payers required not only the treatment of categorical diseases but also some sort of accountability for the outcomes of treatment (Frank et al. 1994). The dynamic model provided no grounds for measuring these outcomes. It could not specify outcomes, the time when a person was cured, the costs and benefits of treatment, or how effectiveness could be demonstrated. The rise of third-party payment for psychiatric treatment exacerbated the absence of accountability in dynamic psychiatry.

The lack of fit between the continua of dynamic psychiatry and reimbursable categories was not a major problem for psychiatry when its clients paid for their own treatments. When private and public third-party payers came to dominate the reimbursement of psychiatric treatment, however, they needed a model of reimbursement that reflected the discrete disorders of medicine. Insurance forms, not the nature of symptoms, demand precise diagnoses. As demand for outpatient therapy rose exponentially among middle-class consumers who used their medical insurance to pay for treatment, the dimensional system could not be sustained. In addition, government programs that funded an increasing amount of psychotherapy also required accountability. Mental health organizations and therapists needed to provide insurers concrete information both on the types of clients they were treating and on the results they were generating (Kirk and Kutchins

1992). Discrete diagnoses were essential for the organizations that were financing mental health treatment. As mental health treatment became more embedded in third-party payment, diagnoses became more essential. Categorical psychiatry was far better suited to the new economics of mental health than was dynamic psychiatry.[10]

Changing Mental Health Politics   Not only the economic, but also the political environment of mental health care began to change radically in the 1970s. The National Institute of Mental Health (NIMH) was created in 1946 to be the federal agency in charge of research, training, and services on mental health and illness. During its early years, the NIMH emphasized research conducted by psychologists, sociologists, and other social scientists and awarded biological scientists less than 15 percent of its grant funds (Kolb, Frazier, and Sirovatka 2000). In the 1960s, the NIMH promoted an expansive agenda of community mental health. At the core of the NIMH agenda was the development of thousands of community mental health centers (CMHCs) whose mandate encompassed not only the treatment of individuals with mental disorders, but also the promotion of broad social changes in the community (Grob 1991a). These CMHCs became involved in efforts to alleviate poverty, to combat juvenile delinquency, to prevent mental disorders from arising in the first place, and to promote positive mental health. In addition, the NIMH sponsored a considerable amount of research on the mental health aspects of a variety of broad social problems. The mandate of public psychiatry had moved well beyond the mental hospital and the outpatient couch to the solution of social and economic problems that presumably underlay mental illness and other social problems.[11]

As the political climate changed from the liberalism of the 1960s to the growing conservatism of the Nixon and Ford presidencies of the 1970s, there was increasing pressure on the NIMH and the CMHCs to retreat from their sweeping social agendas (Kirk 1999). The central role of the NIMH in mental health policy making was drastically scaled back as policy-making power devolved to the states. The devolution of mental health policy from the federal government to the states left the NIMH in search of a new agenda that would replace its efforts at social reform. By the late 1970s, not only Congress but also research-oriented psychiatrists challenged the NIMH's broad focus on social problems. Leading researchers opposed the agency's emphasis on social issues and emphasized the need to focus on questions about specific rigorously defined mental disorders (Kolb, Frazier, and Sirovatka 2000).

A mental health policy dominated by the treatment of specific illnesses fit the increasingly nonactivist climate toward federal government policy making in the 1970s. In the new political context, the biomedical model embodied in diagnostic psychiatry was a highly suitable replacement for the old politics of social change (Kirk 1999). Focusing on research about specific illnesses rather than on broad social problems was a far more astute strategy in the post-1960s political climate. Research priorities shifted to neuroscience and related brain and behavior research and to the epidemiology of specific mental disorders. By the early 1980s, this shift in priorities had proven successful and the NIMH experienced a rapid increase in funding that was directed toward the study of the diagnostic entities found in the DSM-III (Baldessarini 2000).

Lay Groups Advocate Illness Categories   Another change in the political environment lay in the emergence of powerful new lay advocacy groups for the mentally ill. Professional interests had dominated the development of the DSM-III. No organized lay groups opposed the general system of categorical thinking that lay behind the manual.[12] When lay groups became involved in controversies, they generally opposed the inclusion of specific diagnoses, such as homosexuality or premenstrual syndrome, in the manual (Bayer 1987; Figert 1996). Although the interests of professionals were paramount in establishing the system of diagnostic psychiatry, shortly after the adoption of the DSM-III in 1980 powerful lay interest groups emerged that supported and perpetuated a categorical system of illnesses.

During the 1980s a strong lay advocacy group, the National Alliance for the Mentally Ill (NAMI), gained substantial influence in the U.S. Congress and at the NIMH (McLean 1990; Sabshin 1990; Mechanic 1995; Kolb, Frazier, and Sirovatka 2000). The central tenet of this organization, made up mostly of parents whose children suffered from schizophrenia and other psychotic disorders, was that mental illnesses are brain-based disorders caused by biological factors. It fiercely opposed psychodynamic concepts that linked the development of these illnesses to faulty parenting styles and other experiences of early childhood.

The NAMI viewed mental illnesses as categorical, brain-based diseases in order both to destigmatize them and to link them with physical illnesses that emerge because of factors beyond the control of the individual sufferers (and their parents). NAMI also insisted that biologically based research should take primacy over psychodynamic research. Categorical, medical diagnoses suited NAMI's ideology because they were identified with the biomedical model of organic disease, while the continua and family-based causes emphasized in dynamic psychiatry did not. NAMI's advocacy efforts, particularly with Congress and NIMH, the major federal funder of research about mental illness, reinforced the central tenets of diagnostic psychiatry. Hence, the most powerful lay interest group concerned with mental illness welcomed the categorical disease entities found in the new diagnostic system.

Drug Treatments   A final major influence on the development of categorical mental illnesses lay in the growing importance of psychoactive medication in the treatment of disorders. Psychoactive medications, especially tranquilizers such as Miltown, Librium, and Valium, had become widely prescribed during the 1950s and 1960s (Healy 1997). By the 1970s, there had been an explosive growth in the use of drugs to control not only schizophrenia and bipolar disorders but also the widely prevalent conditions of anxiety and depression. By 1980, ten million prescriptions were written for antidepressants alone (Shorter 1997; Healy 1997).

The growing dominance of medications in the treatment of psychiatric disorders reinforced the diagnostic model in two important ways. Most broadly, it enhanced the position of biologically oriented psychiatrists who conceived of psychiatric disorders as biomedical entities. At the same time, the widespread use of medication discredited dynamic practitioners who had denigrated drug treatments as superficial palliatives. Most psychoanalysts were either hostile or, at best, neutral toward the use of medication in treatment (Hale 1995). Dynamic clinicians believed that, unlike insight-oriented therapies, medication only dealt with the surface manifestations but not the underlying causes of problems. Indeed, the focus on overt symptoms found in medication-based treatments was in fundamental intellectual opposition to the dynamic tenet that symptoms were not critical aspects of mental disorders. The widespread use of drugs to cure symptoms challenged the basic principles of dynamic thinking about mental symptoms (Valenstein 1998).

More specifically, the Food and Drug Administration would not approve the marketing of medications unless they were shown to be effective in the treatment of specific illnesses. This model fit the way antipsychotic medications acted on different illnesses (Healy 1997). The phenothiazines, for example, were only used to treat schizophrenia and lithium was only prescribed for bipolar disorders. The illness-specific aspect of antipsychotic medications helped reestablish the Kraepelian distinction between different categories of mental disorder. The illness-specific model used to approve medications meant, however, that once a drug was developed, a specific illness would have to be found that the drug would treat.

Medications for nonpsychotic disorders, however, were rarely illness-specific and the most common medications were prescribed across a wide variety of illness categories. Nevertheless, even when a particular drug works on a broad range of psychological conditions, as is the case with most antidepressant and anti-anxiety medications, it could only be approved and marketed after it was demonstrated to be effective for a particular illness. The FDA requirements, coupled with the explosive growth of medications, insured that diagnostic categories would come to dominate psychiatric thought and practice. The need to conform to the social regulations over medications drove yet another nail into the coffin of dynamic psychiatry.

A PLETHORA OF MENTAL ILLNESSES

A variety of professional, economic, and political reasons thus accounted for the rapid ascendancy of diagnostic psychiatry. The result of the categorical revolution was that, although the DSM-III claimed to be the heir of the Feighner criteria, it encompassed 265 discrete diagnoses, in comparison to the fourteen diagnoses in the Feighner criteria. These expanded to 292 categories in the DSM-III-R and to nearly 400 disorders in the DSM-IV (APA 1980, 1987, 1994).[13] The far greater number of diagnoses in the DSM-III did not, however, mean that it and its successors greatly increased the range of pathology in psychiatry's domain.[14] Indeed, it would have been virtually impossible to expand the near universality of psychopathology found in dynamic psychiatry. Instead, the DSM-III simply categorized behaviors that dynamic psychiatry had already pathologized. It increased the number of specific illness conditions, not the behaviors to which the particular diagnoses referred.

The DSM-III-R and DSM-IV compiled and published since 1980 tinker with particular categories of the DSM-III but make no fundamental changes in the categorical paradigm itself. Just as professional rather than scientific considerations gave rise to the huge number of diagnostic categories, these same considerations ensure that diagnoses are unlikely to leave the system once they enter it. Allen Frances, Spitzer's successor in charge of developing the DSM-IV, states: "We didn't want to disrupt clinical practice by eliminating diagnoses in wide use."[15] Although the newer manuals make it more difficult for new diagnoses to become official illnesses, they also make it very difficult to eliminate a diagnosis from the DSM after its initial appearance (Pincus et al. 1992; Frances et al. 1990, 1991; Widiger et al. 1990, 1991; Skodol 2000).

Once a diagnosis is established, the burden of proof comes to rest on those who wish to remove an illness from the manual, not on those who wish to keep it there (Pincus et al. 1992). For example, while the DSM-III-R added thirty-three diagnostic categories, it eliminated only six (Blashfield, Sprock, and Fuller 1990).[16] With rare exceptions that arise when major values are at stake, as in the controversies over homosexuality or premenstrual syndrome, interest groups rarely arise to demand the removal of diagnoses from illness classifications (Bayer 1987; Figert 1996). In contrast, whatever diagnoses were originally included in the DSM-III are fiercely protected regardless of whether there was any justification for their original inclusion (Kirk and Kutchins 1992). Once a diagnosis has been created, it enters professional curricula, specialists emerge to treat it, conferences are organized about it, research and publications deal with it, careers are built around it, and patients formulate their symptoms to correspond to it. Categories that arose from the professional need to define all the problems of people who entered psychotherapy as distinct illness entities come to seem real.

The splitting of psychological problems into illness categories was a social, not a scientific, necessity. Dynamic psychiatry had created a culture of unhappiness, where people came to view mental health professionals as the legitimate arbiters of suffering. The conditions they brought into treatment reflected a cornucopia of human suffering, existential despair, relational problems, and the like, as well as discrete mental disorders. All of these problems had to fit into the diagnostic boxes of the DSM-III. If psychiatry was to survive as a respected discipline, it had no choice but to adopt a categorical system that would allow it to apply scientific methods, obtain reimbursement, generate research funding, gain approval for medications, and maintain the allegiance of its practitioners. Many of these categories reflect not valid mental disorders, but the necessity to categorize whatever conditions mental health professionals were treating in the United States at mid-century. The problems of clients of psychotherapy who had entered treatment through the influence of the culture of dynamic psychiatry defined what conditions diagnostic psychiatry came to encompass.

CONCLUSION

As is typical in scientific revolutions, diagnostic psychiatry claims to reject virtually every aspect of its discredited dynamic predecessor (Kuhn 1970).

Indeed, the movement from the underlying general mechanisms of dynamic psychiatry to the specific symptom-based categorical entities of diagnostic psychiatry was a conceptual revolution. Yet, diagnostic psychiatry also owes an enormous debt to dynamic psychiatry. If diagnostic psychiatry in one sense is the antithesis of dynamic psychiatry, in another sense the two are deeply symbiotic.

The new psychiatric model did not reject the wide-ranging array of problems that dynamic psychiatry had brought under the umbrella of the psychiatric profession nor the large base of clients who had embraced the culture of dynamic psychiatry. Diagnostic psychiatry inherited both a vast realm of disorders and a large population of potential clients whose threshold of help-seeking from mental health professionals had dropped dramatically (Veroff, Kulka, and Douvan 1981). The new categories of diagnostic psychiatry had to encompass the full array of problems mental health professionals were already treating. Dynamic psychiatry had bequeathed to diagnostic psychiatry not only a legacy of neurotic disorders, but also an array of psychological and behavioral consequences of stressful social arrangements, as well as many forms of social deviance. However opposed to dynamic forms of classification and interpretation diagnostically oriented psychiatrists might have been, they willingly and enthusiastically embraced its generous definition of pathology.

All proponents of scientific revolutions believe that their paradigms represent better and more objective portrayals of natural reality than the models they replaced. They also believe that the paradigms their models replaced are inferior, unscientific systems of thought (Kuhn 1970). The DSM claims to be based on science rather than ideology, on medicine rather than anecdote, and on fact rather than unproven and vague entities. For its advocates, who now include virtually the entire psychiatric community, the illness categories of the DSM provided a more accurate and valid description of clinical reality.

The proponents of the DSM view it as a great triumph of "science over ideology" (Sabshin 1990, 1272; see also Leshner 1999). For them, "The old psychiatry derives from theory, the new psychiatry from fact" (Maxmen 1985, 31). The diagnoses of the DSM are scientific replacements for the near-religious chimeric spirits of dynamic psychiatry. "Scientific evidence" rather than the charismatic authority of "great professors" presumably stands behind the classificatory systems of DSM-III and -IV (Kendler 1990).

Contrary to the claims of its proponents, the new diagnostic framework of the DSM-III did not arise from a new knowledge base. The triumph of a categorical system was not based on evidence that diagnoses were more adequate scientific classifications than dynamic or other alternatives.[17] The developers of this new system did not make empirical comparisons between categorical diagnoses and other possible frameworks. The new system instead imposed a categorical system of diagnoses on phenomena that had previously been considered dimensional. Diagnostic categories emerged in order to raise the prestige of psychiatry, to guarantee reimbursement from third parties, to allow medications to be marketed, and to protect the interests of mental health researchers and professionals.

No valid system of categories could have encompassed the huge range of behaviors that found their way into the DSM-III. The manual did not delineate the proper scope of mental disorder; instead it classified whatever conditions mental health professionals were treating at the time the DSM-III was developed. The proliferation of diagnoses resulted from an awkward marriage between the legitimate intellectual needs of research psychiatrists and the political and economic necessity of including all disorders that were found in clinical practice. The DSM was an adept solution that satisfied the needs of researchers for objects of study amenable to scientific methods and of clinicians for a means to obtain reimbursement without losing clients.

The new diagnostic paradigm solved all at once many aspects of the psychiatric crisis. It divided the life problems and unhappiness that analysis had claimed for psychiatry into suitable disease entities, in the process giving psychiatry the categories that a medical paradigm demanded. Such a paradigm not only linked psychiatry to traditional medical practice but also warded off competition from nonmedical psychotherapeutic professionals. In addition, categorical illnesses fit the demands of third-party payers, which required greater accountability in treatment, and of pharmaceutical companies, which required these illnesses for their products to treat. An illness-based psychiatry was also far more suitable for the more conservative political strategy at the NIMH and for the ideology of family advocacy groups. Changing social circumstances made vague dimensions a liability and specific categories a professional necessity. When symptom-based categories reemerged in psychiatry, they came with a vengeance.

Chapter Four

THE EXTENSION OF MENTAL ILLNESSES INTO THE COMMUNITY

[handwritten: → Insomia, nervousness, → symptoms fear etc.]

Symptom-based categorical illnesses are now firmly embedded in psychiatric practice and research. They have also spread well beyond the particular persons who are treated for these conditions and have become the basis of studies that seemingly demonstrate the pervasiveness of untreated mental disorders in the community. These studies indicate that one fifth of all American adults and children, about 50 million people, suffer from these categorical illnesses each year. They also show that about half of the population has suffered from the most common types of illnesses at some point in their lives (USDHHS 1999). Virtually all articles about particular illnesses that appear in psychiatric and medical journals routinely cite figures that stem from these community studies to indicate their widespread prevalence.[1]

The assumption that mental disorders are extremely common has also diffused from community studies to portrayals of mental illness in the media. An article "Fear Itself" that appeared in the *New York Times Magazine* is typical (Hall 1999a). The article begins with the story of a woman living in Manhattan who has a crippling fear of crossing bridges or using subway tunnels that leads her to develop uncontrollable symptoms of dread whenever she has to leave her home. *[handwritten: > point!]* This story includes the finding that more than 23 million Americans suffer from anxiety disorders that are presumably comparable to this clearly dysfunctional case. *[handwritten: > point]* Another article in this magazine recounts the author's battle with an extreme form of alcohol addiction (Knapp 1999). This story notes that nearly 14 million Americans have alcohol-abuse problems, again equating a clear case of a serious mental disorder with those cases that produce prevalence estimates in the population. Yet another article begins with a description of a man who "has never visited a friend's house because he has never had a friend. He has never dated, either. And he never goes to bars, restaurants or ball games because his chest tightens and he breaks into a sweat when he is around people." The description of this man's social phobia, which clearly seems to indicate a serious internal dysfunction, is followed by the contention that social phobias afflict 19 million Americans, about 7 percent of the population (Raghunathan 1999).

Categorical mental illnesses have thus spread beyond clinical practice and are presumably widespread, even rampant, in the community. The symptoms of the large number of untreated cases are presumed to be equivalent to those of the far smaller number of cases found in clinical treatment. The corresponding claim is that huge numbers of people who suffer from these disorders are not receiving adequate mental health treatment for them (Regier et al. 1993, Hirschfeld et al. 1997). The large estimates of untreated mental disorders become the basis for calls to expand mental health treatment services. The ubiquity of untreated mental disorders, however, does not result from people actually having these disorders but is a product of the classification system that is used to construct them.

CONSTRUCTING MENTAL ILLNESSES IN THE COMMUNITY

The federal agency concerned with research on and policy toward mental illness, the National Institute of Mental Health (NIMH), has been the major sponsor of community studies of mental disorder. As chapter 3 indicated, this agency, like the psychiatric profession in general, was facing a major crisis during the 1970s. From its development in the late 1940s until the early 1970s, the NIMH was the leading force behind an activist mental health agenda (Grob 1991a; Kirk 1999; Kolb et al. 2000). It developed and implemented policies that diminished the role of state mental hospitals, promoted the deinstitutionalization of mental patients, established a broad network of community mental health centers, and sponsored numerous research and policy efforts that assumed broad social and economic changes would promote mental health and prevent mental illness. The new conservative politics of the 1970s, however, forced the NIMH to draw back from its sweeping policy agenda and devolved mental health policy away from the federal government back to the fifty states. At the same time, the NIMH neither developed nor implemented the major policies that would come to dominate federal funding for mental health after the 1960s—Medicare, Medicaid, and Supplemental Security Disability Income.

By the 1970s, the once influential NIMH was becoming peripheral to the most fundamental changes occurring in mental health policy. It had lost its former mission and was in search of another one. The demonstration of the pervasiveness of "real" mental disorders in the community provided the NIMH with a new and important purpose. This purpose was also politically acceptable to the legislators who had to approve the agency's budget. Because the problem to be addressed was now disease conditions, rather than broad social problems, the new direction of the NIMH would be amenable to conservative as well as liberal politics (Kirk 1999).

The construction of mental disorders in community surveys paralleled the movement of psychiatric research and practice from global, nonspecific measures to well-defined categories. Community surveys had been a standard component of social psychiatry since the 1950s. The initial studies of mental illnesses in community populations arose during the heyday of dynamic psychiatry in the 1950s and 1960s (Srole et al. 1962; Leighton 1959; Plunkett and Gordon 1960).[2] These studies had developed broad, continuous, and nonspecific measures of psychological distress based on scales containing general symptoms of depression, anxiety, and psychophysiological disorders (Langner 1962; Macmillan 1957; Weissman, Myers, and Ross 1986). These global scales did not attempt to measure specific types of mental illnesses; during this period these illnesses were not of major concern to mental health professionals. These symptom scales were, therefore, incommensurate with the new system of categorical disorders the DSM-III was developing.

The categorical system of the DSM-III became the model not only for research psychiatrists and clinicians but also for studies of psychiatric disorders in the community. At the same time that the Task Force developing the DSM-III was deliberating in the 1970s, the NIMH decided to launch the first study that would measure the prevalence of particular types of mental disorder in the community (Robins 1986). Researchers from Washington University, the same institution that produced the Feighner criteria that underlay the DSM-III, constructed the Diagnostic Interview Schedule (DIS) that was the basis for the new generation of epidemiological studies. Lee Robins, a sociologist whose husband Eli Robins was a member of the core group of diagnostically oriented psychiatrists at Washington University, was the principal developer of the DIS (Robins 1986). This instrument measured specific diagnostic conditions in community populations that were supposed to be comparable to the major clinical entities—such as depression, social phobia, or generalized anxiety disorder—found in the DSM-III.

Because DSM diagnoses were based entirely upon overt symptoms, epi-

ogists could, with little change, apply diagnoses developed for clini-
ent populations to surveys of the general population in the commu-
he results would presumably provide good estimates of how much
untreated mental disorder existed. These estimates, in turn, would provide
policy makers with knowledge of how much unmet need existed for psychiatric services. From the 1980s to the present, diagnostic models have been
the basis for community studies of psychological disturbance.

The DIS is based on the same categorical, and presumably atheoretical,
logic that informed the DSM-III. It used closed-format questions and answers that trained lay interviewers could administer to gather information
about symptoms. Interviewers were not allowed any discretion in their inquiries regarding the presence of symptoms. In the DIS: "The interviewer
reads specific questions and follows positive responses with additional prescribed questions. Each step in the sequence of identifying a psychiatric
symptom is fully specified and does not depend upon the judgment of the
interviewers" (Leaf, Myers, and McEvoy 1991, 12). There are no degrees
of mental pathology in the DIS. Rather, distinct mental disorders are present or absent—one is or is not clinically depressed, phobic, obsessive-
compulsive, and so on. A diagnosis of depression, for example, stems from
reports of enough symptoms such as sadness, loss of appetite, sleep difficulties, inability to concentrate, and the like. If five symptoms are required
for a diagnosis of depression, persons who report four or fewer symptoms
are not depressed. A diagnosis of anxiety follows from the presence of
enough psychological symptoms such as worries and anxiousness and physiological symptoms such as dizziness, pounding heart, and upset stomach.
Only the presence of symptoms, not their contexts or causes, is relevant for
obtaining diagnoses (Robins and Regier 1991).

The DIS was the basis of the first national study of the prevalence
of mental illness in the community—the Epidemiologic Catchment Area
(ECA) study (Eaton and Kessler 1985; Robins and Regier 1991). The ECA
surveyed more than 18,000 adults in the community and 2,500 persons in
institutions in five sites (New Haven, Durham, Baltimore, St. Louis, and
Los Angeles). It used estimates of the prevalence of disorders in these sites
to generate national estimates of prevalence. The second major community
study of the prevalence of specific psychiatric disorders was the National
Co-Morbidity Survey (NCS), fielded by the NIMH in 1992 (Kessler et al.
1994; Kessler and Zhao 1999). The NCS used the CIDI, a diagnostic instrument similar to the DIS, in a national probability sample.

The findings from the ECA and the NCS are the basis for the estimates regarding the prevalence of mental disorder that are now widely cited in the scientific and popular literature and that form the basis for the claims of the 1999 Surgeon General's Report on Mental Health that 50 million people each year suffer from mental disorders (USDHHS 1999). The ECA estimated that about 16 percent of the population had at least one current psychiatric disorder and about 20 percent had had some disorder over the past year. About a third of the population (32 percent) reported some history of a psychiatric disorder in their lives. When the results of a second ECA survey conducted with the same subjects one year after the original survey were taken into account, the estimates of lifetime prevalence increased from 32 percent to 44 percent of the population (Regier et al. 1998).

The NCS was a single wave sample of about 8,100 persons meant to represent the population of the United States.[3] Its age range of 15–54 years was somewhat lower than the 18–65 age group the ECA sampled. The NCS estimates of lifetime prevalence of psychiatric disorder—48 percent—were even higher than those claimed in the ECA, as was its 29 percent estimate of one-year prevalence. A special concern of the NCS was co-morbid persons who suffer from more than one discrete disorder. It found that 29 percent of respondents reported more than one type of disorder over their lives (Kessler et al. 1994).

Rates of depression, anxiety, and substance abuse disorders were especially high in these surveys. The NCS found that about 10 percent of respondents had a diagnosis of major depression in the past year and that 24 percent reported enough symptoms for a diagnosis of either major depression or dysthymia at some point in their lifetime (Kessler et al. 1994). Rates from the ECA were somewhat lower, with 6.4 percent of respondents reporting major depression over the past year and 18 percent either major depression or dysthymia over their lifetime (Blazer et al. 1994). Both the NCS and the ECA reported a lifetime prevalence rate for some anxiety disorder of about 20 percent. Lifetime rates for substance abuse or dependence disorders were even higher: 28 percent in the NCS and 24 percent in the ECA. Overall, these surveys estimated that nearly a third of the population suffered from the most common psychiatric illnesses over a twelve-month period and nearly half warranted diagnoses of these illnesses over their lifetime (Regier et al. 1998).

A further finding from these studies was how few people seek help for mental disorders. The assumption that there is a large unmet need for mental health services is based on the findings of the ECA and the NCS that showed most people who had presumed psychiatric disorders did not seek professional treatment for them (Regier et al. 1993). The annual prevalence of psychiatric disorder was 28.1 percent in the ECA and 27.7 percent in the NCS. The results from each study indicated a large mismatch between psychiatric need and service reception. In the ECA study less than a third of persons who received psychiatric diagnoses had received any type of professional treatment in the past year (Regier et al. 1993). Data from New Haven, Baltimore, and St. Louis showed that, during the six-month period immediately prior to the interview, only 8.1 to 12.4 percent of individuals with a recent diagnosis had had contact with the mental health specialty sector (Shapiro et al. 1985). The highest proportion of cases in treatment across the three sites was 48.1 percent for schizophrenia. In no diagnostic category did a majority of people with a recent disorder report having sought care for a mental health reason during the preceding six-month period (Shapiro et al. 1985).

The use of community studies to discover the pervasiveness of mental disorder has spread from adults to children. For example, a study of a large, representative group of children in Puerto Rico finds that 49 percent have some kind of mental disorder (Bird et al. 1988). Another indicates that by age twenty-one, 40 percent of young adults in New Zealand have suffered a DIS disorder (Miech et al. 1999). In a study in the United States, 23 percent of twelfth graders have diagnoses of substance abuse disorders alone (Harrison, Fulkerson, and Beebe 1998). These extraordinarily high rates of mental disorders in children presumably demonstrate the need for programs to prevent these disorders from arising in the first place and to provide services to youths who suffer from them.

The findings from these community studies are used to support arguments that mental disorder is a public health problem of vast proportions, that relatively few people with these conditions seek appropriate treatment for them, that untreated mental disorders create vast economic costs, that the amount of mental health services is inadequate, and that many people need to take prescription medications to overcome their suffering (Greenberg et al. 1993; Hirschfeld et al. 1997; USDHHS 1999). In fact, the extraordinarily large number of people who allegedly suffer from categorical mental disorders is a product of symptom-based measures that inevitably overestimate the number of people who have some untreated mental illness.

As explained earlier, mental disorders are internal dysfunctions that are not expectable responses to environmental stressors. The DSM definition of mental disorder explicitly recognizes this when it states: "this syndrome or pattern must not be merely an expectable and culturally sanctioned response to a particular event, for example, the death of a loved one" (APA 1994, xxi). Thus, depression and anxiety stemming from, for example, the dissolution of important social relationships, oppressive employment conditions, loss of a job, or the serious illness of a child should not, according to the DSM definition, be considered signs of mental disorders. Likewise, the DSM definition distinguishes social deviance from internal dysfunctions: "Neither deviant behavior (e.g., political, religious, or sexual) nor conflicts that are primarily between the individual and society are mental disorders unless the deviance or conflict is a symptom of a dysfunction in the individual" (APA 1994, xxii). Heavy drinking that stems from hedonism, delinquency that arises from conformity to subcultural norms, or defiance of authority are not mental disorders when there is nothing wrong with the internal functioning of the individuals who display these behaviors.

The DSM definition thus appropriately distinguishes between mental disorders on the one hand and normal reactions to environmental stressors and social deviance on the other hand. This distinction, however, conflicts with the DSM logic of defining disorders based solely on overt symptoms, regardless of the cause or context of these symptoms. These symptom-based logics are presumably the same in community studies as in clinical practice because the instruments used to classify them, the DSM and the DIS (or CIDI), are virtually identical. This gives rise to the claims that the untreated mental disorders uncovered in community studies are the same kinds of conditions found in clinical practice. In fact, however, the consequences of the use of symptom-based diagnoses in treatment settings differ markedly from the consequences of their use in survey research.

The use of symptom-based diagnoses in clinical practice is unlikely to produce many false positives—people who seek mental health treatment but do not need it (Wakefield 1999b). Most people who receive mental health treatment voluntarily seek professional help. In doing so they indicate that they feel their symptoms are distressing enough and their consequences severe enough to justify professional treatment and that professional treatment can help to alleviate the suffering these symptoms create. Others are in treatment because family members, social workers, teachers, or agents of social control think their behavior warrants some sort of psychological treatment. Thus, before people enter professional treatment, some layperson has already made the judgment that symptoms probably indicate a psychological problem (see Horwitz 1987).

Clinical judgments provide a second level of screening as to what constitutes a legitimate mental health problem. Clinicians must evaluate whether the problems they see are appropriate for mental health treatment (Wakefield 1999b). They can, for example, tell parents who think that their pot-smoking children need psychiatric treatment that smoking marijuana in itself need not indicate a mental health problem. Or they can reassure highly distressed people who are undergoing marital dissolution that their problems are mainly situational rather than internal. Thus, treated groups have undergone two levels of screening, in addition to meeting diagnostic criteria. The symptom-based logic of the DSM is applied within the context of lay and professional judgments that assess whether particular symptoms are signs of mental disorders. The measurement of mental disorders in survey research, however, lacks comparable checks over whether symptoms indicate internal dysfunctions.

A hypothetical example using the DSM definition of bulimia nervosa illustrates the difference between use of symptom-based logic in community surveys and in clinical practice. The major symptoms of bulimia are eating a larger amount of food within a shorter period of time than most people would eat, inappropriate compensatory behavior to prevent weight gain, and binge eating that occurs at least twice a week for three months (APA 1994, 549–50). In some cases, however, the same symptoms might not indicate bulimia but might stem from appropriate rule-following behaviors. For example, wrestlers who must lose weight quickly to qualify for particular weight classes and who then eat large amounts of food as soon as they make weight meet these symptomatic criteria. Yet, their "bulimia nervosa" only occurs during wrestling seasons, arises from conformity to social expectations, and has nothing to do with internal, individual characteristics. Wrestlers who meet the symptomatic criteria for bulimia during wrestling season do not have internal dysfunctions and so are not mentally disordered.

Wrestlers who respond accurately to questions in surveys would affirm items that ask them about reports of binge eating and compensatory efforts to lose weight. Unlike in clinical practice, survey methods do not attempt to differentiate whether symptoms indicate disorders. The interviews or standardized questionnaires used in these methods do not allow for any discretion in inquiries regarding the presence of symptoms. The logic of making diagnoses through the presence of symptoms without regard to the contextual meaning of symptoms would lead to diagnoses of bulimia among wrestlers. The result is that researchers would mistakenly conclude that this disorder is spreading among males, especially among those who participate in wrestling.[4]

The equation of symptoms that might indicate bulimia with bulimic disorders would not be a comparable problem in clinical practice: wrestlers would not seek psychiatric help for bulimia. Although in theory the DSM definition of bulimia nervosa would mistakenly lead to the conclusion that wrestlers are bulimic, in practice, because of the appropriate application of lay and professional judgment, there is little chance that a wrestler would actually be labeled as bulimic.

The hypothetical example of the bulimic wrestlers illustrates a fundamental problem with using symptom-based logics in community surveys: symptoms that represent appropriate responses to environmental circumstances are not distinguished from symptoms that stem from internal dysfunctions. Because both appropriate and inappropriate symptomatic responses to particular contexts are considered signs of mental disorders, the result is to over-count the number of people defined as having these disorders. Thus, a student who is surveyed during the week before she finds out whether or not she has been admitted to medical school might report enough symptoms of anxiety to qualify for a diagnosis of a generalized anxiety disorder. She is not, however, mentally disordered despite the presence of these symptoms if her "disorder" immediately disappears once she finds out she has gained admission. Nevertheless, she would be counted among the 23 million people who suffer from generalized anxiety disorders (USDHHS 1999). Someone else might have had too much to drink at a wedding, an office party, and a birthday celebration over the past year and recall friends commenting on their inebriation. This person could accurately report enough symptoms to be diagnosed with an alcohol dependence disorder. This respondent, although considered one of the 14 percent of Americans with an apparent alcohol disorder, has little in common with someone who persistently uses large quantities of alcohol with problematic consequences (Helzer, Burnam, and McEvoy 1991). A third person might recall symptoms such as depressed mood, insomnia, loss of appetite, or diminished pleasure in usual activities that lasted for longer than two weeks after the breakup of a romantic relationship, the diagnosis of a serious illness in an intimate, or the unexpected loss of a job. Although these symptoms might have dissipated as soon as a new relationship developed, the intimate

· this draws on the ideas that even symptoms are socially constructed! / as well as overrepresentation issue!

recovered, or another job was found, this individual would join the 20 million people who suffer from the "disorder" of depression each year.

The logic of symptom-based diagnoses in community studies considers all of these persons mentally disordered, regardless of the fact that their symptoms do not stem from internal dysfunctions. Unlike clinical practice, community surveys have no checks on whether symptoms are expectable responses to particular situations. Instead, they count all symptoms as indicators of disorders and so overestimate the number of untreated mental disorders in the community. The kinds of symptoms—sadness, anxiousness, bouts of heavy drinking, etc.—that are counted as indicating disorders are common products of ordinary stressors. Therefore, it is even possible that the number of false positives—people who do not have internal dysfunctions but are diagnosed as having a mental disorder—exceeds the number of people who are accurately classified as mentally disordered (Wakefield 1999b).

The following examples of sexual dysfunction, social phobia, major depression, and alcohol use and abuse illustrate how symptom-based logics generate inflated prevalence estimates. They also show how these estimates are created and perpetuated because a number of particular groups have distinct interests in demonstrating the presumed pervasiveness of mental illnesses in the community.

Sexual Dysfunction   A study of sexual dysfunction based on the largest and most representative community study of sexual behavior ever conducted in the United States illustrates how the use of symptom-based logics in survey research inflates rates of presumed mental disorders (Laumann, Paik, and Rosen 1999). This study, which was published in the prestigious *Journal of the American Medical Association (JAMA)*, measures sexual dysfunction with seven symptoms including a lack of interest in sex, anxiety about sexual performance, arousal difficulties, the inability to have an orgasm, difficulty in obtaining erection, or finding sex painful or not pleasurable. It finds that 43 percent of women and 31 percent of men suffered from sexual dysfunctions over the twelve months preceding their participation in the study. These huge numbers result from a failure to use a valid definition of mental disorder that distinguishes internal dysfunctions from expectable results of social stressors or of diminished, but normal, interest in having sex.

Symptoms such as the failure to obtain an erection, to find sex pleasurable, or to be orgasmic can sometimes indicate harmful internal dysfunctions and so can be signs of a mental disorder. Often, however, they can stem from well-adjusted couples who no longer have a strong interest in sexual relationships. They might also stem from boring or inept sexual partners or from unsatisfactory or abusive relationships. Indeed, this study finds that the best predictor of "sexual dysfunction" is low satisfaction with one's sexual partner. If people were to regain normal sexual functioning when they changed sexual partners or when their relationship with their current partner improved, their current symptoms would not indicate an internal dysfunction but instead would reflect a problematic social relationship. The assumption that the presence of symptoms, regardless of what factors account for them, represents an individual dysfunction is unwarranted. A symptom-based definition of sexual dysfunction hopelessly entangles people whose symptoms do stem from internal dysfunctions with those whose symptoms are not the result of any psychological or physiological dysfunction.

The problem with the assumption that all symptoms indicate mental disorder regardless of the meaning or context of these symptoms is not only the resulting highly inflated rates of disorder but also the type of solution that follows. The authors of the *JAMA* study conclude that sexual dysfunction is a "public health" problem that calls for increased provision of medical therapies, especially medications. They assume that the vast numbers of persons with putative sexual dysfunctions are the untreated equivalents of persons who do seek professional help. Yet, clinicians would only see people who define their sexual problems both as internal and as distressing enough to warrant professional help. In contrast, the large number of people in this study whose "sexual dysfunctions" stem from a lack of interest in sex or from relationship problems would not define their problems as psychological nor seek mental health treatment for their supposed symptoms. Indeed, it is not clear what public good would be served by encouraging them to do so.

The authors of this study assume that people with bad or boring interpersonal relationships should remedy their condition by taking drugs that increase their sexual stimulation. Their findings, however, suggest that people would be better advised either to change their relationship with their current partner or to find different partners instead of seeking medication from their physicians. Alternatively, they might be perfectly satisfied with relationships that don't involve much sexual activity. There is no valid reason to consider nearly half of women and one third of men as suffering from the disorder of sexual dysfunction.

What would lead the authors of this widely cited study to take seriously such huge prevalence estimates? The study was done shortly after a new drug, Viagra, came on the market, with sales that exceeded $1 billion in its first year (Hitt 2000).[5] When Viagra was first marketed it was directed toward older men who had problems achieving sexual climax.[6] Shortly thereafter, it became clear that older persons formed only a small portion of the potential market for Viagra because young, sexually capable men were widely using the drug to enhance their sexual performance (Hitt 2000). Subsequent advertising was directed at this much larger market, using attractive young people as models and asking "Not satisfied with your sex life?" Studies that find high prevalence estimates of supposed sexual dysfunctions serve to justify the expansion of the market for Viagra well beyond persons with erectile dysfunctions to any man[7] who wants enhanced sexual performance. Calling people with problems in their interpersonal relationships "sexually dysfunctional" may help the business of the pharmaceutical company that sponsored this research, but it fundamentally mischaracterizes most of the problems the study uncovers.

The example of sexual dysfunctions shows both how easily community studies can generate high prevalence rates and the interests that benefit from these inflated rates. Sexual dysfunctions, however, are not typical types of mental illnesses. Unlike most conditions, it is not difficult to convince people of the benefits that stem from taking Viagra and other sexual stimulants. Both people who have problems in obtaining erections and those who do not will eagerly seek a medication that enhances their sexual pleasure. It is not as easy to convince people with other conditions that they have mental disorders that require medication and other professional treatments.

Social Phobia   Social phobias, also called social anxiety disorders, feature marked and persistent fears of social or performance situations in which embarrassment may occur (APA 1994, 411). Community studies reveal that social phobias are among the most common mental disorders, exceeded in number by only depression and alcohol problems. Pervasive television and print advertisements encourage sufferers to seek medical help for them. Widespread public service announcements likewise urge the many millions of people afflicted with social anxiety disorders to recognize that they have real disorders. An annual National Anxiety Disorders Screening Day has been established to enhance awareness and professional help-seeking for this disorder. It is difficult to avoid the pervasive construction of social phobias as mental disorders in the early part of the twenty-first century.

Social phobias illustrate not only how community studies overestimate rates of disorder, but also how these studies can in large part *create* the disorders they supposedly measure. These conditions did not exist as officially recognized disorders until 1980. The DSM-I and DSM-II did not mention them and they first entered the psychiatric literature only in the late 1960s (Healy 1997, 188). When they first appeared in the DSM-III in 1980, the manual noted that "The disorder is apparently relatively rare" (Cottle 1999, 26). The ECA study provided the first prevalence estimates for social phobias—about 2.75 percent in community populations in the early 1980s (Eaton, Dryman, and Weissman 1991). Social phobias did not truly emerge as significant mental illnesses until the NCS study in the early 1990s, which estimated their lifetime prevalence at 13.3 percent, one out of every eight people in the population (Kessler et al. 1994; Magee et al. 1996).

What led to the near quintupling in the prevalence of social phobias over this ten-year period? Survey questions changed the required criteria for a diagnosis of social phobia from a compelling desire to avoid exposure to social or performance situations to only marked distress in these situations. In the NCS, people received diagnoses of social phobias when they reported an unreasonable fear that leads them to avoid or to feel extremely uncomfortable while doing at least one of the following: public speaking, using the toilet when away from home, eating or drinking in public, feeling foolish when speaking to others, writing while someone watches, or talking in front of small groups of people. The most prevalent responses leading to a diagnosis affirm the question of having an unreasonably strong fear of speaking in public (McHugh 1999, 36).

Why did social phobias suddenly emerge as a major pathological condition of near epidemic proportions? By slightly changing the wording of questions that establish the criteria for this disorder, the NCS presumably established that one of every eight people suffered from this disorder. This created a fertile new market for the antidepressant medications, the SSRIs, that were becoming increasingly popular in the early 1990s.[8] By 1999 the SSRI Paxil was approved for the specific treatment of social phobia, unleashing a barrage of print and television ads aimed at the many persons who report symptoms of this presumed disorder in community surveys. The vast potential market for this medication is less those persons with severe social phobias who are in clinical treatment than the far greater number of persons community studies have uncovered. A spokesperson for the maker of Paxil states that only 5 percent of the population presumably

> main point!

> performed by NIMH

suffering from social phobias receives treatment for them (Raghunathan 1999, C1). The company attempts to reach the 95 percent of putatively untreated sufferers through broadcasting the prevalence estimates of community studies and showing how common these conditions are. One television advertisement for Paxil, for example, features an attractive woman who is extremely nervous before speaking at a gathering of her extended family that might be an anniversary, wedding, or birthday.[9] Such portrayals attempt to convince people both that their discomfort is a mental disorder and that it is an extremely common condition.

Pharmaceutical companies are not the only interests with a stake in high prevalence rates—advocacy organizations for the various disorders also depend on such inflated estimates. The Anxiety Disorders Association of America widely promotes the claim that 19 million Americans suffer from social anxiety disorders. Advocacy groups find such estimates useful because the 19 million people with social phobias can be equated with the far smaller number of people with truly serious mental disorders, presumably lowering the distance between the mentally disordered and others. Public service advertisements from the National Institute of Mental Health likewise encourage people to seek treatment for these "frightening mental illnesses" that afflict 19 million people (Sharkey 1999, E5). These estimates help justify large research budgets for the NIMH even as they enhance the importance of the presumed problem the agency is addressing.

The symptom-based logic of community studies has created these disorders as commonly occurring conditions. It is not surprising that one of eight persons, reflecting back over a lifetime, would recollect having nothing to say on a date, fearfully approaching an oral in-class presentation, or feeling intensely nervous before speaking at an important meeting. Indeed, the advertisements for Paxil capitalize on the fact that, for most people, extreme shyness when called on to speak at public occasions might be the *only* time they display the supposed symptoms of social phobias. Most people rarely have any activities that require them to speak to audiences larger than two or three family members, friends, or colleagues. Their responses to questions that ask, "Have there ever been times when . . . " would naturally refer to unusual situations when they had to toast their sister, honor their parents, or speak for themselves in a class or at a bridal shower, birthday, or wedding. Such questions and subsequent diagnoses will certainly generate huge prevalence estimates, but these estimates will not be valid estimates of social phobias as mental disorders.

Salespeople, teachers, or executives whose jobs require them to speak before large audiences would be well advised to seek professional help when they experience the symptoms of social phobias. Others might justifiably question whether they have a mental disorder or, alternatively, ordinary experiences of discomfort that do not seriously disrupt their normal functioning. There is little evidence that social anxiety disorders are a widespread problem in the population.[10] In the past, people who reported these symptoms rarely sought mental health services: persons with social phobias have a lower rate of help-seeking from mental health professionals than any other disorder except for substance abuse (Katz et al. 1997, 1139). Whether or not the coalition of pharmaceutical manufacturers, advocacy groups, psychiatric researchers, and mental health practitioners will be able to shape the conditions of many millions of untreated nervous and shy people into serious, but treatable, mental disorders is an open question.

Depression Depression is perhaps the most widespread mental disorder and is the cause of an immense amount of human suffering. Any humane social policy will strive to provide people who suffer from depression with adequate mental health services. Yet, until recently depression was limited to those whose symptoms of sadness, withdrawal, hopelessness, and the like were not products of their immediate social circumstances. The major problem in defining depression stems from separating people whose depressive symptoms reflect an internal dysfunction from those who are responding normally to social stressors and whose symptoms will disappear when these stressors abate.

The National Co-Morbidity Survey illustrates how community surveys measure depression (Blazer et al. 1994). The NCS uses two steps to obtain diagnoses of depression based on DSM-III-R criteria. The first is that respondents must affirm at least one stem question that appears at the beginning of the interview. These questions ask: "In your lifetime, have you ever had two weeks or more when nearly every day you felt sad, blue, or depressed?" "Have you ever had two weeks or more when nearly every day you felt down in the dumps, low, or gloomy?" "Has there ever been two weeks or more when you lost interest in most things like work, hobbies, or things you usually liked to do?" and "Have you ever had two weeks or more during which you felt sad, blue, depressed or where you lost all interest and pleasure in things that you usually cared about or enjoyed?" Given the broad nature of these questions and the fact that they have no exclusion

° are racing thoughts even unclicated w DSM
for anxiety + depression (they are for depression)

criteria for the circumstances in which they arose, it is not surprising that
56 percent of the population registered at least one affirmative response
(Blazer et al. 1994). Later in the interview, this group is asked numerous
questions about symptoms of appetite and sleep disturbance, fatigue, and
feelings of sadness, worthlessness, hopelessness, and the like. A computer
program then determines whether respondents meet the criteria for a diagnosis of depression.

these
are
behaviors
relative
to the
person!

In valid cases of depression, symptoms would arise in the absence of any
cause that would expectably give rise to them, be of severity and/or duration disproportionate to their precipitating causes, or persist after the causes
that gave rise to them disappeared (see chapter 1). The DSM definition recognizes the logic of this criterion in stating that bereaved people will normally show signs of depression subsequent to their loss and thus should not
be considered as having a mental disorder. With the exception of short-
term bereavement for major depression, however, all persons in community
studies who report enough symptoms are counted as having the mental disorder of depression. No questions inquire about the context of symptoms.
Symptoms that are severe, longstanding, and indicative of internal dysfunctions are not distinguished from symptoms that are distressing but not severe, transient, or the result of contextual precipitants.

enough
symptoms.
→What is
to little
then?

The resulting diagnoses should accurately encompass persons whose depressions stem from internal causes that are not expectable responses to
environmental circumstances. But in practice they also would include the
reactions of respondents who recall periods of extreme sadness after a romantic breakup, the discovery that a spouse is having an affair, the loss of a
valued job, failure to get a long-awaited promotion, crime victimization, the
devastation of property by natural disaster, or the discovery of an unwanted
pregnancy. Each of these precipitants would normally lead to periods of at
least two weeks that feature enough symptoms to qualify for a diagnosis of
depression (Wakefield 1999). Given the prevalence of stressful events in
ordinary life, people who are responding normally to social circumstances
are likely to make up a large proportion of people in community surveys who
are categorized as having depressive disorders (Turner and Lloyd 1999).

There is nothing wrong with the internal functioning of such persons;
their symptoms are *appropriate* responses to environmental circumstances.
Yet even if their symptoms disappeared as soon as the circumstances that
gave rise to them went away, they are counted as having the mental disorder
of depression. Both people who have expectable responses of sadness to

their environments and those whose sadness is a product of an internal dysfunction meet the diagnostic criteria of depression in community surveys. The result is that the NCS (and ECA) estimate that about 10 percent of respondents have had a case of major depression in the past year and that between 20 and 25 percent have suffered from depression at some point in their lives (Kessler et al. 1994; Blazer et al. 1994).

As with social phobias, a number of groups have a major stake in promoting the notion that depression is a "real" disorder affecting a large proportion of the population. The Consensus Statement of the National Depressive and Manic-Depressive Association, coauthored by twenty prominent psychiatrists, government officials, and mental health advocates and published in the *Journal of the American Medical Association,* illustrates how particular groups promote the findings from community studies about the prevalence of depression (Hirschfeld et al. 1997). The statement's major theme is that depression is an extremely widespread medical illness that strikes about 15 percent of men and 24 percent of women over their lifetimes. Yet, only about one in ten depressed people receives adequate treatment. There is thus a tremendous amount of unmet need for treatments of depression that provide high enough doses of antidepressant medications for long enough periods of time.

The authors of this manifesto believe that depression is vastly undertreated because the cultural beliefs of both laypersons and physicians prevent them from understanding that psychiatric disorders are real illnesses. People who have depressive symptoms have a disease condition that, like untreated physical disorders, requires professional treatment. Untreated cases of depression, no less than untreated cancer, pneumonia, or diabetes cases, are serious public health problems that must be treated with high doses of medication. Although depression is, in fact, a concrete illness defined by its symptoms, many laypersons and even physicians hold mistaken beliefs and "merely thought it was an expected response to a life situation" (Hirschfeld et al. 1997, 337). Lack of knowledge prevents people from seeking medical help and receiving medical treatment. This ignorance must be overcome through educational campaigns. The statement concludes:

> Depression is a pernicious illness associated with long duration of episodes, high rates of chronicity, relapse, and recurrence, psychosocial and physical impairment, and mortality and morbidity—with a 15% risk of death from suicide in patients who have ever been hospitalized for de-

pression. Despite these facts, the vast majority of patients with chronic depression are misdiagnosed, receive inappropriate or inadequate treatment, or are given no treatment at all. (Hirschfeld et al. 1997, 339)

The Consensus Statement thus joins the conditions of persons whose depressive symptoms are clearly serious, ongoing, and dysfunctional with those whose depressions are the expectable results of social circumstances.

Why would this prominent group of researchers, government scientists, and mental health advocates so stridently assert that this dire disorder afflicts such a high proportion of the population each year and, especially, over their lifetimes? As with estimates of social phobias, the most direct benefits of high prevalence estimates of depression accrue to pharmaceutical companies. The greater the number of persons with presumed mental disorders, the larger the market for the hugely successful antidepressants these companies produce. The standard format of pharmaceutical advertisements, which are now prominent both in prime-time television shows and in mass circulation print media, is to feature ordinary people and to cite high prevalence estimates of depression.[11] The message is clear: you are not alone, millions of others share your problem. The explosive growth in sales of antidepressants is testimony to the effectiveness of this appeal. Pharmaceutical companies have also become major funders of both advocacy groups and clinical researchers (Valenstein 1998). The interests of drug companies in promoting their products have thus become highly intertwined with the interests of mental health advocates and mental health researchers in perpetuating the notion that mental disorders are ubiquitous.

The economic benefit to pharmaceutical companies is not the only interest that perpetuates high prevalence estimates of depression. Mental health advocacy groups promote the pervasiveness of depression. Advocates for the seriously mentally ill find high prevalence estimates of depression useful because so many people can tie this condition to their own experiences or to the experiences of family members and friends. When depression is identified as a serious mental disorder, this definition can help decrease the stigma of mental illness, call attention to its widespread nature, and gain more resources for the mental health system. The premise that calling "mental illness an illness just like any other illness," when mental illness is defined as broadly as possible, can lead to greater sympathy for, identification with, and resources dedicated to persons with serious mental disorders (see USDHHS 1999). In this way, advocates hope to reduce the social distance between the mentally disordered and others. If mental disorders affect

↗ does it really?

a broad cross-section of the population, the mentally disordered will cease to be seen as a small, distinct minority with radical differences from most people. Hence, high prevalence estimates lower the distance between the people with serious mental disorders and others, seemingly helping to normalize this population.

In addition to drug companies and advocacy groups, mental health professionals have a stake in the generous counting of mental disorders such as depression in community studies. Because community surveys indicate that only a relatively small proportion of people with putative psychiatric disorders are receiving professional treatment, they allegedly demonstrate the tremendous amount of unmet need for mental health services. Convincing people that their sadness is a real disorder greatly expands the demand for the services of mental health professionals. Epidemiological studies thus underpin efforts to increase the number of persons who seek psychiatric help for their currently unrecognized psychiatric symptoms (Hirschfeld et al. 1997).

Finally, researchers and policy makers benefit from the perceived pervasiveness of mental disorders such as depression. If mental disorders are so widespread, those who study them are dealing not with serious but relatively uncommon problems, but with a public health problem of vast proportions. This enhances the importance of the issues that concern researchers and policy makers. The more people mental disorders afflict, the greater the justification for expanding funding for research and treatment of the sorts of problems that interest researchers and policy makers (Kirk 1999).

These community surveys assume that the conditions they detect are comparable to those that lead people to seek clinical treatment for, say, depression. The marketing of drugs to people suffering from the depressive consequences of social stressors is not necessarily a bad thing. People who have recently undergone separations, layoffs, disappointments, and dissatisfactions might well feel better after taking antidepressant medication. In many cases, the condition that the drug alleviates, however, is not a mental disorder but the ordinary unhappiness that naturally ensues in social life. The assumption that most people who report enough symptoms of depression don't seek treatment for it because of ignorance, stigma, or the cost of seeking mental health treatment is unwarranted (see USDHHS 1999). People may not seek mental health treatment because they *appropriately* view their distress as resulting from interpersonal, occupational, or economic circumstances. In addition, they may realize, often from past occurrences, that after these stressful experiences end, their distress will naturally dissipate over time. These lay views of distressing experiences may be more accurate than the illness models promoted by pharmaceutical companies and mental health professionals.

Alcohol Abuse   After depression, alcohol abuse is the most commonly occurring mental disorder in community studies. As with depression, the symptom-based definitions of alcohol abuse in the community studies that follow DSM definitions ignore the heterogeneous nature of the patterns and frequency of alcohol use and consider all possible symptoms of alcohol use as indicators of a mental disorder, inflating the amount of presumed mental disorders. In the DSM alcohol abuse is defined as a maladaptive pattern of alcohol use leading to clinically significant impairment or distress. It is manifested by at least one of the following consequences over a twelve-month period: a failure to fulfill major social role obligations, recurrent use in hazardous situations such as driving an automobile, recurrent legal problems, or continued use despite interpersonal problems resulting from use (APA 1994, 182–83). The DIS makes diagnoses of alcohol abuse when people have at least one symptom that indicates inappropriate alcohol use (e.g., drinking a fifth or more of liquor in a day, binge drinking, blackouts) and one symptom that might show impaired functioning because of alcohol use (e.g., family objections, physical fights, trouble driving) (Helzer, Burnam, and McEvoy 1991).

None of these criteria, however, refer to whether or not problematic use stems from an internal dysfunction. Instead, some of the criteria that indicate inappropriate alcohol use may be met on occasions where drinking is normative such as at weddings, parties, and other celebrations. Likewise, the criteria that are meant to show impaired functioning need not have anything to do with internal dysfunctions. Most refer to the reactions of either social network members or agents of social control. Hence, a changed social climate with more intolerance for drunken driving can create not only more arrests for driving while intoxicated, but also more mentally ill people. Likewise, having a spouse object to drinking becomes an indicator of a mental disorder rather than an indication of low social tolerance for alcohol consumption. "If you drink or smoke marijuana," Wakefield notes, "your spouse can now give you a mental disorder simply by arguing with you about it, and can cure you by becoming more tolerant!" (Wakefield 1997a, 640).

The logic of equating symptoms, without regard to their context, with diagnoses of alcohol abuse leads to an immense proliferation of alleged mental disorders. The ECA and NCS, for example, find lifetime rates of substance abuse or dependence among 24 percent and 28 percent, respectively, of the population. Even those who conduct these studies note that "The huge lifetime prevalence (for alcohol disorders) for men strains credibility" (Helzer, Burnam, and McEvoy 1991, 84). In fact, many people who fulfill these symptomatic criteria may be in environments that condone heavy substance use. Hence, rates of presumed alcohol disorders are exceptionally high among college-age youth and in lower- and working-class communities (Widom, Ireland, and Glynn 1995; White and Hansell 1997). There may be nothing wrong with the internal mechanisms of people in these contexts, though; rather, it may be that they engage in behavior that is normative within their environments. In other cases, substance use and abuse may indicate expectable responses to stressful social conditions. For example, rates of alcohol and drug use and abuse soar after marital dissolutions and job layoffs (Horwitz 1984; Catalano et al. 1993; Dooley, Catalano, and Wilson 1994; Horwitz, White, and Howell-White 1996; Tausig and Fenwick 1999) The DSM definition of substance abuse, and the community surveys following from this definition, however, do not take into account the social circumstances of substance use and abuse; instead they assume that all symptoms of substance abuse indicate internal dysfunctions. Hence, they use invalid criteria to determine whether or not a particular set of symptoms indicates the presence of a mental disorder.

Although symptom-based logics produce inflated prevalence estimates for alcohol abuse, these estimates cannot be used in the same way as estimates of sexual dysfunctions, social phobias, or depressions to promote the products of pharmaceutical companies. The many millions of presumed alcohol abusers are not likely to seek voluntary help for their disorders; alcohol disorders are the least likely of any condition to be treated in the mental health system, in large part because heavy alcohol consumption is normative among many social groups (Shapiro et al. 1985). Therefore, pharmaceutical manufacturers do not find a large potential market for alcohol disorders, despite their reported high prevalence in the population. Likewise, mental health advocacy groups are ambivalent about the status of alcohol abuse as a mental disorder. The public has a far more negative view of alcoholics (and even more so of drug addicts) than of persons who suffer from disorders such as depression and social phobia (Link et al. 1999; Pescosolido et al. 1999; Swindle et al. 2000). Therefore, linking alcoholism to serious mental illness is not likely to reduce the stigma of mental illness.[12] The high prevalence rates of alcohol abuse and other forms of social devi-

ance generated by community studies do not have the same social currency as sexual dysfunctions, social phobias, or depression.

The use of a symptom-based logic can thus have very different consequences in survey research and in clinical treatment. In contrast to clinical practice, where both clients and therapists apply common-sense judgments to definitions of what symptoms indicate mental disorders, no discretion enters into definitions of mental disorders in community surveys. All symptoms are seen as *prima facie* indicators of mental disorders, without regard to the context or the cause of symptoms. Indeed, because computer programs generate diagnoses, there is no possibility of using lay or professional judgment in deriving diagnoses and resulting estimates of prevalence. Community studies have no way of distinguishing symptoms that indicate appropriate rule-following behaviors, normal responses to stressful life events, or social deviance from those that stem from internal dysfunctions.

Any community survey will inevitably include many people who are depressed and anxious because their spouses are having affairs, they are unable to pay their debts, their children have gotten into trouble, or numerous other distressing life situations. Others will recall getting very drunk at weddings, smoking marijuana at parties, or becoming very nervous before speaking in public. Whenever expectable symptoms that are ubiquitous consequences of stressful life circumstances outnumber symptoms that arise from internal dysfunctions, community surveys will contain large numbers of false positives where people who are not genuinely disordered are counted as if they are (Wakefield 1999b).

In contrast to the large number of false positives community surveys produce, the diagnostic criteria do encompass the symptoms of people who actually have internal dysfunctions. Therefore, there will be few false negatives—people who do have mental disorders will rarely be excluded from diagnostic criteria. The methods of community surveys insure that the number of false positives is far greater than the number of false negatives so that mental disorders will be substantially overcounted (Robins 1985; Wakefield 1999b).

Mental health researchers and others usually take seriously the prevalence rates reported by community studies, instead of questioning the criteria that produce such high rates of disorder. If mental disorders were limited to internal dysfunctions, rates would be far lower. To what extent do community surveys overestimate the prevalence of mental disorders? Ronald Kessler and his colleagues use the following criteria to define rates of serious and persistent mental illness from the data of the NCS and the Baltimore site of the ECA: (1) nonaffective psychosis or mania; (2) major depression or panic disorder with either hospitalization or use of major psychotropic medication; (3) planned or attempted suicide within the past twelve months; and (4) a DSM-III-R disorder accompanied by substantial vocational incapacity and/or serious interpersonal impairment (Kessler et al. 1996, 63). Population projections from these results show that 2.6 percent of the population suffers from a serious and persistent mental illness and 5.4 percent from a serious mental illness—far lower than the prevalence of about 30 percent of people in these studies who are diagnosed with any DSM-III-R disorder in a one-year period (Kessler, Abelson, and Zhao 1998, 19). The magnitude of these differences provides some indication of the extent to which community studies overestimate the prevalence of serious mental disorders.

Because community studies consider *all* symptoms, whether internal or not, expectable or not, deviant or not, as signs of disorder, they inevitably overestimate the prevalence of mental disorder in the community. Symptom-based diagnoses conflate symptoms that are normal and expectable responses to stressful situations or are deviant, but not disordered behaviors, with internal dysfunctions. The rates of various "mental disorders" these studies generate have little to do with the amount of internal dysfunction. A variety of groups, however, have an interest in perpetuating claims about the prevalence of untreated mental disorders.

> main point

> main point

CONCLUSION

Dynamic psychiatry created a continuum between mental disorder and normality, thus breaking down the boundaries between the normal and the pathological. Diagnostic psychiatry then transformed the indistinct pathologies of dynamic psychiatry into the widespread system of symptom-based categorical disorders. By the 1980s, categorical mental illnesses were firmly embedded not only among clinical researchers and therapists but also among epidemiologists and survey researchers. Indeed, it is now virtually impossible to obtain government funding for survey research efforts that do not use categorical diagnoses. Diagnoses are viewed as the only scientifically justifiable way of studying psychological disturbance. The use of symptom-based diagnostic logics that ignore the context or causes of symptoms inevitably led to the proliferation of presumed mental disorders in the community.

Classification schemes arise and persist because they serve various inter-

> Start at. be333 of essay

est groups. Many of the mental disorders uncovered in community surveys are reflections of stressful social conditions and relationships, not of psychological dysfunctions. Just as the many categorical illnesses of the DSM-III emerged primarily out professional self-interest, a number of groups benefit from the demonstration that these illnesses are pervasive in the community. In particular, pharmaceutical companies, mental health advocacy groups, academic researchers, the NIMH, and clinicians have a stake in creating and promoting the finding that at least fifty million people have mental disorders that warrant treatment by mental health professionals each year.

The widespread presence of mental disorder is now a well-established social fact and an essential component of diagnostic psychiatry. It presumably proves the extensive danger to public health posed by mental disorders. The pervasiveness of disorders justifies advocacy efforts, the expansion of mental health services, the promotion of pharmaceuticals, the legitimacy of diagnostic psychiatry, and, ultimately, the reality of these mental disorders itself. Indeed, people might come to interpret nervousness as social phobia, sadness as clinical depression, or persistent drinking as alcoholism. Such a revision would not indicate that people have a more accurate understanding of their problems. Instead, it would demonstrate the power of a social classification system to create the pervasive presence of those conditions it initially set out to measure.

Chapter Five

THE STRUCTURING OF MENTAL DISORDERS

At the end of the twentieth century, the profession of psychiatry adopted a symptom-based, categorical system of mental disorders both to become more medically minded and to maintain its scientific authority over a broad range of human behavior. This categorical system requires the discipline to think about and treat human problems as discrete diseases. Community studies further justify this classificatory system by showing that these conditions are pervasive in untreated populations. The precise definition, high reliability, and refined measurement of each of these categorical mental disorders seemingly proves their reality. Many of these disorders, however, are products of the classification system that defines them rather than natural entities.

The bedrock assumption of diagnostic psychiatry is that overt symptoms indicate discrete underlying mental diseases. Whenever enough symptoms are present to meet the criteria for a diagnosis, a particular mental disorder exists. An anxiety disorder, for example, involves intense fear and dread accompanied by physical sensations such as rapid heartbeat, shortness of breath, and perspiration (USDHHS 1999, 40). A mood disorder features sustained feelings of sadness or elation with disturbances in sleep or appetite, energy level, or concentration (USDHHS 1999, 42). Symptom-based, categorical diagnoses are used to classify a wide range of heterogeneous behaviors including psychoses, neuroses, expectable responses to stressors, and social deviance. The categories of diagnostic psychiatry, however, are not equally useful ways of looking at the variety of behaviors that they try to encompass.

A useful diagnostic system must fulfill certain goals. The self-defined goals of diagnostic psychiatry are the conventional scientific ones of ordering, explaining, predicting, and treating the phenomena so classified (Kendell 1989; Klerman 1977; Goodwin and Guze 1996; Skodol 2000). Ordering is the most basic goal because etiology, prognosis, and treatment all depend on adequate classification (Robins and Helzer 1986). Symptoms that cluster together in predictable ways are used to indicate the presence of a discrete underlying disease. Distinguishing one disease from another also helps differentiate the causes of the different conditions. In addition, knowing what phenomenon is under consideration ought to enable us predict the course of the severity, duration, and frequency of symptoms. Indeed, one prominent psychiatric text states that *"Diagnosis is prognosis"* (Goodwin and Guze 1996, xi). Finally, separating one constellation of symptoms from another ought to indicate different treatments for each. The major intellectual justification for the different entities of diagnostic psychiatry is that they are better able to distinguish distinct etiology, prognosis, and treatment than the vague mechanisms of dynamic psychiatry have been (Robins and Helzer 1986).

Diagnostic measures are thus appropriate when overt symptoms indicate underlying disease entities that have distinct causes, courses, and treatments. However, only a limited number of psychiatric disorders fit this model. The major thesis of this chapter is that the symptoms of most psychological dysfunctions are not direct indicators of discrete underlying disease entities. Instead, most nonpsychotic symptoms stem from general underlying vulnerabilities that may assume many different overt forms, depending on the cultural context in which they arise. Particular symptoms do not indicate underlying diseases; they are symbols that have a more arbitrary connection to what they represent (see Zerubavel 1997, 70). When symptoms are symbols, rather than indicators, the same underlying internal dysfunction finds expression in different overt symptoms and behaviors. Cultural processes, not the unfolding of natural disease, structure the overt manifestation of symptoms into recognizable entities. Because there is little direct correspondence between overt symptoms and specific underlying diseases in most psychiatric conditions, symptom-based diagnoses rarely fulfill the goals of adequate classification schemes. Most of the categorical disorders in diagnostic psychiatry do not predict the cause, course, or treatment of the conditions they are meant to classify.

THE LIMITS OF DIAGNOSTIC MODELS

The categorical measurement model of diagnostic psychiatry is useful for a limited number of conditions. It is most suitable for the conditions of schizophrenia and of the depressive and bipolar affective psychoses that

Kraepelin distinguished (Kraepelin 1896).[1] The symptoms of these disorders cluster into relatively discrete constellations that distinguish them from other conditions. Their essential forms are comparable across widely differing sociocultural contexts (Cancro 2000). In addition, the neurological, genetic, and family backgrounds associated with schizophrenia and the affective psychoses are distinct.[2] Further, as Kraepelin emphasized, when these disorders are not treated their natural courses are very different. Therefore, specific diagnoses are associated with distinct prognoses. Finally, specific diagnoses also help indicate different treatments for these disorders. "For example," Klerman notes, "psychotic patients respond well to neuroleptics; patients with depression respond well to tricyclics and to MAO inhibitors; patients with mania respond well to lithium" (Klerman 1989, 31; see also Cancro 2000). Hence, differential etiology, prognosis, and treatment ideally follow from the ordering of the symptoms of the psychoses into disease entities. Diagnostic psychiatry uses the relatively good fit of categorical models with the psychoses to justify their use with all the conditions found in the DSM (see Robins and Guze 1970; Frances et al. 1991; Pincus et al. 1992). The usefulness of categorical models for psychotic disorders, however, is rarely replicated with other conditions.

At minimum, diagnostic models must be able to distinguish one psychiatric condition from others. The success of all the other justifications for diagnoses—differential prognosis, etiology, and treatment—depends on whether a category identifies a distinct condition. However, the most common forms of nonpsychotic disorders—depression, anxiety, phobias, obsession and compulsion, panic disorders, somatization, and so forth—are very difficult to distinguish from one another (Tyrer 1985). The authors of one leading text of diagnostic psychiatry state: "In our view there are only about a dozen diagnostic entities in adult psychiatry that have been sufficiently studied to be useful" (Goodwin and Guze 1996, vii). Even most of these entities turn out to be highly intertwined: their defining symptoms occur across diagnostic categories and are commonly found in many different types of mental disorders. For example, the same text notes: "Depressions that are indistinguishable symptomatically from primary affective disorder occur commonly in obsessive-compulsive disorder, phobic disorders, panic disorder, somatization disorder, alcohol and drug dependence, and antisocial personality" (Goodwin and Guze 1996, 12).

The two most common types of psychiatric symptoms, depression and anxiety, generally occur together.[3] Most depressed patients have concurrent symptoms of anxiety and many anxious patients are also depressed. In some he co-occurrence of depression and anxiety reaches 90 percent as, Prusoff, and Weissman 1988). Community studies indicate sociation between mood disorder and anxiety disorder is stronger ... the association between two different anxiety disorders (Kessler, Abelson, and Zhao 1998, 15). Furthermore, 80 percent of people with social phobias in community samples also receive a diagnosis of another psychiatric condition (Merikangas and Angst 1995). Clinical studies usually report extremely high rates of depression among people with phobias and high rates of phobia among depressed people (Merikangas and Angst 1995). Likewise, 40 to 50 percent of people with panic disorders and agoraphobia are also depressed (Klerman 1988a; Merikangas, Wicki, and Angst 1994). Panic disorder, which is a type of anxiety disorder, is more closely associated with depressive disorders than with other anxiety disorders (Robins and Helzer 1986; Breier, Charney, and Heninger 1985). More than 80 percent of persons with posttraumatic stress disorder in community studies also receive another psychiatric diagnosis (Breslau et al. 1991). Symptoms of general anxiety are typical in most psychiatric disorders (Breier, Charney, and Heninger 1985). For example, anxious people typically have phobic symptoms and people with phobias are nearly always anxious (Goodwin and Guze 1996, 88). Somatic symptoms are also present in affective, anxiety, and somatization disorders (Goodwin and Guze 1996).

In light of these findings it is not surprising that instruments designed to measure depression are in fact as good in measuring anxiety as in measuring depression (Fechner-Bates, Coyne, and Schwenk 1994). "Indeed," Merikangas and Angst note, "both clinical and epidemiological studies have revealed that the overlap with the specific subtypes of anxiety and between anxiety disorders and depression is far more common than the pure expression of these conditions" (Merikangas and Angst 1995, 297). One may question the point of particular diagnoses when the symptoms of the major disorders are so thoroughly intertwined.

If symptoms overlap to such an extent, how are distinct diagnoses constructed? Diagnostic psychiatry attempts to deal with the inherent crossover of symptoms between different conditions through the category of "comorbidity." People who are comorbid presumably have more than one distinct disease entity. In primary care settings, for example, more than half of people who receive a psychiatric diagnosis have more than one diagnosis; about a third have three or more diagnoses (Spitzer et al. 1994). In the major community study of comorbidity nearly half of respondents with one diagnosis also had another (Kessler et al. 1994).

These findings, however, raise the issue of whether comorbidity indicates the common occurrence of distinct disorders. A better explanation for the co-presence of depressive, anxious, and psychophysiological symptoms in so many disorders might be that symptoms are nonspecific indicators of a common, broad, underlying vulnerability, rather than indications of more than one distinct disease. People who have a single underlying generalized vulnerability to disorder will naturally display a variety of common depressive, anxious, and psychophysiological symptoms (Eaves, Eysenck, and Martin 1989). The particular symptoms that become manifest might not be products of distinct underlying disease processes; instead their occurrence might be influenced by a variety of contextual factors. Diagnostic systems based on assumptions of discrete disorders, however, will count such people as having multiple discrete conditions. As Merikangas and colleagues state:

> The magnitude of comorbidity . . . is in part an artifact of the syndromal approach to diagnostic classification. Accruing evidence from the application of the recent definitions of the subtypes of the affective and anxiety disorders confirms that only a small proportion of individuals exhibit pure forms of these conditions cross sectionally, and even fewer across the life course. (Merikangas et al. 1996, 64)

If arbitrarily defined illness patterns stem from the same underlying condition, they would be inherently "comorbid." Comorbidity may be a product of a classification system that separates a single general syndrome into artificially constructed distinct diseases (Frances et al. 1990). Diagnostic psychiatry's system of ordering faces serious difficulties in distinguishing discrete disease entities.

The second purpose of classificatory systems is to specify distinct etiological factors. Yet many nonpsychotic disorders have common, not distinct, risk factors. Causal factors appear to create general vulnerabilities to psychiatric symptoms, not specific vulnerabilities to depressive, anxiety, and other common disorders (Kendler et al. 1986a). Risk factors, including family histories of any psychiatric disorder, the experience of early trauma, troubled life situations at the time the disorder appears, weak or absent social support systems, and gender predict all kinds of nonpsychotic disorders.[4] In contrast to the common general risk factors for all sorts of disorders, there are virtually no specific etiological causes for any particular nonpsychotic disorder (e.g., Coie et al. 1993; Tucker 1998).

Studies that link family histories to various conditions illustrate the difficulty in maintaining a categorical system of discrete diagnoses. Although family history studies of schizophrenia generally show some specificity in diagnoses, they are the exception rather than the rule (Coryell and Zimmerman 1988). In most cases, people who develop any particular disorder are also likely to have family members with some sort of psychiatric disorder, but their relatives' disorder is often of a different type (von Knorring et al. 1983; Black et al. 1992; Baldessarini 2000). Depressed people are as likely to have family histories of anxiety disorders as of depression and family members of anxious people are as likely to be depressed as to be anxious (Merikangas, Risch, and Weissman 1988). Likewise, those with obsessive-compulsive disorders are not more likely than others to have obsessive-compulsive family members but do have higher family incidence of depressive and other disorders (McKeon and Murray 1987; Black et al. 1992). When diagnostic psychiatrists investigate family histories they often must abandon categorical entities and treat the disorder under study as if it indicates a common vulnerability rather than a specific condition (Merikangas, Prusoff, and Weissman 1988; Mullan and Murray 1989; Smoller and Tsuang 1998). Family studies typically show that a common tendency to develop many possible disorders, not a particular disorder, runs through generations.

Diagnostic psychiatry also fails to distinguish entities with distinct prognoses. Instead, over time there is a large crossover of diagnoses (Tyrer 1985; Stavrakaki and Vargo 1986). People who have been diagnosed with a psychiatric condition are much more likely to be diagnosed with a psychiatric condition in the future, but not necessarily the same one they have, and not necessarily another type that can be predicted from the first type. People who have one diagnosis at one time will be nearly as likely to develop a different diagnosis as to develop the same diagnosis later. Indeed, only a minority of patients retain the same diagnosis over time (Tyrer 1985). People with anxiety disorders become depressed, those with phobias become obsessive-compulsive, or those who are depressed become somaticizers (Kendell 1974; Tyrer 1985). If "diagnosis is prognosis" diagnostic psychiatry generally does not achieve its central purpose (Goodwin and Guze 1996, xi). The idea that nonpsychotic patients have a generalized vulnerability that manifests itself in different, changeable conditions fits the prognosis of the most common conditions better than the notion of discrete diagnoses.

Most diagnoses thus do not distinguish particular conditions, do not differentiate causes, must be abandoned in family studies, and are not very helpful for prognosis. Yet perhaps the most important argument against the categorical entities of diagnostic psychiatry is the failure of diagnoses to indicate distinct treatments for different disorders. The major reason for a categorical diagnostic system is that calling symptom clusters one thing rather than another helps distinguish effective responses to them. This distinction justifies diagnosing specific psychotic conditions, which do respond differently to different treatments (Healy 1997; Klerman 1989).

The medication-specific responses of psychotic conditions, however, are not typical; they do not reflect the manner in which other disorders react to medication. Indeed, the greatest accomplishment of modern psychiatry— the development of efficacious psychotropic medications—provides a strong argument *against* the categories of diagnostic psychiatry for most nonpsychotic conditions. Psychotropic medications for these conditions are not illness-specific but work across different conditions. The most common current medications, the selective serotonin reuptake inhibitors (SSRIs), alter general systems in the brain rather than particular constellations of symptoms (Baldessarini 2000). They are prescribed nonspecifically for depression, anxiety, panic, obsessions, eating disorders, substance abuse and dependence, and generalized distress, among many other conditions (Kramer 1993; Healy 1997). Indeed, they can sometimes generate equal improvement in people who have no disorder at all, compared to those with a diagnosable disorder (Knutson et al. 1998). For most conditions, the classification schemes of diagnostic psychiatry are irrelevant for their most critical purpose—to indicate specific treatments.

The nonspecific actions of the most common medications indicate that categorical diagnoses are probably not valuable tools even for many of the small number of conditions the Washington University group delineated in the Feighner criteria. There seem to be very few distinct, categorical mental diseases aside from the three major disorders that Kraepelin distinguished one hundred years ago: schizophrenia, bipolar disorder, and endogenous depression. Most valid forms of mental illness manifest themselves through broad, changeable, and continuous symptoms, not discrete disease entities.

Aside from the major psychotic disorders, the subject matter of psychiatry does not lend itself to discrete diagnoses. A better explanation for the high crossover of symptoms across diagnostic categories, the interchangeability of diagnoses over time, and the common etiology and treatment of nonpsychotic conditions is that some people have a *general vulnerability* to psychological dysfunctions. With the exception of the psychotic disorders, biological, psychological, or social stresses make people vulnerable to psychological disorders in general, not to particular kinds of disorders. Most of

the many discrete conditions of diagnostic psychiatry might be better regarded as manifestations of a single general syndrome (Hinkle and Wolff
1958; Kramer 1993; Merikangas, Risch, and Weissman 1994; Persons 1986;
Tyrer 1985; Zubin 1977). From a genetic point of view, particular disorders
may be phenotypical variants of the same underlying genes (Wilson 1997;
see also Kendler et al. 1986b).

If people are not prone to develop specific psychiatric disorders, what
determines the particular symptoms they will display? The constellations
of symptoms people develop may stem in large part not from underlying
disease processes but from sociocultural factors that structure general vulnerabilities to disorder into socially appropriate symptomatic displays. A
variety of biological, psychological, and social factors may produce a vulnerability to disorder in general, while the particular disorder that emerges
may reflect sociocultural influences.

THE STRUCTURING OF MENTAL SYMPTOMS

Diagnostic psychiatry assumes that a particular cluster of symptoms indicates a particular disease entity. As reflected in the top part of the figure on
page 115, there is a determinate relationship between the underlying disease
and the resulting cluster of symptoms so that each disease has a distinct set
of indicators that will be invariant across cultures. Psychiatric symptoms
are thought to be analogous to most physical symptoms where, for example,
persistent wheezing, coughing up blood, or a pock may indicate, respectively, asthma, tuberculosis, or smallpox. The relationship between a symptom such as rectal bleeding and a disease such as colon cancer is not an
arbitrary product of cultural convention but a part of the natural world
(Zerubavel 1997, 70). Because there is a direct connection between symptoms and the diseases they represent, the manifestation of symptoms does
not depend on particular cultural contexts; a disease will have the same
symptomatic indicators whether it arises in New York, Nairobi, or Naga-
saki (Wing 1978). However, the model borrowed from medicine where
symptoms indicate specific underlying diseases poorly fits most mental disorders.

Structuring refers to the ways sociocultural factors shape generalized distress into particular outcomes (Cullen 1983). In a very general sense, biological factors may underlie the response of all animal species to stressors.
Experiences of acute trauma or chronic stress effect changes in chemical
and physiological aspects of the central nervous system including altered
metabolic functioning, heightened fear and anxiety, and disturbances in

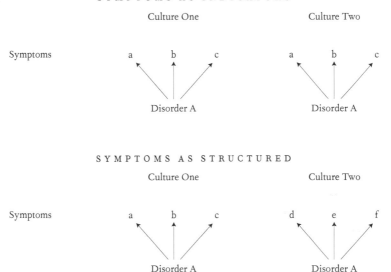

SYMPTOMS AS INDICATORS

Culture One   Culture Two

Symptoms   a   b   c   a   b   c

Disorder A   Disorder A

SYMPTOMS AS STRUCTURED

Culture One   Culture Two

Symptoms   a   b   c   d   e   f

Disorder A   Disorder A

sleep and appetite (Price and Sloman 1987; Cannon 1929; Selye 1956). The human mind, however, must interpret and give meaning to nonspecific psychic and physical disturbances in mood, cognition, feelings, and bodily functions (Kleinman 1988). Although general stress reactions may be rooted in biology, the symbolic systems of culture channel the highly generalized manifestations of stress into culturally specific and culturally recognized entities. As Edward Shorter says: "We must somehow draw upon the cultural symptom pool for models of illness to help us amplify and make sense of our own dim physical perceptions. Otherwise the mind cannot understand what the body is saying" (Shorter 1992, 320).

Whenever painful signs arise people will consider what sort of phenomenon they represent, why they have occurred, the impact they might have on social relationships, and what should be done about them. The answers to these questions are usually not idiosyncratic but are found in social vocabularies that tell people how they ought to interpret their symptoms. The generalized reactions to stress that people suffer may change little over centuries and across societies but the specific ways people ascribe meaning to these states, attribute causes to them, organize them into distinct illness presentations, and seek various sorts of help do alter dramatically.[5]

The bottom part of the figure shows a structuring perspective of mental disorders. In this view symptoms are not direct indicators of an underlying disease. Rather, the same vulnerability to mental disorders can become manifest in different symptomatic indicators from culture to culture. For example, symptoms of depression in the contemporary United States might include despondency, hopelessness, and low self-esteem. In contrast, depression in China might emerge in the form of headaches, lower back pain, and physical fatigue (Kleinman 1986). What factors influence how underlying vulnerabilities become expressed through particular symptomatic manifestations? Three major structuring factors are broad cultural systems of interpretation, identity categories, and professional and media templates of disorder.

The structuring perspective, in contrast to both dynamic and diagnostic psychiatry, emphasizes how cultural forces, not the unconscious or underlying disease entities, are associated with the overt symptoms of mental disorders. People channel distress through interpretive modes that are neither idiosyncratic nor biological but, in large part, collective sociocultural products. Cultures provide publicly available and shared meanings that facilitate certain kinds of symptom interpretations while discouraging others. They structure how people perceive and interpret their symptoms by presenting people with legitimate scripts of illnesses or with alternatives to illness scripts that shape what sensations are attended to or ignored, remembered or forgotten, responded to or neglected.[6]

If the structuring perspective is correct, many of the disorders in the DSM, no less than those in exotic (to us) societies, are culture-bound. Naming a disorder provides a coherent frame that organizes experiences in ways that a specific culture recognizes. The application of a particular illness category, whether posttraumatic stress disorder, panic disorder, social phobia, or depression, shapes diffuse symptoms into structured and meaningful entities. This labeling transforms an incoherent group of physical and psychological symptoms into a culturally recognized entity that provides a socially shared explanation for an otherwise nonspecific condition. To this extent, the form of particular symptom constellations results from the cultural context in which they arise, not from an underlying disease process. Cultural structuring transforms universal processes of distress into different disorders that carry meaning within particular cultural communities (Shorter 1994; Fabrega 1992; Young 1995; Littlewood 1990; Guarnaccia and Rogler 1999; Lopez and Guarnaccia 2000).

In the broadest sense, symptom profiles are structured to fit the illness norms of particular cultures. Within each culture, however, people will embrace symptoms that seem appropriate for their own set of social characteristics. Mental disorders are structured within identity categories that allow people to make sense of their symptoms and life experiences (Brown et al. 1996). The same broad underlying tendency to disorder can take very different forms not only in different sociocultural settings but also within the same culture among men and women, blacks and whites, old and young people, or immigrants and natives among many other possibilities. Because of this, patterns of mental disorder should reflect the major factors that shape personal identities including gender, social status, generation, and ethnicity.[7]

Diagnostic norms of the medical and mental health professions and the interpretations of professional knowledge disseminated in the media also influence the structuring of mental disorders in modern societies (Shorter 1994). Disorders conform to symptom presentations that the medical and mental health communities validate and reward. People who suffer from generalized psychological vulnerabilities or exposure to traumatic stressors are highly suggestible and eager to receive validation of their symptoms (Frank and Frank 1991). Their dependence on professionals can lead them to produce the kinds of symptoms their therapists expect them to have (Scheff 1966; Ofshe and Watters 1994). These symptoms are not unchanging products of diseases; they vary as professional fashions in diagnosis change.

The media are also a major purveyor of the illness templates people use to structure symptom presentations. In the contemporary world, the media often work in tandem with medical authorities and pharmaceutical companies to promote the latest fads and fashions in psychiatric diagnosis. Clients often use the knowledge they obtain from the media and from their informal social networks to preselect those professionals they know will be sympathetic to their self-diagnoses (Abbott 1988; Brown et al. 1996). Professionals and sufferers participate in a common culture of illness display disseminated through the mass media.

The expressions of many nonpsychotic disorders conform to illness styles that reflect cultural, identity, and professional norms of a particular period. Symptom presentations come to be congruent with major styles of culturally recognized illness presentations, to fit the major identity categories of sufferers, and to conform to appropriate displays of illness among medical and mental health professionals and in the mass media. Manifest symptoms of mental disorders vary widely from time to time and place to place according to culturally specific disease definitions and diagnoses. To the extent that these factors, rather than underlying diseases, mold symptoms, the assumptions of diagnostic psychiatry are undermined. A Kraepelian model may fit psychotic disorders where a distinct, biologically rooted disease obtains content from particular cultures.[8] For most psychological disorders, however, discrete diagnostic models are not valuable systems of classification. Symptoms do not indicate specific underlying diseases, so stripping away the cultural overlay would not reveal a natural disease entity (Kleinman 1987). Instead, a generalized vulnerability to many possible symptoms underlies most psychiatric disorders.

[margin note: Main point repeated]

EXAMPLES OF STRUCTURED DISORDERS

[margin note: use it]

[margin note: main point]
[margin note: It fails to do that!]
[margin note: yet they still don't look at culturally specific mental disorders?]

The disorders institutionalized in the DSM are meant to represent universal disease entities rather than culture-bound symptom constellations that arose in Western societies at the end of the twentieth century. Indeed, the DSM places disorders that are presumably culturally specific in an appendix of "culture-bound" disorders that do not conform to Western diagnostic presentations. Diagnostic psychiatry recognizes the presence of "culture-bound" disorders only in *other* cultures (see Rogler 1996). If the structuring perspective is correct, however, many psychiatric disorders are culture-bound in the sense that their symptom constellations are culturally structured rather than manifestations of underlying natural disease processes. The symbolic systems of culture shape universal experiences of suffering into particular idioms of distress appropriate to specific times and places (Shorter 1994).

[margin note: mention this]
[margin note: main point]
[margin note: why? Ex:]

Hysteria Different historical periods structure general symptoms of distress in different ways. The most prominent historical example of a structured disorder is hysteria in late nineteenth-century Europe. Hysteria featured a variety of physical symptoms such as paralysis, fainting, and pain in the absence of an organic cause. It is a particularly good example of the cultural structuring of mental symptoms because it was not a marginal category of disorder in psychiatric thought and practice. Rather, hysteria was a central psychological disorder at the time dynamic psychiatry was founded and was Freud's major interest in the early part of his career (Gay 1988). It was, in the words of a major textbook of psychoanalysis, the "classical subject matter of psychoanalysis" (Fenichel 1995 [1945], 230).

Although the term "hysteria" is of ancient origin, the sorts of symptoms attached to the term varied widely over the course of Western history (Micale 1995). In the nineteenth century, the most prominent symptoms of hysterical illnesses were paralysis of limbs, eyelids, and vocal cords. The stereotypical hysteric of the time was a young woman with disheveled hair, contorted limbs, rolling eyes, and a rigid and writhing body. This uncontrollable motor activity was often accompanied by fainting spells. Perhaps the most famous hysteric, Dora K., suffered from aphonia (periodic loss of voice), chronic attacks of coughing, and dyspnoea (shortness of breath), none of which had a known physical cause (Freud 1963 [1905]).

Sufferers select symptoms from a pool that constitutes legitimate illness in their particular era; their symptoms do not unfold naturally from an invariant disease process (Shorter 1992, 1994). The symptoms of hysteria were collective and widely known in the culture of the time. The new medium of photography provided images of disheveled sufferers with contorted and rigid limbs, wide eyes, and writhing bodies that became templates for this illness (Micale 1995, 149). Doctors also created models of hysteria that taught patients how to display appropriate symptoms. In particular, a leading physician of the time, Jean-Martin Charcot, was celebrated for his public demonstrations of hysterical patients before rapt audiences (Micale 1995, 97). Physicians rewarded patients who displayed these normative symptoms with attention, sympathy, and treatment. Patients then internalized the behaviors the media and physicians inculcated.

Hysterical symptoms were particularly suitable for persons with certain identity traits. Hysterics were overwhelmingly young and female. Edward Shorter notes that most men at the time would no more display symptoms of hysteria than they would wear a dress (Shorter 1992, 221). Instead, men shaped their symptoms into neurasthenia, a grab bag of low-grade psychological symptoms such as dyspepsia, headaches, insomnia, neuralgia, fatigue, and general nervousness that were better suited to the male role than hysteria (Shorter 1992; Caplan 1998).

The prevalence of hysteria in the latter part of the nineteenth century was rapidly followed by its almost complete disappearance over a very short period of time. By the early part of the twentieth century, hysteria had virtually disappeared from the psychiatric landscape of Western cultures. The symptoms typical of hysteria in the late nineteenth century simply no longer existed (Smith-Rosenberg 1972). How could such a prominent illness become extinct so rapidly?

Hysteria disappeared because of the culturally constituted nature of its symptoms.[9] Hysterics in the late nineteenth century who displayed paralysis of bodily organs were speaking a language that was readily understood in the dominant medical theories of the time (Shorter 1992). The dominant reflex theory of disease was compatible with the paralysis and motor symptoms of nineteenth-century hysterics. This theory viewed people as automatons who responded to motor reflexes and so provided validation to hysterical symptoms such as paralysis. The culture of appropriate symptom displays, however, changed rapidly around the turn of the nineteenth century. By the end of the century a model that emphasized the central nervous system and symptoms of pain and fatigue as the basis for disorder had replaced the theory of symptoms as expressions of motor reflexes (Shorter 1992). Once notions of valid illnesses among professionals changed and were disseminated to the lay public, hysterical symptoms went out of fashion.

The new medical frame formed different channels that shaped the legitimate ways to express distress. In particular, the emergence of psychoanalysis led to a new psychological idiom of distress. Cultured women and men who previously had no psychological vocabulary in which to frame their distress could now use the new language of psychoanalysis. The narratives of analysis provided an especially good fit for the life experiences of higher-status females in cosmopolitan urban centers. For such patients, this new psychological literacy meant that expressing distress through production of the physical symptoms of hysteria was no longer necessary, desirable, or normative.

The psychological framework of psychoanalysis led to a new illness vocabulary. At the same time, hysteria lost medical legitimacy after the death of its most charismatic healer, John-Martin Charcot (Micale 1995; Goldstein 1987). His death was quickly followed by the almost complete disappearance of hysteria. The rise and fall of hysteria provides a powerful example of how symptoms that arise through suggestion from a very powerful and charismatic physician can be mistaken for genuine disease entities. Once doctors stopped believing in the particular constellation of hysterical symptoms, patients quit displaying them (Shorter 1992, 196).

Hysteria illustrates how structuring produces distinct mental illnesses. An underlying generalized psychological disturbance becomes manifest through particular symptoms such as fainting or paralyzed limbs that reflect collective cultural notions and the fashions of what the medical profession considers to be appropriate illness displays. These symptom presentations were suitable for certain social groups, particularly young females, in a particular time and place. The symptoms of hysteria were symbols that reflected collective cultural norms; they were not indicators of an underlying disease. Just as sociocultural processes provided a template for hysterical symptoms in the late nineteenth century, they may structure generalized sensations of pain, fatigue, or distress into conditions such as chronic fatigue syndrome, Lyme disease, or fibromyalgia in the contemporary United States (Showalter 1997; Aronowitz 1998; Groopman 2000). One issue the transient nature of hysteria raises is how many current forms of mental disorder represent culturally produced symbolic entities rather than direct indicators of underlying diseases.

Multiple Personality and Recovered Memory Disorders Numerous conditions in the modern world illustrate the structured nature of mental disorders. Multiple personality disorder, recovered memory syndrome, alien abduction, and ritual Satanic abuse, among others, all provide highly structured narratives that shape general vulnerabilities into specific symptom constellations that subcultures of fellow sufferers and some portions of the mental health professions recognize and reward (Showalter 1997).

Multiple personality disorder (MPD) and the associated condition of recovered memory syndrome (RMS) provide particularly striking examples of the structured nature of psychiatric symptoms (Bass and Davis 1988; Fredrickson 1992; Herman 1992; Terr 1994). MPD (renamed dissociative identity disorder in the DSM-IV) involves the presence of more than one, and often many, distinct selves who are not aware of the existence of the other selves. Patients switch back and forth between their various selves seemingly with no knowledge of their alternating personalities. The disorder is nearly always associated with childhood sexual abuse, memories of which were absent until recovered during therapy sessions, often under the influence of hypnosis (Terr 1994).

Although a popular movie in the 1950s, *Three Faces of Eve,* portrayed a woman with three distinct personalities, as late as 1979 only 200 cases of multiple personality disorder had been recorded in the psychiatric literature (Hacking 1995, 8; Ofshe and Watters 1994, 205; McHugh 1992). Even these few early cases were quite different from later instances of MPD, because they featured two or three distinct personalities, instead of the many distinct alters that came to be typical (Hacking 1995, 21). A majority of cases in the 1970s were patients of only two therapists: Cornelia Wilbur, the author of the best-selling novel *Sybil,* and Ralph Allison (Schreiber 1973). Multiple personality disorder gained prominence in the 1980s and by 1990 more than 20,000 cases had appeared in the United States (Ross, Joshi, and Currie 1990; McHugh 1992). One expert estimates that 40,000 cases emerged between 1985 and 1995. The most fervent proponents of the diagnosis claimed that one percent of the U.S. population, or more than two million people, fit the criteria for MPD (Ofshe and Watters 1994, 206).

The publication of *Sybil* in 1973 was the immediate precursor of the MPD epidemic. The discovery of alters in Sybil through hypnosis by her therapist, Cornelia Wilbur, was prototypical of future cases of MPD (Borch-Jacobsen 1997). In contrast to earlier cases of MPD, Sybil had sixteen alternate personalities. As the popularity of *Sybil* grew, more young women surfaced with numerous alters that showed marked similarities to this founding narrative of the disorder. Sybil's background of child abuse also set the stage for future narratives where recovered memories of sexual abuse led to the discovery of a large number of alters.[10]

The narratives of multiple personality disorder and recovered memory syndrome became allied with broader cultural themes that resonated with people who had particular social characteristics. Women, in particular, could relate their personal problems to narratives that focused on early childhood abuse by males. These narratives fit a general model of patriarchal dominance over women that gained prominence in the culture at the time. Men, in contrast, could rarely shape their distressful experiences into the sorts of narratives these diagnoses entailed. Correspondingly, about 90 percent of multiples and recovered memory victims were females (Hacking 1995; Showalter 1997).

Professionals devoted to their study, treatment, and, many would argue, their creation also reinforced the narratives associated with MPD and RMS (Crews 1995; see also Prager 1998). The International Society for the Study of Multiple Personality and Dissociation was founded in 1984. Specialized treatment units developed in respected hospitals, the most famous at Rush-Presbyterian-St. Luke's Medical Center in Chicago. Recalling the demonstrations of Charcot at the Salpêtière, well-known clinicians attached to the movement appeared on television with their star patients who demonstrated their personality alternations before live audiences (Acocella 1998).

The disorder gained prominence in the media and was spread via television talk shows, hundreds of news and magazine stories, popular books, support groups, newsletters, and the Internet (Ofshe and Watters 1994). Accounts of MPD and RMS were featured on the Phil Donahue, Larry King, Oprah Winfrey, and Sally Jessie Raphael shows (Acocella 1998). Prominent celebrities including Roseanne Barr spoke of the multiple personalities they had developed as a result of early experiences with abuse, and best-selling novels such as Jane Smiley's *Thousand Acres* capitalized on the prominence of the recovered memory theme. Despite the fact that multiples and those with recovered memory syndrome generally displayed the most stereotypical features of helpless women, many feminists also strongly advocated their cause as illustrative of victims of patriarchal abuse (Ofshe and Watters 1994; Hacking 1995). Charismatic advocates such as the Harvard psychiatrist Judith Herman and the feminist Gloria Steinem widely promoted MPD and RMS.

Sufferers of the disorder identified with a social movement that included charismatic medical leaders, ritual texts, and strongly held ideological beliefs. Specific subcultures, involving both professionals and sufferers, supported and reinforced these narratives. Support groups, chat rooms, and sympathetic mental health professionals reinforced these messages. A network of therapists arose to provide both sympathy and care and to present coherent narratives of suffering that offered new identities to people who usually had led highly disturbed and disorganized lives (see especially Bass and Davis 1988; Herman 1992).

This movement created and reinforced appropriate illness displays. People who believed they suffered from this disorder molded their symptoms to conform to the dominant stereotypes of the illness. Although MPD never achieved complete respectability as a legitimate disorder among mainstream mental health professionals, the great heterogeneity of contemporary medical and mental health practice insured that sufferers could seek out and find sympathetic professionals who would diagnose and, if necessary, create the illness. Indeed, the best predictor of MPD is having a therapist who believes in the diagnoses (see Hacking 1995). Disturbed and unhappy people take these stereotypical narratives and use them to reorder their own conceptions of their pasts. MPD is a nearly pure case of an iatrogenic disorder "promoted by suggestion and maintained by clinical attention, social consequences, and group loyalties" (McHugh 1992).

When doctors stopped believing in hysterical symptoms, patients at the end of the nineteenth century stopped presenting these symptoms (Shorter 1992, 140–41). In the near future, as the culturally shaped and iatrogenic nature of symptoms of multiple personality disorder and recovered memory syndrome become apparent, they too should become as uncommon as classical symptoms of hysteria. One reason for the declining fortunes of MPD and RMS can be seen in the ever more spectacular presentation of symptoms. Often, sufferers discovered memories of ritualistic Satanic abuse during their childhoods involving thousands of persons, although not one case ever received any corroboration (Hacking 1995, 117). Successful lawsuits

[handwritten margin note: ⟶ evidence that supports a statement, Theory, finding]

against recovered memory therapists and well-publicized demonstrations of the unsubstantiated nature of many accusations of abuse also contributed to the decline of MPD and RMS. The MPD diagnosis of the patient whose case provided the founding narrative of the movement, *Sybil*, was unmasked as fraudulent.[11] The establishment of a countermovement that gained credibility in the media, the Recovered Memory Foundation, also changed the flow of cultural forces away from MPD and RMS (Crews 1995). When professionals stop believing in the legitimacy of these presentations, most patients will stop displaying them. As the social forces that created and sustained the narratives of these conditions disappear, the illnesses will disappear as well. The vulnerabilities that underlie the disorders, however, will remain and become structured into whatever symptoms are suitable for new identity narratives and new fashions of mental health professionals and the media.

Eating Disorders The eating disorders of anorexia and bulimia are other important examples of contemporary structured disorders. Unlike multiple personality disorders, which are relatively marginal to mainstream mental health practice, eating disorders are core diseases in the modern psychiatric canon.[12] Highly respected clinicians and researchers study them, units in prestigious psychiatric facilities are devoted to their treatment, established journals publish many articles about them, and professional organizations are devoted to their study and treatment (e.g., Walsh and Devlin 1998). They are prominent in mainstream culture as well. Programs on eating disorders are now standard parts of educational curricula. Celebrities such as the late Princess Diana have spoken publicly of their problems with these disorders and rumors that many other stars have them are staples of tabloid gossip. Few persons in the contemporary United States, and virtually no adolescent and young adult females, would be unfamiliar with them.

Although scattered cases of eating disorders have been known for hundreds of years, self-induced starvation was historically rare and limited to isolated cases. As recently as 1978, Hilda Bruch, the initial popularizer of anorexia, could call anorexia a "new disease" (Bruch 1978, vii). By 1985, however, "it was nearly impossible to find a young middle-class woman who did *not* know about anorexia nervosa" (Brumberg 1988, 1–2). The current cultural prominence of eating disorders emerged very rapidly and is of recent origin.

Anorexia features sufferers who do not maintain minimal body weights, who have intense and persistent fears of gaining weight, and who obsess over issues of body image (APA 1994, 544–55). Bulimia features recurrent episodes of binge eating followed by compensatory behaviors such as vomiting, laxative use, or intense exercise (APA 1994, 549–50). Compulsive thoughts and obsessive behaviors that center on weight control such as ritualistic eating patterns, excessive and constant exercise, and perfectionist patterns of behavior are central components of the disorders (Brumberg 1988, 28–29). At the extreme, preoccupations with food become obsessive and uncontrollable.

Anorexia and bulimia illustrate how underlying psychological and/or biological vulnerabilities become structured into highly specific illness profiles. In other times and places obsessive-compulsive and/or depressive tendencies would be channeled into different forms.[13] Throughout most of human history people could not take adequate food supplies for granted; the intentional failure to eat (except when it occurs as a well-recognized religious script) would have no credibility (Shorter 1992). The emphasis on thinness as an attribute of female beauty that motivates eating disorders can only structure obsessions and compulsions in modern Western societies where the negative consequences of excessive food consumption are an issue. While eating disorders are currently overwhelmingly Western and, in particular, North American disorders, as the values promoting thin female bodies spread throughout the world the incidence of eating disorders in these societies will likely increase as well.[14]

The cultural symptoms of anorexia resonate only with people in particular social locations. More than 90 percent are female and most also are young, white, and from middle- to upper-middle-class families (Brumberg 1988, 12). Young women, in particular, find a highly specific illness profile in eating disorders into which they can shape their symptoms (Pipher 1994). Over the course of the twentieth century weight standards and, especially, media images of desirable body shapes for women have become ever thinner. Dieting to conform to cultural imperatives is a well-known and widely practiced cultural form that Western women can easily relate to (Brumberg 1988, 231). In addition, a cult of exercise, new to women, emerged in the 1970s that emphasized physical fitness and athleticism. "Compulsive exercising and chronic dieting," Brumberg notes, "have been joined as twin obsessions" (Brumberg 1988, 255). The intense importance of a slim body image for females shapes their psychopathology into culturally appropriate symptom displays.

The cultural script that leads young women to develop eating disorders is incongruent with the experiences of men, as well as with those of women whose cultural groups do not share the ideals of thinness. Desirable male body types have greater variation and do not emphasize extreme thinness. Young men may structure obsessive-compulsive predispositions into more socially acceptable male activities such as body-building or gambling (Hall 1999b; Olivardia, Pope, and Hudson 2000; Pope et al. 2000; see also Pollack 1999).

Media attention both accompanies and precipitates the spread of eating disorders. Celebrities publicly discuss their experiences with eating disorders and anorexia and bulimia become themes in popular books, movies, and television dramas. One account of this disorder indicates that patients in eating disorder units listen obsessively to the music of Karen Carpenter, a popular musician who died from the effects of the disorder (Garrett 1996). Increased cultural attention leads to the development of advocacy groups, support groups, and "a veritable army of health professionals involved in the treatment of eating disorders" (Brumberg 1988, 20). Schools widely disseminate profiles of the signs of the disorder. Journals, conferences, and research careers come to focus on eating problems. Specialized outpatient practices and inpatient units develop to treat them.

The structured nature of eating disorders does not mean that their sufferers do not have internal dysfunctions nor that their symptoms are not real. Rather, it shows how cultures shape generalized vulnerabilities into specific symptom profiles that then become categorical disorders because of cultural, rather than disease, processes. The manifest symptoms of eating disorders, not the underlying vulnerability the symptoms reflect, are cultural constructions. Eating disorders are valid mental disorders, but they are disorders whose symptoms emanate from cultural rather than natural processes.

Depression Structuring affects not only specific symptom presentations but also generalized styles of distress. Depression is the most ubiquitous form of human suffering. Conditions marked by a slowing of metabolic functioning, apathy, and sleep and appetite disturbances are universal. However, cultural forces structure the particular forms these experiences take into a variety of internal psychological symptoms, sensory symptoms, pain, and symptoms of the central nervous system (Shorter 1992).

In modern Western societies where individuals are viewed as independent, self-contained, and autonomous entities, depression is typically experienced through inward forms of psychological suffering (Kleinman 1988; Markus and Kitayama 1991; Littlewood 1990). Western notions of the self, now spreading more broadly throughout the world, emphasize individuality, personal experience, and separation from others. Depressive disorders in Western cultures thus emphasize emotions, personal mood, and subjective experiences of hopelessness, withdrawal, anxiety, and grief (Kirmayer 1984; Fabrega 1989; Karp 1996). The introspective quality of depression that typically features a "phenomenological sinking downwards of the self" focusing on internal psychological states is no less culture-bound than the physiological or social expressions of depression more typical in non-Western groups (Littlewood 1990, 312).

rather than look at the greater picture

In most cultures, symptoms of depression are somatic and emphasize physiological sensations such as exhaustion, weakness, and fatigue (Vega and Rumbaut 1991; Takeuchi, Chun, and Shen 1996; Kleinman 1986). Psychological symptoms of depression such as guilt are less prevalent in non-Western than in Western societies (Jablenski et al. 1981). Indeed, from a comparative perspective, the psychological components of depression that prevail in the modern West are unusual. Depressed Chinese, for example, often emphasize the pain they feel in their lower back (Kleinman 1986). Iranians display distress through "fright illness" and "heart distress" that take meaning from the context of Iranian culture (Good 1977). In many non-Western cultures, illness is understood not as a condition located within the individual but as a disturbance in the affected person's relationships with others (Littlewood 1990; Guarnaccia 1993). Depressed Vietnamese, for example, report shame and dishonor rather than the guilt feelings that characterize depressed Westerners (Kinzie 1982, cited in Kleinman 1987, 451).

Immigrants provide a good quasi-experimental group to test the extent to which culture structures symptoms of depression. If symptoms are cultural products, they should change over time and over generations after people change their sociocultural environments. Symptoms of recent immigrants from non-Western countries should resemble the styles of expression in their countries of origin. Over time, immigrants to Western societies—and especially their children—should adopt illness styles that are appropriate in their new homeland.

David Takeuchi's study of symptom presentation among Asian immigrants to the United States indicates the cultural structuring of symptoms (Takeuchi, Chun, and Shen 1996). It shows how immigrants respond to stressors with symptom displays that are appropriate to their cultural circumstances. In their early years in the United States, Chinese immigrants responded to stressors by developing physiological symptoms. As their length of stay in the United States increased, their stress responses came more and more to emphasize psychological symptoms of depression and anxiety. Likewise, less acculturated Hispanics also express distress through modes more congruent with traditional Latin culture; their growing acculturation leads to expressions similar to more assimilated ethnic groups (Guarnaccia, Angel, and Worobey 1989; Rogler, Cortes, and Malgady 1991).[15]

Research on the symptoms of immigrants thus indicates that psychological reactions to stressors are not universal, but can change according to the cultural context. Physiological styles of symptom expression are not "primitive" and psychological styles are not "sophisticated"; both are cultural idioms that can be appropriate in their particular contexts. Acculturation is related not only to the acquisition of language, fashion, eating tastes, and cultural styles, but also to appropriate expressions of psychological symptomatology.

Gender provides another example of how symptoms of distress can reflect identity categories. Gender attributes structure psychological vulnerabilities in culturally appropriate ways. A consistent finding of contemporary epidemiological research is that, with the exception of relatively comparable sex ratios in the psychoses, most mental disorders are strongly linked to gender. The most common forms of depressive, anxiety, and psychosomatic disorders are about twice as prevalent among women as among men (Weissman and Klerman 1985). Conversely, men report about twice as many acting-out and substance abuse disorders as women (Robins et al. 1984; Kessler et al. 1994). The most common disorder among men, alcoholism, is more than five times more prevalent among men than among women (Helzer, Burnam, and McEvoy 1991). If the structuring perspective is correct, the different sex ratios reflect the fact that certain kinds of illness presentations are more congruent with female or with male categories of identity.

In particular, women tend to focus on and ruminate about the emotional component of painful and threatening experiences, both their own and those of other people (Nolen-Hoeksema 1987). Because women are encouraged to develop feelings of attachment and obligation toward others, they are more likely to channel distress into forms that harm only themselves while refraining from antisocial behaviors (Schwartz 1991). The internalization of feelings that leads to the expression of distress through introspective, anxious, and withdrawn symptoms constitutes a more culturally permissible alternative for women than responses that involve other-directed aggression (Radloff 1975; Rosenfield 1980). The result is that women consistently report about twice as many internalized disorders (such as depression) as men.

In contrast to female styles marked by internalized feelings, men are more likely to channel stress responses through behavioral expressions such as alcohol use, risky behaviors, or violence (Richman 1988; Umberson, Williams, and Anderson 2000). Cultural norms structure distress into these forms because they need not involve introspection and rumination about emotions and so are more compatible with masculine roles. Simultaneously, cultural norms restrain men from expressing symptoms through "feminine" displays of emotion, so men are less likely than women to react to stressors through depression, anxiety, or physical symptoms. Instead, men may channel distress into substance abuse rather than depression; obsessive-compulsive tendencies into gambling rather than anorexia; or anxiety into violence rather than panic disorders (Horwitz and Davies 1994). Gender is such a deeply rooted identity category that it structures underlying vulnerabilities to disorder into gender-appropriate expressions.

> really good point

Structured illnesses emerge in particular times and places from the toolkits of culturally sanctioned symptoms that social groups provide (Shorter 1992, chap. 16). Although broad and universal physiological and psychological sensations often underlie symptoms, people shape these sensations into overt presentations that are congruent with appropriate identity categories and with prevailing fashions in medicine and the media. They receive cultural rewards including diagnoses of legitimate illnesses and support from groups of fellow sufferers and from medical authorities. The collective emergence of these problems, and their absence in other contexts, indicates their socially constructed character.

> argument in nutshell

CONCLUSION

Diagnostic psychiatry uses symptoms to indicate underlying diseases. Only a few discrete diagnoses, however, reflect diagnostic models in which overt symptoms function as indicators and are useful for ordering, predicting, explaining, and treating underlying diseases. While this model is suitable for schizophrenia and the affective psychoses, few other conditions—even those that are valid mental disorders—fit the categories diagnostic psychiatry constructs.

Many nonpsychotic conditions do reflect psychological disorders. Discrete diagnostic entities, however, poorly characterize their nature. The symptom profiles of structured illnesses are often collectively constructed products of particular cultures. The manifestations of common depressive, anxious, and psychophysiological symptoms change over time and across cultures, their symptoms blur indistinguishably into different diagnostic entities, they have no distinct past history in families or distinct prognosis among individuals, and all respond to similar types of treatments. There is little justification for treating them as discrete and natural disease entities.

The overt symptoms of other disorders are almost purely cultural products. Personality and eating disorders, for example, have no universal referents but are found only in Western cultures (Lewis-Fernandez and Kleinman 1995a). George Vaillant observes that borderline and narcissistic personality disorders are usually found only in American cities that have opera houses and psychoanalytic institutes. They are rarely seen in Iowa City or in Mobile and are never present in Tangiers or Bucharest (Vaillant 1984, 543). Although these disorders appear to be characteristics of individuals, they emerge collectively in particular times and places.

The structuring view diverges from the way that researchers who study these disorders, professionals who treat them, and people who suffer from them think of these problems. Each group believes that symptom clusters are direct manifestations of underlying disease entities rather than cultural productions. Instead, a structuring view emphasizes the power of cultural norms and social movements to shape symptoms.[16] It also diverges from social control theories, which assert that professionals impose these illness labels on unwilling sufferers (Kutchins and Kirk 1997). In contrast, because culturally shared discourses shape symptom narratives, people develop symptoms that are congruent with dominant cultural models, identity categories, and medical fashions. Sufferers often actively seek particular diagnoses from mental health professionals or embrace their diagnoses after they receive them.

The structuring view also diverges from debunkers who assume that the cultural shaping of symptoms indicates that the underlying disorders themselves must be cultural products (Showalter 1997). While symptom constellations can be products of particular cultures, it is necessary to distinguish these structured symptom clusters from the vulnerability that produces them. The role of culture in shaping the symptoms of mental disorders does not mean that the underlying disorder is artificial. Because the particular symptom constellations sufferers display are products of particular sociocultural forces does not make their suffering any less real. For them, symptoms are not imaginary or simulated (Shorter 1992).

Mental health professionals often take the symptoms of structured disorders at face value. They create treatment centers and techniques that cater to particular disorders. Psychiatric researchers devote their careers to studying particular disorders and journals arise to publish their results. Support groups emerge to reinforce the reality of the symptoms. Disorders become aspects of social movements that invest in, create, and reinforce the reality of the conditions. Sociologists, however, need to study how these disorders come to be socially defined as real, rather than accept the taken-for-granted notion that diagnostic measures reflect natural entities. There is a valid realm of mental disorders that includes many of these structured disorders, but culture, not nature, influences how most disorders become real both to the people who suffer from them and to those who treat them.

Good point [handwritten marginalia]

Chapter Six

THE BIOLOGICAL FOUNDATIONS
OF DIAGNOSTIC PSYCHIATRY

Diagnostically based psychiatric classification does not dictate any particular cause of mental disorders. It defines discrete disorders by their overt symptoms, not by the causes of these symptoms. In fact, however, biological explanations have attained unquestioned primacy in diagnostic psychiatry. Many prominent works uncompromisingly advocate the biological foundations of mental disorders and such articles dominate the major psychiatric journals.[1] Even those works that emphasize the heterogeneity of possible biological, psychological, and social causes of mental disorders give pride of place to the biological roots of these disorders.[2] The dominant psychiatric model now views mental disorders as diseases of the brain that are the products of malfunctioning neurochemical systems.

The current emphasis on the biological foundations of mental disorders is a *re*-emergence of earlier biological thinking in psychiatry. Before dynamic psychiatry arose at the turn of the nineteenth century, psychiatrists insisted that insanity indicated a physical disease of the brain (Grob 1973; Scull, MacKenzie, and Herevey 1996; Shorter 1997). Over the course of the twentieth century, however, biological theories became associated with reactionary political thought and were stigmatized and discredited. Biological psychiatry was prominent only within asylums, which themselves were marginal in the psychiatric profession (Grob 1991a).

By the 1920s an extreme antihereditarian view dominated the sciences of human behavior (Degler 1991). The most prominent works, such as those of the anthropologists Margaret Mead and Ruth Benedict, placed special emphasis on how cultural patterns shaped thoroughly plastic human traits (Mead 1928, Benedict 1959 [1934]). They radically separated nurture from nature and posited that only the former had any significant impact on human behavior. Subsequently, the rise of eugenic thought in the Nazi movement and the resultant Holocaust destroyed the cultural viability of biological thinking about human behavior after the defeat of Germany in World War II.

During the period of dynamic psychiatry's dominance of psychiatric thought, especially in the 1950s and 1960s, broader cultural currents insured that biological views of human functioning could not be credible. The dominant cultural model only granted that biological functions established before birth set broad parameters for behavioral possibilities (Gerth and Mills 1953). Because cultures were so variable, human behavior showed little uniformity across time and space. All essential aspects of human functioning arose after birth; thus culture, not genetics, molded personality, language, thought, and behavior. The universal biological aspects of behavior were seen as insignificant compared to the great variability in behavior that existed across cultures. Therefore, until the 1970s, few psychiatrists showed any interest in the brain. Those who did had low status in the profession and were usually relegated to positions in state hospitals (Cancro 2000; Eisenberg 1995).

At the beginning of the twenty-first century the intellectual landscape is totally transformed. Genetics is widely recognized as one of the most exciting scientific disciplines and the deciphering of the human genome is hailed as one of the major achievements in the history of science.[3] Evolutionary psychology, which explains human traits as genetic adaptations to environmental conditions, is a major scientific model (Wright 1994; Dennett 1995; Wilson 1998). Likewise, cognitive science, which explores the universal qualities of the human mind, has gained a commanding intellectual presence (Pinker 1997). The models of genetics, evolutionary psychology, and cognitive science reverse the emphasis of the previous cultural model of behavior. They highlight nature, not nurture, and they search for the universal forms rather than the cultural variability of human behavior. The most popular works in these disciplines ridicule previous cultural explanations of human behavior and emphasize how the rigorous truths of biology have supplanted the ideological speculations of the social sciences (see especially Pinker 1997; Wilson 1998; Thornhill, Palmer, and Wilson 2000). Indeed, the study of brains and of genetics now dominates psychiatry (for examples see Andreasen 1984; Detre 1987; Guze 1989; Sabshin 1990; Baldessarini 2000).

The basic principle of the ascendant model underlying current psychiatric thinking is that all mental processes and social actions derive from biological processes in the brain (Kandel 1998, 1999). The summary of prominent biological psychiatrist Nancy Andreasen is typical:

> *The major psychiatric illnesses are diseases . . . caused principally by biological factors, and most of these factors reside in the brain. . . . As a scientific discipline, psychiatry seeks to identify the biological factors that cause mental illness.* This model assumes that each different type of illness has a different specific cause. (Andreasen 1984, 29–30; emphasis in original)

Another prominent review states: "It seems, that we are about to move into a period when genetics will define disease entities in psychiatry" (Mullan and Murray 1989). A third scholar expresses the common view that "there is consistent evidence that nearly all of the psychiatric disorders are familial, and that genetic factors account for a significant proportion of the variance in their etiology" (Merikangas 1995, 44).[4] These views dominate psychiatric curricula, research, and scholarship.

Biological and, in particular, genetic explanations of human behavior are prominent not just in scientific thought but also in the popular images of mental illness presented in the mass media. Science stories in television news and print media are more likely to cover new findings about the genetic roots of mental disorder than findings from other perspectives (Conrad 1997, 2000). Over a very short time, the biological study of human behavior has evolved from a marginal and discredited enterprise to the dominant model of mental illnesses in both academic psychiatry and popular culture.

At present, the basic reality of mental disorders is seen to lie in neurochemicals, receptors, and genes (Luhrmann 2000). This interpretation of the origins of psychiatric problems has become the primary way of looking at them, so much so that other sorts of findings are now often dismissed as unimportant, derivative, or reducible to the primary paradigm. Biological foundations are sought not only for the most serious disorders that gave rise to biological psychiatry in the nineteenth century, but also for the many nonpsychotic conditions catalogued in the DSM.

This chapter considers some of the problems encountered in viewing mental disorders as essentially biological phenomena. If, as this book assumes, current psychiatric classifications embody a very heterogeneous collection of conditions, then the search for biological and genetic foundations will be more likely to succeed for some disorders than for others. In particular, only symptoms that indicate specific underlying diseases can be linked to genetic causes in relatively straightforward ways. Therefore, these explanations have the most promise for psychotic conditions.

When cultural factors structure symptoms, however, the task of joining manifest symptoms to genetic foundations becomes highly problematic. In such cases, biological psychiatry must overcome the problem of how "to define the condition the heredity of which one is attempting to trace" (Smoller and Tsuang 1998, 1152). Biological explanations are even more problematic for expectable distress and for social deviance. There is nothing wrong with people who become depressed or anxious in response to environmental stressors or with those who drink, take illegal drugs, or act out because of cultural norms. Such people respond normally to social conditions; they do not have biological dysfunctions. Despite the problematic relationship of symptoms to underlying mental diseases, diagnostic psychiatry now seeks biological and genetic foundations for virtually all of the conditions it recognizes.

THE BIOLOGICAL VIEW OF MENTAL DISORDER

Biological explanations of mental disorder involve both a theory of human nature and a set of techniques that generate and explain empirical findings. The theory of human nature found in biological psychiatry is based on the assumption that the mind and mental functions are reducible to the operations of the brain (Kandel 1998; Kupfer 1999). Each individual inherits these brain functions, which have evolved over millions of years of human evolution, at conception. Understanding the brain, as opposed to the unconscious or conscious mind, the personality, the soul, or the culture, is the most critical tool for explaining why some people develop mental disorders.

A *reductionist* model is an essential aspect of biological thought.[5] The biological model reduces the operation of complex wholes to the properties of their individual parts. Parts are used to explain wholes; the functioning of parts is not explained by the functioning of the system in which they are elements. In the study of human societies, this means that the group is reduced to its individual members. These individuals, in turn, are defined by the operation of their genes and the neurochemicals in their brains. The principle that mental processes are brain processes "applies to behaviors by single individuals, to behaviors between individuals, and to social behavior in groups of individuals. Viewed in this way, all sociology must to some degree be sociobiology; social processes must, at some level, reflect biological functions" (Kandel 1998, 460). The logic of this model thus reduces mental disorders to disordered molecular or cellular structures in the brain.

Another assumption of the biological model is the *universalism* of its primary object of study, the human brain. Like other organs of the body, the basic nature of the brain does not differ across cultural settings. The essential structure and functioning of the brain transcends social contexts so that the same underlying neurochemical abnormalities will have similar implications wherever and whenever they occur. The biological model thus emphasizes intra- and inter-individual differences in mental disorders that stem from biological and genetic factors; it downplays in these disorders cultural differences that do not result from these factors.

The techniques of biological psychiatry derive from its assumptions about human nature. Science strives for universal laws, not generalizations that are restricted to particular contexts. Biological psychiatry isolates behavior from its contexts much as the natural sciences develop laws about the physical properties of the universe. For example, the laws of thermodynamics hold equally in Africa and Australia and, with appropriate controls, the particular contexts of natural laws can be ignored. Biological psychiatry discovers universal laws through the same methods that have been historically effective in uncovering the natural structure of the physical world because brains are seen as part of the natural rather than the social world. Issues of sampling and context are not prominent because biologically rooted phenomena are presumed to be similar regardless of where and when measurements occur. Therefore, research about the brain can proceed with little regard to social context.

A central task of the methods employed to uncover the biological foundations of mental disorders is to separate the impact of genetic factors from the influence of environmental forces. The genetic roots of mental disorders are present at conception, before people enter the social world. For geneticists, even prenatal influences in the womb are environmental, not genetic. Thus, the meaning of "environment" in biological psychiatry is quite distinct from its meaning in sociology, mainly encompassing factors such as birth injuries, viruses, diet, and infections, not culture and social structure.[6]

Biological studies of mental disorders must overcome the problem of how to unravel genetic from environmental influences when typically the two are highly intertwined. This is because parents transmit not only genes but also cultural practices, habits, knowledge, and many other forms of social behavior to their offspring. Either genetic or social reasons could explain why children acquire mental disorders from their parents. Because genetic and social influences are usually indistinguishable, biological psychiatry must seek unusual situations that can cleanly separate these influences from each other. The attempt to separate genetic from environmental impacts on human behavior is the driving force behind many studies in biological psychiatry.

THE BASIC METHODS OF BIOLOGICAL PSYCHIATRY
Biological psychiatrists have used three major methods to uncover the biological foundations of mental disorders. These are studies of adoption, of twins, and of genetic linkage. Each method has its strengths and limitations.

Adoption Studies Geneticists seek methods that can help disentangle genetic from environmental forces. When people grow up in the same environment with their natural parents or parent, it is difficult or impossible to separate genetic factors from environmental circumstances because parents transmit both. For much of the twentieth century, studies of adoption dominated the attempts to separate the causal importance of genes and environments (e.g., Heston 1966; Kety et al. 1975; Wender et al. 1974).

The logic of adoption studies stems from the fact that the parents who transmit genes to their children are not the same parents who raise these children. The most common type of adoption study begins with known qualities of a biological parent (in nearly all cases the mother) or parents and traces outcomes in their adopted-away children. In theory, biological parents of adopted children contribute all of the genetic variance but none of the environmental variance. Conversely, adoptive parents make no genetic contribution but provide all of the parental environmental influences. Adoption studies typically examine rates of disorder of children born of mentally ill mothers who are raised by nondisordered adoptive parents. The finding that adopted children of mentally ill biological mothers show higher rates of disorder than adopted children of non-ill biological mothers indicates genetic causes of disorder. Conversely, rates of disorder in adopted children that are more comparable to those among adoptive than among biological parents indicate stronger environmental than genetic influences.

Despite their elegant logic, adoption studies are not as powerful in practice as in theory (Cadoret 1991). One uncontrolled factor is that little is known about many biological fathers of adopted children. Often, the paternity of adopted children is unknown; if known, there is seldom any genetic information available. In addition, adoption has variable cultural meanings in different settings. Adoption is not a context-free variable; the meaning of being an adopted child differs across social contexts, regions, countries, and historical eras. Further, adopted children may sometimes be aware of their adopted status and sometimes not, so that the cultural meanings of adoption will influence the behavior of some adoptees but not others. Adoptive parents may or may not be aware of the pathologies of biological parents, including mental illnesses, and may or may not transmit this knowledge to their adopted children. This introduces the possibility that the qualities of biological parents are transmitted to their natural children through social rather than genetic transmission, confounding the influence of genetic with social factors. Similarities between biological parents and their adopted-away children can thus stem from social as well as from genetic transmission (Cadoret 1991).

Although far from perfect, the compelling logic of adoption studies offers great insight into the relative roles of genetic and environmental influences on mental disorders. These studies are no longer as prominent as in the past, in part because of the recognition that they cannot cleanly separate genetic from environmental influences (Cadoret 1991).

Twin Studies　The logic of twin studies inverts that of adoption studies. Adoption studies hold genetic factors constant and vary the environment. They compare how being reared in environments by people who do not share genetic traits influences subsequent behaviors. In contrast, twin studies hold environments constant and compare people with known different genetic endowments who are raised in the same environment (Gottesman and Shields 1976). In addition, while adoption studies compare the transmission of traits from parents to children, twin studies compare siblings of the same generation.

By far the most common type of twin study examines the correlation in a trait among monozygotic (MZ) twin pairs compared to the correlation in the same trait among dizygotic (DZ) twin pairs. These studies proceed from a simple logic that capitalizes on the fact that there are two kinds of twins. MZ twins stem from a single fertilized egg and so are genetically identical. DZ twins are the product of two separate eggs and, like regular siblings, share fifty percent of their genes. The logic of comparing DZ and MZ twin pairs is that while MZ twins are genetically twice as similar to each other as DZ twins, both types of twins presumably share the same familial environment. To the extent that genetic factors influence behavioral traits, MZ twins ought to have twice the rate of concordance in these traits as DZ twins.[7] In contrast, if the environment is the prominent influence, both types of twins should exhibit comparable occurrence of a trait.[8]

Like adoption studies, twin studies are in practice far from the ideal portrayed in the scientific literature. Some of the problems of twin studies stem from the lack of representativeness of twins compared to non-twins. Twins differ from others in the age of mother at birth, placental characteristics, and birth weight. Unlike singletons, twins compete in the womb for space and nutrition, so their prebirth experiences may be quite different (Rose 1991; Wright 1997, 90). Many twin studies also rely on volunteers and are of questionable generality. MZ twins are always overrepresented in these studies relative to DZ twins because of their greater identification with each other and because they have considerably more frequent contact with each other (Rose et al. 1988). Likewise, females typically account for 70 percent of respondents in twin studies although only 50 percent of twins are female (Stein, Jang, and Livesley 1999).

Another shortcoming of twin studies is their inability to determine the extent to which the excessive concordance in traits between MZ compared to DZ twins stems from social rather than genetic factors. For example, compared to DZ twins, MZ twins usually report more similar childhood environments and closer contacts with each other as adults (Kendler et al. 1993). Thus, the greater behavioral and personality similarity of MZ twins may be the consequence, rather than the cause, of social contact (Rose et al. 1988).

The greater physical similarity of MZ twins compared to DZ twins also complicates the separation of genetic and environmental factors. For example, physically attractive people can receive more cultural rewards than physically unattractive people because of social, not genetic, reasons (Buss 1994; Langlois et al. 1995). Because MZ twins resemble each other physically more than DZ twins, they have a greater chance of receiving similar social reactions that, in turn, can influence personality and behavioral traits. The statistical model that divides social from genetic variance in behavioral outcomes, however, attributes all of the greater commonality of MZ compared to DZ twin pairs to genetic rather than environmental influence (Miller 1998; Schwartz 1999). This overstates genetic contributions and understates environmental contributions. Social and genetic factors are always partly confounded in the greater similarity of MZ and DZ twins. Nevertheless, the findings of the relative concordance of mental disorders in MZ and DZ twins provide one way of partially seeing the extent to which mental disorders have a genetic foundation.

Linkage Studies   Recent developments in molecular genetics have set linkage studies on a par with twin and adoption studies as prominent methods in biological psychiatry. Linkage analysis relies on a different logic than adoption and twin studies. It does not attempt to separate genetic from environmental components in behavior. Instead, it analyzes probabilities of certain patterns appearing on the chromosomes of individuals who have known probabilities of genetic similarity. These probabilities are statistically compared to the probabilities of the genetic marker in the population (Weeks and Lange 1988; Lander and Schork 1994). The results of linkage analysis suggest whether or not a particular type of disorder is linked with a particular location on the chromosomes (Risch and Merikangas 1993).

Linkage analysis capitalizes on the fact that pairs of siblings will show more like traits and more unlike traits than a pair of unrelated individuals (Penrose 1934). All people have 22 pairs of non-sex chromosomes and one pair of sex chromosomes. During meiosis, the paired chromosomes split and only one chromosome in each pair is transmitted to a gamete. Two traits on different chromosomes will be inherited independently within the same family, but two traits on the same chromosome will tend to be transmitted together. This leads to the statistical basis for linkage analysis, called the lod (log odds) score, which refers to the probability of linkage between a DNA probe and a disease gene (Martin 1987). If the chances of two siblings sharing a trait far exceeds the frequency of the occurrence of the trait in the general population, the gene on which the trait is located can potentially be identified. Linkage studies are now a major research method in the search for the genetic foundations of mental disorder.

Although linkage studies provide a promising method for uncovering the possible genetic bases for some mental disorders, like adoption and twin studies they have some serious limitations. One problem is that linkage methods were developed for Mendelian disorders that result from a single abnormal gene. These methods have been successful in explaining conditions, such as Huntington's disease, in which a single gene produces the disease, the prevalence is low, the expression of the disease is clear, the disease is easily distinguished from other diseases, and environmental effects are generally inconsequential (Risch and Merikangas 1993; Kendler, Lyons and Tsuang 1991). In contrast to straightforward genetic diseases, the genetics of psychiatric disorders are very complicated. They probably stem from several genes, they have high prevalence, they may be expressed through many different symptoms, they overlap significantly with other disorders, and they are profoundly affected by environmental forces. In addition, the symptoms relatives display often differ from those of the focal individual, so linkage studies must use broad criteria of what counts as a disorder for affected relatives (Risch and Merikangas 1993). When this occurs, the Mendelian assumptions of linkage analysis no longer hold and an overlap with other disorders is virtually assured.[9]

In the absence of a Mendelian pattern of inheritance, sampling strategies become problematic. Detection of a linkage between a specific chromosomal defect and a specific disorder must rely on a probability estimate of how frequently that linkage ought to occur in the general population. The choice of the rate of the disorder in the population has a dramatic effect on estimates of heritability (Risch 1990, 1991). Conditions such as schizophrenia or bipolar disorders can sensibly be studied with these methods because they are spread fairly consistently throughout most populations. A chromosomal anomaly among relatives of schizophrenics, for example, can be probabilistically compared to a relatively constant statistical distribution in the population.

Although, in principle, it is sensible to try and link psychotic disorders to particular locations on chromosomes, in practice, linkage analysis has to date been the source of more embarrassment than accomplishment in biological psychiatry. The most prominent example is a linkage study of bipolar disorder among the Old Amish group in Pennsylvania. This group provides a good opportunity for genetic study because of their large families, clear paternity, and geographic concentration (Egeland and Hostetter 1983). In a widely heralded study, Egeland and her colleagues found "compelling evidence for tight linkage between two DNA sequences located on chromosome 11 and a locus conferring a strong predisposition to bipolar affective disorders" with a probability of more than 10,000 to 1 (Egeland et al. 1987, 784). They draw an apt lesson: "These findings have broad implications for research in human genetics and psychiatry." The lesson, however, is not the one they thought. Two years later a change in information from *two* members of the study sample who became ill after the initial study resulted in a finding of no genetic linkage (Kelsoe et al. 1989). That two people could drop odds from greater than 10,000 to 1 to nonsignificance indicates the great sensitivity of linkage studies to small changes in the prevalence of disorders in the population. Nevertheless, linkage studies have gained tremendous, although as yet unwarranted, currency as indicating the genetically based nature of mental illness.[9]

Linkage studies are even more problematic for nonpsychotic illnesses such as anxiety, depression, or alcohol abuse that are often expectable results of social circumstances, so that prevalence rates vary widely across populations (Lynn and Martin 1997, 371). This variation insures the arbitrariness of any population rate in comparisons with the relatives of people diagnosed with a particular illness. In addition, the same symptoms of these disorders that might sometimes stem from genetic defects also may often arise from environmental circumstances. This is a serious problem in linkage studies because the power to detect linkage is especially weak in disorders that have many false positives (Smoller and Tsuang 1998). In addition, as emphasized in chapter 5, the actual expressions of common symptoms of depression and anxiety are highly variable across cultures. It is therefore difficult or even impossible reliably to link particular symptoms with specific genetic markers (Smoller and Tsuang 1998). Although studies that claim to establish linkage of widespread neurotic traits to a particular gene have appeared and have been widely trumpeted in the media, the chances of successfully replicating them are very low (e.g., Lesch et al. 1996). It is no wonder that linkage attempts in psychiatry have typically resulted in dramatic discoveries, quickly followed by failure to replicate the initial heralded result.

FINDINGS REGARDING THE GENETIC FOUNDATIONS OF MENTAL DISORDERS

Findings from adoption, twin, and linkage studies are far from definitive. In general, however, they provide some evidence for genetic causes of some cases of schizophrenia and bipolar disorder and varying findings for the role of genes in causing nonpsychotic conditions.

Adoption and twin studies of psychotic disorders provide the best evidence for the genetic foundations of some mental disorders. Perhaps the best-known adoption study that traces mental disorder among adopted-away children of mentally ill mothers is Heston's study of fifty-eight children born to schizophrenic mothers in an Oregon mental hospital between 1915 and 1945 (Heston 1966). In each case, the child was removed from the mother within three days of birth and raised in a foster home. Heston compared the rate of schizophrenia that developed when this group reached adulthood with the rate of other children adopted in Oregon during this period, matched for sex and type and length of adoptive placement. Although adopted-away children of schizophrenic mothers had no contact with their biological mothers, 16.6 percent developed schizophrenia themselves, a rate comparable to the proportion of children who develop schizophrenia after growing up in the same home with their schizophrenic mothers. No members of the control group of adoptees developed schizophrenia.

This study strongly implicates genetic factors in the development of schizophrenia.

Most adoption studies are based on data from Scandinavian countries, which have unusually complete records of the life histories of adoptees, including information about natural and foster parents. These studies generally find higher rates of schizophrenia and schizophrenia-like disorders in the biological relatives than in the foster parents of adoptees (Kety et al. 1968, 1975; Rosenthal et al. 1971).[10] In addition, they show higher rates of these disorders in adopted-away children of schizophrenic parents than in control groups of adoptees without schizophrenic parents (Fischer 1971; Kringlen 1978).

As do adoption studies, twin studies show the strongest genetic contributions for schizophrenia and bipolar disorder. Older studies of concordance of schizophrenia showed MZ rates of up to 69 percent with DZ rates less than half as high. More recent studies, based on better samples and more precise diagnostic techniques, show lower rates of concordance that average about 46 percent for MZ twin pairs (Gottesman and Shields 1982; Reiss, Plomin, and Hetherington 1991). A large population-based study shows an even lower concordance of schizophrenia of 31 percent for MZ twins, although DZ twins show a concordance of only 6.5 percent (Kendler and Robinette 1983). In general, MZ twin pairs show about a threefold greater concordance for developing schizophrenia than do DZ twin pairs (Pardes et al. 1989). Studies of the transmission of bipolar disorder also consistently show much higher concordance rates between MZ than between DZ twins (Wender et al. 1986; Bertelson, Harvald, and Hauge 1977). The best studies indicate a heritability of about 60 percent for bipolar disorder (NIMH 1998). It is perhaps more of a surprise for biological psychiatrists that concordance rates for psychotic disorders between MZ twins are so low than that they exceed rates between DZ twins.

Another kind of study compares rates of schizophrenia among the *children* of MZ twins, where one twin has schizophrenia and the other twin does not. These studies, although few in number and based on very small numbers of cases, show equivalent rates of schizophrenia among the offspring of affected and unaffected twins (Fischer 1971; Gottesman and Bertelsen 1989). These findings indicate that genetic transmission, rather than possible deviant parenting by a schizophrenic parent, influences the development of schizophrenia in children.

Unlike adoption and twin studies, which provide good evidence for some genetic basis in many cases of schizophrenic and bipolar disorders, linkage studies have not yet been able to associate particular disorders with particular genes. Although linkage analysis shows much promise to identify more precisely the genes associated with those mental disorders that are genetically transmitted, to date virtually all attempts to replicate initial findings of linkage have failed.[11]

Thus far, convincing evidence for genetic causes has been limited to schizophrenia and bipolar disorder, serious psychotic disorders where it would not be surprising to find genetic influences. The genetic transmission of schizophrenic and bipolar disorders would be expectable because of the strong possibility that these are brain-based disorders. When studies expand beyond psychoses, however, the evidence for genetic influences is considerably more complex.

A number of adoption studies focus on depression. Some find, in support of the genetic hypothesis, that adopted-away children of depressed mothers have more depression than other adoptees (Cadoret 1978; Kety 1985). Others also find higher rates of affective disorders and suicide in the biological relatives of adopted children who have affective disorders (Wender et al. 1986). But, in contrast to studies of adoption and schizophrenia, studies of depression among adopted children often find more support for environmental than for genetic causes. For example, one study found that 48 of 443 adoptees had diagnoses of depression (Cadoret et al. 1985). No traits of their genetic parents were related to depression. Instead, characteristics of their foster parents including psychological problems, alcoholism, and early death predicted depression among adopted children. A Swedish study likewise found no correlation between rates of depression among biological parents and their adopted-away children; psychiatric treatment among adoptive fathers, however, was associated with psychiatric treatment among their foster children (von Knorring et al. 1983). As well, depression among the adopted-away children of depressed mothers was more associated with aspects of their foster families than with qualities of their biological mothers. Other research indicates that depression among adopted children is related to depression in both their biological and their foster relatives (Wender et al. 1986). Overall, studies of depression and adoption indicate a mixed picture of genetic influences, environmental influences, or both.

As do studies of adoption, twin studies report more ambiguous findings about the possible genetic basis of nonpsychotic mental disorders. Some studies show that concordance rates for endogenous depression reflect considerably higher genetic influence than for neurotic depression (McGuffin et al. 1994). A twin study of depression based on an untreated group of about a thousand female twin pairs indicates that many behaviors including depression, anxiety, suicide, and alcohol problems co-occur more frequently among MZ than among DZ twins. However, the differences in concordance for MZ and DZ twins, .48 and .42, is minimal. Further, in this study a history of depression in one twin is a better predictor of a history of depression in another twin than is whether twins are MZ or DZ (Kendler et al. 1995; see Brown 1996). This finding indicates the importance of environmental rather than genetic forces. Other twin studies of panic and anxiety disorders indicate that there are heritable components to these disorders, although environmental influences typically exceed genetic influences (Stein, Jang, and Livesley 1999; Kendler et al. 1989).

Several prominent studies also compare the implications of child-rearing by natural or adopted parents for the development of alcohol disorders in adoptees. Cloninger and colleagues find that adopted children with presumably high genetic risk of developing alcoholism who are raised in middle-class foster homes are not more likely than chance to become alcoholics themselves in later life (Cloninger, Gohman, and Sigvardsson 1981). However, a comparable group of adoptees raised in lower-class foster homes did have higher rates of alcoholism as adults. The environment in which these children were raised determined whether or not their presumed genetic propensity toward alcoholism would be expressed. In another well-known study, Goodwin compared natural-born daughters of Danish alcoholics who were raised by their natural parents with their adopted-away siblings growing up in homes without alcoholic parents (Goodwin et al. 1977). His findings showed that the daughters raised at home with an alcoholic parent had higher rates of alcoholism than their adopted-away siblings. In addition, adopted daughters with and without alcoholic natural parents had comparable rates of alcoholism. These findings support the influence of environmental factors on alcoholism.

However, Goodwin's studies of adoption and alcoholism in Denmark also showed that biological sons of alcoholic parents had equivalent rates of alcoholism whether their biological or their adoptive parents reared them (Goodwin et al. 1973). Rates of alcoholism in adulthood in both groups were higher than among adoptees without alcoholic natural parents. These findings support genetic rather than environmental transmission of alcoholism. Other studies of alcoholism among adoptees support genetic transmission (Cadoret 1978; Cadoret et al. 1985), find no evidence for genetic transmission (Roe and Burks 1945), or obtain mixed results (Cloninger,

Gohman, and Sigvardsson 1981). These results allow some commentators to conclude that genetic factors are more important than environmental factors in producing alcoholism (Merikangas 1990) and others to conclude the opposite (Searles 1988). As with adoption studies, twin studies of alcoholism sometimes show strong genetic effects, sometimes strong environmental effects, and sometimes mixed effects.[12]

Thus, while the evidence lends support for possible genetic foundations for some psychotic disorders, the findings from studies of other disorders are far more complex and open to a variety of interpretations. Some support a genetic explanation, others an environmental explanation; still others offer both explanations (Brown 1996). The claims of the advocates of genetically based psychiatry, however, go well beyond their relatively modest findings to date.

THEORETICAL LIMITS OF BIOLOGICAL PSYCHIATRY

Some general problems that transcend the limitations of particular studies and methods confront attempts to find the comparative impact of genetic and environmental determinants of mental disorders. These problems include the relationship between measured outcomes and underlying genes, the environmentally specific nature of genetic influence, the inadequate measurement of environmental variation, the failure to distinguish individual-level from group-level determinants of outcomes, and the difference between individual and population risks of disorder.

What Is Inherited? The cultural structuring of many mental disorders discussed in chapter 5 creates a central problem in studying how genes influence mental disorders. People inherit genes, not behaviors. Genes do not contain highly specific instructions about human development. What might be genetic are usually certain generalized traits and propensities. Except in rare cases, particular genes are not directly related to particular disease outcomes. The specific outcome that emerges depends on many nongenetic factors, especially the environments in which genes are expressed. This creates a major dilemma regarding how it is possible to connect reliably the outcomes that are measured with the underlying genes that presumably are related to them. Biological psychiatrists often tend to make unwarranted leaps from the existence of genetic differentials to specific human behaviors (Conrad 1997; Valenstein 1998).

The difference between the genotype, which refers to the genetic trait on the chromosome, and the phenotype, which refers to the ways the genotype is expressed, is especially important in the expression of mental disorders.[13] While the genotype is fixed in nature, the phenotypical expressions of the genotype are variable. Traits that stem from identical genes can have quite different manifestations because of different cultural and environmental conditions, among other things. Conversely, similar manifestations of symptoms may stem from different genetic sources.

It is very difficult to study genotypes because of their different phenotypical expressions. As noted in chapter 5, genetic vulnerabilities to most disorders can be molded to fit culturally normative forms of symptoms. Genes might produce general tendencies to disorders, which then obtain their specific forms from many nongenetic factors. The same gene, or combination of genes, could lead to different symptomatic presentations in different environments. For example, males with a genetic tendency toward compulsion may become gambling addicts in one environment, but be obsessive collectors of baseball cards in another context; comparable females might in some cases be fanatical house cleaners and in others develop anorexia nervosa. Although genes might affect how vulnerable people might be to developing a psychiatric disorder, the environment might determine the kind of symptoms they develop (Kendler et al. 1989). Conversely, identical symptoms might develop from genetic predispositions in some people but emerge from environmental precipitants with no genetic basis in others. Another possibility is that symptoms that are products of genetic dispositions might not be socially defined as mental illnesses at all and thus might not elicit any interest from behavioral geneticists. These alternatives greatly complicate the genetic study of mental disorders because of the difficulty in reliably knowing what outcome measures are connected with what genes.

The degree of difficulty of associating overt symptoms with underlying genes should vary according to the type of disorder in question. When symptoms serve as indicators of underlying diseases, as could be the case in schizophrenia or bipolar disorder, the difficulties of identifying possible genes are minimized, although far from eliminated. When, however, various cultural factors affect whether a trait is expressed and, if expressed, what form the trait will take, linking particular disorders with particular genes is highly problematic.

Most mental disorders have expressions that vary widely across cultures. For example, the expression of aggressiveness, hostility, and anger, which may underlie some psychiatric disorders, is extremely variable both between and within cultures (Cole 1996). Even when these traits have genetic bases, their actual manifestations take many forms. For example, the Samoans manifest anger through exaggerated forms of politeness (Freeman 1996, 300). The angrier people get, the more polite they become. Thus, the expression of aggression is so culturally malleable that it might become apparent through the opposite behavior of politeness.

Consider aggression and depression. Certain cultures, such as the Amish, have such powerful restrictions on aggression that overt aggressive behaviors almost never arise (Eaton and Weil 1955). A member of the Amish culture with a putative gene for anger might have a low probability of ever engaging in aggressive actions, but a high probability of developing an affective disorder instead. Even within the same culture, the structuring of disorders might lead women to express a putative genetic tendency to aggression as depression while men with the same genotype might become violent rather than depressed.

Anorexia nervosa illustrates the difficulties of associating specific genes with specific forms of human behavior. As chapter 5 indicated, this disorder is culturally specific: symptoms of anorexia were extremely rare before the 1970s and are typically found in Western postindustrial societies among young white females of relatively high social class backgrounds. Twin studies seemingly indicate that this disorder has a high degree of heritability because both MZ twins are considerably more likely than both DZ twins to develop anorexia (e.g., Walters and Kendler 1995; Wade et al. 2000). Such studies, however, cannot factor in such critical elements as the recent historical emergence of anorexia, its limitation to Western societies, and its predominance among young, wealthy, relatively well-off females.

Given the cultural specificity of the disorder, it is unlikely that genes for *anorexia* underlie the symptoms anorexics display. In other times and places, people with the putative gene or genes that produce anorexia in modern American culture could not have developed the same phenotypical expressions of these genes. The answer to the question "what is a gene for anorexia a gene for?" is unlikely to be "anorexia." Instead, a far more general trait such as compulsion or depression that can have extremely variable manifestations in different contexts is likely to underlie anorexic symptoms.

One-to-one correspondences between genes and behaviors are the exception rather than the rule. Even when they exist, genetic predispositions are often so plastic that cultural rather than genetic influences shape what specific behaviors emerge. Any genetic study faces a difficult challenge of associating particular symptoms with particular genes (Gilger 2000).

Genetic Inheritance Is Environment Specific   The extent to which cultural influences shape the manifestation of putative genetic influences points out a second important limitation of genetic studies. Biological psychiatry assumes that the same genes have similar effects in different environments. Yet, because of cultural structuring, the probability that any genetically based trait will appear changes when the environment changes. People with putative genetic tendencies to various common mental disorders will have varying chances of expressing these tendencies in different environments (Schwartz 1999).

The social context can have a profound influence not only on the form that expresses a possible genetic tendency to disorder, but also on whether a disorder arises at all. For example, the cultural restrictions against alcohol consumption among Mormons make the expression of alcoholism in them far less likely than among the members of the Navaho culture who do not face strict norms regulating drinking (O'Dea 1957; Mail 1989). A Mormon who inherits a gene for alcoholism will therefore have a very different probability of developing alcoholism than a Navaho who inherits the same gene. Likewise, a study that tried to separate the genetic from the environmental contribution to aggressive behavior would show different results among the Amish compared to groups that encourage aggressive expressions among males (Schwartz 1999). Only certain environments might activate genetic tendencies that would otherwise be dormant. Even when activated, these tendencies might be expressed in a wide variety of manifest forms.

Perhaps the best-known current example of a possible genetic underpinning for human behavior stems from Dean Hamer's research on "the gay gene" (Hamer and Copeland 1994). Hamer claims to have isolated a gene that may explain why some people become homosexual. Assume that further research does firmly support this claim.[14] Nevertheless, the environment would determine whether this putative gene is expressed. A person who inherits a "gay gene" in the United States at the beginning of the twenty-first century would be far more likely to engage in homosexual behavior than a person who inherited the same gene at the beginning of the twentieth century or one who lives in most other parts of the world now. Conversely, men who lacked a gene for homosexuality could very well engage in homosexual behavior in fifth-century B.C. Athens, in an English public school, or in a contemporary American prison. The expression of homosexuality is so plastic that even if there is a "gay gene," culture is a very powerful influence on whether or not this potential genetic tendency will be expressed or suppressed.

Minimizing Environmental Influences Whenever environments affect whether and how genetic traits are expressed, the only way to see how genetic and environmental factors influence behavior is to compare these influences systematically in *different* environments (Lieberson 1985; Schwartz 1999). Yet, the sampling design in biological studies of mental disorders and other human behaviors ensures that they cannot answer the questions they claim to resolve about the relative contributions of genes and environment. This is because a basic statistical principle is that only traits that vary in value can have explanatory power (Lieberson 1985). An independent variable that has no variance cannot explain the variance in a dependent variable. When there is little variance in the environment, the only factors that can explain observed variance are individual characteristics, including genetic characteristics (Schwartz 1999). For example, a study of the determinants of heavy drinking only among Irish people could not find that anything about Irish culture is related to that society's high rates of alcoholism without comparative data from other cultures (Bales 1962).

Yet, almost all genetic studies limit the amount of variation in the environment. The design of twin studies, for example, minimizes the variance from environment factors (Segalowitz 1999).[15] Twin studies typically infer all environmental effects from the different degree of concordance in traits between MZ and DZ twin pairs. Most twin studies stem from Scandinavian countries with socially homogeneous populations. This design inevitably increases the proportion of variance that genetic factors account for and limits the proportion that stems from environmental factors. The most prominent twin study in the United States stems from the Virginia Twin Registry (e.g., Kendler et al. 1992, 1993). All of these twins are from the same state, have been raised in the same time period, and are white and female. The sample design itself drastically reduces the amount of possible environmental variance. Because the nature of the sample ensures that the most critical social sources of variance are limited, the most likely sources of variation must stem from nonsocial influences.[16] Common statements, such as that genes and the environment each account for about half of the variation in most human behaviors, stem from studies whose design insures that environmental influences are minimized.[17]

In fact, social and cultural factors are often so uniform and so pervasive that they are rarely recognized.[18] Biological psychiatry has no model that can study the most important social influences, which can only be uncovered in studies that explicitly compare people in very different social contexts. Comparisons of genetic and environmental influences gain validity when more than one distinct environment is an explicit part of the study, rather than when social effects are inferred from differences in concordance rates between MZ and DZ twins. Until such studies are done, conclusions from genetic studies that allocate various percentages of behavioral traits to genetic and to environmental influences are premature.

Inter-Individual and Inter-Group Differences Genetic studies derive their estimates of how much of a trait stems from genetic or from environmental influences by comparing individuals in the same environment. This limits environmental variance and, therefore, inflates genetic influences. This method also ignores group-level factors that can be far more important determinants of mental disorders than individual factors. The focus on inter-individual differences in disorders within the same group leads genetic studies to neglect the consideration of the average levels of the trait in different groups (Brown 1996).

The explanation for why a given individual develops a mental disorder is distinct from why the rate of a disorder in one population is different from the rate of that disorder in another population. Genetic factors can only explain the variation that arises within a given population, while environmental factors are largely responsible for variation that occurs between groups over historical time and across social space. Even when a trait, such as height, is nearly 100 percent heritable within a population, environmental rather than genetic factors can account for wide variation in rates across environments. For example, differences in diet and disease patterns have caused Westerners to be far taller now than they were several generations ago (Silventoinen et al. 2000). Although the height of any particular individual is almost completely genetically determined, the environment can be responsible for a dramatic change in the average height in the population (Schwartz 1999). Whenever the prevalence rates of mental disorders vary substantially across populations, the focus on inter-individual differences will understate environmental influences on the causes of disorders.

Rates of depression illustrate this point. The eminent depression researcher George Brown finds large variations in rates of depression in different settings that range from 2.5 percent in a rural Basque area of Spain to 30 percent in a black urban area of Zimbabwe (Brown 1996). Environmental and cultural differences between the Basques and the Zimbabweans seem to best account for these more than tenfold differentials in depression rates. Assume that the concordance rates of both Basque and Zimbabwean MZ twin pairs for depression are .50 while those of DZ twin pairs in both countries are .25. As the genetic perspective assumes, MZ twin pairs in both countries would show twice the degree of similarity as DZ twin pairs on this trait. The standard formula used to determine heritability would indicate that genes account for 50 percent of the variance in depression and the environment for 50 percent.

Yet, Zimbabwean twins would be more than ten times as likely as Basque twins to become depressed, a figure that the concordance methods of twin studies do not reveal. In fact, the varying environmental influences in these two settings could be far more important than genetic influences in affecting who becomes depressed. It is the particular *method* that compares MZ to DZ twins in a single social context that makes it appear as if genetic influences are equivalent or more important than environmental influences. Until twin studies explicitly consider social variation across groups and not only inter-twin variation, they are incapable of comparing relative influences of genes and environments on any personality or social trait. Even when genetic factors shape which Basques and which Zimbabweans develop mental disorders in every individual case, social factors can determine the mean level of the disorder in these populations (Brown 1996).

When rate differences across settings, as in Brown's studies, are of more than a tenfold magnitude, environmental causes have far more importance than the formula separating determinants of individual traits into genetic and environmental factors grants them. Statements such as: "There has simply been nothing on the environmental side to counter the power of twin and adoption studies" reveal the myopia of the biological view (Wright 1997, 78). While genes might account for which particular individuals develop a disorder in a given setting, the environment can account for why rates of the disorder vary so greatly between settings.

Individual Risk and Population Risk   The focus on inter-individual differences compared to group differences is one factor that contributes to elevating genetic and diminishing social influences in biological psychiatry. Another factor is the failure to distinguish the individual risk of developing a disorder among genetically predisposed persons from the overall risk of developing a disorder within the same population. Genes could be important risk factors for individuals while still being a relatively minor influence on the proportion of people who develop a mental disorder in the population. Even when genetics are powerful risk factors for some individuals, the proportion of people who develop a disorder because of genetic factors might be very small. Schizophrenia, the mental disorder where genetic factors are best established, illustrates this principle.

The twin and adoption studies reviewed above suggest that genetic transmission has an important role in increasing the probability that people with family histories of schizophrenia will themselves become schizophrenic. Indeed, someone with a first-degree relative (parent or sibling) who is schizophrenic will be up to ten times more likely to become schizophrenic than someone who has no family history of schizophrenia (Gottesman and Shields 1976). Nevertheless, genetic factors might play a relatively small role in influencing which individuals in a population develop schizophrenia.

Most researchers posit that schizophrenia occurs in about one percent of people in most populations (e.g., Sartorius et al. 1986). Therefore, it would be the close relatives of this one percent of the population who are at considerably elevated risk of developing schizophrenia themselves. In such relatively rare disorders, however, the vast majority of the population with no family history of schizophrenia will account for far more cases than those who do have family histories of this disorder, because there are so many more of them.

A population-based study of 1.75 million children born of Danish women between 1935 and 1978 illustrates this point (Mortensen et al. 1999). Consistent with genetic research, people whose mothers, fathers, or siblings had schizophrenia were more than nine times more likely to develop schizophrenia than people with no affected parents or siblings. Yet because of the relatively low prevalence of schizophrenia in the population, only a small minority of people who develop schizophrenia have a family history of this disorder; about 5.5 percent of cases of schizophrenia in Denmark stem from people with affected parents or siblings. In contrast, about 35 percent of cases are attributable to birth in an urban rather than a rural area. Place of birth accounts for far more cases of schizophrenia in the population than family history.

These results suggest that even in disorders where genetic factors considerably elevate individual risk, environmental factors are more important determinants than genetic factors of who develops schizophrenia. This is true even for those mental disorders where there is a high probability of genetic transmission in persons with a family history of the disorder. These environmental forces could include factors such as increased exposure to viruses during pregnancy or other perinatal complications, living conditions in urban areas, or other stressors that are more common in urban than in rural areas. This fact is rarely emphasized, however, in scholarly or media accounts of the findings from biological psychiatry.

GENETICS AS IDEOLOGY

The most common social scientific criticisms of genetic studies of human behavior attack the reactionary political implications of such studies (Lewontin, Rose, and Kamin 1984; Gould 1981). Critics of studies that purport to demonstrate the genetic basis of intelligence, race, or gender, for example, emphasize how these studies uphold a repressive status quo and make current social hierarchies seem inevitable. These political critiques, however, poorly fit biologically based explanations of mental disorders.

The political implications of biological psychiatry are closer to liberal than to conservative values. The notion that mental illness is genetically transmitted so that the mentally ill are victims of a brain disease, rather than people who choose to behave in certain ways, is generally associated with a liberal viewpoint. In addition, the medication-based treatments that result from biological studies do not uphold the status quo, but they can create positive changes in the lives of people with serious psychiatric conditions. Indeed, medication may have done more to alleviate psychotic symptoms than any other therapeutic mode. The result is that biological views are now associated with optimism about the possibility of fundamentally changing the lives of persons with serious mental disorders (Kramer 1993). From the point of view of liberal politics, biological psychiatry is progressive, not reactionary. In contrast, conservative commentators usually promote the opposing view that individual choice, rather than biological compulsion, is responsible for mental symptoms (see especially Szasz 1961). Regardless of whether the intellectual principles of biological psychiatry are right or wrong, they do not repress the mentally ill.

The politics of biological psychiatry and mental illness, therefore, do not parallel the politics of biology and other human behaviors such as intelligence, race, or gender roles (see Kamin 1974; Gould 1981; Lewontin 1992; Tavris 1992). The major problem of studies that assert the biological foundations of mental disorders is their tendency to overstate the impact of genetic, as compared to social, influences on behavior. It is now commonplace to hear sweeping conclusions about the genetic foundations of mental disorders. One book on twin studies concludes: "The science of behavioral genetics, largely through twin studies, has made a persuasive case that much of our identity is stamped on us from conception; to that extent our lives seem to be pre-chosen—all we have to do is live out the script that is written in our genes" (Wright 1997, 143–44). "The results are clear and consistent," another popular book concludes; "overall, heredity accounts for roughly 50 percent of the variation in the samples of people that have been tested, environmental influences for the other 50 percent" (Miller 1998, 23). A prominent twin researcher confidently concludes: "about two-thirds of the reliable variance in measured personality traits is due to genetic influence" (Bouchard 1994, 1700). Even more extreme is Hamer's exultation: "Finding close to 100 percent inherited covariance between personality factors and psychiatric symptoms is truly astounding" (Hamer and Copeland 1998, 68).

Research on the genetic aspects of mental disorder is surely useful and important. This model, however, too often reduces mental disorders to purely organic conditions (see Karp 1996; Luhrmann 2000). The major problem with the ideology of biological psychiatry lies in its reluctance to explore its limitations, its overgeneralization of results, and its failure to develop adequate measures of the environment. Its most fervent promoters view their work not as a useful framework that is one way of approaching nature, but as the one true way to study reality (Wilson 1998; Pinker 1997; Bouchard et al. 1990). Yet, generalizing from comparisons of MZ and DZ twins to genetic and environmental contributions to human behavior will surely result in an impoverished understanding. This is especially true when research does not consider contextual effects, examine environmental variation, or even measure different social environments at all.

CONCLUSION

Genes have attained cultural status as icons (Nelkin and Lindee 1995). Both scientific and popular reports associate the presumed demonstration of a genetic influence with the primary causes of human behavior. They fail to note the nonspecific, limited, and contextual effects of genes. Instead, genes are assumed to be the basic level of reality to which other factors are reduced (Kandel 1998; Pinker 1997). The pendulum of the dominant scientific thought community has swung from a denial of biological effects on human behavior to a primary focus on the brain (Eisenberg 1995).

The current cultural power of biological models makes it seem as if biological influences are more fundamental than social influences. For example, Merikangas states: "The key to alcoholism is likely to reside in the effects of alcohol on the brain" (Merikangas 1990, 19). From a purely biological viewpoint, there is nothing objectionable about this statement. It would, however, be equally plausible to say that the key to alcoholism—and most other mental disorders—resides in cultural forces, because of the immense variation across social groups, societies, and historical time in rates of heavy drinking.

It is undoubtedly the case that knowledge about the structural and functional qualities of the brain has soared in the past decade (Schwartz 1999). Likewise, methods of assessing brain structure and function have grown far more advanced and precise. The discovery of neurotransmitters and receptors has created the potential for sophisticated manipulation of psychiatric symptoms. As yet, however, despite the rhetoric to the contrary, these advances have not led to significant advances in knowledge about the *causes* of mental disorders. It is quite possible that even in the near future the causes of some cases of some psychotic disorders will be linked to a set of particular chromosomes. If the argument of this work is correct, however, these advances will only occur for a very limited number of serious psychological dysfunctions, not for the broader range of disturbances that biological psychiatry now seeks to explain.

Thus far, in the study of mental disorders advances in neuroscience have mainly resulted in improved psychopharmacology. At this writing, the ascendant belief that "mental illnesses are brain diseases" is due far more to the cultural belief that only biologically based illnesses are "real" illnesses than to any empirical findings that the causes of mental disorder are brain-based. The view that real illnesses must have biological causes is, paradoxically, a cultural construction. Advocacy groups lobby for genetic and biological views of mental disorder because if a mental illness is regarded as an organic brain disorder then it is presumably less likely that the individual will be blamed and stigmatized for the condition (see especially Hirschfeld et al. 1997). It is no wonder that people often make prodigious efforts to show that their illnesses are really physical.[19]

Yet, even when genetic correlates of disorders are shown, particular biological treatments do not logically follow.[20] Indeed, social changes often hold more promise than biological changes in altering most diseases (Dubos 1959). For example, improved living conditions, diets, and patterns of behavior are more responsible for better contemporary physical health and longevity than particular medical treatments. Likewise, changing patterns of sexual partnering accounted for both soaring rates of AIDS during the 1980s and their more recent steep decline in the United States (Shilts

1987; Bayer 1989). There is no necessary association between biological causes and effective treatment and prevention of disorders.

It will not be surprising if there are biological foundations for many cases of the most serious psychological dysfunctions. However, the most radical proponents of genetic determinism proclaim: "For almost every behavioral trait so far investigated, from reaction time to religiosity an important fraction of the variation among people turns out to be associated with genetic variation. This fact need no longer be subject to debate" (Bouchard et al. 1990, 227). Such assertions are currently grounded far more in ideology than in evidence. The cost of the ascendancy of biological psychiatry has been to minimize arguably more powerful sources of individual distress: culture and social structure.

Chapter Seven

SOCIAL CAUSES OF DISTRESS

Diagnostic psychiatry minimizes the importance of social causes of mental disorder. This orientation naturally results from its emphasis on internal, genetic causes of disorder, which contradicts the social focus on external, environmental causes. For diagnostic psychiatry, social causes might precipitate disorders in vulnerable people but they are rarely the primary cause (e.g., Heston 1988; Guze 1989; Kandel 1998).

This emphasis on nonsocial causes of valid mental disorders is not necessarily misplaced. Biological and psychological causes plausibly explain many internal dysfunctions. Yet, a major unresolved (and usually unstated) problem for diagnostic psychiatry is that the vicissitudes of social life naturally produce much depression, anxiety, and grief. These products of stressful social environments often feature symptoms common to disorders such as major depression, dysthymia, or generalized anxiety disorder. Likewise, heavy drinking, drug use, and criminal behavior that are not products of internal dysfunctions are symptomatically no different from the mental disorders of alcohol abuse, drug dependence, or antisocial personality disorder. Symptoms alone can never distinguish "normal" unhappiness, anxiety, and deviance from mental disorders. Only symptoms that reflect a disorder "in the person" and not those that are expectable responses to social environments are mental disorders.

A critical flaw of diagnostic psychiatry is its failure to separate symptoms that are normal responses to stressful environments from those where some internal psychological mechanism is functioning inappropriately (Wakefield 1992a). Sociological attention is best directed toward conditions that are *not* mental disorders—that is, toward the expectable psychological consequences of stressful social arrangements (Aneshensel, Rutter, and Lachenbruch 1991). This chapter illustrates how social factors that are external to individuals are responsible for many of the conditions now mistakenly viewed as mental disorders.[1]

SOCIAL CAUSES OF DISTRESS

Sociologists emphasize a variety of causes for psychological distress. Many sociological studies focus on the mental health consequences of stressful life events (e.g., Holmes and Rahe 1967; Dohrenwend and Dohrenwend 1974, 1981; Wheaton 1990). These include, among many others, divorce, unemployment, physical illness, and the death of close relations. Typical studies in this tradition sum the number of such events that individuals experience into an overall stress index, which is then correlated with levels of distress. Most of this research reports consistent, although modest, relationships between experiences of stressful life events and the development of distressing conditions (Rabkin and Struening 1976; Mirowsky and Ross 1989b; Thoits 1983). Life events that are both negative and uncontrollable such as combat experiences, serious criminal victimizations, untimely bereavement, or severe abuse as a child are particularly powerful causes of adverse mental health outcomes (Dohrenwend 2000).

Sociological studies also emphasize how persistent social stressors often account for distressful psychological conditions (Avison and Turner 1988; Pearlin 1989; Aneshensel 1992; Turner, Wheaton, and Lloyd 1995; Wheaton 1999). Chronic conditions do not come and go, as is the case for many stressful life events, but are rooted in ongoing circumstances (Pearlin et al. 1981; Link and Phelan 1995; Pearlin 1999; Wheaton 1999). Social environments that feature high rates of poverty, instability, unemployment, dilapidated housing, neighborhood disorganization, crime, and broken families are associated with high rates of distress (e.g., Aneshensel and Sukoff 1996; Ross, Reynolds, and Geis 2000). For example, the median rate of psychological disturbance in community studies is 36 percent in the lowest social class, compared to 9 percent in the highest social class (Link and Dohrenwend 1980). Other work in this vein shows how marital, sex, and age differences in distress reflect patterned differences in structural conditions between these groups (e.g., Eaton and Muntaner 1999; Avison 1999; Rosenfield 1999; Williams and Harris-Reid 1999; Mirowsky and Ross 1999). Social factors associated with distress, therefore, are often persistent and chronic and not disturbances of some preexisting state of equilibrium.[2]

Another major sociological tradition relates characteristics of interpersonal networks to the production of distress. Work in this tradition derives states of mental health from characteristics of role relationships rather than from individual qualities. Some of this work shows how strong interpersonal ties protect people from becoming distressed, while weak ties leave them vulnerable to distress (e.g., House, Landis, and Umberson 1988; Horwitz, McLaughlin, and White 1998; Turner 1999). Other studies focus on how the differential distribution of power in relationships is related to mental health (e.g., Horwitz 1982b; Rosenfield 1992). A final type of sociological study ties cultural systems of beliefs, values, and meanings to mental health (e.g., Idler 1987; Simon 1997).

The sociological emphasis on social causes of distress such as life events, chronic stressors, social relationships, and collective meaning systems is similar to conceptions of stressors among members of the lay community. When population samples are asked about their perceptions of the major causes of "nervous breakdowns," the four most common responses are "stress," problems of others in the social network, work and school problems, and financial problems (Swindle et al. 2000). This list is remarkably similar to the most common stressors that drove English patients in the seventeenth century to seek psychological treatment: "the most common stresses Napier's clients experienced were conflicts with their families, lovers, and neighbors, the loss of their loved ones slain by disease, and fear of poverty and want" (MacDonald 1981, 74).

What makes this variety of factors *social* causes? Social causes are external to any particular individual (Durkheim 1951 [1897]). Acute and chronic social conditions, the strength and degree of dominance in social relationships, and systems of cultural meaning do not reside within physical organisms but stem from environments that exist independently of any given individual.[3] They are not aspects of individuals acquired at conception and so are not transmitted genetically. Likewise, social causes differ from psychological causes such as motivation, self-esteem, or fatalism in that they are properties of the external environment, not of individuals. The distinctive emphasis of sociological studies lies in how social relationships, social groups, social structures, social institutions, and cultural systems of meaning affect distress and well-being. "The distinguishing mark of sociological inquiry," Pearlin notes, "is its effort to uncover patterns and regularities shared by people whose social characteristics and circumstances are similar" (Pearlin 1989, 242). Much distress emerges from factors that are neither aspects of particular individuals nor universal properties of the human species but elements of social environments.

While social causes are external to given individuals, not all external causes are social. People who are struck by lightning or infected by viruses are victims of nonsocial external causes. Social causes are not only external but also *collective* (Lukes 1975; Zerubavel 1997). Social meaning systems affect what factors particular groups consider to be stressful. A stressor in one group need not have stressful consequences in another. Poverty, for example, is not inherently stressful but only becomes so because of cultural definitions in particular contexts. The sparse resources of a serf in feudal Europe need not have been a source of distress because they were viewed as inevitable and unchangeable. Social stressors are therefore external conditions that relevant collective meaning systems define as likely to produce distress.

SOCIAL CAUSATION AND SOCIAL SELECTION

Sociological studies assume the causal primacy of social factors on distress. They posit that variations in social environments and roles *precede* and lead to variations in individual states of mental health (Aneshensel 1992). Social explanations show how aspects of the social context, which individual traits in these contexts cannot explain, are associated with variations in psychological conditions. This endeavor requires explicit attention to the question of whether mental health and distress are the consequences or the causes of various social arrangements.

For the past century, sociologists have assumed that social conditions are fundamental causes of psychological outcomes. Durkheim's *Suicide* provides the classic statement of this position (Durkheim 1951 [1897]). Durkheim emphasized that groups featuring strong social integration display lower suicide rates than less integrated groups. Rates of suicide vary across countries, states, communities, and neighborhoods as a function of the strength of social bonds within these units. Therefore, married people, people with children, and those with high rates of participation in social groups account for fewer suicides than single, divorced, or widowed people, childless people, and those with weaker group ties. A century of sociological research after Durkheim likewise has assumed that aspects of social contexts and relationships are responsible for resulting states of mental health (House, Landis, and Umberson 1988; Thoits 1999).

The demonstration that the social precedes the psychological inverts the assumption of biological psychiatry that genetically determined personality characteristics affect the kinds of social structures and relationships people enter. Biological psychiatry explains social structures through the characteristics of the individuals within them rather than the opposite (Kendler et al. 1991; Plomin et al. 1990; Scarr and McCartney 1983).[4] One prominent article, aptly titled *How People Make Their Own Environments: A Theory of Genotype-Environment Effects,* concludes that "most differences among people arise from genetically determined differences in the experiences to which they are attracted and which they evoke from their environments" (Scarr and McCartney 1983, 433). In this view, social experiences stem from genotypes that guide people's choices regarding social activities, relationships, and life experiences. Twin research that indicates MZ twins have more similar religious beliefs, divorce rates, and types of life events than DZ twins also presumably supports the contention that genetic traits lead people to evoke and select their environments (Bouchard et al. 1990; Bouchard 1994; Lykken et al. 1992; Kendler et al. 1993).

From the biological perspective, life events that sociologists consider to be the cause of psychological distress—suffering robbery or assault, illness or injury, or marital or financial problems—have stronger genetic than environmental influences, because they occur more frequently among both identical twins than among both fraternal twins. For example, the finding that MZ twin pairs are more likely to be robbed than are DZ twin pairs presumably indicates their genetic propensity to enter risky situations (Kendler et al. 1993).[5] A study of identical twins who are reared apart concludes that twins are so similar because they "tend to elicit, select, seek out, or create very similar effective environments and, to that extent, the impact of these experiences is counted as a genetic influence" (Bouchard et al. 1990, 227–28).[6] Best-selling syntheses of cognitive science and sociobiology highlight this research as demonstrating how the genetic traits of individuals precede and cause social experiences (Pinker 1997; Wilson 1998; Wright 1994). A hundred years after Durkheim showed how presumably individual conditions such as suicide resulted from variations in social environments, biological psychiatry has reversed the causal chain between social structure and psychological experience.

The argument that individual traits shape selection into social contexts is not implausible (Turner and Wagenfeld 1968; Dohrenwend and Dohrenwend 1969). Individuals, especially members of modern individualist societies, often consciously choose what environments they want to enter. For example, to find a high proportion of gay people in large, urban communities would not indicate that anything about this particular social environment leads people to be gay. Instead it may indicate that gay people move to areas where there are many other gay people. In such cases, people seek those environments that are most compatible with their personal characteristics.

Issues of selection are particularly important in studies of mental disorders because psychological dysfunctions can create personal limitations that lead people to enter or to stay out of certain kinds of social environments. For example, if schizophrenia limits the ability of individuals to attain high-status jobs, there would be, and is, an inverse correlation between socioeconomic status and schizophrenia (Hollingshead and Redlich 1958; Dohrenwend et al. 1992). This correlation, however, arises because the mental condition leads to the social status, rather than because the social status produces the individual condition. Indeed, one of the most important early studies of schizophrenia initially argued that the social isolation of inner-city areas was a primary cause of the higher rates of schizophrenia found in central cities (Faris and Dunham 1939). An author of this study later discovered, however, that people with schizophrenia were more likely to move to the inner city from other areas, so the initial assumption of causal order was backwards (Dunham 1959). The most impressive recent study of selection also shows that selection is more important than causation in producing the relationship between low socioeconomic status and schizophrenia (Dohrenwend et al. 1992).[7] Sociological studies must demonstrate that social factors are responsible for the development of individual conditions in ways that biological or psychological factors cannot explain better. This chapter shows that much psychological distress is external, collective, and expectable, rather than internal, individual, and non-normative.[8]

VARIABILITY IN TIME AND SPACE

The stressful aspects of social arrangements are neither idiosyncratic individual traits nor universal qualities of the human species, but instead are rooted in the collective structural and cultural systems of social groups. To the extent that social factors are responsible for states of psychological well-being and distress, there should be wide variation in these states across groups. Social explanations emphasize that relative constants, such as gene pools, generally cannot cause large variations in rates of disorder across historical time and social space. In contrast, biological explanations emphasize genetic traits that are relatively constant at the group level across social and temporal contexts. Therefore, social explanations emphasize variability in rates of disorder in different groups, while biological explanations stress uniformity in these rates.

The demonstration of a social cause of mental disorder must, however, go beyond indicating differences in rates of disorder between social groups. Gene pools, viruses, or psychological differences between individual group members, among multitudes of other possible causes, could lead to different base levels and inter-group differences in rates of mental disorders. A social explanation must show how social factors account for differences in these rates in ways that differ from biological or psychological explanations. The study of birth cohorts and mental disorders provides one way to compare the biological and social views.

Birth Cohorts and Mental Disorders　A birth cohort is a group of people born in a particular time and place. The study of birth cohorts, or generations, provides an especially good way to compare how social and genetic experiences affect mental disorders. It is a social concept that does not have a biological basis; cohorts and genes influence behavior in opposite ways. The period when they were born defines the particular birth cohort an individual belongs to—e.g., birth in a particular decade or during particular historical periods such as the Depression or the baby boom. Genetic factors are irrelevant to a person's generational position, which is solely determined by historical and social experiences. Karl Mannheim, the sociologist most closely associated with the concept, defines a generation as follows:

> The fact of belonging to the same . . . generation or age group . . . endows the individuals sharing in them with a common location in the social and historical process, and thereby limits them to a specific range of potential experience, predisposing them for a certain characteristic mode of thought and experience, and a characteristic type of historically relevant action. (Mannheim 1952, 291)

Because they have a common period of birth, members of the same generation or birth cohort share distinct life experiences as well.

The study of cohort influences on distress is especially useful because the concept of a birth cohort *inverts* the logic of genetic transmission. Genes are wholly transmitted from parents to children and do not change across generations, except in atypical cases where mutations occur. In contrast to genetic effects that remain stable over time, generational effects can show sharp divergences and rapid change over time. Generational effects are acquired in Lamarckian fashion: traits that one generation develops, rather than inherits, can be passed on to future generations and new generations can develop their own distinctive behaviors.[9] While Lamarckian inheritance is thoroughly repudiated in genetics, people do inherit acquired social and cultural traits from their parents as well as develop new traits of their own (e.g., Mannheim 1952; Ryder 1965; Cain 1967).

Generational effects on mental disorder thus reflect social influences that genetic mechanisms cannot account for. One way to examine generational effects on mental disorders is by comparing rates of disorder among same-age members of different birth cohorts across historical time. Members of different generations have many experiences in common that are different from the experiences of members of other generations. These include differences in experiencing different historical events, marriage and divorce rates, occupational and educational opportunities, and changes in fashion, lifestyle, cultural patterns, and worldviews (e.g., Elder 1974; Wohl 1979; Thornton and Rodgers 1987). To the extent that social factors cause mental disorders, rates of disorders in same-age members of successive birth cohorts over time should diverge substantially. In contrast, if genetic factors are responsible for disorders, age-specific rates should remain relatively stable across generations.

Unfortunately, information on generational change in mental disorders is limited because useful data regarding changing rates have only been collected in recent years. A rare exception is Goldhamer and Marshall's study of first admissions to public and private mental institutions and nursing homes in Massachusetts between 1840 and 1940 (Goldhamer and Marshall 1953). When controlled for changing life spans and population size, rates of psychoses remained stable over the entire hundred-year period examined (Goldhamer and Marshall 1953). Age-adjusted rates indicate that hospitalizations for mental illness were relatively constant over this period for persons under fifty years of age. This finding supports the biological assumption that cohort influences, which showed great fluctuations over this period, are not strong causal factors in rates of psychoses.

The stable temporal rates of the psychoses in this study, however, are exceptional; incidence of other disorders fluctuates across generations. Changing rates of depression, for example, support the social rather than the genetic expectation. Persons of the same age who are born in different periods have very different rates of depression. Rates of depression have been rising in the United States for as long as they have been systematically recorded (Klerman 1988b). As the figure on page 166 indicates, there has been a steady rise in depression in subsequent cohorts born over ten-year intervals between the early and late parts of the twentieth century in the United States. Epidemiological studies, rates of treated depression, and studies of rates of depression among relatives of persons in treatment for depression all show higher rates of depression among people born after World War II than among those born before. In addition, successive birth

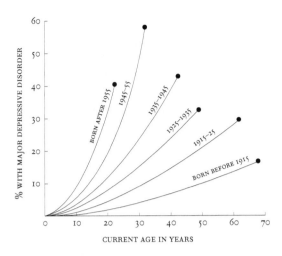

SOURCE: Adapted from Klerman 1988b, 9.

cohorts report a consistently lower average age of onset for the disorder (Klerman 1988b).[10]

Rates of substance abuse are even more strongly linked than depression is to generational changes. Social explanations emphasize how these conditions often reflect normative aspects of cultural environments, especially of youth cultures, in particular times and places. Therefore, they should show large variations over time. In contrast, biological explanations emphasize brain functioning and genetics, which do not vary so rapidly across generations.

The evidence about rates of substance abuse strongly supports social, rather than genetic, explanations. For example, the National Co-Morbidity Survey (NCS) separates respondents into four age cohorts: 15- to 24-year-olds born between 1966 and 1975, 25- to 34-year-olds born between 1956 and 1965, 35- to 44-year-olds born between 1946 and 1955, and 45- to 54-year-olds born between 1936 and 1945 (Warner et al. 1995). The results indicate a higher prevalence of age-adjusted substance abuse in successively more recent cohorts. Despite their greater risk of exposure, the oldest group had the *lowest* lifetime rate of substance use dependence—2.9 percent, compared to 8.5 percent, 9.5 percent, and 7.3 percent in progressively younger age cohorts. For example, 2.1 percent of respondents in the oldest cohort reported a history of substance dependence by age 24, compared to 17.3 percent of the youngest cohort. This means that there is an 800 percent difference in the chances of a 24-year-old having had a substance dependence disorder, depending on whether they were born between 1966 and 1975 or between 1936 and 1945. These generational effects seem far greater in magnitude than possible genetic influences on rates of these disorders.

The results of the NCS mirror the findings from many other studies that show the increasing prevalence of substance use and dependence among cohorts born after World War II (Anthony and Helzer 1991; Burke et al. 1991; Helzer, Burnam, and McEvoy 1991). Even taking into account the biases in these findings that could stem from differential recall, willingness to admit use, and mortality across cohorts, the large difference in rates of substance use disorders across cohorts cannot stem from genetic changes. All studies of other nonpsychotic disorders show dramatic changes in rates of these disorders across generations. This variability over time indicates social influences.[11]

Cohort effects, rather than genetic effects, better account for the higher prevalence rates of nonpsychotic disorders found in members of different birth cohorts. Different generations have many different structural and cultural experiences in common with each other that differ from those of other generations. The various aspects of social life that birth cohorts encompass, however, do not allow for the specification of exactly how generation is related to mental disorder. Factors in the social environment such as increasing individualism, divorce, economic insecurity, tolerance for substance use, and the like can be associated with the rising rates of disorder among young people. The findings about generation and nonpsychotic mental disorders thus indicate that something about social experience influences rates of these disorders, although they do not specify what social forces produce this large variation over time.

Cross-Cultural Variations in Mental Disorders   Social explanations emphasize variability in rates of disorders across social space as well as through historical time. If social explanations are correct, different societies should display different rates of distress and well-being that reflect differences in their collective social environments. In contrast, if genetic factors are responsible for mental disorders rates should not show much variation across groups.

Comparable to the relatively constant rates of psychoses over time, rates of psychotic disorders show limited variance across groups. The best-known comparative study of schizophrenia, by the World Health Organization (WHO), shows relatively similar rates of core cases of this disorder in very different cultural contexts (Sartorius, Jablensky, and Shapiro 1978).

Standardized assessment techniques applied to first admission patients in nine different cultures produced fairly constant incidence rates of schizophrenia. A follow-up study that used the same instruments in twelve sites in ten countries also found similar rates of schizophrenia when strict criteria were used, leading the authors to conclude that "the 'central' schizophrenic syndrome may be occurring with approximately equal probability in different populations" (Sartorius et al. 1986, 924). These findings, however, hold only when restrictive criteria for defining schizophrenia are used (Kleinman 1988; Hopper 1992). When broader definitions are included, rates of new cases of schizophrenia per 10,000 population fluctuate from 1.5 in Denmark to 4.2 at a rural site in India. Nevertheless, even these differences are far less than the variability in nonpsychotic disorders.

In contrast to the fairly comparable rates of core cases of schizophrenia, rates of less serious disorders vary widely across societies. For example, cross-cultural studies of rates of depression indicate large variations across social groups. These rates, according to DSM-III criteria, vary from 2.4 percent in a rural Basque area of Spain to 30 percent in an urban, black area of Zimbabwe (Brown 1996). Although it is possible that genetic factors might influence which particular Basques or Zimbabweans become depressed, they cannot account for the more than tenfold difference in the mean levels of depression in these groups. Other studies indicate that rates of major depression are far higher in Western countries, including Canada (8.6 percent), the United States (10.1 percent) and New Zealand (12.6 percent), than in other cultures such as Puerto Rico (4.6 percent), Korea (3.4 percent), or Taiwan (0.9 percent) (Horvath and Weissman 1995; Kessler et al. 1994). Other disorders, such as social phobias, range from 1.7 percent in Puerto Rico to 16 percent in Basel, Switzerland (Merikangas et al. 1996). Rates of alcohol and drug dependence show even larger variations across national contexts (Merikangas et al. 1996). One cross-national study of alcoholism finds the highest lifetime prevalence rate (23 percent) among a Native American population and the lowest (0.45 percent) in Shanghai, China (Helzer and Canino 1992). Other diagnoses, including attention deficit disorder and multiple personality disorder, are virtually nonexistent outside the United States (Livingston 1997; Hacking 1995).

These studies indicate that the focus on intra-individual differences found in biological psychiatry presents a limited view of mental disorders. Most mental disorders show a degree of social variation that the biological qualities of individuals cannot explain. The statement that "there has simply been nothing on the environmental side to counter the power of twin and adoption studies" indicates the tunnel vision of many current commentators (Wright 1997). Such statements reflect the focus of biological psychiatry on intra-individual differences and ignore the powerful influence of social factors on rates of mental disorder across societies. These historical and cross-cultural differences reflect social forces that are not reducible to properties of genes or of brains.

CONSEQUENCES OF SOCIAL STRESSORS

The high variability in rates of many mental disorders across time and space indicates the importance of sociological influences. Another way to examine the importance of social factors on mental disorders is to see whether different individuals in the same circumstances will have comparable reactions to social stressors. If they do, psychological conditions would at least partly be expectable products of social circumstances. Likewise, when social influences are dominant, the same individuals would have different psychological reactions when their social situations change.

The most common type of sociological research associates the occurrence of stressful life circumstances with resulting rates of distress. This research indicates that interpersonal difficulties are especially powerful determinants of distress (Brown and Moran 1994; Weissman and Paykel 1974). Further, this research shows that marital dissolution is among the most stressful types of interpersonal difficulty.[12] I will use research on marital dissolution as an example of how stressful social circumstances predictably lead to psychological distress.

The study of marital dissolution is a good example of the sociological perspective on mental health. It indicates how people who respond normally to stressful events can mistakenly be called "mentally disordered." The DSM definition of mental disorder that excludes syndromes that are "merely an expectable and culturally sanctioned response to a particular event, for example, the death of a loved one" would seemingly not count people who are undergoing the distress of marital dissolution as among the mentally disordered (APA 1994, xxi). Yet, no such exclusion is present either in the manual for clinical use or in community studies that rely on DSM definitions. A social perspective, however, indicates that the distress of most people undergoing marital dissolution is not an internal dysfunction, but rather a normal response to a highly stressful situation.

Marital dissolution is also a good example of a social stressor because of the pervasive influence it exerts on mental health.[13] Separated and divorced people show far higher levels of psychological distress, alcohol abuse, and outpatient and inpatient mental health treatment than married people.[14] For instance, married people report fewer than half as many alcohol related problems as those undergoing marital dissolution (Umberson 1987; Waite 1995). People undergoing marital dissolution suffer not only from the stress of the divorce process itself, but also from a change in social relationships, valued social roles, living conditions, financial resources, social identities, and stigma (Pearlin 1989). Such a broad upheaval of one's entire social situation should *expectably* produce major negative consequences on mental health among psychologically normal individuals.

Rates of marital dissolution have changed dramatically in recent decades; increasing divorce rates are one of the most significant social trends over the past century (Thornton and Rodgers 1987). Between 1960 and 1980 rates of divorce more than doubled. In a longer-term perspective, divorce was virtually absent in the United States in 1860, increased very slowly but steadily until the early 1960s, and then increased very sharply until the 1980s when it began to stabilize (Cherlin 1992). Now, about half of marriages end in divorce. Although divorce rates have risen for all groups, there are still wide variations across regional, ethnic, generational, and religious groups and especially across groups with different labor force participation of women (Kitson, Babri, and Roach 1985; Cherlin 1992). Neither the huge fluctuations in marital dissolution over time nor their variations in social space can be manifestations of genetic tendencies.[15]

It is, however, possible that some genetically influenced psychological traits precede and influence the events leading to marital dissolution. Chronic depression or substance abuse, for example, can provoke marital dissolutions (Mastekaasa 1992). In this sense, individual factors such as depression or heavy drinking could set the social process of marital dissolution in motion. Longitudinal studies of marital dissolution represent a quasi-experimental situation because the social status of an individual at one point in time is compared to the same individual's (different) social status at a different point in time. Qualities of individuals that do not change, such as their genetic inheritance, are in effect held constant when the same individual is compared at different times. The environment varies while genetic qualities do not.

A longitudinal study of a representative sample of about 1,300 residents of New Jersey provides good evidence of how marital dissolution influences mental health (Horwitz, White, and Howell-White 1996). This is one of the few studies to measure psychological conditions that precede the period of marital dissolution as well as those that follow. The three groups of subjects in this study were initially sampled between 1979 and 1981 when they were twelve, fifteen, or eighteen years old. The sampling design insured that they were representative of the population of New Jersey at the time. They were subsequently interviewed three additional times, the last time around 1993 when they were twenty-five, twenty-eight, or thirty-one years old. There was a 90 percent retention rate of subjects across the four interview periods.

By the last interview, about half of the sample had married. Of those who had married, a quarter were separated or divorced. The design of this study allows for the comparison of the mental health of those who remained married with those whose marriages dissolved, and of individuals in the married and dissolution groups with themselves at the earlier time. In these ways, the impact of marital dissolution on resulting states of mental health can be shown after controlling for the effect of psychological characteristics that might have been responsible for the marital dissolution.

The stressful impact of marital dissolution is clear. During the seven years between the last two interviews, rates of depression among people who get and remain married fall 23 percent and rates of alcohol problems among the stably married tumble by 57 percent. These rates reflect the maturing of people as they move out of late adolescence and enter marital, family, and work roles in young adulthood (Hirschi 1969; Horwitz and White 1991; Labouvie 1996).

The situation is quite different for the group whose marriages dissolve over this period. Their levels of depression rise by 17 percent while their levels of alcohol problems increase by 55 percent. The contrast in rates of alcohol problems among stably married women and women whose marriages dissolved is especially strong. While rates of alcohol problems among stably married women are less than a third of their rates seven years earlier, women whose marriages dissolved reported almost twice the number of alcohol problems as in the previous period.

Could premarital psychological states account for the higher rate of depression and alcohol problems among people whose marriages dissolve? Multivariate statistical analysis shows that premarital states of mental health only account for about 15 percent of the impact of marital dissolution on depression. Earlier rates of alcohol problems have no influence on the impact of marital dissolution on alcohol problems. These results indicate that marital dissolution is far more likely to be the cause than the consequence of much higher levels of depression and alcohol problems. They also confirm the findings of other longitudinal studies of the mental health consequences of marital dissolution. After taking into account pre-dissolution states of mental health and other psychological factors, marital dissolution is associated with less well-being and with more depression, anxiety, and alcohol and drug problems (Menaghan and Lieberman 1986; Doherty, Su, and Needle 1989; Amato and Rogers 1997; Aseltine and Kessler 1993).

These findings should not be surprising. People who are undergoing marital dissolution *expectably* suffer from numerous psychological problems. These problems are symptomatically identical to mental disorders but are expectable reactions to highly stressful situations. They do not result from genetic or psychological factors, but develop from the extremely stressful social circumstances that marital dissolution generates. The argument that genetic influences cause life events finds little support in one of the most common and most stressful life experiences (compare McGue and Lykken 1992).

The case of marital dissolution illustrates a broader principle about social relationships and mental health. The absence or loss of social relationships or the presence of conflictual or unfulfilling social relationships often entails many negative psychological consequences. Indeed, the single most common precipitant for entry into mental health treatment is problems with social relationships (Kadushin 1969; Olfson and Pincus 1994a). Conversely, individuals with strong social ties, much social support, and positive relationships generally have good mental health (House, Landis, and Umberson 1988). Consequently, many symptoms that are called "mental disorders" in community surveys and that form the basis for implausibly high rates of mental disorders are not disorders at all but expectable results of stressful social situations (Wakefield 1999b). People who are distressed because of stressful social conditions are reacting normally; they do not have mental disorders.

CONSEQUENCES OF ONGOING SOCIAL ROLES
Marital dissolution illustrates a social situation that has relatively discrete temporal boundaries. Another social cause of distress can stem from stable life conditions. Unlike life events whose stressful quality stems from the changes they entail, the chronic and ongoing nature of some social conditions and social roles can cause distress in individuals (Wheaton 1999).

One especially important chronic social stressor is the degree of dominance and oppression in social relationships. The differential distribution of power characterizes all relational systems. Masters and slaves lie on one extreme of a continuum where egalitarian partnerships are on the other extreme. Dominance and dependence can only exist within an interdependent relationship; power is a characteristic of relationships, not of individuals (Mirowsky 1985). Further, dominance and dependence are not individual characteristics: someone who is the dominant party in one relationship might be the dependent party in another. A man who enjoys patriarchal dominance at home might be a powerless subordinate at work. His wife may be totally dependent on him but dominate their children.

The far-ranging, deeply embedded, and highly consequential nature of relational positions of dominance should have significant consequences for psychological distress. In general, mental health should vary directly with domination and inversely with subordination in systems of social relationships.[16] Dominants can express feelings toward subordinates more freely and so can vent frustrations and aggressions openly in a downward direction. Subordinates, however, are much more limited in their capacity to vent emotions upward and so would be more likely to express them through signs of depression, anxiety, or psychophysiological symptoms that do not directly confront the dominant party. Because they fear punishment from dominants, dependents must often internalize hostile emotions and consequently develop physiological or neurotic symptoms (Levy 1976; Horwitz 1982b). For example, when a master rapes a servant, the victim's choice is often between disgrace and silence with consequent depression (see, for example, MacDonald 1981, 88). Gender differences in distress illustrate the impact that systems of relational dominance have on mental health.

Gender and Distress   One of the most striking aspects of psychological disorders is their strong connection to gender. Only schizophrenic and bipolar disorders, which are about evenly distributed between men and women, show little variance in sex ratios (Weissman and Klerman 1977, 1985). Unlike the psychoses, rates of nonpsychotic mental disorders, expectable distress, and deviant behavior are all strongly sex-specific. Most nonpsychotic disorders and distress consistently show sex ratios of about two women to every man (Kessler et al. 1994; Nolen-Hoeksema 1987; Weissman and Klerman 1977; Culbertson 1997). Girls and women constitute about 90 percent of cases of conditions such as anorexia and multiple personality disorder. In contrast, men account for the large majority of cases of most forms of deviance including substance use disorders, antisocial personality disorders, oppositional disorders, and the like (Dohrenwend and Dohrenwend 1976; Zent 1984). With the exception of the psychoses, most psychological disturbances are strongly sex-linked.

Sociologists have posited two major types of explanations for the striking sex differences in rates of most nonpsychotic mental disorders. Both emphasize how gender—the culturally defined nature of women's and men's roles—rather than biological sex accounts for the styles and rates of mental disorders. The first explanation, discussed in chapter 5, focuses on how gender-specific identity categories channel symptom expressions of distress in different directions for men and women. Cultural norms lead women to react to stressful situations through internalized responses while men respond through more externalized reactions. These explanations provide one possible reason for gender differences in the response to stressful conditions.

Explanations that focus on how cultural roles channel distress in gender-specific ways can address why men and women have distinct *reactions* to stressors, but not whether men and women have different *rates* of distress. A different type of explanation, one that focuses on the nature of dominance and submission found in the social roles of men and women, explains these differential rates. This explanation posits that the greater structural dependence of women compared to men accounts for the higher rates of distress women display (Rosenfield 1999). Note, however, that this explanation is grounded in roles of dominance and submission, not in any qualities of either sex or gender *per se*.

Gender differences in distress should be deducible, in part, from power relationships. Not femaleness, but the prevalence of women in subordinate roles, could account for the greater incidence of distress among women. If so, when women possess dominant roles and men subordinate roles, gender differences in distress should reverse themselves. Likewise, when men and women have relatively egalitarian roles, rates of distress should be relatively equal as well. The relationship between gender and distress might be grounded in social structure and culture, not in biology.

Women as Dependents Throughout most of recorded human history women have been dependent on men. In most times and places, women have been in subordinate relationships with husbands, fathers, and brothers (Lerner 1987; Tomes 1990). As in Western societies, most cases of mental disorder in anthropological reports about pre-industrial societies arise among women rather than men. Studies in a wide variety of contexts show that unmarried women who have been frustrated in love or married women who have been neglected or rejected by their husbands are especially prone to depression-like symptoms (Lewis 1966; Lambek 1979; Messing 1959; Counts 1980). For example, typical patients in the Zar therapeutic cults in northern Ethiopia are "married women, who feel neglected in a man's world in which they serve as hewers of wood and haulers of water" (Messing 1959, 320).

MacDonald's (1981) study of the clients of a seventeenth-century physician in England also shows that the link of interpersonal oppression, gender, and psychological distress is of long-standing origin in the West. Of 2,039 cases where mental disturbance led to consultation, more than 60 percent involved women. Their most common problems were conflicts with husbands, lovers, and parents. The strong patriarchal values in this society enforced the dependency of women on their husbands or parents with few or no means of redress. "[T]he bondage they found most troubling," MacDonald notes, "subordinated daughters to parents, wives to husbands, rather than peasants to lords" (MacDonald 1981, 40). Such oppression without hope of direct remedy would naturally lead to the higher levels of distress among women.

Patriarchal arrangements in the contemporary world are also strongly linked to distress. Consider the case of a typical client of a folk psychotherapist in Korea who

> had been supporting her family since her husband's business failed. The husband . . . had been chronically unemployed, spending his days lounging at home and his evenings out drinking up her meager earnings. He often beat her, accusing her of hiding money from him. If she complained, he would tell her to get lost. (Harvey 1976, 192)

Not the husband, however, but the wife becomes distressed enough to seek help from a therapist. Likewise, women in highly traditional patriarchal relationships in Pakistan report three to six times more psychosomatic symptoms than men (Mumford et al. 1996). A study of Pakistani women shows that they consider their husbands' violence, indifference, infidelity, or preference for their own families as the most common source of their distress (Karasz 1997). In Great Britain, as well, problematic relationships with men are the most likely sources of depression in women (Brown and Harris 1978).

The findings from contemporary U.S. studies regarding gender-linked dominance and submission mirror the comparative and historical evidence.

Overall, married women consistently report more distress than married men (Gove and Tudor 1973; Radloff 1975; Mirowsky and Ross 1989b). In particular, women who are in powerless positions relative to their husbands or other male partners are consistently more likely to be depressed (Mirowsky 1985; Aneshensel, Frerichs, and Clark 1981). Employment is the best indicator of relative power between married partners. Housewives, as a rule, have fewer resources than their husbands and constricted options outside of the marriage (Rosenfield 1992). Women with independent economic resources have access to sources of power that can equalize the relationship between spouses. When other factors such as the type and level of demands from the job are held constant, employed wives report less distress than housewives (Horwitz 1982b; Menaghan 1989; Lennon and Rosenfield 1992). Women who have greater control in their jobs are especially likely to have lower levels of depression (Lennon 1994). Furthermore, the greater the amount of income a wife has relative to her husband's income, the better her mental health (Rosenfield 1989; see also Kessler and McRae 1982). The relative power a wife has compared to her husband predicts how much distress she will have.

Gender Comparable Roles   If the structural positions of men and women in interpersonal relationships are related to their levels of psychological well-being and disturbance, then men and women who hold comparable structural positions should also show relatively comparable rates of disorder. This finding would be deducible from a social, but not from a biological, explanation of sex differences in distress.

One test of this thesis lies in comparing rates of distress among men and women who share common structural positions (Lennon 1987). Like women, men who become distressed are rarely in dominant positions but are most likely to be young, unmarried, and in marginal social and economic positions (Horwitz 1982a, 78; see also Horwitz 1977). In African societies, for example, men who enter therapy are typically young bachelors who have been unable to establish independent families (Lewis 1966). The same holds in contemporary American society (Leaf and Bruce 1987). Further, if dominance and oppression account for sex differences in distress, single men and women should have more comparable rates of distress than married people, because the structural roles of single people of both sexes are relatively comparable. In contrast to the greater distress of wives compared to husbands, unmarried men and women do report similar rates of distress (Gove 1972; Radloff 1975; Horwitz 1982b). Indeed, in the National

Co-Morbidity Survey, among people aged twenty to thirty where the structural roles of men and women are relatively similar, rates of depression among men are actually higher than among women (Kessler et al. 1994).

The comparability of distress among single men and women suggests that structural aspects of social roles are associated with rates of distress. Another indication of the social basis of distress lies in the impact of unemployment. Married men who lose their jobs also lose the foundation of their dominant roles in their families. These men report far more distress than any other role category of men or of women (Radloff 1975; Horwitz 1982b; Menaghan 1989; Simon 1998). An even greater variation in family roles arises when wives have more power than their husbands, as indicated by relative income and participation in household chores. In those rare households where wives earn more income and do not do more household labor than their husbands, gender differences in mental health reverse: dependent husbands report more distress than their dominant wives (Rosenfield 1992).

Just as inequitable relationships predict distress, egalitarian relationships should be associated with mental health. For example, when Pakistani women have more egalitarian household relationships they report fewer symptoms of distress and higher levels of well-being (Chandra et al. 1995). Likewise, in his classic work on depression, George Brown finds that the best protection against depression among middle- and working-class English women lies in intimate and confiding, rather than inequitable, relationships with husbands or boyfriends (Brown and Harris 1978). Similarly, husbands and wives in households that feature relatively equal divisions of labor report more equivalent levels of distress than those in households with imbalanced divisions of labor. As well, spouses in marriages where husbands and wives share power report comparable levels of depression in contrast to inegalitarian marriages where wives report more distress and husbands less distress (Kessler and McRae 1982; Mirowsky 1985; Rosenfield 1992).

Not sex *per se* but powerless positions that women occupy more frequently than men are associated with sex differences in distress. Dominance and dependence are social phenomena. Inequity, not femaleness, produces distress (Mirowsky 1985).

Cultural Meanings of Dominance and Dependence The findings regarding dominance and dependence and mental health in human societies are consistent with ethological studies that show dependent animals of other species display more depression-like symptoms than dominant ones (Sloman,

Konstantareas, and Dunham 1979; Price and Sloman 1987). Indeed, research with primates provides even stronger evidence than human studies for the critical social influence of dominance and subordination because, unlike human studies, it can experimentally test the differential impact of social positions. When monkeys are moved from groups where they are dominant to groups where they are subordinates, their serotonin levels, which are associated with depression, drop by nearly 40 percent (Raleigh and McGuire 1984). Conversely, serotonin levels in monkeys who change status from dependent to dominant increase by nearly 50 percent. Social dominance predicts levels of serotonin, not vice versa. Serotonin levels may be brain characteristics, but their levels vary in response to the structural qualities of social relationships. The consequences of dominance and subordination arise not only among humans but also among other primates.

There is a major difference, however, between dominance and oppression in human and in nonhuman groups. The degree to which dominance and subordination affect human mental health is a function of social *expectations* of gender appropriate levels of dominance and subordination (Simon 1995, 1998). Cultural expectations can mitigate or exacerbate the role of dependence on depression. Dependence is less distressing for women who share prevailing and coherent cultural belief systems that dictate female subordination than it is for women whose cultures do not provide them with meaning systems to justify their oppression (Levy 1976). Thus, women who do more housework than their husbands do not suffer more distress when they believe their greater contributions are justified; only those who feel their unequal contributions are unjust are likely to suffer more distress (Lennon and Rosenfield 1994).

Conversely, just as cultural ideologies can lessen the impact of dependence on depression for women, they can amplify the detrimental mental health impact of subordination for men. Unemployment, for example, is considerably more distressing for men than for women. Men who have spousal and parental but not wage-earner roles show more distress than any other role category of men, while the same role pattern is associated with little depression for women (Horwitz 1982b; Menaghan 1989). The identical role configuration associated with little power leads to more distress among husbands than among wives because it is less culturally acceptable for men than for women. Not only unemployment, but also relative income levels between spouses, is associated with different mental health consequences for men and women. Men whose wives earn more than they do show more depression than other men, but wives with higher-earning husbands do not show elevated levels of distress (Rosenfield 1992). Hence, dominance and dependence are not solely aspects of the amount of power people have, but also of cultural expectations about what are appropriate levels of power for men and women to hold. These expectations are not idiosyncratic; they are products of collective systems of meaning.

Because they are part of collective meaning systems, expectations of dominance and subordination are not constant, but change over time. In recent decades, increasing gender egalitarianism has decreased expectations of male dominance and female subordination. These changing norms may explain why in the 1960s men whose wives were employed suffered from more depression than men married to housewives, while by the 1980s female employment was not related to more depression among men (Rosenfield 1980, 1989). Husbands no longer associated their wives' employment with their own dependency, although those with wives that earned more than they did still had worse mental health. Changing expectations associated with different social roles may also explain why over time rates of male distress are becoming more equivalent to rates of female distress. Trends toward greater female participation in the labor force have closed the depression gap between males and females, more by increasing the distress of men than by decreasing the distress of women (Kessler and McRae 1981). Which social statuses are dominant and which are subordinate at any particular time are both culturally defined and historically contingent.

Structural positions of dominance and subordination are related to male and female rates of distress. Relationships with power imbalances produce imbalances in distress, while egalitarian relationships equalize distress. Powerless positions, whether occupied by men or women, are associated with much distress. Conversely, dominant positions are associated with less distress. Because powerlessness is socially defined as a more feminine than masculine trait, powerless men may be even more prone to distress than powerless women, both because they are subordinates and because they depart from social role expectations.[17] This social cause is deducible from relational structures but not from the characteristics of individuals.

CONCLUSION

Social factors do not equally affect all types of mental illnesses. The relative lack of variability across time and space in rates of psychotic disorders suggests that these disorders do not primarily arise because of social influences. Social and cultural factors do have significant impacts on how serious mental disorders are defined and treated, as well as on their courses over time, but these factors do not seem to be their fundamental causes. When strong associations appear between social factors and serious mental illnesses, such as the strong relationship between social class and schizophrenia, the mental condition is more likely to produce the social status than the other way around (Dohrenwend et al. 1992). The lack of social variance in serious mental disorders is consistent with the contention of diagnostic psychiatry that serious mental disorders are diseases with strong biological components. It is also consistent with the emphasis biological psychiatry places on the genetic causes of these disorders.

The situation is different with other conditions diagnostic psychiatry considers as mental disorders. Rates of the most prevalent disorders—depression, generalized anxiety, and substance abuse—all vary widely across social contexts. Rates of expectable distress and deviant behavior also fluctuate over time and space in ways that biological psychiatry cannot explain (e.g., Brown 1996; Castillo 1997). The magnitude of inter-group and inter-period differences indicates that social factors are influential causes of widespread psychological conditions including depression, anxiety, and substance abuse as well as of generalized distress.

Psychological well-being and distress commonly stem from external and collective social factors. Happiness and sadness, ebullience and distress, conformity and disobedience are associated with social conditions and cultural beliefs. They arise from acute life events, chronic life circumstances, social roles, and collective systems of meaning. Their symptoms may be identical to those of internal dysfunctions, but they are not mental disorders because people who experience them are not responding inappropriately or dysfunctionally. Social and cultural systems lead people's lives to be fulfilling or boring, meaningful or anxious, filled with joy or dread. Unhappiness, fearfulness, hopelessness, fatigue, and distress often arise in normal individuals trying to function in difficult social circumstances. Likewise, they often disappear when the social circumstances that give rise to them change for the better. Psychological conditions that fluctuate with social situations indicate normality, not mental disorders.

Chapter Eight

DIAGNOSTIC PSYCHIATRY AND THERAPY

Therapy refers to the deliberate efforts of socially designated healers to change disturbing thoughts, feelings, and behaviors (Frank and Frank 1991). Greatly oversimplifying, there have historically been two major types of therapy: psychotherapies and medication therapies. Contemporary diagnostic psychiatry encompasses both styles of therapy. Although psychiatrists now learn both psychotherapy and medication therapy and these approaches exist in uneasy alliance with each other, they are in fact distinct in many important aspects (Luhrmann 2000).

Psychotherapies produce changes by using cultural symbols and so rely on the power of language and human understanding to heal mental suffering (see especially Frank and Frank 1991; Jackson 1999). The personal qualities, interpersonal relationships, and cultures of both therapists and clients are integral aspects of these therapies. In contrast to psychotherapies, medication-based therapies rely on physical substances that act directly on brains (Kramer 1993; Healy 1997). The personal characteristics of healers who prescribe medication, of sufferers who take them, and of the relationships between the two are less consequential than in psychotherapy; a dose of medication administered to an individual should have the same effect regardless of which physician administers it. Likewise, the same medication administered to people of different cultures ought to produce similar neurochemical changes in their brains.[1]

This chapter first examines the basic nature of psychotherapy and medication therapy. It then considers how research on the effectiveness of therapies proceeds. Next, it turns to the results of effectiveness studies and their implications for the premises of diagnostic psychiatry. If these premises are correct, distinguishing discrete mental disorders from one another should lead to more effective treatments for each. In fact, distinct diagnoses are for the most part irrelevant to the efficacy of both medication and psychotherapies.

PSYCHOTHERAPY AND MEDICATION THERAPIES
Throughout history, psychotherapies have been a dominant means of changing personalities (Kiev 1964, 1972; Ellenberger 1970; Jackson 1999). Psychotherapies use symbolic systems to heal the minds of sufferers and so are rooted in philosophical and religious systems of healing. For most of the twentieth century, dynamic psychiatry was the most prominent form of psychotherapy (Hale 1995). Although psychoanalysis is no longer a dominant style, most current psychotherapies are indebted to the general ideas that Freud developed. These include a focus on personal biography, close attention to early childhood experiences, careful scrutiny of the language used in therapy, and the use of an intense interpersonal relationship between clients and therapists to change personalities. This chapter focuses on the broad class of psychotherapies that use self-understanding to produce positive changes among clients.

At present, no particular type of psychotherapy dominates. Instead, most therapists incorporate an eclectic variety of approaches that may focus on emotions, cognitions, or behaviors (Hale 1995). Yet, regardless of their particular techniques and theories, all psychotherapies share common elements. Jackson summarizes these elements:

> to provide an attentive, listening ear; to allow confiding, confessional, and cathartic moments; to comfort and console; to evoke and deal with emotions; to arouse and sustain hope; to provide thoughtful suggestion or persuasion; to integrate explanation or interpretation with these other ingredients; to promote self-understanding. . . . (Jackson 1999, 391)

In the most general sense, psychotherapeutic systems show individuals how to understand disturbing experiences within the context of their personal life histories (Berger and Luckmann 1967).

Psychotherapies are thus grounded in hermeneutics: the process of understanding the meanings of human behavior (Jaspers 1964; Burke 1969; Gadamer 1982). The particular ways in which psychotherapeutic processes occur are inconsequential compared to the common processes that bring about change (Frank and Frank 1991). Both healers and sufferers try to understand the meaningful nature of symptoms within some larger framework of knowledge. This framework defines what kinds of problems people have, how they came to develop these problems, and the most appropriate and efficacious cure for them. Psychotherapeutic interventions inherently involve intense interpersonal interactions. The personal relationships that develop between the two parties are thus essential aspects of psychotherapy, as are the personal qualities of both sufferers and healers.

In therapy, people learn what sorts of mental phenomena they should attend to and what they should ignore, what events to remember and what to forget, which experiences are significant and which ones are not (cf. Zerubavel 1997). In each of these aspects, people participate in therapy and learn how to be patients as members of particular cultural communities. Definitions of the nature, causes, and cures for problems are only meaningful and can only be embraced if they are compatible with the meaning systems of clients. Hence, it makes no more sense to psychoanalyze a Haitian peasant than to exorcise voodoo spirits from a resident of the Upper West Side of Manhattan (Berger and Luckmann 1967).

Because psychotherapies rely on shared meaning systems to change symptoms, the evaluation of their effectiveness does not easily fit traditional scientific methods. The "truth" of the interpretations clients and therapists make does not lie in how closely they resemble some assumed state of reality but rather in their plausibility to the patient (Frank and Frank 1991, 72). The interpretations of their problems that people find plausible depend on what narratives of suffering have credence in their culture. In addition, each person's biography invites multiple interpretations that can change over time and in different circumstances. What sorts of factors people select or ignore, emphasize or downplay are affected as much by aspects of their present situation as by what presumably happened in their pasts (Prager 1998). Many changeable factors, including the particular life circumstances of clients, their rapport with a particular therapist, and the current credence of a form of therapy in a particular culture, always influence whether psychotherapies will be effective. Psychotherapies are intrinsically tied to particular cultural contexts and to particular kinds of people who accept the sorts of understandings that a psychotherapeutic system provides. It is difficult, therefore, to use traditional scientific methods to evaluate whether psychotherapies achieve their goals.

Diagnostic psychiatry also encompasses therapies that use medication to alter the brain. The proximate historical origins of biological therapies lie not in dynamic psychiatry but in the asylum psychiatry that emerged in nineteenth-century mental institutions. Modern treatments that emphasize the use of psychoactive medications stem from the Kraepelian tradition that classifies and groups symptoms according to their responses to treatment (Healy 1997).

The use of medication to treat symptoms is grounded in theories of scientific medicine, not in theories of hermeneutic understanding. These therapies assume that the treatment of mental disorders is not fundamentally different from the treatment of bodily illnesses (Luhrmann 2000). Medications act directly upon the physical organism to change the neurochemistry of the brain. Because of this, psychiatrists who prescribe medication need to know only what types of symptoms and diseases their patients have, not what their symptoms mean or what kind of people they are. Although patients must interpret the changes in neurochemistry that medications produce and synthesize these changes into meaningful biographical contexts, the changes themselves are not products of symbolic manipulations but stem from chemical alterations in the brain.

Unlike psychotherapists, psychiatrists who prescribe medication do not even need to know the language of the people they treat. American psychotherapists, who could use mutually held knowledge systems to treat the problems of their clients in Beverly Hills, would be unable to deal with a Malaysian who believes that his penis has shrunk into his body. In contrast, the same medication may have similar effects on the brains of residents of California or Malaysia. Therefore, prescribers of medication stand outside of culture in ways that psychotherapists cannot.[2] The origins, ideologies, and practices of psychotherapies and medication-based therapies diverge in almost every respect.

Unlike the difficulties they face in evaluating psychotherapeutic changes, classical scientific methods are suitable for evaluating the effectiveness of medications. The answer to the question of whether a medication is effective lies in analyzing data that are separable from the perspectives of both patients and therapists. In principle, experimental designs can measure how much change in symptoms different drug treatments produce.

WHAT MAKES THERAPIES EFFECTIVE?

The culturally appropriate standards for evaluating therapies derive from more general norms of scientific legitimacy. Over the course of the twentieth century, the legitimacy of any technique or policy has come to depend on quantifiable demonstrations of effectiveness (Porter 1995). No process, including the exploration of the deepest recesses of the psyche, is immune to demands that it demonstrate production of concrete and quantifiable benefits. States, corporations, and scientific institutions require numerical justifications to prove that the policies they implement actually seem to work.

The demand for quantitative results is especially powerful in medicine. At the beginning of the twentieth century, case studies that supported theoretical intuition that some medical treatment was effective were standard bases of legitimacy of the treatment (Starr 1982; Hale 1995, chaps. 17, 18). By mid-century, however, the criteria of effectiveness in medicine had changed from the earlier reliance on case studies to the comparison of groups that received some sort of treatment with those that did not. Medical norms demanded that statistical tests, not clinical intuition, prove efficacy. To maintain its position as a medical specialty psychiatry was required to replace the subjective, intuitive, and broad standards of dynamic psychiatry with the quantifiable and measurable techniques that were the source of medical legitimacy.

An additional pressure to quantify standards of effectiveness came from the third-party funders of therapy. For the first half of the twentieth century most clients of psychotherapy paid for services out of pocket and so no institution pressed for accountability in treatment outcomes (Grob 1991a; Hale 1995). In the 1950s insurance companies became prominent sources for funding psychotherapy, and in the 1960s the federal government began to finance a large proportion of outpatient therapy. By the 1990s private and public third parties paid for most psychotherapy; only about one in seven patients now pays solely out of pocket for psychiatric treatment (Zarin et al. 1998). Third-party payment requires not only the treatment of some distinct condition but also some quantifiable justification that the technique used is efficacious. In contrast to the period when dynamic psychiatry flourished, the legitimacy of therapy now rests on demonstrations of effectiveness according to traditional standards of scientific methodology.

Proving the effectiveness of a therapeutic technique is not simple. It requires showing, first, that the otherwise natural course of symptoms changes in a favorable direction; second, that this improvement occurs *because of* the technique; third, that some *particular* aspect of the technique rather than some generic aspects of therapy produces improvement; and finally, that the improvement is greater than what would have occurred in the absence of the therapy. The central issue in the study of therapeutic effectiveness is the appropriate comparison group for people who undergo therapy. Is the rate of improvement for people in a specific type of therapy higher than for those who used a different type of therapy, joined a gym, started yoga lessons, went to religious confession, began a new relationship, talked to friends, or did nothing at all? The need for an adequate comparison group is especially acute because people often enter therapy when they have "hit rock bottom." Their psychological states at the time they enter therapy are so poor that it is far more likely their mental health will improve than that it will decline, even in the absence of therapy. Therefore, without any therapeutic intervention, a regression to the mean effect is expectable. Demonstrations of effectiveness must try to control for this expectable improvement.

Another difficulty in obtaining an adequate comparison group lies in the natural course of the conditions that lead people to seek therapy. If many people enter therapy because of romantic crises, bereavement, and problems with spouses, children, parents, jobs, or careers, symptoms will naturally abate when these crises are over. Therapy might appear to be successful because many problems would be resolved over time, even without professional intervention. If so, the attribution of success to therapy could be a spurious result of the alleviation of or the adjustment to the crises that led to the distressful symptoms. The success rate of therapy can only be evaluated above and beyond the proportion of cases that would have improved without professional treatment.

A further difficulty in evaluating the effectiveness of therapy is that people who enter treatment are pre-socialized to believe in the benefits of whatever techniques they receive. People are far more prone to accept than to doubt what they are told, so when they are told that something, such as therapy, will work, they will naturally accept this statement as true (Gilbert 1991). Regardless of the actual benefits of therapy, people who enter treatment are highly motivated to recover and to believe that therapy can help them, particularly when the persons applying the technique are prestigious, culturally sanctioned healers. This tendency is especially strong for highly distressed people whose personal and social resources are depleted. Hence, people who receive therapy may improve when they are told that a technique will help them, regardless of what that technique actually does (Frank and Frank 1991). A large proportion of this improvement could stem from the generic belief that therapy is effective, rather than from the particular impact of a specific treatment.

Finally, the scientific evaluation of therapy demands the standardization of therapeutic techniques. Scientific models must minimize variation in how therapists apply a particular technique to make sure that instruments measure the same thing. This insures that the evaluation is testing the effectiveness of the particular technique rather than the personal qualities of those who are applying the technique. Therefore, evaluations of the effectiveness of any therapy that conform to traditional scientific methods must use standardized protocols.

EVALUATING MEDICATION THERAPIES

Medication is the class of drugs that are intentionally used to treat illnesses. For centuries chemists and druggists have dispensed herbal and chemical compounds for the relief of nervous complaints (Healy 1997, 15–16). In the United States, until the early years of the twentieth century, coca and opiates were widely used for many nonspecific mental and physical complaints. The first antipsychotic drug, chlorpromazine, was discovered in 1952; this was followed by discovery of the first antidepressant drug, imipramine, in 1957. By the 1960s, physicians and psychiatrists widely prescribed tranquilizers, barbiturates, and bromides to outpatients with mental health problems (Shorter 1997).

An explosive growth in the use of psychotropic medications began in the mid-1980s with the development of the antidepressants called SSRIs (selective serotonin reuptake inhibitors). Within specialized psychiatric practice alone, between 1985 and 1994 the number of visits where an antidepressant was prescribed nearly tripled, from 4.2 million to 11 million visits (Olfson et al. 1998). These antidepressants penetrated not only psychiatric and medical practice but also popular culture and everyday discourse, most notably through Peter Kramer's best-selling *Listening to Prozac* (Kramer 1993). In the past, people who entered therapy might have expected to learn about sexual repression. Now, they are more likely to expect to find out something about their brain chemistry.

Although drugs create changes in the brain, people must interpret the changes in mental sensations that drugs produce. The interpretations people make of these sensations are neither purely universal nor idiosyncratic, but are influenced by cultural systems of meaning (Lin, Poland, and Anderson 1995; Rudorfer 1996). Drug therapies have cultural meanings that, in part, create the conditions for their effectiveness. People now learn about medications through stories and advertisements in print and video media as well as in everyday conversations and they expect that drugs will help them. They have often heard from friends, relatives, the media, and professionals what sorts of psychic and physical changes they will experience from, for example, taking Prozac. These preconceptions affect their actual experiences so that the impact of the drug is not independent of the social expectations connected with the drug. Whether people will start taking a medication and continue its use depends on their interpretations of the sorts of changes it produces (Karp 1996). Medications are not isolated from cultural belief systems but draw upon socially shared systems of meaning that promote their effectiveness. Thus, the impact of drugs could stem from cultural expectations for success, rather than from the biological impact of the drug itself.

Procedures that utilize an experimental treatment and a placebo where neither the patient nor the therapist knows what treatment is administered can in large part isolate the particular effects of a medication. In medical research, the concept of a "placebo" has traditionally referred to a biologically inactive form of medication, although more recently placebo groups often receive an active medication with established effectiveness.[3] Some people are given a pill with an active substance and others an identical pill with no active medication or a different medication. Ideally, random allocation selects which subjects are in the experimental and which in the placebo group. Most medication trials are "double-blind," meaning that neither subjects nor therapists know who ingests the test drug and who gets the placebo. When two groups of subjects think they are receiving the same treatment but only one group actually gets the treatment, the specific effect of the treatment can in principle be isolated.

The use of placebos to evaluate medical treatments originated around 1945 (Pepper 1945; Shepherd 1993). In the United States, placebo trials were mandated for psychotropic medications in 1962 (Healy 1997). At this time the Food and Drug Administration was authorized to approve only drugs, including psychoactive drugs, that could demonstrate efficacy in placebo-controlled, double-blind trials. Drugs could not go onto the market until they were proven to be effective agents for the treatment of specific disorders, although once approved they could be used to treat other disorders. Double-blind, randomized placebo controls quickly became the major method of establishing legitimacy for medical treatments

Double-blind, randomized placebo trials of medications can help separate how much clinical improvement results from the medication itself and how much from other factors such as cultural expectations, regression to the mean, patient or physician preconceptions, the particular type of doctor-patient relationship, or the spontaneous remission of symptoms. The extent to which cultural expectations influence effectiveness is controlled in placebo trials because on average both people who receive the placebo and those who receive the test medication have the same expectations of improvement. The placebo group also provides a control for factors such as the tendency for many symptoms to improve over time, the attention people get from participating in the research project, and the benefits of repeated assessments (Klerman et al. 1994). Any added improvement of the treated group compared to the placebo should be due to the actual impact of the drug, rather than to the expectations attached to its use. Thus, the difference between placebo and medicated groups occurs after controls for the most probable spurious effects of therapy. Finally, randomization of subjects into treatment and control groups is sensible because the brains on which medications work should not differ across subject groups. Success rates due to placebo effects are thus subtracted from success rates due to a medication to obtain the true rate of recovery due to the medication.

The standardization of technique that scientific methodology demands thus fits studies of the effectiveness of medication. Because medication acts on brains, aspects of the personality of the therapist and the interaction between therapists and clients should not have major impacts on the effectiveness of medications. Drugs prescribed by cold and aloof physicians should be just as effective as those prescribed by warm and sympathetic dispensers.[4] Standardizing the administration and dosage of medication does not violate the principles of medication therapies but enhances the purity of the evaluation. Therefore, standard principles of medical research are suited to the evaluation of medication therapies.

Results of Medication Studies   Double-blind placebo trials of medication are developed from the assumption that a particular condition is treatable with a specific drug. This assumption holds for most medical conditions. For example, penicillin cures staphylococcal infections and insulin controls the symptoms of diabetes. The model of specificity was imported from medicine to become the governing standard for psychoactive drugs (Healy 1997).

Research about the efficacy of medication shows that antipsychotic medications treat particular kinds of disorders and so generally conform to the principle of specificity. Since the development of the phenothiazines in 1952 thousands of studies, including many double-blind placebo studies, show that these medications do produce more improvement in symptoms among schizophrenics than placebo treatment or treatment with other medications.[5] The phenothiazines, however, control the positive symptoms of schizophrenia better than the negative symptoms and produce severe side effects in many users (Breier et al. 1994). More recently, clozapine has proven effective in helping both the positive and the negative symptoms of schizophrenia with fewer of the side effects associated with the phenothiazines. Studies of the effects of clozapine establish that positive effects are particularly strong for severely treatment resistant individuals as well as for more moderately symptomatic schizophrenic outpatients (Kane et al. 1988; Breier et al. 1994). Although clozapine does not work for all persons with schizophrenia, it does reduce symptoms and postpone relapses more than older antipsychotic medications.[6]

Schizophrenia, but not other conditions, responds to the phenothiazines and clozapine. Overall, there is little doubt that these medications are "antischizophrenic" agents, not general tranquilizers. Likewise, bipolar conditions respond favorably to particular medications (Cade 1949; Schou et al. 1954; Gershon and Yuwiler 1960). Since 1954 lithium, a naturally occurring element, has been used to relieve the symptoms of bipolar disorders. As with the antischizophrenic medications, lithium only produces positive changes in bipolar patients and bipolar patients often only respond to the class of lithium-related drugs.

Thus, studies of the way medication works with the major psychoses show parallels with the model of specific diseases: different disorders respond distinctly to different medications (Klerman 1989). The phenothiazines and clozapine help control the symptoms of schizophrenia and lithium those of manic-depression, but neither drug works well with other conditions. Although these findings are widely used to justify the categorical system of diagnostic psychiatry, in fact they are the exceptions, not the rule, for how psychotropic medications generally work.

The findings of effectiveness studies of drugs for nonpsychotic conditions differ from those for psychotic disorders. Two findings stand out from research on the way medication alters symptoms of commonly occurring disorders such as depression, generalized anxiety, panic disorders, obsessive-compulsive conditions, anorexia, and many other disorders as well as general distress. The first is that a wide range of different kinds of drugs act to relieve symptoms of a broad variety of different kinds of nonpsychotic conditions. Although the SSRIs were initially heralded as major breakthroughs in the treatment of these conditions, in fact they are no more effective than older classes of antidepressants.[7] Major and minor tranquilizers, tricyclics, MAOIs, and SSRIs all facilitate improvement of symptoms and all have roughly similar degrees of effectiveness (Healy 1997, 261). These classes of drugs often have little to do with each other in a pharmacological sense. None is clearly superior to the others in alleviating distress, and all are helpful in treating the symptoms of various disorders.[8]

Secondly, and most importantly, medications for most nonpsychotic disorders are not illness-specific. The so-called "antidepressants" work equally well for a broad range of disorders including panic, obsessive, and phobic conditions, as well as depressive and anxious states (Healy 1997, 71). They are also widely used for substance use and eating disorders and for general distress among both adults and children. Moreover, these medications are also promoted as ways to enhance the personalities of *normal* people by improving self-esteem, self-confidence, interpersonal relationships, and achievement (see especially Kramer 1993).[9] These drugs are mislabeled as "antidepressants"; their nonspecific effects are more compatible with the terms "antineurotics" or, better, "psychic energizers" (Loomer, Saunders, and Kline 1957; see Healy 1997).

Diagnostic psychiatry claims to classify discrete disease entities. A major justification for the classification of categorical illnesses is that particular conditions will respond to particular medications. Medications do act in disease-specific ways for schizophrenic and bipolar conditions. Yet, the ways psychotic disorders respond to drugs is distinct from the effect of medication on other disorders. "Antidepressant" medications work across a wide range of conditions; they respect neither the borders of different diseases nor the border between disease and nondisease. These findings are more compatible with the assumption that various nonpsychotic conditions are manifestations of a common underlying vulnerability than with the assumption that they are discrete entities. The effects of "antidepressant" medications are more congruent with noncategorical, continuous models of mental symptoms than with distinct diagnoses. Medications can improve most conditions, but they generate this improvement in ways that are inconsistent with the basic tenets of diagnostic psychiatry.

Limitations of Medication Studies   The finding that psychotropic medications improve psychological conditions is routinely used to support not only the scientific basis of diagnostic psychiatry but also more sweeping claims that mental illness is a brain disease that arises from chemical imbalances. The reasoning is that if altering brain chemistry can change disordered conditions then brain chemistry must be a prominent reason why the condition developed in the first place (Kandel 1998). Using this logic, prominent educational campaigns use the effectiveness of drug treatments to equate psychological disorders with "real" biological illnesses (Hirschfeld et al. 1997). These arguments now dominate academic psychiatry, science reporting in the media, and a large part of the culture. There are, however, a number of reasons to doubt this claim. What are the more general implications of the finding that medications, compared to placebos, relieve symptoms in many people?

First, the argument backward from the successful effect of a drug to the cause of a disease is a logical mistake. It does not follow from the fact that drugs produce changes in the brain that the original brain state that is changed constitutes a mental disorder.[10] All drugs, including not only psychotropic medications but also alcohol and illegal substances, create changes in brain chemistry. For example, alcohol often loosens people's inhibitions but these inhibitions do not constitute a mental disorder (Mc-Hugh 1999). In addition, medications affect equally symptoms that arise from many causes, whether marital dissolution, early childhood trauma, or genetic transmission. Aspirin can relieve headaches that arise because of a stressful day at work, but a deficiency of aspirin did not cause the headaches. The assumption that psychic pain has neurological causes because it is alleviated by drug treatment rightly assumes that brain chemistry is associated with particular states of mind. But it wrongly gives these biological events causal priority over nonbiological events. Faulty marriages, disturbing relationships, oppressive work conditions, and the like are common causes of psychological distress. That people who suffer the psychic results of these situations feel better after they take medication does not indicate a particular cause of their distress.

There is another important limitation to what conclusions can be derived from medication studies. The gold standard of these studies, the double-blind randomized placebo trial, creates as pure as possible a situation to show that a medication does better in changing symptoms *than the absence of the medication*. People in distress who take antidepressants usually feel better than those who take pills that contain no medication or that contain a different medication. Something about the medication produces changes in behavior over and above the expectations of patients, personalities of therapists, treatment context, and other expectations that a pill implies in a particular culture. These studies, however, say nothing about whether a medication is superior to alternatives other than medication.

How does the effectiveness of the medication compare with entering a new career, joining a gym, going to religious confession, or returning to school? Would a disorder respond better to an entirely different kind of therapy than to medication (Marks et al. 1993)? Would people who suffer from distressing romantic relationships gain more from entering new relationships than from taking an antidepressant? We cannot, of course, design an experimental study that provides people with new romantic partners, so we don't know. But the finding that receiving a particular medication is superior to not receiving this medication indicates nothing about the effectiveness of medication compared to alternatives such as changing social circumstances or providing other sorts of therapies.

In fact, the ways that medications work *challenge* the basic tenets of diagnostic psychiatry. Medications do act in disease-specific ways for schizophrenic and bipolar conditions. Yet, with other conditions they do not respect the boundaries that diagnostic psychiatry draws. Further, studies that compare the changes in personality that antidepressants produce in presumably healthy people with those experienced by people who have some sort of disorder find that the SSRIs work on the disordered and nondisordered alike (Knutson et al. 1998). Psychotropic medications not only fail to respect particular diagnostic entities but also make no distinction between psychiatric disorders and other behaviors.

Thus, the relief in psychiatric symptoms that medications produce does not indicate that what has been relieved is a specific disease. Indeed, the way psychoactive medication works for nonpsychotic conditions is not consistent with the notion that psychiatric symptoms are indicators of distinct, categorical entities. Rather, their wide-ranging effects are more compatible with the assumption that a common, general vulnerability underlies many psychiatric conditions than with the assumption that different specific disease states produce particular kinds of symptoms. The paradoxical challenge that psychopharmacology presents to diagnostic psychiatry is that the effects of psychoactive medications for nonpsychotic conditions are more congruent with continuous and generalized models of symptoms than with the categorical nosology of diagnostic psychiatry.

EVALUATING PSYCHOTHERAPIES

Although it is prudent to resist the more extreme claims for the benefits of medication, drug treatments do have favorable impacts on many psychological conditions. Does psychotherapy have the same impact? A major problem in addressing this question is that double-blind randomized placebo methods that are suitable for evaluating medications are poorly suited to test the effectiveness of psychotherapies (see especially Seligman 1995).

Medication studies control the potentially powerful effects of cultural expectations by comparing the success rates of groups that receive a placebo with those that receive a test medication, where neither patients nor therapists know which condition they are in. The placebo group provides a benchmark of the number of people who would have recovered without the particular medication (Shepherd 1993). The success rate of the medication stems not from the proportion of patients who took a particular drug that improved but from the portion of successes that occur over and above the rate of recovery in the placebo group. There is, however, nothing in psychotherapeutic research that can compare to the double-blind placebo standard in tests of medication.

A pure double-blind placebo group in tests of psychotherapy is conceptually impossible. In psychotherapy research, neither patients nor therapists can be blinded to whether or not they get a certain treatment: their membership in the treatment group is a component of the therapy. Evaluations of psychotherapy thus face a difficult task in finding an appropriate comparison group that could indicate what results would occur in the absence of therapy. Yet, to maintain scientific legitimacy psychotherapy researchers must find some way to control for recoveries that stem from regression to the mean, from the abating of crises that led people to develop symptoms, or from informal help outside of therapy. Further, these evaluations face the difficult task of controlling for the extent to which recovery stems from a particular form of therapy or from elements that are common to all forms of psychotherapies.

These problems are exacerbated by the fact that psychotherapy shares many of its fundamental elements with other cultural systems of meaning including religion and other belief systems and with natural systems of social support including friendship, kinship, and romantic relationships. All human interaction draws upon verbal symbols to affect behavior. When people deal with suffering, they draw upon encouragement, empathy, and advice from members of their informal networks. A critical question is the extent to which psychotherapy from mental health professionals is more effective than support people can obtain from nonspecific, cultural systems of meaning and from their informal social relationships.

The dilemmas of psychotherapy research do not stop there. The relationship between the therapist and the patient is an essential aspect of psychotherapeutic treatments. The sorts of factors that placebos are intended to control for, such as patient expectations of help, trust in a particular therapist, or the qualities of the interaction between patient and therapist should not be eliminated through the standardization of treatment because they are major *components* of psychotherapy. The reception of the "same" psychotherapy from a cold and aloof or from a warm and empathic therapist is an altogether different experience. Unlike the impact of medications, the practice of psychotherapy is inherently linked to the qualities of the therapist, the patient, and the particular relationship between them (Frank and Frank 1991; Jackson 1999). These aspects cannot be controlled in order to obtain the "real" effect of therapy without distorting the most essential aspects of psychotherapeutic encounters. Standardizing the implementation of psychotherapy does not create a more scientific evaluation; instead it eliminates an essential aspect of therapeutic techniques—the particular relationship that develops between therapist and client. Conformity to traditional scientific models of assessment thus insures that the results of effectiveness studies will have little or no relationship to the actual practice of psychotherapy (Persons 1991; Seligman 1995).[11]

Finally, the randomization of subjects into treatment and control groups that is essential to conventional scientific evaluations fundamentally *distorts* the operation of psychotherapy. People naturally select psychotherapies that are most congruent with their worldviews: feminists seek feminist therapists, Jews enter psychoanalysis, Hispanics select spiritualists.[12] Randomizing Hispanics into feminist therapy, Jews to treatment from spiritualists, or feminists into psychoanalysis is not a sensible way of evaluating the effectiveness of any of these treatments. Randomization ensures that the therapy will *not* be evaluated in the way it actually works in the natural world where people choose therapies that fit their cultural backgrounds.

Paradoxically, the better the study design in terms of traditional scientific methods, the *less* relevant the evaluation will be to the actual practice of psychotherapy. In this respect, the evaluation of psychotherapy fundamentally differs from studies of drug efficacy where the nature of the therapeutic encounter between patient and therapist is much less relevant. Despite the questionable relevance of standardized evaluation techniques, and especially of double-blind, randomized placebo trials, the pressures to produce quantifiable proof of effectiveness became overwhelming in the latter part of the twentieth century (Porter 1995). Psychotherapy researchers were forced to find some analogue to the double-blind, randomized methods of their colleagues who evaluate the effectiveness of medications regardless of how sensible these procedures might be when applied to psychotherapy.

Eysenck's Studies of Psychotherapeutic Effectiveness   Psychoanalysis is the prototype for most psychotherapies in the twentieth century. It developed around a case study method that focused on interpreting individual cases, not around statistical comparisons of large groups of people. In analysis, patients recall fragments of past experiences and attempt to construct coherent narratives from them, an enterprise that does not lend itself to standardized methods of evaluation. The goal of understanding psychodynamic processes in individuals is so vague that even defining improvement is difficult (Grob 1991a).

During the first half of the century, the lack of demonstrated effectiveness of dynamic techniques was not considered a major problem (Hale 1995). Dynamic psychiatrists did not think that the deep understanding of behavior that is at the heart of successful treatment was susceptible of precise measurement. Its practitioners therefore showed little interest in evaluating the effectiveness of analytic methods. This reluctance to evaluate the effectiveness of dynamic treatments proved impossible to sustain.

The first major attack on the resistance of dynamic psychiatry to standardized evaluations came in 1952. In that year the British psychologist Hans Eysenck published a sweeping indictment of the effectiveness of psychoanalytic therapies (Eysenck 1952). Eysenck's review, based on the evaluation of twenty-four studies, became the basis for an explosion of effectiveness research over the following several decades. Eysenck, an opponent of psychoanalysis, examined studies that tried to assess whether psychoanalysis was more likely than alternative forms of therapy to produce positive changes in mental health. At the time of his initial review, virtually no study compared rates of recovery between groups of people treated in psychotherapy with those who had comparable psychological conditions but received no treatment. Eysenck, however, insisted that only studies that compared the proportion of patients who improved because of psychotherapy with the proportion whose symptoms underwent "spontaneous remission"—that is, would have disappeared without therapeutic intervention—could demonstrate the effectiveness of psychotherapy.

Eysenck used two studies as benchmarks of how many patients would have improved in the absence of psychotherapy. The first examined patients who entered the New York state hospital system who were not treated but were discharged as recovered or improved. The second examined insurance claims of disability due to neurosis of patients who received, at most, superficial levels of therapy from general physicians. Both of these studies indicated that about two-thirds of patients with psychiatric difficulties recovered without significant amounts of professional intervention. He then used this two-thirds figure as the comparative standard for the recovery rates of patients in psychotherapy.

Eysenck drew three general conclusions from his review. First, he claimed that rates of recovery among patients treated with psychotherapy did not exceed the rate of spontaneous remission in presumably untreated groups of neurotics. Although a majority of patients in psychotherapy did recover, this number was comparable to the rate that would have recovered anyway without any therapy. Thus, psychotherapy provided no benefits beyond those that would have occurred naturally. Second, psychoanalysis was no more effective than any other form of psychotherapy. Indeed, Eysenck claimed that the particular form of therapy had no effect on recovery rates—none exceeded the rate of spontaneous remission. Third, the only exception to the second claim was that therapies based on behavioral methods had better results than other therapies. Recovery rates in behavioral treatments, which ignored patients' states of mind and focused solely on changing their behaviors, exceeded recovery rates due to psychotherapy or to spontaneous remission. Eysenck concluded that only behavioral methods should be used in the scientific treatment of psychological disorders; psychotherapies and, especially, psychoanalysis were not effective and should not receive public support.

Thirteen years later Eysenck considered the results of those few subsequent studies of psychotherapeutic effectiveness that used control groups, nonsubjective measures of improvement, and measures at more than one point in time (Eysenck 1965). He claimed that his second review reaffirmed his initial conclusions. These scientifically more adequate studies uniformly found that psychotherapy, especially psychoanalysis, did not produce improvement beyond what would be expected in the absence of any therapy. Again, the sole exception was that people treated with behavioral methods based on learning theory more often and more quickly improved than those treated through psychotherapy or those who were not treated at all.

Eysenck's reviews set the agenda for subsequent studies of psychotherapeutic research. These studies deal with three major issues. First, does the success rate of psychotherapy exceed the rate of recovery in comparable untreated populations? Second, do all types of psychotherapies have comparable success rates or are some types better than others? Finally, what is the impact of professional training on therapeutic success?

Is Psychotherapy Effective? Eysenck's highly negative evaluation of psychotherapeutic effectiveness generated a huge subsequent body of research. The meta-analyses Smith and Glass published in 1977 and 1980 are the best-known reviews of this research (Smith and Glass 1977; Smith, Glass, and Miller 1980). Meta-analyses take a large number of studies, place their results on a standardized metric, and average their effects. They then compare the standardized effect on groups in all studies that received a treatment to the standardized effect among all groups that did not receive the treatment. Smith and Glass concluded that their analysis of 375 studies contradicted Eysenck's main conclusion. Their results indicated that members of groups obtaining therapy did better than groups that did not get therapy. The magnitude was such that the average person who received therapy did better than 75 percent of persons in untreated control groups (Smith and Glass 1977). Subsequent studies confirmed that a high proportion of people, often approaching 80 percent, who enter psychotherapy benefited from it. Meta-analyses that only incorporated studies using randomized assignments to treatment and control groups supported the contention that treated groups do better than untreated controls (Landman and Dawes 1982). As Eysenck found, however, subsequent reviews fail to find that the effectiveness of psychoanalytic therapies exceeds that of any other type of therapeutic technique (Fisher and Greenberg 1996; see also Wallerstein 1986; Henry et al. 1994).

Most psychotherapy researchers accept Smith and Glass's central conclusion that a high percentage of patients who enter psychotherapy benefit from it and reject Eysenck's assertion that psychotherapy has no effectiveness (Shapiro and Shapiro 1982; Lipsey and Wilson 1993; Seligman 1995). Indeed, the two-thirds rate of spontaneous remissions Eysenck used as his comparison point for psychotherapeutic effectiveness is highly suspect.[13] Nevertheless, the techniques meta-analyses use to indicate treated groups improve more often than untreated groups are also problematic (Shadish and Sweeney 1991; Omer and Dar 1992; Kazdin and Bass 1989). Foremost is the difficulty of finding an adequate comparison group against which to judge the effectiveness of psychotherapeutic treatment.

A common method of obtaining a control group is to divide people who have sought therapy into those who are randomly assigned to therapy and those who are put on a waiting list for treatment (Robinson, Berman; and Neimeyer 1990; Lambert and Bergin 1994; Greenberg, Elliott, and Lietaer 1994). The wait-listed group presumably provides a control for the treated group because it is composed of people who have comparable levels of distress and of motivation to use professional help to get well. The rates of recovery in this group are used to show how often treated groups would have recovered in the absence of treatment. Meta-analyses do indicate that people who receive psychotherapy have higher recovery rates than those who are wait-listed for therapy but do not receive it (Robinson, Berman, and Neimeyer 1990).

Yet, it is unlikely that wait-list groups provide the kind of controls for recovery in psychotherapy that placebos do in studies of medication. People who seek therapy are strongly motivated to get well. This could exacerbate the difference between those who are given therapy and those who are wait-listed because the expectations of the former group are fulfilled but those of the latter group are not (Lambert and Bergin 1994). In addition, entering therapy gives people a sense of hopefulness and optimism that can itself help alleviate common symptoms such as despair and helplessness. In contrast, placement on a wait list can exacerbate feelings of despondency. Further, it is highly unlikely that wait-listed patients do nothing while waiting for therapy. Instead, they may often pursue a wide variety of strategies to alter their condition, including high rates of self-medication and substance abuse that may compound their problems. Most are also likely to seek outside advice and counseling about their problems, some of which is likely to be good, some not so good. It is possible that these coping strategies, rather than the absence of professional therapy, are responsible for the lower rates of recovery of wait-listed groups of people who seek but do not receive psychotherapy.

Other studies use other alternatives to obtain analogues to placebos in medication trials.[14] The best-known, most ambitious, and most important study of the effectiveness of psychotherapy is the NIMH Treatment of Depression Collaborative Research program. This study involved a large group of researchers at several different sites in the 1980s (Elkin et al. 1985, 1989; Imber et al. 1990; Elkin 1994). Its major purpose was to compare the relative effectiveness of interpersonal therapy and cognitive-behavioral therapy. Interpersonal therapy relied on Klerman's and Weissman's method of helping patients identify their interpersonal problems and improve their relationships with others (Klerman et al. 1984). Cognitive behavioral treatment used Beck's approach, which focuses on changing clients' distorted perceptions and beliefs about themselves and the world (Beck et al. 1979).

The study was developed to approximate a "pure" scientific experiment with carefully delineated diagnoses, highly standardized treatments, and highly skilled therapists. It addressed the critical question of finding a comparison group for psychotherapeutic treatment by using a group of patients treated with imipramine hydrochloride, a tricyclic antidepressant that was the most common antidepressant at the time of the study. The medication group also received minimal clinical support. In addition, to ensure that improvement in all treated conditions was not due to the common factor associated with raising hopes and expectations of improvement, a placebo group was created that received a placebo pill and minimal clinical support and encouragement. The study randomly assigned a total of 239 patients with "pure" cases of major depression to one or another of the cognitive-behavioral, interpersonal, drug, or placebo groups at three research sites (Pittsburgh, Oklahoma City, and Washington, D.C.). A total of twenty-eight carefully selected and experienced therapists participated in the study. In an attempt to control for factors such as the effect on treatment of personalities of therapists, all groups used carefully standardized manuals with specific treatment protocols.

Results for subjects who completed the sixteen-week treatment schedule indicate that all four groups, including the placebo group, improved over the treatment period on all outcome measures and in all sites, although the medication group improved more quickly than the other groups. Results from longer-term term follow-up at six, twelve, and eighteen months after treatment showed few differences across the four treatment conditions (Shea et al. 1992). Differences in rates of relapse across the four conditions were small. "Although there was significant improvement from pre- to post-treatment for all treatment conditions," the principal investigator summarized, "there were surprisingly few significant differences among the treatments at termination" (Elkin 1994, 130). The absence of differences was due more to the good outcome for patients in the placebo condition than to the poor performance of the psychotherapies. Indeed, patients in the condition of clinical management with placebo pill had the lowest rates of relapse of any group (Elkin 1994, 128).

Another major finding of the study, however, was a clear difference in effectiveness of treatments across subjects with varying severity of psychiatric conditions. For severely depressed patients, medication was clearly better and placebo treatment clearly worse. In contrast, less severely depressed patients showed comparable responses to all treatments, including the placebo condition. The finding that medication is clearly more effective than psychotherapy for more severely depressed patients but not for more mildly depressed patients conforms to the results of many other studies (WPA Dysthymia Working Group 1995; Katon et al. 1995; Frank et al. 1990).[15]

The most elaborate study of psychotherapeutic effectiveness ever done, then, shows that, for persons who are not severely depressed, a placebo treatment that consists of a twenty- to thirty-minute-per-week discussion with an experienced psychotherapist leads to a reduction of symptoms comparable to drug therapy or to more elaborate forms of psychotherapy. In addition, all four groups, including the placebo group, showed significant improvement from pre- to post-treatment. A meta-analysis of treatments for depression that indicates no significant differences between groups that receive psychotherapy and those that receive a placebo or general attention but not therapy also confirms these findings (Robinson, Berman, and Neimeyer 1990).[16]

These findings would seem to indicate that mildly depressed persons benefit as much from sensible clinical management of depression and generic social support as from either medication or therapy (Healy 1997, 251).[17] Neither interpersonal nor cognitive-behavioral psychotherapy provided more protection against relapse for less depressed patients than did the placebo and neither helped seriously depressed patients more than medication. These findings are congruent with the notion that many people with relatively mild symptoms of depression suffer from distress that is rooted in social experiences and that can be alleviated through basic forms of social support.

Are Some Types of Psychotherapies More Effective Than Other Types? One conclusion of many studies of psychotherapeutic effectiveness, including the NIMH Collaborative Study, is that different types of psychotherapies have equivalent effects. Where researchers differ is on whether all forms of psychotherapy are equally effective or equally ineffective. Eysenck drew the latter conclusion, that no form of psychotherapy is effective. In contrast, a well-known survey of the comparative impact of psychotherapies derived exactly the opposite conclusion, which it called the "dodo bird" effect: "everyone has won and all must have prizes" (Luborsky, Singer, and Luborsky 1975). This analysis found little or no difference in the effectiveness of group vs. individual approaches, time-limited vs. time-unlimited approaches, client-centered vs. traditional therapies, or behavior therapy vs. psychotherapy. The authors also find an "amazing" lack of match between types of treatments, types of patients, and levels of effectiveness (Luborsky, Singer, and Luborsky 1975, 1004). There were only two exceptions. One is that psychotherapy combined with medical treatment was better than medical treatment alone for people with psychosomatic symptoms. The other was that, as Eysenck found, behavioral therapy is the best treatment for circumscribed problems such as phobias. "All of the forms of psychotherapy benefit all types of patients," Luborsky and colleagues summarize, "yet not one of the psychotherapies, even dynamic, offers much evidence of special benefits for specific types of patients" (Luborsky et al. 1993, 541; see also Fisher and Greenberg 1996).

Smith, Glass, and Miller's meta-analysis also concluded that similar proportions of patients improved regardless of the nature of the psychotherapy they receive (Smith, Glass, and Miller 1980; see also Stein and Lambert 1984; Dawes 1994; Seligman 1995). Likewise, the NIMH Collaborative Study found no differences between cognitive and interpersonal therapies (Elkin et al. 1989).[18] Comparable findings hold for the treatment of alcoholism, where equivalent recovery rates are found among inpatients and outpatients, brief and extended treatment, and various types of treatment (Miller and Hester 1989). The lack of variation in effectiveness between psychotherapeutic techniques, with the exception of behavioral techniques for circumscribed problems, is a consistent finding (Fisher and Greenberg 1996).[19]

What explains the finding that all styles of therapy are equally effective? Improvement in psychotherapy might arise from generalized social support that therapists provide troubled people rather than from anything having to do with a particular technique (Frank and Frank 1991). Social support creates feelings of being valued, understood, and helped. These feelings are generalized benefits of supportive social interaction, not benefits that stem from particular psychotherapies. While both its clients and its practitioners believe that they are engaging in a very special sort of relationship, the beneficial aspects of this relationship could indicate the generic value of social support, not the value of a particular kind of psychotherapy.

If psychotherapeutic effectiveness stems from generic processes of social support, then a factor common to all types of therapy accounts for their effectiveness. A helping relationship with a therapist would account for why there are neither winners nor losers in the contest for the best psychotherapy (Luborsky, Singer, and Luborsky 1975). The provision of social support is a general factor that cuts across all therapeutic styles. The common aspects of therapy are more consequential than the differences between therapies for generating positive changes.

It seems possible to test the extent to which psychotherapeutic effectiveness rests on generic rather than specific grounds. As noted above, the gold standard of medical research, the double-blind placebo trial, allows researchers to separate the real effects of a medication from benefits that occur solely from expectations of help. Because a true double-blind placebo trial of psychotherapy is impossible, the concept of a placebo has a different meaning in psychotherapeutic than in medical research. In psychotherapeutic research, placebo groups are those that receive generic attention and support but no specific type of therapy. The proportion of patients who recover in placebo groups, over and above the proportion who recover with no treatment, indicates how *common* factors shared by all forms of therapeutic interventions, such as empathy, warmth, and encouragement, influence outcomes (Frank and Frank 1991). Thus, in psychotherapy, a placebo effect does not indicate the illusion of help, as it does in tests of medications; instead it indicates the presence of a common factor of social support that cuts across all forms of treatment.

Lambert and Bergin's summary of various meta-analyses shows little difference between patients who receive general placebo treatment and those who receive specific forms of psychotherapy: the typical patient in psychotherapy is better off than 79 percent of people who get no treatment (Lambert and Bergin 1994, 150). Yet, the typical placebo patient is better off than 66 percent of controls not getting treatment. These findings indicate that a powerful factor accounting for the success of psychotherapy is the common effect of entering a therapeutic relationship, regardless of the particular character of that relationship.

The findings regarding the importance of the placebo effect in psychotherapy indicate that beneficial psychotherapeutic effects need not involve intense time and effort. Recall the findings of the NIMH Collaborative Study that used a placebo condition that combined a nonmedicated pill with general support and encouragement (Elkin et al. 1989). People in this placebo condition who were not severely depressed did as well as those who received more intensive psychotherapy or cognitive-behavioral therapy. All forms of psychotherapy may work, but they work because of their common supportive nature, not because of the particular systems of knowledge they use (Frank and Frank 1991).

Whatever common factors produce this placebo effect also account for why the type of therapist, type of therapy, and length of treatment make little difference in the effectiveness of psychotherapy. The most likely explanation for the equivalent effectiveness of psychotherapies is that all successful therapies provide social support by creating a warm and empathetic relational context.[20] When these elements are present, therapy will succeed; when they are absent, therapy fails. Therapists who possess these qualities, regardless of their allegiance to a particular mode of psychotherapy, will be successful. According to Jackson, the qualities for effective psychological healing are: "a respectful and interested way of listening; a readily felt trustworthiness; a compassionate and sympathetic response to those who suffer; a capacity for arousing and sustaining hope; and a calm response to disturbing or frightening clinical states" (Jackson 1999, 392). The relatively random distribution of therapists with good interpersonal skills into various forms of treatment may account for the finding that all psychotherapeutic schools are equally effective. The generic aspect behind the effectiveness of all psychotherapies also might explain another finding of psychotherapy research: professionals are not more effective clinicians than nonprofessionals.

Are Professionals Better Therapists Than Others? A third general conclusion of studies of psychotherapeutic effectiveness is that professional training has little impact on the success of therapists. Smith, Glass, and Miller's review indicated that therapists with Ph.D.'s, M.D.'s, or no advanced degree at all produced equivalent results (Smith, Glass, and Miller 1980). Berman and Norton's comprehensive review confirmed the irrelevance of professional credentials: professionally trained therapists and paraprofessionals had comparable levels of effectiveness (Berman and Norton 1985). This finding held across all types of problems, all types of treatments, and all types of outcomes. Other reviews likewise conclude that the outcomes of therapists with varying training do not differ (Stein and Lambert 1984; Luborsky et al. 1986). Considerable research indicates that neither the content of therapies, the particular systems of knowledge, nor the type of professional training of therapists produce therapeutic success. Neither does experience, type of degree, nor disciplinary allegiance predict therapeutic effectiveness.

The finding that professionals don't have higher success rates than others would follow if psychotherapy is a generic form of social support. The common qualities of effective therapists have to do with their empathy, warmth, and genuineness (Frank and Frank 1991). These qualities do not stem from formal knowledge systems or from specific techniques and so cannot be taught in clinical training programs. Indeed, peer evaluations of psychotherapists focus on their qualities as people rather than on their technical expertise (Luhrmann 2000, 182). Paradoxically, protocols that force clinicians to use standardized techniques in order to compare different types of therapy eliminate precisely the most important component of therapeutic success—the personal qualities of the therapist. Warm, insightful, and intuitive laypersons should be successful psychotherapists while highly trained therapists who are cold and aloof should not be. No amount of coursework, training, or experience can create the qualities that lead to successful psychotherapy.

Psychotherapy usually succeeds because distressed people obtain a form of social support that they value and expect to help them. The effectiveness of social support depends on whether providers are insightful, empathetic, warm, and genuine. Therapists cannot learn these qualities in programs of professional training. Various kinds of professionals do not differ from each other or from nonprofessionals because successful therapy depends more on intuitive than on professional knowledge. Psychotherapy does work but its success stems from mechanisms comparable to those that shape other forms of supportive interaction. The best predictor of the effectiveness of therapy is the quality of the therapeutic relationship (Orlinsky, Grawe, and Parks 1994). This is what we would expect if therapy were a generic type of supportive relationship.

CONCLUSION

Psychotropic medications effectively treat serious mental disorders. Indeed, it is irresponsible to overlook drug treatments as one component of care for the seriously mentally ill (Klerman 1990). The primary needs of persons with serious mental illness lie in obtaining the social and economic resources that enhance their quality of life. But psychotropic medications provide the psychological stability that allows the seriously mentally ill to live adequate lives in the community. The benefits of psychotherapy with the seriously mentally ill, however, have yet to be demonstrated (Klerman et al. 1994).

For nonpsychotic disorders, the most common criticism of medications is that they are palliatives that ignore the more fundamental underlying problems that lead to particular symptoms. In this view, psychotherapy, not medication, must address people's basic problems. Psychotherapeutic approaches to mental health, however, do not seem to be better than biological approaches.[21] The effects of current medications may be overstated but they help many people and hurt few. Medications are not forced upon unwilling clients because of the interests of drug companies and third-party payers. The current craze for psychoactive medications benefits pharmaceutical manufacturers, but it persists because consumers find fast and easy relief for distress with antidepressant drugs.

There is nothing wrong with using medications to make people suffering from problems in living feel better. In modern society, and perhaps in all societies, bad marriages and other interpersonal relationships as well as social and economic conditions underlie much psychological distress. Treatment with medication may be preferable to letting people suffer until their social situation has changed. It is not necessary to embrace the more sweeping claims of the proponents of psychoactive medications to advocate their usefulness in addressing many forms of distress. The fundamental causes for much or even most psychic distress lie in social relationships and social organization, but medication therapies provide practical ways of alleviating the distress that arises from stressful social circumstances.[22]

What should be resisted are not the benefits of medication but the broader ideology of its proponents that these benefits entail biological causes of human behavior. Psychiatrists and their allies increasingly promote the view that chemical imbalances account for both why mental disorders emerge and how they are best controlled. Neurochemistry is one aspect of a far more complex reality. The biological and cultural success of the antidepressants, however, is compatible with many alternative interpretations. Indeed, future historians of early twenty-first-century psychiatry might ask: "why didn't they realize that poor social relationships, not neurochemicals, created distress?"

Specific medications help schizophrenia and bipolar disorders and the antidepressants alleviate the distress of most other conditions. In addition, cognitive-behavioral approaches have clear benefits for circumscribed problems. As well, time-limited, structured forms of psychotherapy are helpful for many problems. What is the appropriate role of the longer-term psychotherapies based on talk between patients and therapists? Unlike medication, which works better than its absence, there is little evidence indicating that psychotherapy produces better results than generic social support. Psychotherapy, of course, should be available to people who think they benefit from it. Whether their private or public insurance plans should pay for this form of social support is another question. It may be that the psychotherapies should be regarded as forms of social support or techniques to achieve self-improvement that seekers could voluntarily purchase just as they join health clubs, singles groups, and sports teams.

Diagnostic psychiatry encompasses an uneasy mixture of two radically different approaches to the treatment of mental disorder: drug treatment and psychotherapy. With the exception of psychotic mental illnesses, research indicates that the ways both types of therapies change symptoms are incongruent with the assumptions of diagnostic psychiatry. Both drug and talk therapies work generically across most of the discrete entities of the

DSM. The way in which drug treatments affect symptoms usually undermines, rather than reinforces, the basic principles of diagnostic psychiatry because these treatments are generic rather than illness-specific. Likewise, the impact of psychotherapy stems from its general provision of social support rather than from specific techniques.

One important reason (if not the most important) for distinguishing different psychological disorders is to specify different treatments for different conditions. Yet, the comparable impact of "antidepressants" for quite different conditions seemingly indicates that highly specific diagnostic classifications are not useful for treatment purposes. Similarly, the way psychotherapies work is also not specific to distinct disorders but is generalized across diagnostic conditions. If treatments are nonspecific, the major justification for specific diagnoses collapses. The way therapies work is more congruent with the view that most mental disorders are not discrete diseases but variants of nonspecific psychic conditions and human problems.

Conclusion
MENTAL ILLNESSES
AS SOCIAL CONSTRUCTIONS

Prototypical classifications of mental illnesses are generally, and perhaps even universally, rooted in extreme deviations from normal psychological functioning. Throughout history, social groups have judged that certain kinds of phenomena lie outside the boundaries of sanity and have labeled these conditions "mental illnesses" regardless of the particular names they call them or the particular frameworks they use to classify them (Horwitz 1982a; Jackson 1986). Historically, however, these classifications have been applied to only a small number of severely disturbed conditions. This limited use of mental illness labels has now changed beyond recognition. The variety of conditions currently regarded as mental illnesses, the large numbers and wide distribution of people who presumably suffer from these illnesses, and the great number of professionals who treat them are unprecedented. The reasons mental illnesses have proliferated in modern life stem from specific social and historical circumstances and from the interests of particular groups that benefit from classifying psychological conditions as states of illness.

By the time the diagnostic revolution embodied in the DSM-III emerged in 1980, mental health professionals had already pathologized a broad and heterogeneous range of human conditions and influential groups had already accepted these professionals as the socially legitimate experts entitled to define and treat these conditions. Over the first two-thirds of the twentieth century, the model of dynamic psychiatry broadened the definition of the pathological from the psychoses to encompass conditions such as anxiety, hysteria, sexual perversions, and character disorders (Roazen 1992; Rieff 1961; Lunbeck 1994; Hale 1995; Grob 1991a). In dynamic psychiatry, these pathologies were not sharply defined entities but indeterminate manifestations of underlying unconscious mechanisms (Freud 1960 [1924], 1964

[1933]). Common processes led to both neurotic and presumably normal behaviors and so the pathological was continuous with, rather than distinct from, the ordinary. Dynamic clinicians sought the causes of psychological disturbances in repressed intrapsychic experiences and their treatments in explorations of the inner depths of the psyche.

The major initial appeal of dynamic psychiatry was to Jews, bohemians, intellectuals, and artists who used dynamic explanations to focus on their inner lives and to reject the claims of traditional moral systems. These clients found in the tenets of dynamic psychiatry not only cures for their particular symptoms but also solutions to their interpersonal problems and answers to their quest for meaning in life (Rieff 1966; Grob 1991a). By midcentury, such explanations had spread beyond an intellectual elite to exert considerable influence on mainstream culture (Hale 1995; Shorter 1997). Dynamic practitioners came to treat people who were dissatisfied with their careers, their marriages, their lives, and their selves as well as involuntary clienteles of delinquents, criminals, alcoholics, and other deviants (Lunbeck 1994; Jones 1999).

The loose classification system of dynamic psychiatry, which emphasized indistinct and vague unconscious processes, was suitable during a period in which the mental health professions did not require a rationalized, quantitative system of thought about mental disorder. Once professional, economic, and organizational circumstances changed, however, the practical weaknesses of the dynamic system became apparent. In particular, dynamic classifications were not amenable to precise systems of measurement. For psychiatrists, this weakness jeopardized their central claim to legitimacy as members of a medical specialty and rendered them vulnerable to clinical psychologists and social workers who were as capable as physicians in providing dynamic forms of treatment (Abbott 1988). In addition, the outcomes of dynamic treatment were difficult to measure, a defect that became more pressing after third-party funding for therapy became widespread and stimulated demands for accountability (Wilson 1993). Dynamic treatments also gave short shrift to the use of medications, a growing problem as various tranquilizing drugs came to be commonly prescribed for a variety of ills. They also had little to offer persons who suffered from psychotic disorders, a limitation that became especially important once persons with serious mental illnesses left mental institutions and entered community settings during the 1960s and 1970s. How much insight into human behavior the system of dynamic psychiatry offers is controversial.[1] What is certain is that the dynamic model of mental disorder became unsuitable both for maintaining professional legitimacy and for adapting to the changed social and economic circumstances of the psychiatric profession.

The replacement of the vague, opaque, and continuous unconscious mechanisms of the dynamic system with the incommensurate system of precisely defined, symptom-based disease entities in the DSM-III was not gradual; it was a total transformation of the system of psychiatric thought over a short period of time (Wilson 1993; Kirk and Kutchins 1992; McCarthy and Gerring 1994). In contrast to the very general classifications of disorder found in dynamic psychiatry, which are based on underlying explanatory mechanisms, diagnostic psychiatry defines diseases through the presence of overt symptoms, regardless of their causes. It regards diseases as discrete natural entities that exist in the brain and that generate the particular symptoms a person displays. These qualities of diseases allow them to become the objects of scientific claims that can be made apart from the social contexts and personalities in which they arise (e.g., Sabshin 1990; Maxmen 1985; Kendler 1990). Such abstractions of diseases from particular personality dynamics would be unthinkable in the dynamic model. Furthermore, the diagnostic model seeks the primary causes of disorder in disturbed brains rather than in dysfunctional childhoods. It therefore moved the treatments of disorders from intrapsychic explorations to searches for the best medication to relieve symptoms.

Shifting the focus of study to distinct diseases resolved the crisis that had imperiled the legitimacy of the psychiatric profession during the 1970s. If psychiatrists were to be treated as "real" physicians, then they needed to treat "real" diseases. Symptom-based diseases provided researchers with entities that could be separated from particular persons and contexts, reliably measured, compared across sites, and quantified.[2] When conditions are formulated as diseases rather than as unconscious mechanisms, problems in human relationships, or deviant behaviors, psychiatrists can also participate in high-status areas of neuroscience such as brain imaging and linkage analysis instead of being relegated to the study of personal troubles. A classification system based on discrete diseases that were analogous to the diseases treated in other areas of medicine enhanced the status claims of psychiatrists at a time when their position as physicians was extremely shaky.

The initial proponents of diagnostic psychiatry were a group of research-oriented psychiatrists who were able to capture the most powerful positions in their profession during the 1970s (Kirk and Kutchins 1992). They defeated their psychoanalytic opponents in political battles and replaced the dynamic paradigm with a model that relied on symptom-based categorical diseases (Bayer and Spitzer 1985). This group, committed to the norms of biomedicine, had a legitimate need to construct disorders that were measurable, quantifiable, and suitable as objects of research. They were also able to transform the agenda of the National Institute of Mental Health, the major resource for funding research about mental illness, from efforts that involved large-scale community changes to studies that featured the new categorical illnesses as their objects (Kirk 1999; Baldessarini 2000; Kolb, Frazier, and Sirovatka 2000). Biological, epidemiological, and economic studies of specific diseases have dominated the research agenda of the NIMH ever since.

Although a classification system based on discrete diagnostic categories arose because of the needs of research psychiatrists, it quickly spread well beyond the research psychiatrists to clinicians and to the broader culture. Discrete mental disorders had a number of qualities that were more appealing to clinicians than the blurry continua of the dynamic model. In particular, discrete mental disorders reclassified the loosely defined psychoneuroses of the clients of dynamic psychiatry into specific, categorical disorders. This reclassification fit the needs of clinicians who were receiving an increasing amount of their income from third parties (Wilson 1993). Insurers would be more likely to reimburse professionals for treating diseases than for analyzing unconscious mechanisms or solving generic human problems. Quantifiable disease conditions thus provided both administratively useful knowledge that enhanced the rationality of payment systems and financial incentives for clinicians to embrace categorical disorders (Grob 1991a; Hale 1995). Furthermore, the *large* number of categorical disorders in the DSM maintained the entire array of personal troubles and disruptive behaviors that clinicians were already treating, however foreign the logic of symptom-based disease conditions initially was to them. Most clinicians, as well as researchers, came to embrace the symptom-based logic of diagnostic psychiatry.

The disease-based classification system became dominant not only because of intraprofessional concerns but also because of the interests of a variety of extraprofessional groups. The pharmaceutical industry has had an especially important role in promoting the reclassification of a broad range of conditions as specific diseases (Valenstein 1998; Raghunathan 1999; Cottle 1999). In particular, pharmaceutical companies can only gain approval for and market products that are seen as treating discrete disease entities (Healy 1997). Drug companies can market Viagra to treat erectile dysfunctions but not to enhance sexual performance, can promote Ritalin to address the symptoms of attention deficit disorder but not to calm behavioral problems, can claim that Paxil alleviates social anxiety disorders but not shyness. Although the conditions that the tremendously profitable products of drug companies deal with may actually be general human problems, they must be formulated as diseases to become the objects of drug treatments. Immense print and televised advertising campaigns now transmit images of these specific mental illness entities to the public. These campaigns have been wildly successful: three of the seven most prescribed drugs of any sort are now mood elevators.[3] Both the psychiatric and lay communities participate in a shared culture of using medications to treat distressing conditions.

Moreover, drug companies have a major interest in showing not only that generic human problems are diseases but also that these diseases are widespread in the population. For example, various estimates from community surveys indicate that 19 million people have generalized anxiety disorders, 19 million suffer from social phobias, and more than 19 million have major depressions.[4] Because they use the same symptom-based logic as the DSM, these surveys encompass within their definitions of mental disorders persons whose symptoms stem from a variety of stressful social arrangements and freely chosen behaviors, as well as those who suffer from internal dysfunctions. They thus invariably generate large numbers of persons who presumably have specific mental disorders, providing a valuable rhetorical tool for expanding the market for various medications (Robins et al. 1984; Kessler et al. 1994; Regier et al. 1998; Laumann, Paik, and Rosen 1999; USDHHS 1999).

The acceptance of specific mental diseases has spread to the broader culture not only through the marketing efforts of pharmaceutical companies but also through the efforts of advocacy groups. Although empirical studies focus on the rare cases when social movements opposed including particular diagnostic categories such as homosexuality and PMS in the DSM, in fact the most powerful advocacy groups concerned with mental illness have been among the most fervent supporters of diagnostic psychiatry (McLean 1990). Groups such as the National Alliance for the Mentally Ill embrace the idea that mental illnesses are specific diseases because of the moral advantages of disease classifications. These classifications not only name things but also instruct people how they ought to act toward the objects so classified (Conrad and Schneider 1992). Conditions that are considered diseases are assumed to arise because of biological processes the affected individuals cannot control (Parsons 1951, 428–79). Unlike people who intentionally violate social norms or who suffer from problems in living, people who have diseases are the victims, not the agents, of their conditions. Treatment, not punishment or stigmatization, is considered the appropriate response to them.

Powerful advocacy groups argue vehemently that mental illness is a brain disease (Hatfield 1987). This view allows them to equate the schizophrenic and bipolar conditions with "real" diseases of the body, both decreasing the stigma of these conditions and deflecting parental responsibility for why their children became disturbed. Estimates that show how widespread in the population mental disorders are also provide advocacy groups with a tool to reduce the distance between the mentally ill and the normal and the stigma accorded mental illness. The influence these groups have attained in both legislative bodies and in the NIMH has been a major force in promoting the disease-based view of diagnostic psychiatry (see especially USDHHS 1999).

The embrace of diagnostic psychiatry has gone well beyond particular social movements concerned with mental illnesses to large segments of the lay community. Depression, alcohol abuse, eating disorders, panic attacks, and the like are all now widely seen as mental diseases. They often form the basis for cover stories in national magazines, themes of television talk shows and series, best-selling books, and science reporting in the news media.[5] These popular outlets raise public consciousness of these disorders and can help shape the symptoms of troubled people to conform to the disease conditions they read about and view. These template images of disease can lead individuals to seek professional help for these conditions and/or to join one of the many self-help groups that focus on the particular diagnostic categories of the DSM. Ultimately, the classification system of diagnostic psychiatry can create the entities it claims to represent (Fleck 1979 [1935]; Zerubavel 1997). Diagnoses that initially arose to provide researchers a useful tool for the reliable study of standardized sets of symptoms eventually become seemingly real conditions that people believe they suffer from.

Mental health professionals rarely impose labels of mental illness on resistant clients; instead, professionals and clients alike are more likely to participate in a shared culture of medicalized mental disorders.[6] The categorical illnesses of diagnostic psychiatry provide people with coherent explanations and point to specific treatments for troubling conditions. Most generally, biological explanations of problems, including personal problems, have far greater cultural credence in contemporary Western societies than they did for most of the twentieth century. Conceptions that define mental illnesses as stemming from chemical imbalances or from brain diseases are congruent with broader intellectual trends that emphasize biological factors and downplay the role of social conditions in explaining human behavior.[7] For many, the conviction that they suffer from a chemical imbalance that can be corrected through drug therapy defines their problem in a way that not only excuses them from blame but also offers them the hope of a quick and easy cure (McHugh 1999). For others, the notion of a brain disease can explain underachievement, excuse misbehavior, or provide an alternative to punishment (Conrad and Schneider 1992; Parsons 1951; Fingarette 1988). Occasionally, labels such as "learning disability" can lead to special considerations. Paradoxically, people who have the psychotic conditions that most warrant the use of disease categories are the most likely to fervently *reject* these classifications (Estroff 1981; Kaufmann 1999).

Mental illnesses, as they are construed at the beginning of the twenty-first century, have little resemblance to older stereotypes of madness but instead are seen as common, pervasive, and ubiquitous. Nor do they resemble the neurotic conditions that dynamic psychiatry featured. Over a short time, not only researchers, but also clinicians, other groups concerned with the response to mental illnesses, clients of mental health professionals, and the general public have come to consider mental illnesses as disease entities. Although some opposition to mental illness classifications arises from time to time, in general the categories of diagnostic psychiatry have gained broad acceptance in educational, occupational, political, and cultural institutions.[8] This acceptance, however, results less from advances in the scientific understanding of mental disorders that disease classifications have brought about than from the many advantages these classifications have for a variety of professional and lay groups (McCarthy and Gerring 1994).

THE LIMITS OF SOCIAL CONSTRUCTIONISM

The social constructionist view can explain how a medicalized categorical system of mental illnesses emerged and has persisted during a particular historical era, but it cannot evaluate the adequacy of this classification system. Because disease classifications are contingent upon social factors does not mean that mental disorders are reducible to historically specific categories or to whatever conditions are defined as such in various social groups (Danziger 1990; Aronowitz 1998). Only criteria that stem from outside a social constructionist perspective can judge the validity of any particular system of classification.

The various diagnostic conditions in the current DSM did not enter the manual because they meet any conceptual standards determining what are valid mental disorders. Instead, these diverse conditions are classified as "mental disorders" because they were among the problems clients of mental health professionals brought into treatment. The same knowledge system classifies, among many other conditions, hallucinations, delusions, and bizarre thoughts and behaviors, heavy and problematic consumption of alcoholic beverages or illegal drugs, inexplicable fears of leaving one's home, unhappiness following from the painful process of marital dissolution, disruption and inattention in classrooms, or persistent vomiting of food to maintain a desirable body image. The disease model that is now applied to all of these heterogeneous conditions is far better suited to understanding some of them than others.

I have used two very general standards to evaluate the usefulness of diagnostic classifications. The first requires that a condition be a valid mental disorder. Valid mental disorders exist when something is wrong with the functioning of a psychological mechanism and when these dysfunctions are defined as socially inappropriate (Wakefield 1992a, 1992b, 1993). This definition distinguishes valid mental disorders from both normal responses to stressful environments and social deviance (APA 1994, xxi–xxii). Mental disorders indicate that people have *dysfunctional* psychological mechanisms, not conditions that represent appropriate responses to stressful conditions or conformity to cultural norms. This concept is congruent with the DSM definition of mental disorder, although not with the actual way this manual applies this definition to particular disorders.

The second criterion is whether or not a condition is usefully viewed as a "disease." Diseases exist when underlying natural pathological processes produce particular sets of symptoms. Conversely, different constellations of symptoms serve as indicators of specific underlying disease entities. The fundamental model of diagnostic psychiatry is appropriate when valid mental disorders are also diseases. Carefully distinguishing discrete diseases from one another is useful because it aids in establishing distinct causes, prognoses, and treatments for each condition. Few of the many entities in the current classification scheme of diagnostic psychiatry meet both of these criteria.

Psychoses All societies carve out as distinct phenomena seemingly senseless and incomprehensible behaviors that are severe deviations from social norms (Horwitz 1982a; Jackson 1986). Calling the various psychotic conditions "mental disorders" fits a natural distinction that has been commonly made in human groups (Murphy 1976). In addition, the psychotic disorders of schizophrenia, bipolar conditions, and psychotic forms of depression conform to disease-based models. Their forms do not differ widely across social and historical contexts, so the symptoms of these disorders seem to indicate underlying disorders (Goldhamer and Marshall 1953; Sartorius, Jablensky, and Shapiro 1986). Genetic studies indicate that many cases of these disorders have biological foundations. Different psychotic disorders also respond distinctively to medication, so differential diagnoses are consequential for specific treatment regimens (Klerman 1989).

The social implications that stem from calling conditions "mental disorders" also seem to be appropriate for people who suffer from psychotic disorders. The psychological severity and resulting social dysfunctions of these disorders indicate a compelling case for providing social and treatment services for this population. Policies that increase resources for adequate mental health services for these individuals warrant public support, and people with these conditions who do not receive adequate professional services should be encouraged to get them (Mechanic 1999). These services, however, must emphasize housing, financial assistance, and coping skills with daily needs and crises at least as much if not more than they stress medication and therapy (Bachrach 1980; Stein, Test, and Marx 1980; Beard, Propst, and Malamud 1982; Mechanic and Rochefort 1992; Rosenfield and Neese-Todd 1993; Breakey 1994).

Diagnostic psychiatry takes the psychoses as models for other conditions and assumes that other putative mental disorders are analogous to the psychoses (Robins and Guze 1970; Klerman 1989). In fact, however, few other conditions fit the disease model that is useful for defining, studying, and treating the psychoses.

Nonpsychotic Disorders   Nonpsychotic mental disorders include anxiety disorders, nonpsychotic depressions, sexual dysfunctions, somatoform disorders, dissociative disorders, addictions, and eating disorders. The boundaries of these conditions are vague and usually difficult to define. Clear cases include people whose depressions persist in the absence of social circumstances that would explain them; who have crippling compulsions, obsessions, phobias, and anxieties that lack rational explanation; who are unable to function sexually despite the desire to do so; who are unable to refrain from repeated self-injurious behaviors; or who have persistent physiological problems without any physical cause. People who have symptoms of these disorders have valid mental disorders as this definition is used here:

all have psychological mechanisms that are not working properly and all deviate from socially defined standards of appropriate functioning.

That nonpsychotic disorders are valid mental disorders does not necessarily mean that the categorical system of diagnostic psychiatry is the best way to classify them. Symptom-based classifications assume that symptoms are indicators of underlying natural disorders. Unlike psychotic conditions, where this assumption generally holds, manifestations of nonpsychotic conditions vary widely across social contexts and are structured to fit the illness norms of particular groups (Kleinman 1988; Lopez and Guarnaccia 2000). Anxiety disorders that might feature the perceived shrinking of the penis into one's body in one context might appear as an obsession in a different context (Yap 1965). In one culture, depression might manifest itself through sadness, grief, and hopelessness; in another, this disorder might present solely through physical symptoms (Kleinman 1988). Other conditions such as eating disorders or particular sexual dysfunctions might be virtually nonexistent in most societies other than our own (Brumberg 1988; Vaillant 1984). The symptoms of nonpsychotic disorders are not straightforward indicators of underlying diseases; instead they vary widely across times and places.

Because the symptoms of these disorders are often culturally structured, it is difficult to use them to construct diagnoses that differentiate the causes, courses, and treatments of various disorders. The variety of nonpsychotic conditions do not seem to have distinct causes; instead, they have common risk factors including generalized family histories of psychiatric disorders, occurrences of early traumatic events, disturbances of family functioning, and experiences of severe and uncontrollable stressors (e.g., Kramer 1993; Tyrer 1985; Zubin 1977; Coie et al. 1993; Dohrenwend 2000). This could indicate that a general vulnerability produces a tendency to develop any of these conditions, not that distinct causes are responsible for particular diseases.

Attempts to associate particular symptoms with specific underlying disorders are especially problematic for studies that explore the genetic roots of such disorders. Such studies face the dilemma of how to define the condition the heredity of which they are attempting to trace (Smoller and Tsuang 1998, 1152). The same underlying genetic constellation can produce numerous different symptomatic conditions, making it difficult to use manifest symptoms to indicate particular disease conditions. In addition, the prognoses of the various nonpsychotic disorders are rarely predictable from the particular diagnoses. Instead, people who get one diagnosis at a particular time very often get other diagnoses later on (Tyrer 1985). Likewise, with the exception of some circumscribed conditions such as phobias, neither medications nor psychotherapies respect the boundaries of particular diagnostic categories but work across a variety of nonpsychotic conditions (Healy 1997).

Although the categorical system of diagnostic psychiatry might not be a useful way of classifying most nonpsychotic disorders, it can sometimes *create* the disorders it claims to classify (Hacking 1999). People use the classifications their cultures provide to translate broad and undifferentiated feelings of emotional pain and unease into recognizable categories. Before the advent of diagnostic psychiatry, these were Freudian categories of "repression," "projection," "displacement," and the like. Now, diagnoses of panic disorder, social anxiety, depression, anorexia, or bulimia are the culturally approved frameworks that shape vulnerabilities into the diagnoses that mental health professionals, as well as the broader society, promote (Wilson 1993). Whether viewing these conditions as discrete diseases leads to more understanding than seeing them as manifestations of unconscious mechanisms or of social conditions remains an open question.

The social policy issues surrounding nonpsychotic disorders are more complex than those surrounding the psychoses. People whose depressions, anxieties, compulsions, and addictions stem from internal dysfunctions should be encouraged to seek professional mental health treatment. Although they rarely work in disease-specific ways, medications and specific and directive forms of psychotherapy produce positive results in most people who receive them (e.g., Antonuccio et al. 1999; WPA Dysthymia Working Group 1995; Luborsky et al. 1993). For some people, however, illness categories can promote self-identification as helpless victims and dependency on mental health professionals. For others, mental health professionals can create iatrogenic disorders such as multiple personality disorder that they then purportedly treat (Showalter 1997). Policies that promote parity between mental and physical illnesses should take into account conditions under which professional attention can stimulate or exacerbate, instead of alleviate, mental disorders (see Klerman et al. 1992; Scheff 1966).

The study and treatment of distinct disorders is firmly embedded in the mental health professions and is unlikely to change soon. Sociologists, however, need not accept the assumption that the various nonpsychotic disorders are discrete entities. Instead, they should specify the various sorts of cultural factors that structure symptoms into a variety of forms, examine the historical rise and fall of these symptom presentations, and attempt to specify when professional treatment helps or harms particular conditions.

Distress   Current classifications of mental illness encompass distressful conditions that are appropriate responses to stressful social conditions. These conditions are not mental disorders when they dissipate after the conditions that gave rise to them disappear. Only psychological conditions that are of a severity and duration disproportionate to the circumstances in which they arise or that remain long after the stressors that caused them have disappeared are mental disorders (Wakefield 1999b).[9] Social conditions can often cause internal dysfunctions, but many common depressive, anxious, and psychophysiological symptoms that stem from social conditions are not internal dysfunctions. The symptom-based logics of diagnostic psychiatry, however, mistakenly conflate normal responses to stressful conditions with mental disorders.

The confounding of distress and mental disorder is a particular problem in community studies. Diagnostic decisions in clinical practice allow the use of lay and professional common-sense judgments about whether a particular condition is or is not a mental disorder. In contrast, community studies use computer programs, which are based on the presence of sufficient numbers of symptoms for each particular condition, to generate diagnoses. All symptoms—those that are temporary, transient, and responsive to particular stressors as well as those that are longstanding, deeply rooted, and internal—are counted as potential indicators of particular disorders (Wakefield 1999b). They thus count anxiety that is adaptive to particular situations or unhappiness that naturally results from stressful social situations as symptoms of mental disorders (Robins and Regier 1991; Kessler et al. 1994). Because widespread stressors produce the same symptoms of depression, anxiety, and/or heavy consumption of alcohol seen in depressive, anxiety, and substance use disorders, community studies invariably overcount mental disorders in untreated samples. The logic used to classify symptom-based disorders, not the actual presence of mental disorders, accounts for the high prevalence estimates of community studies.

The kinds of situations that produce distress—romantic breakups, marital disturbances, problems at school or on the job, physical illnesses, failure to achieve aspirations—are widespread and intrinsic to social life. People whose symptoms arise because of social stressors and whose symptoms disappear when these stressors abate are responding normally to their situations, yet the application of symptom-based logics of classification in community studies transforms the suffering of ordinary people into psychiatric disorders (Robins and Regier 1991; Kessler et al. 1994; Laumann, Paik, and Rosen 1999). The resulting high prevalence estimates of mental disorders help to market pharmaceuticals, to bolster the rhetorical arguments of advocacy groups, to increase demand for the services of mental health professionals, and to secure increased funding for mental health researchers and agencies (e.g., Kirk 1999; Valenstein 1998). Prevalence estimates thus become normative tools that justify certain social practices. There are better alternatives than the discrete disease classifications of diagnostic psychiatry for viewing the expectable consequences of stressful social arrangements. Classifications that view distress as broad, as continuous, and as manifest in multiple ways are more useful than the specific, discrete, and singular categories of diagnostic psychiatry (Mirowsky and Ross 1989a; Aneshensel, Rutter, and Lachenbruch 1991).

The psychological consequences of stressful social arrangements are not specific disease entities (Cassell 1974, 1976). Humans (and other animals) respond to stressors with general, nonspecific reactions that include depressive, anxious, and psychophysiological symptoms (Selye 1956; Cassell 1974; Hinkle and Wolff 1958; Hinkle 1987). Psychological symptoms of disinterest, hopelessness, and helplessness are usually accompanied by physical symptoms of tiredness, fatigue, weakness, reduced motor activity, and problems with sleep and appetite. Stress reactions also often include symptoms of anxiousness, fearfulness, and digestive problems (Selye 1956). These symptoms overlap many diagnoses and so correlate very highly with other measures of depression, anxiety, and self-esteem.[10] Scales that measure broad and nonspecific symptoms of distress provide the best measures of the psychological consequences of stressful social arrangements.[11]

In contrast to the outcomes of diagnostic psychiatry that are discrete entities—so that one either is or is not schizophrenic, phobic, depressed, and such—the distress that results from stressful social circumstances is continuous (Mirowsky and Ross 1989a). There are no sharp cut points between people under stress and those who are not, so the consequences of chronic and acute stressors are not categorical illness entities but gradations of distress (Angst and Merikangas 1997; Harrison, Fulkerson, and Beebe 1998). Categorical diagnoses are appropriate for some conditions and for some purposes, but superimposing categories on what are essentially continuous phenomena of depression and anxiety leads to less, not more, accurate systems of classification (Mirowsky and Ross 1989a).

Finally, unlike symptoms of disease that emerge from underlying biological processes, cultural forces shape the symptoms of distress into socially appropriate styles of expression. The cultural structuring of distress means that members of different social groups including social classes, ethnicities, sexes, and generations can respond to stressors in different ways. For example, if women are more likely than men to respond to stressors with depression and anxiety then the sole use of an internalized outcome measure such as depression can underestimate the stressful impact of these stressors on men. An adequate comparison of the stressful consequences of social arrangements would have to include measures of the typical ways that *both* men and women respond to stressors. Accurate comparisons of how different social groups respond to the stressful consequences of social arrangements should not rely on single outcomes but should include measures that typify how each group under study responds to stressors. These considerations suggest that the psychological consequences of stressful social conditions should be viewed not as distinct mental illness entities, but rather as broad, continuous, and diverse.

The conflating of distress and mental disorder in diagnostic psychiatry raises difficult policy issues. Current government policy defines mental disorders as broadly as possible, emphasizes the many people with presumed disorders who do not seek professional treatment, and encourages all people who have these putative disorders to seek professional mental health treatment.[12] A possible consequence of using expansive definitions of mental disorders in formulating public policy is to reinforce a mental health system that is already oriented toward treating people who apparently are struggling with problems of living but who do not have mental disorders. A major legacy of dynamic psychiatry is that many people view mental health professionals as social experts who can help them deal with the problems they face with family members, romantic relationships, failed careers, and dissatisfied lives. How widespread are such conditions in the current mental health system? It is impossible to answer this question with any precision but the answer is certainly "quite pervasive."

The Epidemiologic Catchment Area Study found that, despite a very generous definition of mental disorder that indicates more than a quarter of the population had a mental illness over the past year, nearly half of persons who receive treatment from mental health professionals do not have a diagnosable mental disorder (Regier et al. 1993). The National Co-morbidity Study, although it indicated that half of the population has some lifetime mental disorder, also showed a high use of mental health services among the other half of the population, the half with *no* lifetime history of psychiatric disorder (Katz et al. 1997). A third large national study, the Medical Expenditures Survey, also found that most heavy users of psychotherapy (those making more than twenty visits in the previous year) were in generally good health, did not report serious psychiatric symptoms, and did not have major functional impairments (Olfson and Pincus 1994b, 1290).[13] Although data about the conditions of the users of mental health services are very poor, they suggest that many of the clients of mental health professionals are distressed but not mentally disordered.

If the argument of this book is correct, many of the fifty million Americans who meet the criteria for a mental disorder in community studies do not have valid disorders but suffer from distress that is rooted in stressful social arrangements and that will disappear when these situations improve. For such individuals, it is not clear that professional mental health treatment produces better responses than social and political efforts to change stressful situations, or than talking with friends and other intimates about these situations. It is also arguable that the current mental health system overemphasizes the treatment of generic life problems instead of internal dysfunctions. It is debatable whether public policy should emphasize expansive definitions of mental disorder and the widespread use of professional mental health services or, alternatively, direct mental health services toward people with psychological dysfunctions who need them the most. Policies that directly confront the social sources of distress such as poverty, economic insecurity, social isolation, issues of childcare and jobs among dual-career couples, or care for the disabled elderly might do more to eliminate distress than encouraging people to seek mental health treatment.

Social Deviance   Diagnostic psychiatry encompasses a fourth general category of behaviors, which are often defined as forms of social deviance. "Deviance" is a vague term that is difficult to define with precision but it generally refers to behaviors that violate social norms of right and wrong conduct (Parsons 1951; Black 1976; Horwitz 1990). Decisions about whether or not deviant behaviors indicate mental illnesses are especially problematic: many comparable behaviors can be viewed as either violations of social norms or individual dysfunctions (in general, see Fingarette 1988; Toby 1998). When heavy drinking, persistent cocaine use, juvenile delinquency, career criminality, or disruptive behavior should be viewed as, respectively, substance abuse, substance dependence, conduct disorder, antisocial personality disorder, or attention deficit disorder is always a difficult question. Social value judgments will invariably play a large part in whether a condition is viewed as a chosen deviant act that should be subject to punishment or a compelled psychological dysfunction that ought to be treated. The problem of diagnostic psychiatry is that its symptom-based logics make no distinction between symptoms that are products of internal dysfunctions and those that stem from chosen, although socially disvalued, activities.

Internal dysfunctions can sometimes produce the kinds of symptoms that indicate antisocial personality disorder, substance abuse and dependence disorders, conduct disorder, attention deficit disorder, and the like. These same symptoms, however, can emerge because of collective, normative, and external causes in people whose psychological functioning is normal. In such cases, norm violations do not indicate underlying diseases but stem from the choices that rational individuals make to engage in socially disvalued behaviors.

Many causes, apart from individual dysfunctions, might lead psychologically normal individuals to engage in social deviance. One theoretical tradition explains behaviors such as crime, delinquency, and gambling as attempts by people, especially those in disadvantaged social groups who lack legitimate means, to achieve valued social ends (e.g., Merton 1938; Cloward and Ohlin 1960). In this view, socially valued goals of success, not individual dysfunctions, motivate thieves and drug dealers no less than stockbrokers or pharmaceutical salespersons. Another major sociological theory emphasizes that much drinking, drug use, gambling, and defiance of authority is the result of *conformity* to subcultural norms (e.g., Sellin 1938; Shaw and McKay 1942). Gaining the approval of one's peers, which is a trait of normal individuals, drives people in certain social groups to engage in activities that the norms of other groups define as deviant. A third prominent theory stresses that, unless strong social institutions are present to stop them, people will naturally engage in hedonistic drinking, thievery, lying, promiscuous sex, and the like (e.g., Hirschi 1969). From this point of view, deviance results from a lack of external constraints and not from the presence of internal dysfunctions.

There are, therefore, a number of reasons why normal individuals might participate in activities diagnostic psychiatry defines as mental disorders. Such diagnoses are neither valid mental disorders nor indicators of underlying diseases. Symptom-based logics, however, inevitably conflate deviance with disease, expanding the range of abnormal behavior beyond the bounds of reason. Medicalized definitions of deviance are not only conceptually inadequate but also potentially wasteful. Normal individuals who choose to engage in deviant activities are unlikely to define themselves as in need of mental health treatment, do not want this kind of treatment, and will not benefit from treatment if forced to enter it. Only substantial amounts of coercion can enforce treatment for such populations.

Laypersons are far more skeptical of applying the logic of diagnostic psychiatry to social deviance than to the other major types of conditions the mental health professions currently regard as diseases. In contrast to the widespread acceptance of the disease categories of diagnostic psychiatry for other conditions, the public is far more ambivalent or hostile toward classifying deviance as disease (Link et al. 1999; Pescosolido et al. 1999). In general, people believe that in most circumstances individuals choose to drink heavily, to take illegal drugs, to commit criminal and delinquent acts, or to misbehave, and they reject the idea that a disease compelled these behaviors.[14] Classifying such activities as diseases, with the resulting diminution of responsibility and prescription of treatment, contradicts deeply held social values. Therefore, diagnostic psychiatry faces the greatest difficulties in applying its disease frameworks to conditions that violate social norms.[15]

Medicalized frameworks that classify discrete mental diseases can be useful ways of studying some mental disorders. The valid range of these classifications, however, is far narrower than their current application not only to the psychoses, but also to nonpsychotic disorders, to the normal consequences of stressful social arrangements, and to deviant behaviors.

THE FUTURE OF DIAGNOSTIC PSYCHIATRY

The notion that the mentally ill suffer from discrete diseases is so thoroughly embedded in the knowledge system and organization of the psychiatric profession that these conditions seem to be the only possible subject matter of the discipline (Lurhmann 2000). They have also become fundamental aspects of undergraduate and graduate curricula in psychology and other mental health disciplines and of common belief systems about mental illness in the broader culture (Conrad and Schneider 1992). Educational campaigns sponsored by government agencies, advocacy groups, professional organizations, and pharmaceutical companies widely promote the idea that mental illnesses are diseases (Paykel et al. 1997; Hirschfeld et al. 1997; USDHHS 1999; Olfson et al. 2000). These campaigns assure sufferers that they have genuine disease conditions that are best treated by medical and mental health professionals. Experiences with distinct mental disorders are also the theme of many talk shows, television programs, and popular news stories.[16] Social movements composed of sufferers of these diseases have arisen that provide face-to-face reinforcement of their reality. The Internet, as well, features voluminous information, advice, and interaction about these disorders. The belief that mental illnesses are distinct diseases has such great cultural resonance at present that it is difficult to imagine that they are anything but natural and unchangeable entities.

Most of the diseases of diagnostic psychiatry that are now taken for granted, however, are historically contingent and will persist only as long as specific groups have a stake in regarding them as "diseases." Just as the categorical classifications of diagnostic psychiatry emerged because they justified valued social practices, they will persist as long as they continue to fit prevailing socioeconomic conditions. When these diseases no longer meet the interests of various groups, they will disappear and alternative systems of classification will emerge. I conclude this book with some speculations about circumstances that might reinforce the power of specific mental disease entities as well as those that might destabilize the current classification system of diagnostic psychiatry.

At present, the same social conditions that gave rise to an extensive categorical system of mental illnesses should also ensure its continuation. The entire enterprise of training, research, and treatment in psychiatry and other mental health disciplines is based on the reality of categorical diseases. Government policy toward funding research about mental illness also is grounded in the categorical system of disorders and does not encourage alternative ways of thinking about distressful conditions. There also seems to be little doubt that medications will continue to be the treatment of choice for mental disorders into the foreseeable future. The highly profitable marketing of psychoactive drugs is predicated on the presence of discrete disease conditions and current regulatory systems for bringing new drugs onto the market demand proof that a medication is effective for a specific disease (Healy 1997).

The current system for reimbursing the treatment of mental illnesses also should perpetuate the idea that these conditions are diseases. In particular, the spread of managed care throughout the health care system should increase pressures to limit reimbursement to the treatment of particular disease entities (Mechanic 1999; Kiesler 2000). Managed care approaches, while diverse, rely on strategies that reduce health expenditures by eliminating unnecessary services and by using less expensive alternatives instead of more expensive kinds of treatments (Mechanic 1998b). The entities of diagnostic psychiatry seem to meet the demands of managed care organizations to treat specific conditions and not more general personality or social problems. The emphasis on medication therapies rather than on long-term psychotherapies is especially congenial to the logic behind managed mental health care. The disease conditions of diagnostic psychiatry are thus congruent with the current organization of the health care system, which emphasizes various managed care approaches.

Although the categorical system of diagnostic psychiatry is deeply entrenched, several factors might lead to alternative ways of viewing mental disorders. While external social, cultural, and economic factors may account for why a profession develops a particular system of classification, if this system fails to order its domain adequately, it may eventually collapse (Abbott 1988). It could become increasingly apparent that the underlying bases of most mental disorders do not fit the categorical system diagnostic psychiatry imposes on them (e.g., Kendler and Gardner 1998). Just as researchers initially developed these illnesses to enhance the rigor of their studies, an intellectual crisis may develop over time as they realize that the disease categories they use fail to provide distinct explanations, prognoses, and treatments for the conditions they theoretically reflect.

A particularly important source of change in the categorical system might emerge from future developments in genetic research. If the argument presented in this book is correct, with a small number of exceptions, specific genes or combinations of genes do not produce specific disorders. Instead, genetic factors might produce broad vulnerabilities to generalized depressive, compulsive, or addictive traits, which sociocultural and other factors structure into a variety of particular forms. A disorder such as anorexia, for example, could be a cultural manifestation of such generalized vulnerabilities, not a product of a gene or complex of genes that are specific for anorexia or for eating disorders. If so, a categorical system that defines disorders through their manifest symptoms will hinder rather than help the search for the genetic foundations of mental disorders. Once researchers gain greater understanding of these foundations, they are not likely to continue to endorse the current disease-based system. The intellectual weaknesses of a categorical system are not sufficient to lead to its demise, but they may help stimulate its eventual replacement.

Another factor that might undermine the classification system of diagnostic psychiatry is the tremendous success of current psychotropic medications. The most publicly visible component of diagnostic psychiatry, the widespread use of antidepressant medications, contradicts the discrete logic on which the classification system is based (Kramer 1993; Healy 1997). These drugs do not treat specific psychiatric conditions, but help alleviate many forms of human unhappiness without regard to diagnoses. The same medications are prescribed across a range of nonpsychotic and distressing conditions including depression, anxiety, anorexia, panic, obsession-compulsion, substance abuse, and many others. With the exception of psychotic conditions, diagnoses rarely determine specific prescription practices. The efficacy of drug treatments not only does not depend on distinct illness categories but also is not congruent with the categorical logic on which diagnostic psychiatry is built.

The logical flaws of the classification system of diagnostic psychiatry would not be sufficient causes for its replacement. Socioeconomic factors could also be sources of change in the categorical system. Specific disease entities impose economic disadvantages, as well as advantages, for mental health professionals. Many people have some symptoms but do not meet the full criteria for the most common psychiatric disorders such as depression or anxiety (Pincus et al. 1992; Angst, Merikangas and Preisig 1997; Kessler et al. 1997). For example, if five symptoms are necessary to diagnose depression, the problems of people who have four symptoms are not reimbursable. Categories thus not only create reimbursable conditions but also preclude reimbursement for treatment of conditions that do not meet full criteria.

The realization that categorical logic excludes, as well as includes, symptom-based conditions has already given rise to a potentially important countermovement to categorical thinking. This movement defines "shadow syndromes" or "subthreshold conditions" as points on a continuum of mental disorder, which all can become reimbursable (Frances et al. 1991; Angst and Merikangas 1997).[17] People who have some symptoms but who do not meet full-blown criteria for diagnoses are especially abundant in primary medical care settings. Robert Spitzer, the primary force behind the development of the categorical system of the DSM-III, has more recently developed a new instrument for diagnosing mental disorders in these settings. It allows physicians to screen their patients in only eight minutes for the most common symptoms of depression, anxiety, psychosomatic disorders, and eating disorders. Spitzer's study of 1,000 patients in primary care settings indicates that only 19 percent are symptom-free while about 40 percent nearly or fully meet criteria for psychiatric disorders (Spitzer et al. 1994). The study concludes that reimbursement from third parties could result in the widespread adoption of this measure. The extent to which these "shadow syndromes," which potentially encompass much of human activity, can in fact become reimbursable will affect the future of diagnostic psychiatry. Once mental health professionals see a greater advantage in treating conditions that fall outside the boundaries of categorical disorders, their enthusiasm for discrete diseases could diminish.

The pharmaceutical industry, which up to now has been among the most fervent proponents of diagnostic psychiatry, is another interest group that might benefit from the demise of the categorical system. At some time in the future, categorical illnesses might detract from, rather than enhance, the potential market for psychotropic medications. The same logic that creates "shadow syndromes" and "subthreshold conditions" also opens up new markets of patients who presumably need prescription medications (Valenstein 1998). Far more people have some symptoms of the most common psychiatric disorders than meet the full criteria for these disorders. "Subthreshold conditions" that are based on continua rather than on categories could create enormous new markets for psychoactive medications. While current government regulations preclude the marketing of medications for nonspecific conditions, it would, as Healy notes, take "little more than a minor stroke of a politician's pen" to change these regulations (Healy 1997, 255). Such a change could help precipitate a collapse of the current disease-based diagnostic system.

The spread of managed care for the treatment of mental health problems is also likely to have a major influence in limiting the sweep of the diagnostic system. Although, as noted above, the pressures to impose limits on treatment that managed care systems present are congruent with a categorical system of diseases, they are especially suitable to a *narrow* categorical system. Managed care organizations may well come to apply intense pressure to contract the expansive categories of diagnostic psychiatry, especially those that involve deviant behavior and problems in living (Mechanic and McAlpine 1999). Indeed, the continuing spread of managed care is likely to be a major source of downsizing the categorical system, although not of changing the logic behind disease-based mental illnesses.

The future of diagnostic psychiatry is therefore in some doubt. Although the categorical logic on which it is based seems secure, not long ago the "unconscious," "repression," "sublimation," "projection," and the like were equally firmly embedded realities. While powerful forces ensure the perpetuation of distinct mental diseases, internal developments in genetic research and external changes in the socioeconomic environment of psychiatry might lead to the eventual demise of the categorical system. The persistence of mental diseases will ultimately depend on what factors best serve the interests of the mental health professions within the restraints changing socioeconomic conditions impose upon them.[18]

While mental illnesses are social constructions, *something* is being constructed. The conditions that are classified can be construed in many, but not in unlimited, ways. Constructing some kinds of disturbed human behaviors as diseases fits some conditions better than others. Those who are concerned with mental health and illness should not assume either that mental illness labels are appropriate whenever they are applied or that they are never appropriate. Instead, they should strive to specify when people have internal dysfunctions or, alternatively, when they are making normal responses to the social situations in which they find themselves. Ultimately, they need to consider when restoring normality is best accomplished by changing individuals and when it is best done by transforming social conditions.

Notes

INTRODUCTION: THE PROLIFERATION OF MENTAL ILLNESSES

1 See Rosen 1968 for how ancient and medieval societies defined mental illness. Good anthropological examples of definitions of mental illness in small-scale groups are Kiev 1964, Kleinman 1988, and Littlewood 1990.

2 Representative portrayals of the mentally ill in premodern Western societies are Foucault 1965, Grob 1966, Rothman 1971, and MacDonald 1981. More generally, see Horwitz 1982a: chap. 2.

3 The political conflict between dynamic psychiatrists and research psychiatrists resulted in the elimination of the term "neurosis" from the body of the DSM-III and subsequent diagnostic manuals (see Bayer and Spitzer 1985). Nevertheless, it can be a useful descriptive term that refers to the psychosexual, psychosomatic, anxious, and depressed conditions that were the focus of dynamic psychiatry.

4 Good illustrations of the spread of dynamic psychiatry in the United States are Grob 1991a, Lunbeck 1994, Hale 1995, and Herman 1995.

5 See the many writings of Robert Spitzer, the major figure behind the development of the DSM-III (e.g., Spitzer, Sheehy, and Endicott 1977; Spitzer and Endicott 1978; Spitzer, Williams, and Skodal 1980; Bayer and Spitzer 1985; Spitzer 1991).

6 For the best general discussion of medicalization see Conrad and Schneider 1992.

7 Illustrative statements of the philosophy behind diagnostic psychiatry are Klerman 1977; Robins and Helzer 1986; and any of the Spitzer articles in note 5. See Nathan 1994 for a viewpoint from the perspective of clinical psychology. Kirk and Kutchins 1992 present the most extensive critique of this position.

8 Wakefield 1996 provides a succinct critique of the latest version of the DSM.

9 For representative examples see Blazer et al. 1994 for depression; Lesch et al. 1996 for anxiety; Magee et al. 1996 for social phobia; Laumann, Paik, and Rosen 1999 for sexual dysfunction; and Wender 1987 for attention deficit disorder.

10 The major community studies of mental illness are the Epidemiologic Catchment Area study summarized in Robins and Regier 1991 and the National Co-Morbidity Survey summarized in Kessler et al. 1994.

11 See any issue of the major journals of the psychiatric profession, *The American Journal of Psychiatry* and *The Archives of General Psychiatry*.

12 See especially the Report of the Surgeon General on Mental Health, which on its first page proclaims as its primary goal: "Every person should be encouraged to seek help

when questions arise about mental health, just as each person is encouraged to seek help when questions arise about physical health" (USDHHS 1999, 3). See also Hirschfeld et al. 1997.

13 Hirschfeld et al. 1997, Paykel et al. 1997, and Olfson et al. 2000 are representative of professional efforts to promote public awareness of mental illness. The most comprehensive statement of this point of view is found in the Surgeon General's Report on Mental Health (USDHHS 1999).

14 Pincus et al. 1998 present recent statistics on the use of medication.

15 These figures are derived from 1996 sales. See *New York Times Magazine*, 23 November 1997, 17. Representative statements of the impact of new antidepressants are Wurtzel 1997 and Slater 1998. See also Schatzberg 2000. For critical views see Breggin 1991 and Glenmullen 2000.

16 See Dawes 1994 and Herman 1995 for the spread of psychologists into many areas of modern life, Tucker 1999 for the rise of the therapeutic ethic in modern corporations, and Sonnenstuhl 1996 for alcohol and mental health programs in the workplace. See Nolan 1998 for a discussion of the rise of mental health programs in prisons and other government institutions and Nicholi 1987 for the emergence of psychiatrists as advisors to professional sports teams. A good general overview of this trend is found in Conrad 1992 and Conrad and Schneider 1992.

17 See Shorter 1997 for a view that denigrates the position of psychoanalysis in the history of psychiatry.

18 For the general philosophical underpinnings of the constructionist position see Rorty 1989. For a broad discussion of controversies about the constructionist position see Hacking 1999.

19 See especially Berger and Luckmann 1967; Zerubavel 1997. See Brown 1995 for a good summary of the use of the constructionist perspective in medical sociology. Examples of anthropological studies that use this point of view are Gaines 1992, Nuckolls 1992, and Young 1995.

20 Portions of the following section are adapted from Horwitz (1999, 68–72).

21 See Fadiman 1997 for an excellent portrayal of cross-cultural differences in conceptions of seizure disorders.

22 In contrast to his theoretical presentation, Scheff actually used the concept of residual rule-breaking as synonymous with psychiatric symptoms, not as a quality of cultural rules. See Horwitz 1979.

23 See Bayer 1987 for homosexuality, Figert 1996 for premenstrual syndrome, and Scott 1990 and Young 1995 for posttraumatic stress disorder.

24 For general statements of this view see Spector and Kitsuse 1977, Schneider 1985, Conrad and Schneider 1992.

25 The absence of a universal standard of comparison is particularly problematic in anthropological research on mental illness. Anthropologists often reject the possibility of obtaining definitions of mental disorders that are valid across cultures. For example, the foremost anthropologist of mental illness, Arthur Kleinman, states: "Depressive illness and dysphoria are thus not only interpreted differently in non-Western societies and across cultures; they are constituted as fundamentally different forms of social reality" (1988, 5). However, this comparison requires that there be something in both non-Western and Western groups that reflects the common concept of "depression." See also Fabrega 1989, 1992; Hopper 1992.

26 Conrad (1992) makes the related point that sociologists who adopt constructionist

views usually provide strong critiques of medicalized conceptions of illness without providing alternatives to medicalized views.

27 See Bayer 1987 for a discussion of the controversy over whether homosexuality is a disease or a lifestyle and Hahn 1995 for a more general discussion of the necessity of a definition of mental disorder that transcends particular cultural contexts.

28 Likewise, the Surgeon General's Report provides the following definition: "Mental illness is the term that collectively refers to all diagnosable disorders" (USDHHS 1999, 5).

29 See Waxler 1974 and 1979, Jenkins 1988, and Lewis-Fernandez and Kleinman 1985b for examples of culturally specific influences on psychotic disorders.

30 This does not mean that social theories are irrelevant to the study of psychotic disorders. Social factors may be responsible for the content of symptoms that become manifest, the course of the disorder, and the social response to the disorder, among other things. See Horwitz 1982a; Estroff 1981; Link, Dohrenwend, and Skodol 1986.

31 See chapter 5 of this book.

32 It may also be the case that disorders such as schizophrenia that best fit the disease model are also more continuous than discrete. See Tsuang 2000.

33 See Aronowitz 1998 for chronic fatigue syndrome and Lyme disease, Kroll-Smith and Floyd 1997 for multiple chemical sensitivity, and Groopman 2000 for fibromyalgia. See also Showalter 1997. The fact that some people who claim to have the symptoms of these maladies do not actually have them does not, of course, mean that all sufferers from these conditions do not have physical diseases.

34 This was a dominant theme of the now dormant Neo-Freudian school in the 1930s and 1940s. See, in particular, Horney 1937, Fromm 1941. See also the work of the historian Edward Shorter, especially 1992 and 1994.

35 See Finlay-Jones and Brown 1981 for the alternative argument that anxiety and depression have distinct social precipitants.

36 Good statements of appropriate sociological approaches to psychiatric outcomes are found in Mirowsky and Ross 1989a and Aneshensel, Rutter, and Lachenbruch 1991.

37 See Abbott 1988 for an excellent synthesis of how status concerns drive professional knowledge.

CHAPTER ONE: A CONCEPT OF MENTAL DISORDER

1 See also Devereux's classic analysis of the shaman as a mentally disordered person (Devereux 1980 [1956]).

2 See, for example, Robins et al. 1984, Kessler et al. 1994. The definition in the Surgeon General's Report on Mental Health is typical: "*Mental illness* is the term that refers collectively to all diagnosable mental disorders" (USDHHS 1999, 5).

3 The best statements of Wakefield's position are found in Wakefield 1992a, 1992b, and 1993. See the August 1999 issue of the *Journal of Abnormal Psychology* for a variety of critiques of Wakefield's position and Wakefield's response to these critiques.

4 Lewis 1953 provides the classic statement of this position. See also Klein 1978; Wakefield 1992a, 1992b, and 1993.

5 Compare Bell (1985), who argues that religious practices of self-starvation are analogous to eating disorders, with Brumberg (1988), who claims they are different. Brumberg's argument is consistent with the one presented here.

6 See Toby 1998 for a critique of the ability to control conduct as a way of defining mental disorders.

7 Even some physical conditions such as blindness and deafness that used to be consen-

sual are now contested. Some advocacy groups for the blind and the deaf deny the dysfunctional quality of sightlessness or lack of hearing and redefine these as positive conditions (Gates 2000).

8   Various social groups also do not regard certain physical illnesses as diseases. Malaria, for example, is such a common condition in some Amazonian groups that they do not define it as a disease. See Mechanic 1978.

9   The distinction between mental and physical disorders on the dimension of social inappropriateness is one of degree, not of kind. The degree of social inappropriateness is relevant to whether dysfunctions such as physical disabilities or pain conditions are socially defined as diseases.

10 The universality of depression is not limited to humans. A large ethological literature indicates that most mammals display depression-like symptoms in certain types of highly stressful conditions, e.g. Price and Sloman 1987.

11 See Cardozo et al. 2000 for an example of PTSD among a war-ravaged civilian population. See Barker 1991 for an excellent fictional portrayal of the psychological consequences of combat.

12 For example, the *New York Times*, 23 December 1999, reports that archaeologists have estimated through an analysis of drinking cups that each mourner at a Phrygian funeral in 700 B.C. consumed an average of a gallon of a mixture of grape wine, barley beer, and mead.

13 See Wakefield 1999b for a critique of these estimates.

CHAPTER TWO: THE EXPANSION OF MENTAL ILLNESSES
IN DYNAMIC PSYCHIATRY

1   Freud 1958 [1900]. In addition to Freud's own voluminous works, there is possibly more secondary literature about Freud than about any major figure of the twentieth century. Good examples are Rieff 1961; Gay 1988; Roazen 1992; and Robinson 1993. The recent secondary literature tends to be harshly critical of Freudian thought. See, e.g., Grunbaum 1984; Masson 1984; Crews 1995.

2   In general, dynamic psychiatry explains symptomatic conditions as conflicts between instinctual demands and their repression by the defensive forces of the ego. See Fenichel 1995 [1945]. The unconscious, which contains unclassified material that stands outside of reality, time, order, and logic, is driven to discharge this material into consciousness. The conscious mind, however, resists expressing the socially unacceptable contents of unconscious drives. Instead, it reformulates drives and instincts into socially acceptable forms. This conflict between unconscious pressures to discharge drives and conscious pressures to repress their direct expression leads to anxiety and many other psychological symptoms. Sufferers, however, are aware neither of the meaning of their manifest symptoms nor of the underlying dynamics that give rise to them.

3   Freud states: "It follows from the nature of the facts which form the material of psychoanalysis that we are obliged to pay as much attention in our case histories to the purely human and social circumstances of our patients as to the somatic data and the symptoms of the disorder" (1963 [1905], 178).

4   This individualistic emphasis is also true of the group therapies based on dynamic principles that emerged in the 1960s. Although these took place in group settings, they emphasized the uniqueness of each individual personality and promoted self-actualization, not attachment to the group. See the discussion and references in Horwitz 1982a, 176–82.

5   See also Hale 1995, chaps. 14–16; Herman 1995.

6   See especially Freud's analyses of Dora K. (1963 [1905]), Little Hans (1924 [1909]), and the Wolf Man (1989 [1918]).

7   Grob 1991a, Lunbeck 1994, Hale 1995, and Herman 1995 provide excellent descriptions of these developments. Wilson 1993 provides a succinct overview of this process that is compatible with the analysis presented here.

8   See Jones 1999 for a detailed portrayal of the emergence of the child guidance movement.

9   The many films of Alfred Hitchcock, such as *Vertigo, Marnie,* and *Spellbound,* provide especially good illustrations of this attitude.

10   See also Shorter 1997.

11   Redlich and Kellert (1978, 22) note that "In 1975 only 45% of psychiatric residents rated psychoanalysis as an important tool compared with almost universal acclaim in 1950."

CHAPTER THREE: THE EMERGENCE OF
DIAGNOSTIC PSYCHIATRY

1   See, for example, Fuller 2000, Horwich 1994, and Margolis 1993 for differing viewpoints on Kuhn's perspective

2   See especially the film version of Kesey's *One Flew Over The Cuckoo's Nest* and Rosenhan 1973.

3   See also the critique of Faust and Miner 1986.

4   The static emphasis of the categorical model is especially ironic in view of its claims to be "Neo-Kraepelian." Kraepelin's model emphasized the unfolding of symptoms over time rather than their static manifestations.

5   The role of schizophrenia in establishing the credentials of diagnostic psychiatry parallels the role of syphilis in creating a scientific basis for psychiatry in the early part of the twentieth century. See Lunbeck 1994.

6   Psychoanalysts did fiercely contest the basic rationale behind the DSM-III. By the late 1970s, however, diagnostically minded research psychiatrists were able to defeat their psychoanalytic opponents and to remove the neurotic process from the body of the DSM-III to an appendix. See Bayer and Spitzer 1985; Kirk and Kutchins 1992.

7   The inclusion of Acute Stress Disorder in the DSM-IV further expands the range of potential problems that can be encompassed in the categorical diagnostic system. See Marshall, Spitzer, and Liebowitz 1999 for an argument that this disorder actually does not encompass as many conditions as it should.

8   The various personality disorders were placed on a different dimension, called Axis II, from the many particular diagnoses that were placed on Axis I. The multiaxial nature of the DSM-III, although important, is not critical to the argument presented here.

9   See, for example, "compulsive buying" disorder in Black et al. 1998. See also Kirk and Kutchins 1994 for a critique of "handwriting disorder."

10   The subsequent growth of managed care and accompanying limits on mental health treatment has intensified pressures to make specific diagnoses. See Luhrmann 2000, chap. 6.

11   See Grob 1991a for the best overview of the development of the NIMH and the CMHCs. Duhl and Leopold 1968 provide a representative statement of the philosophy of the CMHC movement at the time. See Kolb, Frazier, and Sirovatka 2000 for the view of some of the major participants in the changes that occurred in the NIMH between the 1940s and the 1990s.

12 An exception was orthodox psychoanalysts who broadly demeaned the notion that the neuroses could be captured by symptom-based categories. See Bayer and Spitzer 1985; Kirk and Kutchins 1992.

13 The DSM-V is scheduled for publication in 2002.

14 The claim that the DSM expanded the range of pathology is typical. See, for example, Rogler 1997, Kutchins and Kirk 1997, Davis 1997.

15 Quoted in *New York Times*, 19 April 1994, C1.

16 In fact, the six diagnostic categories that were removed were renamed as aspects of other diagnoses.

17 For example, psychometrically based dimensions provide a radical alternative to the categorical logic of the DSM-III. See, for example, Eysenck, Wakefield, and Friedman 1983.

CHAPTER FOUR: THE EXTENSION OF MENTAL ILLNESSES INTO THE COMMUNITY

1 See any issue of the *American Journal of Psychiatry* or *Archives of General Psychiatry*.

2 See Dohrenwend and Dohrenwend 1982 for a good overview of trends in community studies over time.

3 A second wave of data collection for the NCS is ongoing at the time of this writing.

4 The example is not purely hypothetical. Several psychiatrists report an increase in the incidence of men with eating disorders, especially among those who participate in sports such as wrestling. See Gilbert 1996; Markel 2000.

5 Two of the authors of the JAMA article are consultants to Pfizer, the maker of Viagra.

6 Most notably, Robert Dole, the former Republican presidential candidate, became the major initial spokesmen for the benefits of Viagra.

7 One of the major, as yet unsuccessful, efforts of pharmaceutical companies is to develop a female counterpart to Viagra. See Grady 1999. Also see the Web site www.viacreme.nu.

8 The growing interest in social phobias began in the late 1980s when studies indicated that patients in clinical treatment responded to the drug phenelzine (Healy 1997, 189; Liebowitz et al. 1991). However, the major proponent of this disorder, psychiatrist Michael Liebowitz, notes that pharmaceutical companies develop strong interest in a mental disorder when its prevalence begins to reach nearly 10 percent of the population. See Raghunathan 1999.

9 Some print ads for Paxil, in contrast, feature a tormented man with his head against the wall.

10 It is, however, possible that contemporary American culture has changed to the point that shyness is less acceptable than in the past as part of a well-adjusted personality. In general, see Kramer 1993.

11 See, for example, any advertisement for Xoloft, Paxil, or Prozac. For illustrative media stories see Hall 1999a, Knapp 1999, Raghunathan 1999.

12 This perhaps explains the exclusion of alcohol disorders from the major advocacy document of the mental health movement, the Surgeon General's Report on Mental Health. See USDHHS 1999.

CHAPTER FIVE: THE STRUCTURING OF MENTAL DISORDERS

1 There is a growing movement that questions the discrete nature of even diagnoses of the psychoses and argues that continuous rather than discrete models better reflect the

nature of these disorders. See Tsuang, Stone, and Faranoe 2000 for schizophrenia and Mullan and Murray 1989 and Kendler and Gardner 1998 for affective disorders.

2 For schizophrenia see Rosenthal 1970; Gottesman and Shields 1982; Goodwin and Guze 1996, chap. 2. For affective disorders see Gershon et al. 1982; Weissman et al. 1984; Kramer 1993.

3 Kendell 1974; Tyrer 1985; Stavrakaki and Vargo 1986; Breier, Charney, and Heninger 1985; Eaves, Eysenck, and Martin 1989; Angst, Merikangas, and Preisig 1997; Zimmerman, McDermut, and Mattia 2000.

4 For a dissenting view see Finlay-Jones and Brown 1981.

5 See Leventhal et al. 1997 for a general discussion of interpretive schemes of illness. For an application of broad interpretive schemes to psychiatric symptoms in the eighteenth and nineteenth centuries see Shorter 1992.

6 See especially Kleinman 1988. For general discussions of the role of culture in shaping categories of interpretation see Berger and Luckmann 1967, Swidler 1986, Zerubavel 1997, Dimaggio 1997.

7 Mental disorders are far more structured than physical disorders because they affect deeply rooted conceptions of the self. The implications for the self of having diabetes or pneumonia are not comparable to those of psychiatric disorders. Therefore, symptoms of physical disorders are far less likely than those of mental disorders to be structured to fit appropriate notions of personal identity. See Fabrega 1989.

8 For contrasting views see Littlewood 1990; Hopper 1992.

9 See Wallace 1972 for a different view that interprets hysteria as a biological disease caused by calcium deficiencies.

10 An anomaly of *Sybil* is that, unlike future narratives, Sybil's mother rather than her father perpetrated her putative abuse.

11 Dr. Herbert Spiegel has revealed that Cornelia Wilbur, the author of *Sybil*, knew that her patient did not in fact have multiple personalities but exploited the sensationalistic aspects of her symptoms to create a popular and salable book. See Borch-Jacobsen 1997.

12 For example, Goodwin and Guze's (1996) classic text includes them as one of only twelve major mental disorders.

13 Pardes et al. (1989, 441) report some findings that suggest anorexia is a genetic variant of affective illness.

14 A study cited in the *New York Times* reports a rise in eating disorders among young females in the Fiji islands. See Goode 1999.

15 See also Furnam and Malik 1994 for a study of how younger South Asian immigrants to Britain come to display Western models of depression.

16 The structuring view also contrasts with the earlier views of the culture and personality school that symptoms stemmed from deeply rooted and culturally specific socialization processes that arose in early childhood. See, for example, Whiting and Child 1953; Gorer and Rickman 1949.

CHAPTER SIX: THE BIOLOGICAL FOUNDATIONS
OF DIAGNOSTIC PSYCHIATRY

1 E.g., Kandel 1998, Andreasen 1984, Sabshin 1990. See also Eaves, Eysenck, and Martin 1989 and Plomin, Owen, and McGuffin 1994 for the application of the genetic perspective to more general personality traits and social behaviors.

2 A good example of this approach is found in the Surgeon General's Report on Mental Health: "Mental disorders are characterized by abnormalities in cognition, emotion or mood, or the highest integrative aspects of behavior, such as social interactions or planning of future activities. These mental functions are all mediated by the brain. It is, in fact, a core tenet of modern science that behavior and our subjective mental lives reflect the overall workings of the brain. Thus, symptoms related to behavior or our mental lives clearly reflect variations or abnormalities in brain function" (USDHHS 1999, 39).

3 See, e.g., the cover of the July 3, 2000, issue of *Time*.

4 For similar statements see Kessler, Abelson, and Zhao 1998, 18; Tsuang 2000, 490.

5 Both opponents (e.g., Lewontin, Rose, and Kamin 1984, Lewontin 1992) and proponents (e.g., Wilson 1997) of the biological model agree on its reductionist nature. Although reductionism is often used as an epithet in social science, in biology it generally has a positive connotation.

6 The following statement, while extreme, is not atypical: "The 'environment' matters, of course, but contrary to popular belief, the most important environmental factors are not rearing, education, or social status. Rather, they are random and uncontrollable experiences such as the precise concentrations of a particular chemical in the brain, or something apparently minor like a childhood case of measles. While we like to imagine ourselves to be the carefully crafted products of our upbringing and education, we are actually shaped by the same sort of chaotic events that make each snowflake unique" (Hamer and Copeland 1998, 9). See Susser and Lin 1992 for a good example of a biological view of environmental factors.

7 The estimate of heritability is the squared correlation of concordance in a trait among monozygotic (MZ) twins, less the concordance rate among dizygotic (DZ) twins. For example, if the correlation between rates of depression is .50 between MZ twins and .28 between DZ twins, the heritability is $.50 - .28 = .22 \times 2 = 44$ percent. Heritability (h^2) has a possible range from 0 to 1. See Schwartz 1999.

8 In addition to showing the extent of heritability, twin studies divide the environment into shared and nonshared components. They use the formula b (behavior) $= h^2 + c^2 + e^2$, where h^2 is genetic heritability, and environmental variance is divided into the shared environment, c^2, and the nonshared environment, e^2. C^2 refers to the environment twins share, such as growing up in the same family, same neighborhood and community, same social class, and the like. E^2 indicates nonshared environmental experiences both within the family (such as birth order effects, differential parental treatment, or the impact of sibs on each other) and outside the family (such as different peer, school, work, or family experiences). See Schwartz 1999.

9 Studies of other disorders show comparable failure to replicate initial findings of linkage to particular chromosomes. For example, four studies find evidence for a gene associated with schizophrenia on chromosome 6 but two other studies fail to confirm this result (see Peltonen 1995; Hallmeyer et al. 1992; Kennedy et al. 1988). Likewise, the finding of a genetic linkage for panic disorder in one prominent study had to be retracted after further investigation failed to confirm this linkage (see Crowe et al. 1987; Lander and Schork 1994). Similarly, the purported discovery of a gene for alcoholism failed to be replicated in further research. For the discovery of the presumed gene for alcoholism see Blum et al. 1990; Noble et al. 1991. For the failure to replicate these findings see Parsian and Cloninger 1991. Merikangas (1995, 47) summarizes the state of the

field: "Despite a decade of intensive effort to identify the genetic basis of bipolar disorder, there is still not a single replicated linkage or association finding for this condition or any of the other major psychiatric disorders."

10 For a critique of this work see Lewontin, Rose, and Kamin 1984. See Mendlewicz and Rainer 1977 for a study of manic-depression and adoption.

11 Compare Hamer et al. 1993 with Rice et al. 1999; Crowe et al. 1987 with Lander and Schork 1994; Blum et al. 1990 with Bolos et al. 1991.

12 For evidence of strong environmental but weak genetic influences on alcohol problems see Searles 1988; Grove et al. 1990; and Han, McGue, and Iacono 1999. For studies that show strong genetic but weak environmental effects see, e.g., Prescott and Kendler 1999; Jang, Vernon, and Livesley 2000. The relative strength of genetic influence varies considerably depending upon factors such as sex, age, and the way alcohol problems are defined in a particular study.

13 See Singer 1985 or any other genetics text.

14 In fact, the latest research fails to replicate Hamer's findings regarding a "gay gene." See Rice et al. 1999.

15 If most biological studies maximize the possibility of finding genetic variance by minimizing environmental variance, others use haphazard sampling designs that do not systematically measure environments at all. This is particularly true of studies of the type often considered the "holy grail" of biological research about human behavior: studies of identical twins who are reared apart. Such studies cannot examine mental disorders because of their small sample sizes and so they are not directly relevant to the concerns of this book. I would note that although many researchers see this design as the strongest possible test of genetic influences, in fact they have no control whatsoever for the environments of twins but infer environmental effects from the difference in correlations of a trait between MZ and DZ twins. In addition, and contrary to established scientific norms, researchers provide virtually no information about their samples and it appears that many of their subjects actually were raised in quite similar circumstances, often by close relatives. See especially the work of Thomas Bouchard (e.g., Bouchard et al. 1990; Bouchard and McGue 1990; Bouchard 1994).

16 Adoption studies, as well as twin studies, minimize possible environmental variance. Parents whose biological children are adopted are younger, poorer, from more socially disorganized backgrounds, less likely to be married, and have more problems with substance abuse than parents who raise their natural children. These traits are also associated with nongenetic sources of psychopathology such as poor prenatal health care and diet. Conversely, adoptive parents are more likely than the general population and far more likely than the biological parents of adopted children to be older, better off financially, socially respectable, and free of psychopathology. The chance of attaining a statistical correlation between environmental factors and pathology declines when there is little variation in the environment. The relatively uniform higher social standing and low incidence of pathology among adoptive parents reduces the range of environmental variation and thus the probability of attaining a correlation between the environment and pathology among adoptive children. The socially structured nature of adoption thus affects the statistical probabilities of correlations between the traits of biological parents, adoptive parents, and children. See Cadoret 1991; Lieberson 1985. For twin studies see Rose et al. 1988.

17 See, for example, Bouchard 1994; Rowe 1994; Plomin and Daniels 1987; Harris 1998. This problem is particularly acute when there is great variation in the prevalence of symptoms in different environments, as with most types of mental disorders. Conditions such as schizophrenia that have relatively similar prevalence rates in different environments do not face the same difficulties.

18 As Marshall McLuhan reportedly remarked: "It's a cinch (that) fish didn't discover water" (cited in Segall, Lonner, and Berry 1998, 1101).

19 The efforts of Gulf War veterans to demonstrate that their symptoms result from physical, rather than mental, causes provide a good illustration of the social fact that only diseases with perceived biological causes have social legitimacy. Hence, the Gulf War Syndrome that many veterans of this conflict believe they have only becomes a legitimate disease if it results from chemical exposure. If there is no physical cause, symptoms are "merely" mental and their bearers are stigmatized and considered unmanly. See Showalter 1997; Fukuda et al. 1998.

20 The converse of this principle, that disorders with social causes may benefit from biological treatments, is also true. For example, medications will often effectively deal with symptoms of depression or anxiety that stem from problems of living (see Kramer 1993).

CHAPTER SEVEN: SOCIAL CAUSES OF DISTRESS

1 The "biopsychosocial" model is one common way of looking at the relationship between social, biological, and psychological causes of mental disorder (USDHHS 1999). This model integrates all types of variables in order to maximize explanatory power in predicting mental disorder. This chapter takes a contrasting view that the external and collective aspects of social causes can best be seen as different in fundamental ways from the internal and individual nature of biological causes and so does not try to integrate social with biological causes. Both models have their advantages and disadvantages.

2 In this regard, studies of chronic stressors diverge from the classic models of stress that emerged from the biological literature, which emphasize that life *changes* rather than that chronic conditions produce distress (see Cannon 1929; Selye 1956; Hinkle and Wolff 1958).

3 Externality indicates that social facts are independent of any particular individual, not that they have a reality independent of any individual. See Lukes 1975.

4 See also Myers and Diener 1995; Lykken and Tellegen 1996.

5 The power of genetic makeup over social experiences is seemingly so great that identical twins reared apart actually come to resemble each other more in later life than twins who were reared together, supposedly because genetic influences on memory affect what events people remember. See Plomin et al. 1990.

6 The same author regards the social environment is no more than "noise" that masks the genetic determination of personality. See Bouchard 1994, 1701.

7 The same study, however, shows that social causation is more important than selection in affecting depression in women and substance abuse and antisocial personality in men.

8 This view of social causes is narrower than the common view many sociologists hold, which regards psychological traits such as self-esteem, locus of control, fatalism, mastery, and the like as causal sources of distress. I do not consider these as social causes because they are internal qualities of individuals, not social properties that are external to

particular individuals. Because they are internal traits of individuals, they should intrinsically correlate with mental disorder, which is the variable to be explained. For example, the association of low self-esteem with depression is in part tautological because low self-esteem is an intrinsic aspect of, not a cause of, depression. In contrast, limiting social factors to aspects of environments that are external to particular individuals more clearly separates the causes from the consequences of distress.

9   Lamarck was a French biologist whose writings preceded Darwin's. He believed that the traits humans acquired as adaptations to their environments could be passed on to their offspring.

10 The same trends hold in Puerto Rico, Taiwan, and Lebanon. See Cross-national Collaborative Group 1992.

11 Recent epidemiological studies also consistently show a finding that is anomalous for biological psychiatry but consistent for the social perspective: rates of lifetime prevalence of nearly all disorders are equivalent or higher among younger than among older age groups (see Robins et al. 1984; Kessler et al. 1994). This contradicts the biological perspective because older people have had more years of possible exposure to the disorder. It is consistent with the cohort perspective that predicts diverse rates of disorder among different age groups because of the various sorts of experiences different cohorts have had. In particular, it is consistent with the evidence noted above that rates of depression and substance use have been rising in recent cohorts.

12 Not much has changed over the course of Western history. MacDonald (1981, 99) reports that in seventeenth-century England "Marital problems were very common among . . . disturbed clients, and most of those who complained about turbulent unions were women."

13 The pervasive impact of marital dissolution on mental health is limited to groups where marital status is an important determinant of prestige, resources, and social roles. For example, among the Tiv of West Africa, divorce has few consequences for social roles and relationships (see Bohannon 1957). In such groups divorce should not produce major mental health consequences.

14 For reviews of this large literature see Bloom, Asher, and White 1978; Gerstel and Reissman 1984; Kitson, Babri, and Roach 1985; Kitson and Morgan 1990; Ross, Mirowsky, and Goldstein 1990; Waite 1995.

15 In contrast, McGue and Lykken (1992) argue that the causes of divorce are largely genetic because both MZ twins are more likely to get divorced than both DZ twins.

16 As Aristotle noted, an insult from an inferior leads to anger, while an insult from a dominant leads to sadness (cited in Price and Sloman 1987, 96S).

17 See the work of Rosenfield (1983) on the disproportionate sanctions to "deviant deviants" who deviate from gender roles in sex-inappropriate ways.

CHAPTER EIGHT: DIAGNOSTIC PSYCHIATRY AND THERAPY

1   These chemical changes must, of course, be interpreted through categories that different cultures provide. See Lin, Poland, and Anderson 1995; Rudorfer 1996.

2   This does not mean that cultural and interpersonal factors are irrelevant to the study of the efficacy of medications (see Lin, Poland, and Anderson 1995; Rudorfer 1996; Fisher and Greenberg 1997). They are, however, of less importance compared to psychotherapy, where they are integral aspects of treatment.

3   The original use of placebos was as inactive medications. See Pepper 1945. More recently, the notion of a placebo in drug treatment has altered. The presence or absence

of side effects of the medication can lead people to guess whether they are in the experimental or the control group. In addition, ethical concerns often dictate that an experimental treatment be compared to a treatment with known effectiveness, rather than to a placebo. Therefore, placebo treatments now often compare an experimental drug with a different drug of relatively known effectiveness rather than with an inert pill. See Antonuccio et al. 1999.

4 See Fisher and Greenberg 1997 for a dissenting view.

5 Historically, the most important study is the NIMH Collaborative Study of phenothiazines (1964). See Swazey 1974 and Gelman 1999 for extended commentaries about this study. See Pickar and Hsiao 1995 and Thase and Kupfer 1996 for examples of more recent studies. As Valenstein (1998) demonstrates, current pharmaceutical research is completely intertwined with the interests of private drug companies. The dependency of researchers on the sponsorship of pharmaceutical companies may serve to increase the chances that positive findings regarding effectiveness will be reported and negative findings will be ignored, thus inflating the degree to which medications seem to be effective.

6 See Meltzer et al. 1993 for an optimistic view of clozapine. See Wahlbeck et al. 1999 for a more tempered assessment from a meta-analytic study.

7 http://www.ahcpr.gov/clinic/deprsumm.htm 3/19/99; WPA Dysthymia Working Group 1995. The belief that the SSRIs are far better than the older antidepressants is largely a result of Kramer's (1993) wildly popular, but anecdotal, accounts of the total transformations in personality that his patients underwent after taking Prozac.

8 Klerman's comprehensive review of antidepressant studies (1989) indicates that for major depression, medications were effective in 50 percent of cases compared to 32 percent for placebo. For dysthymic disorders, 59 percent of cases actively treated showed improvement, compared to 37 percent treated with placebo. Strangely, this evidence for the efficacy of medication has sometimes been taken to indicate that medication and placebo therapy have equivalent effect. See Horgan 1999. See Quitkin et al. 2000 for a critique of these claims.

9 Knutson et al. 1998 present evidence that the SSRIs relieve the symptoms of normal people as much as they do those of the disordered.

10 The prominent American psychiatrist Adolph Meyer made a similar argument (see Caplan 1998, 110).

11 Hohmann (1999) provides an excellent model for the evaluation of therapeutic interventions that is more suitable for evaluating the actual operation of therapeutic programs than are traditional approaches.

12 See Marx and Spray 1972; Horwitz 1982a; Rogler and Cortes 1993; Padgett et al. 1994; Scheffler and Miller 1989; Shorter 1997; Sue 1988; Takeuchi, Uehara, and Maramba 1999. See also Seligman 1995.

13 See Zetzel 1965 and Strupp 1965 for critiques of Eysenck's assertion that two thirds of untreated neurotics recover.

14 Studies do not consider people in the community who have comparable psychological conditions but who seek various kinds of help from nonprofessionals. Effectiveness studies assume that support is equivalent to professional support so "untreated" means "not obtaining professional mental health treatment." Yet, this assumption lumps diverse informal responses ranging from isolated individuals who do nothing to relieve their distress or who self-medicate in damaging ways to people who discuss their problems with

many trusted and empathetic friends. Professional psychotherapy may be better than the former alternative but not the latter. If psychotherapy represents a more generic form of social relationship, people who obtain support in their informal networks should get the same benefit as those who enter psychotherapy. The best possible measure of the effectiveness of professional psychotherapy may be a comparison between people in psychotherapy and those who talk about their problems with trusted friends and family members but not with professionals.

15 DeRubeis et al. (1999), in a meta-analysis, argue to the contrary, claiming that cognitive-behavioral therapy and antidepressant medication have comparable effectiveness for severely depressed patients.

16 In contrast to severely depressed patients, about 50 to 70 percent of mildly depressed patients respond to placebos. See Thase 1999; Hamburg 2000.

17 This also conforms to the recommendations of the WPA Dysthymia Working Group (1995, 180) that brief psychotherapies are the most efficacious method of treating mild to moderate depressions.

18 The finding that cognitive-behavioral therapy did not show greater benefits than interpersonal therapy and the placebo condition in the NIMH Collaborative Study appears to be the exception to the bulk of research. Cognitive-behavioral methods do seem to be more effective than other forms of psychotherapies in treating not only phobias but also obsessive-compulsive disorders, panic attacks, and bulimia among other conditions. See, for example, Marks et al. 1993; Wilson and Fairburn 1993; Persons, Thase, and Crits-Christoph 1996.

19 I do not consider behavioral treatments to be psychotherapeutic techniques because they do not rely on the manipulation of verbal symbols. Their effectiveness in improving particular symptoms does seem to be superior to psychotherapy.

20 The parallel between professional therapy and generic support is, of course, not exact, as patients who lose their ability to pay their therapists will quickly find out. In general, see Schofield 1964.

21 Some studies that question the benefits of psychotropic medications argue that psychotherapeutic approaches are more effective. The rigorous standards they apply to tests of medications, however, are considerably relaxed when they argue for the presumed effectiveness of psychotherapy. See especially Glenmullen 2000.

22 Indeed, some prominent psychopharmacologists claim that because individuals can regulate their psychological states as well as their physicians can, the most common antidepressants, which usually have benefits without major negative side effects, should be available over the counter, like pain relievers or anti-allergy medications. In the future, it may be possible to purchase antidepressants at the supermarket (see Healy 1997).

CONCLUSION: MENTAL ILLNESSES AS SOCIAL CONSTRUCTIONS

1 Positive answers are found in Rieff 1961, Gay 1988, Robinson 1993, and Fisher and Greenberg 1996. For negative views see Crews 1995, Grunbaum 1984, and Masson 1984.

2 For a contrasting view that the new entities of diagnostic psychiatry did not improve the reliability of their measurement, see Kirk and Kutchins 1992.

3 *New York Times Magazine*, 23 November 1997. The major work that propelled the SSRIs into public consciousness is Kramer 1993. See Glenmullen 2000 for a critique of these medications.

4 For generalized anxiety disorder see Sharkey 1999; for social phobia see Raghunathan 1999; for depression see Clinton and Hyman 1999.

5 E.g., *People*, 9 November 1998, 12 April 1999; *Newsweek*, 26 January 1998. Best-selling books about mental illness also emphasize that they are "real" diseases. See especially Rapoport 1989, Styron 1992, Jamison 1995.

6 Borges and Waitzkin (1995) illustrate how clients of primary care physicians can be more likely to want their physicians to prescribe psychotropic medications than their physicians are willing to provide them with these prescriptions. See Kutchins and Kirk (1997) for a contrasting view that the illnesses of the DSM are imposed upon unwilling victims.

7 This trend is most apparent in the vast publicity given to the completion of the human genome. See, for example, *Time*, 3 July 2000. See Conrad 2000 for a general sociological critique of this trend.

8 For the general acceptance of medicalized notions of mental illnesses see Conrad 1992, Conrad and Schneider 1992. Opposition to medicalized categories has emerged in several areas. One such camp is opposed to the widespread prescription of antidepressants to ever younger age groups, including preschoolers. See Zito et al. 2000. Opposition also emerges when medical labels are applied to behaviors such as alcohol and drug abuse that have traditionally been viewed as forms of social deviance. In addition, there is widespread skepticism about the use of disease categories when they result in social advantages, as the controversy over the Americans with Disabilities Act illustrates. See Mechanic 1998a.

9 The use of terms such as "disproportionate" or "long after" in judging whether or not the symptoms of people who have experienced social stressors indicates that mental disorders inherently require the use of social value judgments. Thus, such definitions always have a social component.

10 The CES-D (Radloff 1977), for example, which is supposed to measure depression, is about as strongly related to diagnoses of anxiety disorders, including panic, agoraphobia, social phobia, generalized anxiety disorder, and obsessive-compulsive disorder, as it is to depression. See Fechner-Bates, Coyne and Schwenk 1994.

11 Examples are the Langner scale (Langner 1962), the Health Opinion Survey (Macmillan 1957), and the CES-D (Radloff 1977). Early stress researchers including Cannon (1929), Dubos (1959), Selye (1956), Hinkle and Wolff (1958), and Cassell (1974, 1976) emphasized how the outcomes of external stressors were not specific but reflected a general adaptational syndrome that encompassed numerous negative outcomes.

12 See especially the Surgeon General's Report on Mental Health (USDHHS 1999). See also Regier et al. 1993; Narrow et al. 1993; Hirschfeld et al. 1997.

13 The 3 percent of the population who use formal psychotherapeutic services each year account for 14 percent of the total ambulatory costs in the medical system.

14 A full elaboration of this assertion would require many qualifications. For example, people are more willing to apply disease frameworks to the misbehavior of their intimates than they are to apply such frameworks to the deviance of strangers. See Horwitz 1982a.

15 This ambivalence is seen in many ways. The Americans with Disabilities Act, for example, explicitly exempts from protection conditions produced by illegal drug use. See Mechanic 1998a. Likewise, mental health advocacy groups do not link conditions of serious mental illness to alcohol and drug disorders. The Surgeon General's Report on men-

tal health, for example, does not address issues concerning drug and alcohol disorders (see USDHHS 1999).

16 A few examples include the publicity generated by the disclosures of the late Princess Diana's bulimia, Roseanne Barr's recovered memory syndrome, Tipper Gore's depression, and Howard Stern's obsessive-compulsive disorder.

17 This movement gained popular notice in a cover story in *Newsweek*, 26 January 1998.

18 Recent critiques of the psychiatric profession, especially Luhrmann 2000 and Glenmullen 2000, argue for the reemergence of psychotherapy grounded in the dynamic rather than in the diagnostic tradition. Such a development is highly unlikely for many reasons: psychotherapies are far more costly and time-consuming than medication therapies, they appeal to a narrower cultural spectrum, and they show little evidence of effectiveness beyond the generalized social support they provide.

——— References ———

Abbott, A. 1988. *The System of the Professions*. Chicago: University of Chicago Press.

Acocella, J. 1998. "The Politics of Hysteria." *The New Yorker*, 6 April 1998, 64–79.

Alarcon, R. D. 1995. "Culture and Psychiatric Diagnosis: Impact on DSM-IV and ICD-10." *Cultural Psychiatry* 18:449–65.

Alexander, F. 1948. *Fundamentals of Psychoanalysis*. New York: W. W. Norton.

Amato, P. R., and S. J. Rogers. 1997. "A Longitudinal Study of Marital Problems and Subsequent Divorce." *Journal of Marriage and the Family* 59:612–24.

American Psychiatric Association (APA). 1952. *Diagnostic and Statistical Manual of Mental Disorders*. Washington, D.C.: American Psychiatric Association.

———. 1968. *Diagnostic and Statistical Manual of Mental Disorders*, 2d ed. Washington, D.C.: American Psychiatric Association.

———. 1980. *Diagnostic and Statistical Manual of Mental Disorders*, 3d ed. Washington, D.C.: American Psychiatric Association.

———. 1987. *Diagnostic and Statistical Manual of Mental Disorders*, 3d ed., revised. Washington, D.C.: American Psychiatric Association.

———. 1994. *Diagnostic and Statistical Manual of Mental Disorders*, 4th ed. Washington, D.C.: American Psychiatric Association.

Andreasen, N. 1984. *The Broken Brain: The Biological Revolution in Psychiatry*. New York: Harper & Row.

Andreasen, N., and D. Black. 1995. *Introductory Textbook of Psychiatry*. Washington, D.C.: American Psychiatric Press.

Aneshensel, C. S. 1992. "Social Stress: Theory and Research." *Annual Review of Sociology* 18:15–38.

Aneshensel, C. S., R. R. Frerichs, and V. A. Clark. 1981. "Family Roles and Sex Differences in Depression." *Journal of Health and Social Behavior* 22:379–93.

Aneshensel, C. S., C. M. Rutter, and P. A. Lachenbruch. 1991. "Social Structure, Stress, and Mental Health." *American Sociological Review* 56:166–78.

Aneshensel, C. S., and C. A. Sukoff. 1996. "The Neighborhood Context of Adolescent Mental Health." *Journal of Health and Social Behavior* 37:293–310.

Angst, J. K., and R. Merikangas. 1997. "The Depressive Spectrum: Diagnostic Classification and Course." *Journal of Affective Disorders* 45:31–40.

Angst, J. K., R. Merikangas, and M. Preisig. 1997. "Subthreshold Syndromes of Depression and Anxiety in the Community." *Journal of Clinical Psychiatry* 58:6–10.

Anthony, J. C., and J. E. Helzer. 1991. "Syndromes of Drug Abuse and Dependence." In *Psychiatric Disorders in America: The Epidemiologic Catchment Area Study*, ed. L. N. Robins and D. A. Regier, 116–54. New York: Free Press.

Antonuccio, D. O., W. G. Danton, G. Y. DeNelsky, R. P. Greenberg, and J. S. Gordon. 1999. "Raising Questions about Antidepressants." *Psychotherapy and Psychosomatics* 68:3–14.

Aronowitz, R. A. 1998. *Making Sense of Illness: Science, Society, and Disease.* New York: Cambridge University Press.

Aseltine, R. H. Jr., and R. C. Kessler. 1993. "Marital Disruption and Depression in a Community Sample." *Journal of Health and Social Behavior* 34:237–51.

Auden, W. H. 1991. "In Memory of Sigmund Freud." In *Collected Poems*, 273–76. New York: Vintage.

Avison, W. R. 1999. "Family Structure and Process." In *A Handbook for the Study of Mental Health: Social Contexts, Theories, and Systems*, ed. A. V. Horwitz and T. L. Scheid, 228–40. New York: Cambridge University Press.

Avison, W. R., and R. J. Turner. 1988. "Stressful Life Events and Depressive Symptoms: Disaggregating the Effects of Acute Stressors and Chronic Strains." *Journal of Health and Social Behavior* 29:253–64.

Bachrach, L. L. 1980. "Overview: Model Programs for Chronic Mental Patients." *American Journal of Psychiatry* 137:1023–30.

Back, K. F. 1973. *Beyond Words: The Story of Sensitivity Training and the Encounter Movement.* New York: Penguin.

Baldessarini, R. J. 2000. "American Biological Psychiatry and Psychopharmacology, 1944–1994." In *American Psychiatry after WWII: 1944–1994*, ed. R. W. Menninger and J. C. Nemiah, 371–412. Washington, D.C.: American Psychiatric Press.

Bales, R. F. 1962. "Attitudes toward Drinking in Irish Culture." In *Society, Culture and Drinking Patterns*, ed. D. J. Pitman and C. R. Snyder, 157–87. Carbondale: Southern Illinois University Press.

Barker, P. 1991. *Regeneration.* New York: Penguin.

Bart, P. B. 1974. "Ideologies and Utopias of Psychotherapy." In *The Sociology of Psychotherapy*, ed. P. Roman and H. M. Trice, 9–57. New York: Jason Aronson.

Bass, E., and L. Davis. 1988. *The Courage to Heal.* New York: Harper & Row.

Bayer, R. 1987. *Homosexuality and American Psychiatry: The Politics of Diagnosis.* Princeton, N.J.: Princeton University Press.

———. 1989. *Private Acts, Social Consequences: AIDS and the Politics of Public Health.* New York: Free Press.

Bayer, R., and R. L. Spitzer. 1985. "Neurosis, Psychodynamics, and DSM-III: A History of the Controversy." *Archives of General Psychiatry* 42:187–96.

Beard, J. H., R. N. Propst, and T. J. Malamud. 1982. "The Fountain House Model of Psychiatric Rehabilitation." *Psychosocial Rehabilitation* 5:47–54.

Beck, A. T., A. J. Rush, B. F. Shaw, and G. Emery. 1979. *Cognitive Therapy of Depression.* New York: Guilford.

Bell, R. M. 1985. *Holy Anorexia.* Chicago: University of Chicago Press.

Benedict, R. 1934. "Anthropology and the Abnormal." *Journal of General Psychology* 10:59–80.

———. 1959 [1934]. *Patterns of Culture.* New York: New American Library.

Berger, P. L., and T. Luckmann. 1967. *The Social Construction of Reality: A Treatise in the Sociology of Knowledge.* Garden City, N.Y.: Doubleday Anchor.

Berman, J. S., and N. C. Norton. 1985. "Does Professional Training Make a Therapist More Effective?" *Psychological Bulletin* 98:401–7.

Bertelson, A., B. Harvald, and M. Hauge. 1977. "A Danish Twin Study of Manic-Depressive Disorder." *British Journal of Psychiatry* 130:330–51.

Bird, H. R., G. Canino, M. Rubio-Stiper, M. S. Gould, J. Ribera, M. Sesman, M. Woodbury, S. Huertas-Goldman, A. Pagan, A. Sanchez-Lacay, and M. Moscos. 1988. "Estimates of the Prevalence of Childhood Maladjustment in a Community Survey in Puerto Rico." *Archives of General Psychiatry* 45:1120–26.

Black, D. 1976. *The Behavior of Law.* New York: Academic Press.

———. 1983. "Crime as Social Control." *American Sociological Review* 48:34–45.

Black, D. W., R. Noyes, R. B. Goldstein, et al. 1992. "A Family Study of Obsessive-Compulsive Disorder." *Archives of General Psychiatry* 49:362–68.

Black, D. W., S. Repertinger, G. R. Gaffney, and J. Gabel. 1998. "Family History and Psychiatric Comorbidity in Persons with Compulsive Buying: Preliminary Findings." *American Journal of Psychiatry* 155:960–63.

Blashfield, R. K. 1982. "Feighner et al., Invisible Colleges, and the Matthew Effect." *Schizophrenia Bulletin* 8:1–8.

Blashfield, R. K., June Sprock, and A. Kenneth Fuller. 1990. "Suggested Guidelines for Including or Excluding Categories in the DSM-IV." *Comprehensive Psychiatry* 31:15–19.

Blazer, D. G., R. C. Kessler, K. A. McGonagle, and M. S. Swartz. 1994. "The Prevalence and Distribution of Major Depression in a National Community Sample: The National Comorbidity Survey." *American Journal of Psychiatry* 151:979–86.

Bloom, B. L., S. J. Asher, and S. W. White. 1978. "Marital Disruption as a Stressor: A Review and Analysis." *Psychological Bulletin* 85:867–94.

Blum, K., E. P. Noble, P. J. Sheridan, A. Montgomery, et al. 1990. "Allelic Association of Human Dopamine D2 Receptor Gene in Alcoholism." *Journal of the American Medical Association* 263:2055–60.

Bohannon, P. 1957. *Justice and Judgment among the Tiv.* London: Oxford University Press.

Bolos, A. M., M. Dean, A. Lucas-Derse, M. Ramsburg, G. L. Brown, and D. Goldman. 1991. "Population and Pedigree Studies Reveal a Lack of Association between the Dopamine D2 Receptor Gene and Alcoholism." *Journal of the American Medical Association* 264:3156–60.

Borch-Jacobsen, M. 1997. "The Making of a Disease: An Interview with Herbert Spiegel." *New York Review of Books,* 24 April.

Borges, S., and H. Waitzkin. 1995. "Women's Narratives in Primary Care Medical Encounters." *Women and Health* 23:29–42.

Bouchard, T. J. Jr. 1994. "Genes, Environment, and Personality." *Science* 264:1700–1701.

Bouchard, T. J. Jr., D. T. Lykken, M. McGue, N. L. Segal, and A. Tellegen. 1990. "Sources of Human Psychological Differences: The Minnesota Study of Identical Twins Reared Apart." *Science* 250:223–28.

Bouchard, T. J. Jr., and M. McGue. 1990. "Genetic and Rearing Environmental Influences on Adult Personality: An Analysis of Adopted Twins Reared Apart." *Journal of Personality* 58:263–92.

Breakey, W. R., ed. 1994. *Integrated Mental Health Services: Modern Community Psychiatry.* New York: Oxford University Press.

Breggin, P. R. 1991. *Toxic Psychiatry: Why Therapy, Empathy, and Love Must Replace the Drugs, Electroshock, and Biochemical Theories of the New Psychiatry.* New York: St. Martin's.

Breier, A., R. W. Buchanan, B. Kirkpatrick, O. R. Davis, D. Irish, A. Summerfelt, and W. T. Carpenter. 1994. "Effects of Clozapine on Positive and Negative Symptoms in Outpatients with Schizophrenia." *American Journal of Psychiatry* 151:20–26.

Breier, A., D. S. Charney, and G. R. Heninger. 1985. "The Diagnostic Validity of Anxiety Disorders and Their Relationship to Depressive Illness." *American Journal of Psychiatry* 142:787–97.

Breslau, N., G. C. Davis, P. Andreski, and E. Peterson. 1991. "Traumatic Events and Post-traumatic Stress Disorder in an Urban Population of Young Adults." *Archives of General Psychiatry* 48:216–22.

Brodbeck, M. 1968. "General Introduction." In *Readings in the Philosophy of the Social Sciences*, ed. M. Brodbeck, 1–11. New York: Macmillan.

Brown, B., P. Nolan, P. Crawford, and A. Lewis. 1996. "Interaction, Language and the 'Narrative Turn' in Psychotherapy and Psychiatry." *Social Science and Medicine* 43:1569–78.

Brown, G. W. 1996. "Genetics of Depression: A Social Science Perspective." *International Review of Psychiatry* 8:387–401.

Brown, G. W., and Tirril Harris. 1978. *Social Origins of Depression: A Study of Psychiatric Disorder in Women.* New York: Free Press.

Brown, G. W., and Patricia Moran. 1994. "Clinical and Psychosocial Origins of Chronic Depressive Episodes I: A Community Survey." *British Journal of Psychiatry* 165:447–56.

Brown, P. 1995. "Naming and Framing: The Social Construction of Diagnosis and Illness." *Journal of Health and Social Behavior* (extra issue):34–52.

Bruch, H. 1978. *The Golden Cage: The Enigma of Anorexia Nervosa.* Cambridge: Harvard University Press.

Brumberg, J. J. 1988. *Fasting Girls: The History of Anorexia Nervosa.* Cambridge: Harvard University Press.

Burgess, A. W., and L. L. Holstrum. 1974. "The Rape Trauma Syndrome." *American Journal of Psychiatry* 131:981–86.

Burke, K. 1969. *A Rhetoric of Motives.* Berkeley: University of California Press.

Burke, K. C., J. D. Burke, D. S. Rae, and D. A. Regier. 1991. "Comparing Age of Onset of Major Depression and Other Psychiatric Disorders by Birth Cohorts in Five U.S. Community Populations." *Archives of General Psychiatry* 48:789–95.

Burton, R. 1948 [1621]. *The Anatomy of Melancholy*, ed. Floyd Dell and Paul Jordan-Smith. New York: Tudor.

Buss, D. M. 1994. *The Evolution of Desire: Strategies of Human Mating.* New York: Basic Books.

Cade, J. 1949. "Lithium Salts in the Treatment of Psychotic Excitement." *Medical Journal of Australia* 36:349–52.

Cadoret, R. J. 1978. "Evidence for Genetic Inheritance of Primary Affective Disorder." *American Journal of Psychiatry* 135: 463–66.

———. 1991. "Adoption Studies in Psychosocial Epidemiology." In *Genetic Issues in Psychosocial Epidemiology*, ed. M. T. Tsuang, K. S. Kendler, and M. J. Lyons, 33–46. New Brunswick, N.J.: Rutgers University Press.

Cadoret, R. J., T. W. O'Gorman, E. Heywood, and E. Troughton. 1985. "Genetic and Environmental Factors in Major Depression." *Journal of Affective Disorders* 9:155–64.

Cain, L. D. Jr. 1967. "Age Status and Generational Phenomena: The New Old People in Contemporary America." *The Gerontologist* 7:83–92.

Cancro, R. 2000. "Functional Psychoses and the Conceptualization of Mental Illness." In

American Psychiatry after WWII: 1944–1994, ed. R. W. Menninger and J. C. Nemiah, 413–29. Washington, D.C.: American Psychiatric Press.

Cannon, W. B. 1929. *Bodily Changes in Pain, Hunger, Fear and Rage*, 2d ed. New York: Appleton.

Caplan, E. 1998. *Mind Games: American Culture and the Birth of Psychotherapy.* Berkeley: University of California Press.

Cardozo, B. L., A. Vergara, F. Agani, and C. A. Gotway. 2000. "Mental Health, Social Functioning, and Attitudes of Kosovar Albanians following the War in Kosovo." *Journal of the American Medical Association* 284:569–77.

Cassell, J. 1974. "Psychosocial Processes and 'Stress': Theoretical Formulations." *International Journal of Health Services* 4:471–82.

———. 1976. "The Contribution of the Social Environment to Host Resistance." *American Journal of Epidemiology* 104:107–23.

Castillo, R. J. 1997. *Culture & Mental Illness: A Client-Centered Approach.* Pacific Grove, Calif.: Brooks/Cole.

Catalano, R., D. Dooley, G. Wilson, and R. Hough. 1993. "Job Loss and Alcohol Abuse: A Test Using Data from the Epidemiologic Catchment Area Project." *Journal of Health and Social Behavior* 34:215–26.

Center for Mental Health Services. 1996. *Mental Health, United States, 1996*, ed. R. A. Manderscheid and M. A. Sonnenschein. DHHS Pub. No. (SMA)96–3098. Washington, D.C.: U.S. Government Printing Office.

———. 1998. *Mental Health, United States, 1998*, ed. R. A. Manderscheid and M. J. Henderson. DHHS Pub. No. (SMA)99–3285. Washington, D.C.: U.S. Government Printing Office.

Chandra, P., M. Sudha, A. Subbarathna, S. Rao, et al. 1995. "Mental Health in Mothers from a Transitional Society: The Role of Spouse Supportiveness." *Family Therapy* 22:49–59.

Cherlin, A. J. 1992. *Marriage, Divorce, Remarriage*, rev. ed. Cambridge: Harvard University Press.

Chesler, P. 1972. *Women and Madness.* New York: Doubleday.

Clifford, C. A., R. M. Murray, and D. W. Fulker. 1984. "Genetic and Environmental Influences on Obsessional Traits and Symptoms." *Psychological Medicine* 14:791–800.

Clinton, H. R., and S. Hyman. 1999. "Mental Illness Is a Disease." In *How Should Mental Illness Be Defined?*, ed. T. I. Rodeff and L. K. Egendorf, 37–41. San Diego, Calif.: Greenhaven Press.

Cloninger, C. R., M. Gohman, and S. Sigvardsson. 1981. "Inheritance of Alcohol Abuse: Cross Fostering Analysis of Adopted Men." *Archives of General Psychiatry* 38:861–68.

Cloward, R., and L. Ohlin. 1960. *Delinquency and Opportunity.* New York: Free Press.

Coie, J. D., N. F. Watt, S. G. West, J. D. Hawkins, J. R. Asarnow, H. J. Markman, S. L. Ramey, M. B. Shure, and B. Long. 1993. "The Science of Prevention: A Conceptual Framework and Some Directions for a National Research Program." *American Psychologist* 48:1013–22.

Cole, M. 1996. *Cultural Psychology: A Once and Future Discipline.* Cambridge: Harvard University Press.

Conrad, P. 1992. "Medicalization and Social Control." *Annual Review of Sociology* 18:209–32.

———. 1997. "Public Eyes and Private Genes: Historical Frames, News Constructions, and Social Problems." *Social Problems* 44:139–54.

———. 2000. "Medicalization, Genetics and Human Problems." In *The Handbook of Medical Sociology*, ed. C. Bird, P. Conrad and A. Fremont, 5th ed., 322–43. Upper Saddle River, N.J.: Prentice-Hall.

Conrad, P., and Joseph Schneider. 1992. *Deviance and Medicalization*, 2d ed. Philadelphia: Temple University Press.

Cooper, J., R. Rendell, B. Burland, L. Sharpe, J. Copeland, and R. Simon. 1972. *Psychiatric Diagnosis in New York and London*. London: Oxford University Press.

Coryell, W., and M. Zimmerman. 1988. "The Heritability of Schizophrenia and Schizoaffective Disorder." *Archives of General Psychiatry* 45:323–27.

Cottle, M. 1999. "Selling Shyness." *The New Republic*, 2 August, 24–29.

Coulter, J. 1973. *Approaches to Insanity: A Philosophical and Sociological Study*. New York: Wiley.

Counts, D. A. 1980. "Fighting Back Is Not the Way: Suicide and the Women of Kaliai." *American Ethnologist* 7:332–51.

Crews, F. 1995. *The Memory Wars: Freud's Legacy in Dispute*. New York: New York Review Book.

Cross-National Collaborative Group. 1992. "The Changing Rate of Major Depression: Cross-National Comparisons." *Journal of the American Medical Association* 268:3089–3105.

Crowe, R. R., R. Noyes, A. F. Wilson, R. C. Elston, and L. J. Ward. 1987. "A Linkage Study of Panic Disorder." *Archives of General Psychiatry* 44:933–37.

Culbertson, F. M. 1997. "Depression and Gender: An International Review." *American Psychologist* 52:25–31.

Cullen, F. T. 1983. *Rethinking Crime and Deviance Theory: The Emergence of a Structuring Tradition*. Totowa, N.J.: Rowman & Allanheld.

Danziger, K. 1990. *Constructing the Subject: Historical Origins of Psychological Research*. New York: Cambridge University Press.

Davis, K. 1938. "Mental Hygiene and the Class Structure." *Psychiatry* 1:55–65.

Davis, L. J. 1997. "The Encyclopedia of Insanity." *Harper's*, February, 61–66.

Dawes, R. M. 1994. *House of Cards: Psychology and Psychotherapy Built on Myth*. New York: Free Press.

Decker, H. S. 1991. *Freud, Dora, and Vienna 1900*. New York: Free Press.

Degler, C. N. 1991. *In Search of Human Nature: The Decline and Revival of Darwinism in American Social Thought*. New York: Oxford University Press.

Dennett, D.C. 1995. *Darwin's Dangerous Idea: Evolution and the Meaning of Life*. New York: Simon & Schuster.

DeRubeis, R. J., L. A. Gelfand, T. Z. Tang, and A. D. Simons. 1999. "Medications versus Cognitive Behavior Therapy for Severely Depressed Outpatients: Meta-analysis of Four Randomized Comparisons." *American Journal of Psychiatry* 156:1007–13.

Detre, T. 1987. "The Future of Psychiatry." *American Journal of Psychiatry* 144:621–25.

Devereux, G. 1980 [1956]. *Basic Problems in Ethnopsychiatry*. Chicago: University of Chicago Press.

Dimaggio, P. 1997. "Culture and Cognition: An Interdisciplinary Review." *Annual Review of Sociology* 23: 263–88.

Doherty, W. J., S. Su, and R. Needle. 1989. "Marital Disruption and Psychological Well-Being." *Journal of Family Issues* 10:72–85.

Dohrenwend, B. P. 2000. "The Role of Adversity and Stress in Psychopathology: Some Evidence and its Implications for Theory and Research." *Journal of Health and Social Behavior* 41:1–19.

Dohrenwend, B. P., and B. S. Dohrenwend. 1969. *Social Status and Psychological Disorder: A Causal Inquiry.* New York: Wiley.

————. 1976. "Sex Differences and Psychiatric Disorders." *American Journal of Sociology* 81:1447–54.

————. 1982. "Perspectives on the Past and Future of Psychiatric Epidemiology." *American Journal of Public Health* 72:1271–79.

Dohrenwend, B. P., I. Levav, P. E. Shrout, S. Schwartz, G. Naveh, B. G. Link, A. E. Skodol, and A. Stueve. 1992. "Socioeconomic Status and Psychiatric Disorders: The Causation-Selection Issue." *Science* 255:946–52.

Dohrenwend, B. S., and B. P. Dohrenwend, eds. 1974. *Stressful Life Events: Their Nature and Effects.* New York: Wiley-Interscience.

————. 1981. *Stressful Life Events and Their Contexts.* New Brunswick, N.J.: Rutgers University Press.

Dooley, D., R. Catalano, and G. Wilson. 1994. "Depression and Unemployment: Panel Findings from the Epidemiologic Catchment Area Study." *American Journal of Community Psychology* 22:742–65.

Dowdall, G. 1996. *The Eclipse of the State Mental Hospital: Policy, Stigma, and Organization.* Albany: State University of New York Press.

Dubos, R. 1959. *Mirage of Health: Utopias, Progress, and Biological Change.* New York: Harper & Row.

Duhl, L., and R. Leopold. 1968. *Mental Health and Urban Social Policy: A Casebook of Community Action.* San Francisco: Jossey-Bass.

Dunham, H. W. 1959. *Sociological Theory and Mental Disorder.* Detroit: Wayne State University Press.

Durkheim, E. 1966 [1895]. *The Rules of the Sociological Method.* New York: Free Press.

————. 1951 [1897]. *Suicide: A Study in Sociology.* New York: Free Press.

Eaton, J. W., and R. J. Weil. 1955. *Culture and Mental Disorders.* Glencoe, Ill.: Free Press.

Eaton, W. W., A. Dryman, and M. M. Weissman. 1991. "Panic and Phobia." In *Psychiatric Disorders in America,* ed. L. Robins and D. Regier, 155–79. New York: Free Press.

Eaton, W. W., and L. G. Kessler. 1985. *Epidemiological Field Methods in Psychiatry: The NIMH Epidemiologic Catchment Area Project.* Orlando, Fla.: Academic Press.

Eaton, W. W., and C. Muntaner. 1999. "Socioeconomic Stratification and Mental Disorder." In *A Handbook for the Study of Mental Health: Social Contexts, Theories, and Systems,* ed. A. V. Horwitz and T. L. Scheid, 259–83. New York: Cambridge University Press.

Eaves, L. J., H. J. Eysenck, and N. G. Martin. 1989. *Genes, Culture and Personality: An Empirical Approach.* New York: Academic Press.

Edgerton, Robert B. 1966. "Conceptions of Psychosis in Four East African Societies." *American Anthropologist* 68:408–25.

Egeland, J. A., D. S. Gerhard, D. L. Pauls, J. N. Sussex, K. K. Kidd, C. R. Allen, A. M. Hostetter, and D. E. Housman. 1987. "Bipolar Affective Disorders Linked to DNA Markers on Chromosome 11." *Nature* 325:783–87.

Egeland, J. A., and A. Hostetter. 1983. "Amish Study I: Affective Disorders among the Amish." *American Journal of Psychiatry* 140:56–61.

Eisenberg, L. 1995. "The Social Construction of the Human Brain." *American Journal of Psychiatry* 152:1563–75.

Elder, G. H. Jr. 1974. *Children of the Great Depression: Social Change in Life Experience*. Chicago: University of Chicago Press.

Eldridge, L. D. 1996. "'Crazy Brained': Mental Illness in Colonial America." *Bulletin of the History of Medicine* 70:361–86.

Elkin, I. 1994. "The NIMH Treatment of Depression Collaborative Research Program: Where We Began and Where We Are." In *Handbook of Psychotherapy and Behavior Change*, ed. A. E. Bergin and S. L. Garfield, 4th ed., 114–41. New York: John Wiley & Sons.

Elkin, I., M. B. Parloff, S. W. Hadley, and J. H. Autry. 1985. "NIMH Treatment of Depression Collaborative Research Program: Background and Research Plan." *Archives of General Psychiatry* 42:305–16.

Elkin, I., T. Shea, J. T. Watkins, et al. 1989. "National Institute of Mental Health Treatment of Depression Collaborative Research Program: General Effectiveness of Treatments." *Archives of General Psychiatry* 46:971–82.

Ellenberger, H. F. 1970. *The Discovery of the Unconscious: The History and Evolution of Dynamic Psychiatry*. New York: Basic Books.

Estroff, S. E. 1981. *Making It Crazy: An Ethnography of Psychiatric Clients in an American Community*. Berkeley: University of California Press.

Evidence Report/Technology Assessment: Number 7. 1999. Agency for Health Care Policy and Research. http:/www.ahcpr.gov/clinic/deprsumm.htm.

Eysenck, H. J. 1952. "The Effects of Psychotherapy: An Evaluation." *Journal of Consulting Psychology* 16:319–24.

———. 1965. "The Effects of Psychotherapy." *International Journal of Psychiatry* 1: 99–142.

Eysenck, H. J., J. A. Wakefield Jr., and A. F. Friedman. 1983. "Diagnosis and Clinical Assessment: The DSM-III." *Annual Review of Psychology* 34:167–93.

Fabrega, H. 1989. "Cultural Relativism and Psychiatric Illness." *The Journal of Nervous and Mental Disorders* 177:415–25.

———. 1992. "The Role of Culture in a Theory of Psychiatric Illness." *Social Science and Medicine* 35:91–103.

Fadiman, A. 1997. *The Spirit Catches You and You Fall Down*. New York: Farrar, Straus, and Giroux.

Faris, R.E.L., and H. W. Dunham. 1939. *Mental Disorders in Urban Areas*. Chicago: University of Chicago Press.

Faust, D., and R. A. Miner. 1986. "The Empiricist and His New Clothes: DSM-III in Perspective." *American Journal of Psychiatry* 143:962–67.

Fechner-Bates, S., J. C. Coyne, and T. L. Schwenk. 1994. "The Relationship of Self-Reported Distress to Depressive Disorders and Other Psychopathology." *Journal of Consulting and Clinical Psychology* 62:550–59.

Feighner, J. P., E. Robins, S. B. Guze, R. A. Woodruff, G. Winokur, and R. Munoz. 1972. "Diagnostic Criteria for Use in Psychiatric Research." *Archives of General Psychiatry* 26:57–63.

Fenichel, O. M. 1995 [1945]. *The Psychoanalytic Theory of Neurosis*. New York: W. W. Norton.

Figert, A. E. 1996. *Women and the Ownership of PMS: The Structuring of a Psychiatric Disorder*. New York: Walter de Gruyter.

Fingarette, H. 1988. *Heavy Drinking: The Myth of Alcoholism as a Disease*. Berkeley: University of California Press.

Finlay-Jones, R., and G. W. Brown. 1981. "Types of Stressful Life Events and the Onset of Anxiety and Depressive Disorders." *Psychological Medicine* 11:803–15.

Fischer, M. 1971. "Psychoses in the Offspring of Schizophrenic Monozygotic Twins and Their Normal Co-Twins." *British Journal of Psychiatry* 18:43–52.

Fisher, S., and R. P. Greenberg. 1996. *Freud Scientifically Reappraised: Testing the Theories and Therapy.* New York: John Wiley & Sons.

———. 1997. "The Curse of the Placebo: Fanciful Pursuit of a Pure Biological Therapy." In *From Placebo to Panacea: Putting Psychiatric Drugs to the Test*, ed. S. Fisher and R. P. Greenberg, 3–56. New York: John Wiley & Sons.

Fleck, L. 1979 [1935]. *Genesis and Development of a Scientific Fact.* Chicago: University of Chicago Press.

Foucault, M. 1965. *Madness and Civilization: A History of Insanity in the Age of Reason.* New York: Pantheon.

———. 1973. *The Birth of the Clinic.* New York: Random House.

Frances, A. J., M. B. First, T. A. Widiger, G. M. Miele, S. M. Tilly, W. W. Davis, and H. A. Pincus. 1991. "An A to Z Guide to DSM-IV Conundrums." *Journal of Abnormal Psychology* 100:407–12.

Frances, A. J., H. A. Pincus, T. A. Widiger, W. W. Davis, and M. B. First. 1990. "DSM-IV: Work in Progress." *American Journal of Psychiatry* 147:1419–48.

Frank, E., D. J. Kupfer, J. M. Perel, C. Cornes, D. B. Jarrett, A. G. Mallinger, M. E. Thase, A. B. McEachran, and V. J. Grochocinski. 1990. "Three-Year Outcomes for Maintenance Therapies in Recurrent Depression." *Archives of General Psychiatry* 47:1093–99.

Frank, J. D., and J. B. Frank. 1991. *Persuasion and Healing: A Comparative Study of Psychotherapy*, 3d ed. Baltimore, Md.: Johns Hopkins University Press.

Frank, R. G., T. G. McGuire, D. A. Regier, R. W. Manderscheid, and A. Woodward. 1994. "Paying for Mental Health and Substance Abuse Care." *Health Affairs* 1:337–42.

Fredrickson, R. 1992. *Repressed Memories.* New York: Simon & Schuster.

Freeman, D. 1996. *Margaret Mead and the Heretic.* New York: Penguin.

Freud, Sigmund. 1915–1917. *Introductory Lectures on Psychoanalysis.* In *Standard Edition of the Complete Works of Sigmund Freud*, ed. James Strachey, vol. 16. London: Hogarth Press.

———. 1924 [1909]. *Analysis of a Phobia in a Five-Year-Old Boy.* London: Hogarth Press.

———. 1924. *On the History of the Psychoanalytic Movement.* In *Standard Edition of the Complete Works of Sigmund Freud*, ed. James Strachey, vol. 14. London: Hogarth Press.

———. 1927. *The Problem of Lay Analysis.* New York: Brentano.

———. 1928. *The Future of an Illusion.* New York: Liveright.

———. 1930. *Civilization and Its Discontents.* New York: Norton.

———. 1958 [1900]. *The Interpretation of Dreams.* In *Standard Edition of the Complete Works of Sigmund Freud*, ed. James Strachey, vols. 4 and 5. London: Hogarth Press.

———. 1960 [1914]. *The Psychopathology of Everyday Life.* New York: Macmillan.

———. 1960 [1924]. *A General Introduction to Psychoanalysis.* New York: Washington Square Press.

———. 1963 [1905]. *Dora: An Analysis of a Case of Hysteria.* New York: Collier.

———. 1964 [1933]. *New Introductory Lectures on Psychoanalysis.* London: Hogarth Press.

———. 1989 [1918]. "The History of an Infantile Neurosis ("Wolf Man")." In *The Freud Reader*, ed. Peter Gay, 400–426. New York: W. W. Norton.

———. 1989 [1923]. "Notes Upon a Case of Obsessional Neurosis ("Rat Man")." In *The Freud Reader*, ed. Peter Gay, 309–50. New York: W. W. Norton.

———. 1989 [1924]. "Three Essays on the Theory of Sexuality." In *The Freud Reader*, ed. Peter Gay, 240–91. New York: W. W. Norton.

Fromm, E. 1941. *Escape from Freedom*. New York: Rinehart.

Fukuda, K., R. Nisenbaum, G. Stewart, et al. 1998. "Chronic Multisymptom Illness Affecting Air Force Veterans of the Gulf War." *Journal of the American Medical Association* 280: 981–88.

Fuller, S. 2000. *Thomas Kuhn: A Philosophical History for Our Time*. Chicago: University of Chicago Press.

Furnam, A., and R. Malik. 1994. "Cross-Cultural Beliefs about Depression." *International Journal of Social Psychiatry* 40:106–23.

Gadamer, H. G. 1982. *Truth and Method*. New York: Crossroad.

Gaines, A. D. 1992. "From DSM-I to III-R; Voices of Self, Mastery and the Other: A Cultural Constructivist Reading of U.S. Psychiatric Classification." *Social Science and Medicine* 35:3–14.

Garrett, C. J. 1996. "Recovery from Anorexia Nervosa: A Durkheimian Interpretation." *Social Science and Medicine* 43:1489–1506.

Gates, A. 2000. "In the World of the Deaf, Hearing Poses Dangers." *New York Times*, 25 October, E5.

Gay, P. 1988. *Freud: A Life for Our Times*. New York: W. W. Norton.

Gelman, S. 1999. *Medicating Schizophrenia: A History*. New Brunswick, N.J.: Rutgers University Press.

Gershon, E. S., J. Hamovit, J. J. Guroff, et al. 1982. "A Family Study of Schizoaffective, Bipolar I, Bipolar II, Unipolar, and Normal Control Probands." *Archives of General Psychiatry* 39:1157–67.

Gershon, S., and A. Yuwiler. 1960. "Lithium Iron: A Specific Pharmacological Approach to the Treatment of Mania." *Journal of Neuropsychiatry* 1:229–41.

Gerstel, N., and C. K. Reissman. 1984. "Marital Dissolution and Health: Do Males or Females Have Greater Risk?" *Social Science and Medicine* 20:627–35.

Gerth, H., and C. W. Mills. 1953. *Character and Social Structure: The Psychology of Social Institutions*. New York: Harcourt, Brace & World.

Gibbs, J. P. 1981. *Norms, Deviance, and Social Control*. New York: Elsevier.

Gilbert, D. T. 1991. "How Mental Systems Believe." *American Psychologist* 46:107–19.

Gilbert, S. 1996. "More Men May Seek Eating-Disorder Help." *New York Times*, 28 August, C9.

Gilger, J. W. 2000. "Contributions and Promise of Human Behavioral Genetics." *Human Biology* 72:229–55.

Glenmullen, J. 2000. *Prozac Backlash: Overcoming the Dangers of Prozac, Zoloft, Paxil, and Other Antidepressants with Safe, Effective Alternatives*. New York: Simon & Schuster.

Goffman, E. 1961. *Asylums: Essays on the Social Situation of Mental Patients and Other Inmates*. Garden City, N.Y.: Doubleday.

———. 1971. *Relations in Public: Microstudies of the Public Order*. New York: Harper.

Goldberg, D., and P. Huxley. 1980. *Mental Illness in the Community: The Pathway to Psychiatric Care*. London: Tavistock.

Goldhamer, H., and A. W. Marshall. 1953. *Psychosis and Civilization: Two Studies in the Frequency of Mental Disease*. Glencoe, Ill.: The Free Press.

Goldstein, J. 1987. *Console and Classify: The French Psychiatric Profession in the Nineteenth Century*. New York: Cambridge University Press.

Good, B. J. 1977. "The Heart of What's the Matter: The Semantics of Illness in Iran." *Culture, Medicine and Psychiatry* 1:25–58.

Goode, E. 1999. "Study Finds TV Trims Fiji Girls' Body Image and Eating Habits." *The New York Times*, 20 May, A17.

Goodwin, D. W., and S. B. Guze. 1996. *Psychiatric Diagnosis*, 5th ed. New York: Oxford University Press.

Goodwin, D. W., F. Schulsinger, L. Hermansen, S. B. Guze, and G. Winokur. 1973. "Alcohol Problems in Adoptees Raised Apart from Alcoholic Biological Parents." *Archives of General Psychiatry* 28:238–43.

Goodwin, D. W., F. Schulsinger, N. Moller, S. Mednick, and S. Guze. 1977. "Psychopathology in Adopted and Nonadopted Daughters of Alcoholics." *Archives of General Psychiatry* 34:1005–1009.

Gorer, G., and J. Rickman. 1949. *The People of Great Russia*. London: Cresset.

Gottesman, I. I., and A. Bertelson. 1989. "Confirming Unexpressed Genotypes for Schizophrenia." *Archives of General Psychiatry* 46:867–72.

Gottesman, I. I., and J. Shields. 1976. "A Critical Review of Recent Adoption, Twin, and Family Studies of Schizophrenia: Behavioral Genetics Perspectives." *Schizophrenia Bulletin* 2:360–401.

———. 1982. *Schizophrenia: The Epigenic Puzzle*. New York: Cambridge University Press.

Gould, S. J. 1981. *Mismeasure of Man*. New York: W. W. Norton.

Gove, W. R. 1972. "The Relationship between Sex Roles, Marital Status and Mental Illness." *Social Forces* 51:34–44.

Gove, W. R., and Jeanette Tudor. 1973. "Adult Sex Roles and Mental Illness." *American Journal of Sociology* 78:812–35.

Grady, D. 1999. "Sure, We've Got a Pill for That." *New York Times*, 14 February, E1, 5.

Greenberg, L., R. Elliott, and G. Lietaer. 1994. "Research on Experiential Psychotherapies." In *Handbook of Psychotherapy and Behavior Change*, 4th ed., ed. A. E. Bergin and S. L. Garfield, 509–39. New York: John Wiley.

Greenberg, P. E., L. E. Stiglin, S. N. Finkelstein, and E. R. Berndt. 1993. "The Economic Burden of Depression in 1990." *Journal of Clinical Psychiatry* 54:405–18.

Griesinger, W. 1845. *Die Pathologie und Therapie der psychischen Krankheiten fur Aerzte und Studirende*. Stuttgart: Krabbe.

Grob, G. N. 1966. *The State and the Mentally ill: A History of Worcester State Hospital in Massachusetts, 1830–1920*. Chapel Hill: The University of North Carolina Press.

———. 1973. *Mental Institutions in America: Social Policy to 1875*. New York: The Free Press.

———. 1985. "The Origins of American Psychiatric Epidemiology." *American Journal of Public Health* 75:229–36.

———. 1990. "World War II and American Psychiatry." *The Psychohistory Review* 19:41–69.

———. 1991a. *From Asylum to Community: Mental Health Policy in Modern America*. Princeton, N.J.: Princeton University Press.

———. 1991b. "Origins of DSM-I: A Study in Appearance and Reality." *American Journal of Psychiatry* 148:421–31.

Groopman, J. 2000. "Hurting All Over." *The New Yorker*, 13 November, 78–92.

Grove, W. M., E. D. Eckert, L. Heston, T. J. Bouchard Jr., N. Segal, and D. T. Lykken. 1990. "Heritability of Substance Abuse and Antisocial Behavior: A Study of Monozygotic Twins Reared Apart." *Biological Psychiatry* 27:1293–1304.

Grunbaum, A. 1984. *The Foundations of Psychoanalysis: A Philosophical Critique*. Berkeley: University of California Press.

Guarnaccia, P. J. 1993. "Ataques de Nervios in Puerto Rico: Culture-Bound Syndrome or Popular Illness?" *Medical Anthropology* 15:157–70.

Guarnaccia, P. J., R. Angel, and J. L. Worobey. 1989. "The Factor Structure of the CES-D in the Hispanic Health and Nutrition Examination Survey: The Influences of Ethnicity, Gender, and Language." *Social Science and Medicine* 29:85–94.

Guarnaccia, P. J., and L. H. Rogler. 1999. "Research on Culture-Bound Syndromes: New Directions." *American Journal of Psychiatry* 156:1322–27.

Guze, S. B. 1989. "Biological Psychiatry: Is There Any Other Kind?" *Psychological Medicine* 19:315–23.

Hacking, I. 1995. *Rewriting the Soul: Multiple Personality and the Sciences of Memory*. Princeton, N.J.: Princeton University Press.

———. 1999. *The Social Construction of What?* Cambridge: Harvard University Press.

Hahn, R. A. 1995. *Sickness and Healing: An Anthropological Perspective*. New Haven, Conn.: Yale University Press.

Hale, N. G. Jr. 1995. *The Rise and Crisis of Psychoanalysis in the United States: Freud and the Americans, 1917–1985*. New York: Oxford University Press.

Hall, S. S. 1999a. "Fear Itself." *New York Times Magazine*, 28 February, 42 ff.

———. 1999b. "The Bully in the Mirror." *New York Times Magazine*, 22 August, 30–35.

Halleck, S. L. 1971. *The Politics of Therapy*. New York: Science House.

Hallmeyer, J., W. Maier, M. Ackenheil, et al. 1992. "Evidence Against Linkage of Schizophrenia to Chromosome 5q11-q13 Markers in Systematically Ascertained Families." *Biological Psychiatry* 31:83–94.

Hamburg, S. R. 2000. "Antidepressants Are Not Placebos." *American Psychologist* 55:761–62.

Hamer, D., and P. Copeland. 1994. *The Science of Desire: The Search for the Gay Gene and the Biology of Behavior*. New York: Simon & Schuster.

———. 1998. *Living with Our Genes*. New York: Anchor.

Hamer, D., S. Hu, V. L. Magnuson, N. Hu, and A.M.I. Pattatuci. 1993. "A Linkage between DNA Markers on the X Chromosome and Male Sexual Orientation." *Science* 261:321–27.

Hamilton, V. L., C. L. Broman, W. S. Hoffman, and D. S. Renner. 1990. "Hard Times and Vulnerable People: Initial Effects of Plant Closing on Autoworkers' Health." *Journal of Health and Social Behavior* 31:23–40.

Han, C, M. K. McGue, and W. G. Iacono. 1999. "Lifetime Tobacco, Alcohol and Other Substance Use in Adolescent Minnesota Twins." *Addiction* 94:981–93.

Harris, J. R. 1998. *The Nurture Assumption: Why Children Turn Out the Way They Do*. New York: The Free Press.

Harrison, P. A., J. A. Fulkerson, and T. J. Beebe. 1998. "DSM-IV Substance Use Disorder Criteria for Adolescents: A Critical Examination Based on a Statewide School Survey." *American Journal of Psychiatry* 155:486–92.

Harvey, Y. K. 1976. "The Korean Mudang as a Household Therapist." In *Culture-Bound Syndromes, Ethnopsychiatry, and Alternate Therapies*, ed. W. Lebra, 189–200. Honolulu: University Press of Hawaii.

Hatfield, A., ed. 1987. *Families of the Mentally Ill: Meeting the Challenges*. New Directions for Mental Health Services, no. 34. San Francisco: Jossey-Bass.

Healy, D. 1997. *The Anti-Depressant Era*. Cambridge: Harvard University Press.

Helzer, J. E., A. Burnam, and L. T. McEvoy. 1991. "Alcohol Abuse and Dependence." In *Psychiatric Disorders in America*, ed. L. Robins and D. Regier, 81–115. New York: The Free Press.

Helzer, J. E., and G. Canino. 1992. "Comparative Analysis of Alcoholism in 10 Cultural Regions." In *Alcoholism in North America, Europe and Asia*, ed. J. E. Helzer and G. Canino, 289–308. New York: Oxford University Press.

Hemingway, E. 1964. *A Moveable Feast*. New York: Scribner's.

Henry, A. J., and J. F. Short Jr. 1954. *Suicide and Homicide: Some Economic, Sociological, and Psychological Aspects of Aggression*. New York: The Free Press.

Henry, W. P., H. H. Strupp, T. E. Schacht, and L. Gaston. 1994. "Psychodynamic Approaches." In *Handbook of Psychotherapy and Behavior Change*, 4th ed., ed. A. E. Bergin and S. L. Garfield, 467–508. New York: John Wiley & Sons.

Herman, E. 1995. *The Romance of American Psychology: Political Culture in the Age of Experts*. Berkeley: University of California Press.

Herman, J. 1992. *Trauma and Recovery*. New York: Basic Books.

Heston, L. L. 1966. "Psychiatric Disorders in Foster Home Reared Children of Schizophrenic Mothers." *British Journal of Psychiatry* 112:819–825.

———. 1988. "What About the Environment?" In *Relatives at Risk for Mental Disorder*, ed. D. L. Dunner, E. S. Gershon, and J. E. Barrett, 205–13. New York: Raven Press.

Hinkle, L. E. 1987. "Stress and Disease: The Concept after 50 Years." *Social Science and Medicine* 25:561–66.

Hinkle, L. E., and H. G. Wolff. 1958. "Ecologic Investigations of the Relationship between Illness, Life Experiences, and the Social Environment." *Annals of Internal Medicine* 49:1373–88.

Hirschfeld, R. M., M. B. Keller, S. Panico, et al. 1997. "The National Depressive and Manic-Depressive Association Consensus Statement on the Undertreatment of Depression." *Journal of the American Medical Association* 277:333–40.

Hirschi, T. 1969. *Causes of Delinquency*. Berkeley: University of California Press.

Hitt, J. 2000. "The Second Sexual Revolution." *New York Times Magazine*, 20 February, 34 ff.

Hohmann, A. A. 1999. "A Contextual Model for Clinical Mental Health Effectiveness Research." *Mental Health Services Research* 1:83–92.

Holland, A. J., A. Hall, R. Murray, G.F.M. Russell, and A. H. Crisp. 1984. "Anorexia Nervosa: A Study of 34 Twin Pairs and One Set of Triplets." *British Journal of Psychiatry* 145:414–19.

Hollingshead, A. B., and F. C. Redlich. 1958. *Social Class and Mental Illness: A Community Study*. New York: John Wiley & Sons.

Holmes, T. H., and R. H. Rahe. 1967. "The Social Readjustment Rating Scale." *Journal of Psychosomatic Research* 11:213–18.

Hopper, K. 1992. "Some Old Questions for the New Cross-Cultural Psychiatry." *Medical Anthropology Quarterly* 7:299–330.

Horgan, J. 1999. "Placebo Nation." *New York Times*, 21 March, Section 4, 15.

Horney, K. 1937. *The Neurotic Personality of Our Time*. New York: W. W. Norton.

Horvath, E., and M. Weissman. 1995. "Epidemiology of Depression and Anxiety Disorders." In *Textbook in Psychiatric Epidemiology*, ed. M. T. Tsuang, M. Tohen, and G. Zahner, 317–44. New York: John Wiley.

Horwich, P., ed. 1994. *World Changes: Thomas Kuhn and the Nature of Science*. Cambridge: MIT Press.

Horwitz, A. V. 1977. "The Pathways into Psychiatric Treatment: Some Differences between Men and Women." *Journal of Health and Social Behavior* 18:169–78.

———. 1979. "Models, Muddles, and Mental Illness Labeling." *Journal of Health and Social Behavior* 20:296–300.

———. 1982a. *The Social Control of Mental Illness.* New York: Academic Press.

———. 1982b. "Sex-Role Expectations, Power, and Psychological Distress." *Sex Roles* 8:607–23.

———. 1984. "The Economy and Social Pathology." *Annual Review of Sociology* 10:95–119.

———. 1987. "Help-Seeking Processes and Mental Health Services." In *Improving Mental Health Services: What the Social Sciences Can Tell Us,* ed. D. Mechanic, 33–45. San Francisco: Jossey-Bass.

———. 1990. *The Logic of Social Control.* New York: Plenum.

———. 1999. "The Sociological Study of Mental Illness: A Critique and Synthesis of Four Perspectives." In *Handbook of the Sociology of Mental Health,* ed. C. S. Aneshensel and J. C. Phelan, 57–78. New York: Plenum.

Horwitz, A. V., and L. Davies. 1994. "Are Emotional Distress and Alcohol Problems Differential Outcomes to Stress? An Exploratory Test." *Social Science Quarterly* 75:607–21.

Horwitz, A. V., J. McLaughlin, and H. R. White. 1998. "How the Negative and Positive Aspects of Partner Relationships Affect the Mental Health of Young Married People." *Journal of Health and Social Behavior* 39:124–36.

Horwitz, A. V., and J. S. Mullis. 1998. "Individualism and Its Discontents: The Response to the Seriously Mentally Ill in Late Twentieth Century America." *Sociological Focus* 31:119–33.

Horwitz, A. V., and H. R. White. 1991. "Marital Status, Depression, and Alcohol Problems among Young Adults." *Journal of Health and Social Behavior* 32:221–37.

Horwitz, A. V., H. R. White, and S. Howell-White. 1996. "The Use of Multiple Outcomes in Stress Research: A Case Study of Gender Differences in Responses to Marital Dissolution." *Journal of Health and Social Behavior* 37:278–91.

House, J., K. Landis, and D. Umberson. 1988. "Social Relationships and Health." *Science* 241:540–45.

Idler, E. L. 1987. "Religious Involvement and the Health of the Elderly: Some Hypotheses and an Initial Test." *Social Forces* 66:226–38.

Imber, S. D., P. A. Pilkonis, S. M. Sotsky, I. Elkin, et al. 1990. "Mode-Specific Effects among Three Treatments for Depression." *Journal of Consulting and Clinical Psychology* 58:352–59.

Jablensky, A., N. Sartorius, W. Gulbinat, and G. Ernberg. 1981. "Characteristics of Depressive Patients Contacting Psychiatric Services in Four Cultures." *Acta Psychiatrica Scandinavica* 63:367–83.

Jackson, S. W. 1986. *Melancholia and Depression: From Hippocratic Times to Modern Times.* New Haven, Conn.: Yale University Press.

———. 1999. *Care of the Psyche: A History of Psychological Healing.* New Haven, Conn.: Yale University Press.

Jamison, K. R. 1995. *An Unquiet Mind: A Memoir of Moods and Madness.* New York: Vintage.

Jang, K. L., P. A. Vernon, and W. J. Livesley. 2000. "Personality Disorder Traits, Family

Environment, and Alcohol Misuse: A Multivariate Behavioural Genetic Analysis." *Addiction* 95:873–88.

Janik, A., and S. Toulmin. 1973. *Wittgenstein's Vienna.* New York: Simon and Schuster.

Jaspers, K. 1964. *The Nature of Psychotherapy: A Critical Appraisal.* Chicago: University of Chicago Press.

Jenkins, J. H. 1988. "Conceptions of Schizophrenia as a Problem of Nerves: A Cross-Cultural Comparison of Mexican-Americans and Anglo-Americans." *Social Science and Medicine* 12:1233–43.

Jones, K. W. 1999. *Taming the Troublesome Child.* Cambridge: Harvard University Press.

Kadushin, C. 1969. *Why People Go to Psychiatrists.* New York: Atherton Press.

Kamin, L. 1974. *The Science and Politics of IQ.* Potomac, Md.: Erlbaum.

Kandel, E. R. 1998. "A New Intellectual Framework for Psychiatry." *American Journal of Psychiatry* 155:457–69.

———. 1999. "Biology and the Future of Psychoanalysis: A New Intellectual Framework for Psychiatry Revisited." *American Journal of Psychiatry* 156:505–24.

Kane, J., G. Honigfeld, J. Singer, H. Meltzer, and the Clozaril Collaborative Study Group. 1988. "Clozapine for the Treatment-Resistant Schizophrenic: A Double-Blind Comparison with Chlorpromiazine." *Archives of General Psychiatry* 45:789–96.

Kaplan, B., and D. Johnson. 1964. "The Social Meaning of Navaho Psychopathology and Psychotherapy." In *Magic, Faith and Healing,* ed. A. Kiev, 203–30. New York: The Free Press.

Karasz, A. 1997. *Role Strain and Symptoms in a Group of Pakistani Immigrant Women.* Ph.D. dissertation, Graduate and University Center of the City University of New York.

Karp, D. A. 1996. *Speaking of Sadness.* New York: Oxford University Press.

Katon, W., M. Von Korff, E. Lin, E. Walker, G. E. Simon, T. Bush, P. Robinson, and J. Russo. 1995. "Collaborative Management to Achieve Treatment Guidelines: Impact on Depression in Primary Care." *Journal of the American Medical Society* 273:1026–31.

Katz, S. J., R. C. Kessler, R. G. Frank, P. Leaf, E. Lin, and M. Edlund. 1997. "Utilization of Mental Health Services in the United States and Ontario: The Impact of Mental Health Morbidity and Perceived Need for Care." *American Journal of Public Health* 87:1136–43.

Kaufmann, C. L. 1999. "An Introduction to the Mental Health Consumer Movement." In *A Handbook for the Study of Mental Health: Social Contexts, Theories and Systems,* ed. A. V. Horwitz and T. L. Scheid, 493–507. New York: Cambridge University Press.

Kazdin, A. E., and D. Bass. 1989. "Power to Detect Differences between Alternative Treatments in Comparative Psychotherapy Outcome Research." *Journal of Consulting and Clinical Psychology* 57:138–47.

Kelsoe, J. R., E. I. Ginns, J. A. Egeland, et al. 1989. "Re-evaluation of the Linkage Relationship between Chromosome 11p Loci and the Gene for Bipolar Affective Disorder in the Old Order Amish." *Nature* 342:238–343.

Kendell, R. E. 1974. "The Stability of Psychiatric Diagnoses." *British Journal of Psychiatry* 124:352–56.

———. 1989. "Clinical Validity." *Psychological Medicine* 19:45–55.

Kendell, R. E., J. E. Cooper, and A. G. Gourlay. 1971. "Diagnostic Criteria of American and British Psychiatrists." *Archives of General Psychiatry* 25:123–30.

Kendler, K. S. 1990. "Toward a Scientific Psychiatric Nosology: Strengths and Limitations." *Archives of General Psychiatry* 47:969–973.

Kendler, K. S., and C. O. Gardner. 1998. "Boundaries of Major Depression: An Evaluation of DSM-IV Criteria." *American Journal of Psychiatry* 155:172–77.

Kendler, K. S., A. C. Heath, N. G. Martin, and L. J. Eaves. 1986a. "Symptoms of Anxiety and Depression in a Volunteer Twin Population: The Etiological Role of Genetic and Environmental Factors." *Archives of General Psychiatry* 43:213–21.

———. 1986b. "Symptoms of Anxiety and Symptoms of Depression: Same Genes, Different Environments?" *Archives of General Psychiatry* 44:451–57.

Kendler, K. S., A. C. Heath, M. C. Neale, R. C. Kessler, and L. J. Eaves. 1993. "Alcoholism and Major Depression in Women: A Twin Study of the Causes of Comorbidity." *Archives of General Psychiatry* 50:690–98.

Kendler, K. S., R. C. Kessler, A. C. Heath, M. C. Neale, and L. J. Eaves. 1991. "Coping: A Genetic Epidemiological Investigation." *Psychological Medicine* 21:337–46.

Kendler, K. S., R. C. Kessler, E. E. Walters, C. MacLean, M. C. Neale, A. C. Heath, and L. J. Eaves. 1995. "Stressful Life Events, Genetic Liability, and Onset of an Episode of Major Depression in Women." *American Journal of Psychiatry* 152:833–42.

Kendler, K. S., M. Lyons, and M. T. Tsuang. 1991. "Introduction." In *Genetic Issues in Psychosocial Epidemiology*, ed. M. T. Tsuang, K. S. Kendler, and M. J. Lyons, 1–11. New Brunswick, N.J.: Rutgers University Press.

Kendler, K. S., M. Neale, R. C. Kessler, A. C. Heath, and L. J. Eaves. 1992. "A Twin Study of Recent Life Events and Difficulties." *Archives of General Psychiatry* 50:789–96.

Kendler, K. S., and C. D. Robinette. 1983. "Schizophrenia in the National Academy of Sciences–National Research Council Twin Registry: A 16-Year Update." *American Journal of Psychiatry* 140:1551–62.

Kendler, K. S., R. L. Spitzer, and J.B.W. Williams. 1989. "Psychotic Disorders in DSM-III R." *American Journal of Psychiatry* 146:953–62.

Kennedy, J. G. 1987. *The Flower of Paradise: The Institutionalized Use of the Drug Qat in North Yemen.* Dordrecht: Reidel.

Kennedy, J. L., L. A. Giuffra, H. W. Moises, L. L. Cavalli-Sforza, A. J. Pakstis, J. R. Kidd, C. M. Castiglione, B. Sigren, L. Wettenberg, and K. K. Kidd. 1988. "Evidence Against Linkage of Schizophrenia to Markers on Chromosome 5 in a Northern Swedish Pedigree." *Nature* 336:167–70.

Kesey, K. 1962. *One Flew Over the Cuckoo's Nest.* New York: Signet.

Kessler, R. C., J. M. Abelson, and S. Zhao. 1998. "The Epidemiology of Mental Disorders." In *Advances in Mental Health Research: Implications for Practice*, ed. J.B.W. Williams and K. Ell, 3–24. Washington, D.C.: NASW Press.

Kessler, R. C., P. A. Beglund, S. Zhao, et al. 1996. "The 12-Month Prevalence and Correlates of Serious Mental Illness (SMI)." In *Mental Health, United States, 1996*, ed. R. Manderscheid and M. A. Sonnenschein, 59–70. Washington: U.S. Government Printing Office.

Kessler, R. C., K. A. McGonagle, S. Zhao, C. B. Nelson, M. Hughes, S. Eshleman, H. Wittchen, and K. S. Kendler. 1994. "Lifetime and 12-Month Prevalence of DSM-III-R Psychiatric Disorders in the United States: Results from the National Comorbidity Survey." *Archives of General Psychiatry* 51:8–19.

Kessler, R. C., and J. A. McRae Jr. 1981. "Trends in the Relationship between Sex and Psychological Distress: 1957–1976." *American Sociological Review* 46:443–52.

———. 1982. "The Effect of Wives' Employment on the Mental Health of Married Men and Women." *American Sociological Review* 47:216–27.

Kessler, R. C., and S. Zhao. 1999. "The Prevalence of Mental Illness." In *Handbook for the*

Study of Mental Health: Social Contexts, Theories, and Systems, ed. A. V. Horwitz and T. L. Scheid, 58–78. New York: Cambridge University Press.

Kessler, R. C., S. Zhao, D. G. Blazer, and M. Swartz. 1997. "Prevalence, Correlates, and Course of Minor Depression and Major Depression in the National Comorbidity Survey." *Journal of Affective Disorders* 45:19–30.

Kety, S. S. 1985. "Interactions between Stress and Genetic Processes." In *Stress in Health and Disease*, ed. M. R. Zanes. New York: Brunner/Mazel.

Kety, S. S., D. Rosenthal, P. H. Wender, and F. Schulsinger. 1968. "The Types and Prevalence of Mental Illness in the Biological and Adoptive Families of Adopted Schizophrenics." In *The Transmission of Schizophrenia*, ed. D. Rosenthal and S. S. Kety, 345–62. Oxford: Pergamon.

———. 1975. "Mental Illness in the Biological and Adoptive Families of Adopted Individuals Who Have Become Schizophrenic." In *Genetic Research in Psychiatry*, ed. R. R. Fieve, D. Rosenthal, and H. Brill. Baltimore, Md.: Johns Hopkins University Press.

Kiesler, C. A. 2000. "The Next Wave of Change for Psychology and Mental Health Services in the Health Care Revolution." *American Psychologist* 55:481–87.

Kiev, A. 1964. "The Study of Folk Psychiatry." *Magic, Faith, and Healing*, ed. A. Kiev, 3–35. New York: The Free Press.

———. 1972. *Transcultural Psychiatry*. New York: The Free Press.

Kinzie, D. 1982. "Development and Validation of a Vietnamese Language Depression Rating Scale." *American Journal of Psychiatry* 139:1276–81.

Kirk, S. A. 1999. "Instituting Madness: The Evolution of a Federal Agency." In *Handbook of the Sociology of Mental Health*, ed. C. Aneschensel and J. Phelan, 539–62. New York: Plenum.

Kirk, S. A., and H. Kutchins. 1992. *The Selling of DSM: The Rhetoric of Science in Psychiatry*. New York: Aldine de Gruyter.

———. 1994. "Is Bad Writing a Mental Disorder?" *New York Times*, 20 June, A17.

Kirmayer, L. 1984. "Culture, Affect, and Somatization." *Transcultural Psychiatric Research Review* 21:159–88.

———. 1994. "Rejoinder to Professor Wakefield." In *Controversial Issues in Mental Health*, ed. S. A. Kirk and S. D. Einbinder, 7–20. Boston: Allyn & Bacon.

Kitson, G. C., K. B. Babri, and M. J. Roach. 1985. "Who Divorces and Why: A Review." *Journal of Family Issues* 6:255–93.

Kitson, G. C., and L. A. Morgan. 1990. "The Multiple Consequences of Divorce: A Decade Review." *Journal of Marriage and the Family* 52:913–24.

Klein, D. F. 1978. "A Proposed Definition of Mental Illness." In *Critical Issues in Psychiatric Diagnoses*, ed. R. F. Spitzer and D. F. Klein, 41–71. New York: Raven Press.

———. 1999. "Harmful Dysfunction, Disorder, Disease, Illness, and Evolution." *Journal of Abnormal Psychology* 108:421–29.

Kleinman, A. 1986. *Social Origins of Distress and Disease: Depression, Neurasthenia, and Pain in Modern China*. New Haven, Conn.: Yale University Press.

———. 1987. "Anthropology and Psychiatry: The Role of Culture in Cross-Cultural Research on Illness." *British Journal of Psychiatry* 151:447–54.

———. 1988. *Rethinking Psychiatry: From Cultural Category to Personal Experience*. New York: The Free Press.

Klerman, G. L. 1977. "Mental Illness, the Medical Model, and Psychiatry." *The Journal of Medicine and Philosophy* 2:220–43.

———. 1988a. "Overview of the Cross-National Collaborative Panic Study." *Archives of General Psychiatry* 45:407–12.

———. 1988b. "The Current Age of Youthful Melancholia: Evidence for Increase in Depression among Adolescents and Young Adults." *British Journal of Psychiatry* 152:4–14.

———. 1989. "Psychiatric Diagnostic Categories: Issues of Validity and Measurement." *Journal of Health and Social Behavior* 30:26–32.

———. 1990. "The Psychiatric Patient's Right to Effective Treatment: Implications of Osheroff v. Chestnut Lodge." *American Journal of Psychiatry* 147:409–18.

Klerman, G. L., M. Olfson, A. C. Leon, and M. M. Weissman. 1992. "Measuring the Need for Mental Health Care." *Health Affairs* 11:24–33.

Klerman, G. L., M. M. Weissman, J. Markowitz, I. Glick, et al. 1994. "Medication and Psychotherapy." In *Handbook of Psychotherapy and Behavior Change*, 4th ed., ed. A. E. Bergin and S. L. Garfield, 734–82. New York: John Wiley.

Klerman, G. L., M. M. Weissman, B. J. Rounsaville, and E. S. Chevron. 1984. *Interpersonal Psychotherapy of Depression*. New York: Basic Books.

Knapp, C. 1999. "The Glass Half Empty." *New York Times Magazine*, May 9: 19–20.

Knutson, B., O. M. Wolkowitz, A. W. Cole, T. Chan, E. A. Moore, R. C. Johnson, J. Terpstra, R. A. Turner, and V. I. Reus. 1998. "Selective Alteration of Personality and Social Behavior by Serotonergic Intervention." *American Journal of Psychiatry* 155:373–79.

Kolb, L. C., S. H. Frazier, and P. Sirovatka. 2000. "The National Institute of Mental Health: Its Influence on Psychiatry and the Nation's Mental Health." In *American Psychiatry after WWII: 1944–1994*, ed. R. W. Menninger and J. C. Nemiah, 207–31. Washington, D.C.: American Psychiatric Press.

Kraepelin, E. 1896. *Psychiatrie. Ein Lehrbuch fur Studirende und Aerzte*, 5th ed. Leipzig: Johann Ambrosius Barth.

Krafft-Ebing, R. 1904. *Text Book of Insanity*. Philadelphia: F. A. Davis.

Kramer, M. 1977. *Psychiatric Services and the Changing Institutional Scene, 1950–1985*. Washington, D.C.: National Institute of Mental Health.

Kramer, P. D. 1993. *Listening to Prozac: A Psychiatrist Explores Antidepressant Drugs and the Remaking of the Self*. New York: Viking.

Kringlen, E. 1978. "Adult Offspring of Two Psychotic Parents, with Special Reference to Schizophrenia." In *The Nature of Schizophrenia: New Approaches to Research and Treatment*, ed. L. Wynne, 9–24. New York: John Wiley.

Kroll-Smith, S., and H. H. Floyd. 1997. *Bodies in Protest: Environmental Illness and the Struggle over Medical Knowledge*. New York: New York University Press.

Kuhn, T. 1970. *The Structure of Scientific Revolutions*, 2d ed. Chicago: University of Chicago Press.

Kupfer, D. J. 1999. "Research in Affective Disorders Comes of Age." *American Journal of Psychiatry* 156:165–67.

Kutchins, H., and S. A. Kirk. 1997. *Making Us Crazy: DSM: The Psychiatric Bible and the Creation of Mental Disorders*. New York: The Free Press.

Labouvie, E. 1996. "Maturing Out of Substance Use: Selection and Self-Correction." *Journal of Drug Issues* 26:457–76.

Laing, R. D. 1960. *The Divided Self*. London: Tavistock.

———. 1967. *The Politics of Experience*. New York: Pantheon.

Lambek, M. 1979. "Spirits and Spouses: Possession as a System of Communication among the Malagasy Speakers of Mayotte." *American Ethnologist* 7:318–31.

Lambert, M. J., and A. E. Bergin. 1994. "The Effectiveness of Psychotherapy." In *Handbook of Psychotherapy and Behavior Change*, 4th ed., ed. A. E. bergin and S. L. Garfield, 143–90. New York: John Wiley & Sons.

Lander, E. S., and N.J. Schork. 1994. "Genetic Dissection of Complex Traits." *Science* 265:2037–47.

Landman, J. T., and R. M. Dawes. 1982. "Psychotherapy Outcome: Smith and Glass' Conclusions Stand Up Under Scrutiny." *American Psychologist* 37:504–16.

Langlois, J. H., J. M. Ritter, R. J. Casey, and D. B. Sawin. 1995. "Infant Attractiveness Predicts Maternal Behaviors and Attitudes." *Developmental Psychology* 31:464–72.

Langner, T. S. 1962. "A Twenty-two Item Screening Score of Psychiatric Symptoms Indicating Impairment." *Journal of Health and Social Behavior* 3:269–76.

Laumann, E. O., A. Paik, and R. C. Rosen. 1999. "Sexual Dysfunction in the United States: Prevalence and Predictors." *Journal of the American Medical Association* 281:537–44.

Leaf, P. J., and M. L. Bruce. 1987. "Gender Differences in the Use of Mental-Health-Related Services: A Reexamination." *Journal of Health and Social Behavior* 28:171–83.

Leaf, P. J., M. B. Livingston, G. L. Tischler, M. M. Weissman, C. E. Holzer, and J. K. Myers. 1985. "Contact with Health Professionals for the Treatment of Psychiatric and Emotional Problems." *Medical Care* 23:1322–37.

Leaf, P. J., J. K. Myers, and L. T. McEvoy. 1991. "Procedures Used in the Epidemiologic Catchment Area Study." In *Psychiatric Disorders in America*, ed. L. Robins and D. Regier, 11–32. New York: The Free Press.

Leighton, A. H. 1959. *My Name is Legion*. New York: Basic Books.

Lemert, E. M. 1962. "Paranoia and the Dynamics of Exclusion." *Sociometry* 25:2–20.

Lennon, M. C. 1987. "Sex Differences in Distress: The Impact of Gender and Work Roles." *Journal of Health and Social Behavior* 28:290–305.

———. 1994. "Women, Work, and Well-Being: The Importance of Work Conditions." *Journal of Health and Social Behavior* 35:235–47.

Lennon, M. C., and S. Rosenfield. 1992. "Women and Mental Health: The Interaction of Job and Family Conditions." *Journal of Health and Social Behavior* 33:316–27.

———. 1994. "Relative Fairness and the Division of Housework: The Importance of Options." *American Journal of Sociology* 100:506–31.

Lerner, G. 1987. *The Culture of Patriarchy*. New York: Oxford.

Lesch, K., D. Bengel, A. Heils, S. Z. Sabol, B. D. Greenberg, S. Petri, J. Benjamin, C. R. Muller, D. H. Hamer, and D. L. Murphy. 1996. "Association of Anxiety-Related Traits with a Polymorphism in the Serotonin Transporter Gene Regulatory Region." *Science* 274:1527–31.

Leshner, A. I. 1999. "Science Is Revolutionizing Our View of Addiction—and What to Do About It." *American Journal of Psychiatry* 156:1–3.

Leventhal, H., Y. Benyamini, S. Brownlee, M. Diefenbach, E. A. Leventhal, L. Patrick-Miller, and C. Robitaille. 1997. "Illness Representations: Theoretical Foundations." In *Perceptions of Health and Illness: Current Research and Applications*, ed. K. J. Petrie and J. A. Weinman, 19–45. Amsterdam: Harwood Academic Publishers.

Levy, R. 1976. "Psychosomatic Symptoms and Women's Protest: Two Types of Reaction to Structural Strain in the Family." *Journal of Health and Social Behavior* 17:121–33.

Lewis, A. 1953. "Health as a Social Concept." *British Journal of Sociology* 4:109–24.

Lewis, I. M. 1966. "Spirit Possession and Deprivation Cults." *Man* 1:307–29.

Lewis-Fernandez, R., and A. Kleinman. 1995a. "Culture, Personality, and Psychopathology." *Journal of Abnormal Psychology* 103:67–71.

———. 1995b. "Cultural Psychiatry: Theoretical, Clinical, and Research Issues." *Cultural Psychiatry* 18:433–48.

Lewontin, R. C. 1992. *Biology as Ideology: The Doctrine of DNA.* New York: HarperCollins.

Lewontin, R. C., S. Rose, and L. J. Kamin. 1984. *Not in Our Genes.* New York: Pantheon.

Lieberson, S. 1985. *Making It Count: The Improvement of Social Research and Theory.* Berkeley: University of California Press.

Liebowitz, M. R., F. R. Schneir, E. R. Hollander, et al. 1991. "Treatment of Social Phobia with Drugs Other than Benzodiazepines." *Journal of Clinical Psychiatry* 52, supp. 11:10–15.

Liefer, R. 1969. *In the Name of Mental Health: The Social Functions of Psychiatry.* New York: Science House.

Lilienfeld, S. O., and L. Marino. 1995. "Mental Disorder as a Roschian Concept: A Critique of Wakefield's 'Harmful Dysfunction' Analysis." *Journal of Abnormal Psychology* 104:411–20.

Lin, K. M., R. E. Poland, and D. Anderson. 1995. "Psychopharmacology, Ethnicity and Culture." *Transcultural Psychiatry* 32:3–40.

Link, B. G., and B. P. Dohrenwend. 1980. "Formulation of Hypotheses about the True Prevalence of Demoralization in the United States." In *Mental Illness in the United States: Epidemiological Evidence,* ed. B. P. Dohrenwend et al., 114–32. New York: Praeger.

Link, B. G., B. P. Dohrenwend, and A. E. Skodol. 1986. "Socio-economic Status and Schizophrenia: Some Occupational Characteristics as a Risk Factor." *American Sociological Review* 51:242–58.

Link, B. G., and J. Phelan. 1995. "Social Conditions as Fundamental Causes of Disease." *Journal of Health and Social Behavior,* extra issue:80–94.

Link, B. G., J. C. Phelan, M. Bresnahan, A. Stueve, and B. Pescosolido. 1999. "Public Conceptions of Mental Illness: Labels, Causes, Dangerousness, and Social Distance." *American Journal of Public Health* 89:1328–33.

Littlewood, R. 1990. "From Categories to Contexts: A Decade of the 'New Cross-Cultural Psychiatry.'" *British Journal of Psychiatry* 156:308–27.

Lipsey, M., and D. Wilson. 1993. "The Efficacy of Psychological, Educational, and Behavioral Treatment: Confirmation from Meta-analysis." *American Psychologist* 48:1181–1209.

Livingston, K. 1997. "Ritalin: Miracle Drug or Cop-Out?" *The Public Interest* 129:3–18.

Loomer, H. P., J. C. Saunders, and N. S. Kline. 1957. "A Clinical and Pharmaco-dynamic Evaluation of Iproniazid as a Psychic Energiser." *Psychiatric Research Reports* 8:129–41.

Lopez, S. R., and P. J. Guarnaccia. 2000. "Cultural Psychopathology: Uncovering the Social World of Mental Illness." *Annual Review of Psychology* 51:571–98.

Luborsky, L., P. Crits-Christoph, A. T. McLellan, G. Woody, W. Piper, B. Liberman, S. Imber, and P. Pilkonis. 1986. "Do Therapists Vary Much in Their Success? Findings from Four Outcome Studies." *American Journal of Orthopsychiatry* 56:501–12.

Luborsky, L., L. Diguer, E. Luborsky, B. Singer, D. Dickter, and K. A. Schmidt. 1993. "The Efficacy of Dynamic Psychotherapies: Is It True that 'Everyone Has Won and All Must Have Prizes'?" In *Psychodynamic Treatment Research: A Handbook for Clinical Practice,* ed. N. Miller, L. Luborsky, J. Barber, and J. Docherty, 497–516. New York: Basic Books.

Luborsky, L., B. Singer, and L. Luborsky. 1975. "Comparative Studies of Psychotherapies: Is It True That 'Everyone Has Won and All Must Have Prizes'?" *Archives of General Psychiatry* 32:995–1008.

Luhrmann, T. M. 2000. *Of 2 Minds: The Growing Disorder in American Psychiatry.* New York: Alfred A. Knopf.

Lukes, S. 1975. *Emile Durkheim: His Life and Work.* London: Penguin.

Lunbeck, E. 1994. *The Psychiatric Persuasion: Knowledge, Gender, and Power in Modern America.* Princeton, N.J.: Princeton University Press.

Lykken, D. T., and A. Tellegen. 1996. "Happiness Is a Stochastic Phenomenon." *Psychological Science* 7:186–89.

Lykken, D. T., M. McGue, A. Tellegen, and T. J. Bouchard Jr. 1992. "Emergenesis: Genetic Traits that May Not Run in Families." *American Psychologist* 47:1565–77.

Lynn, R., and T. Martin. 1997. "Gender Differences in Extraversion, Neuroticism, and Psychoticism in 37 Nations." *The Journal of Social Psychology* 137:369–73.

MacDonald, M. 1981. *Mystical Bedlam: Madness, Anxiety, and Healing in Seventeenth-Century England.* New York: Cambridge University Press.

Macmillan, A. M. 1957. "The Health Opinion Survey: Technique for Estimating Prevalence of Psychoneurotic and Related Types of Disorder in Communities." *Psychological Reports* 3:325–39.

Magee, W. J., W. W. Eaton, H. J. Witchen, K. A. McGonagle, and R. C. Kessler. 1996. "Agoraphobia, Simple Phobia, and Social Phobia in the National Comorbidity Survey." *Archives of General Psychiatry* 53:159–68.

Maier, W., and K. Merikangas. 1996. "Co-occurrence and Cotransmission of Affective Disorders and Alcoholism in Families." *British Journal of Psychiatry* 168:93–100.

Mail, P. D. 1989. "American Indians, Stress, and Alcohol." *American Indian and Alaskan Native Mental Health Research* 3:7–26.

Mannheim, K. 1952. "The Problem of Generations." In *Essays on the Sociology of Knowledge*, ed. K. Mannheim, 276–320. New York: Oxford University Press.

Margolis, H. 1993. *Paradigms and Barriers: How Habits of Mind Govern Scientific Beliefs.* Chicago: University of Chicago Press.

Markel, H. 2000. "Anorexia Can Strike Boys, Too." *The New York Times*, 25 July, F7.

Marks, I. M., R. P. Swinson, M. Basoglu, et al. 1993. "Alprazolam and Exposure Alone and Combined in Panic Disorder with Agoraphobia." *British Journal of Psychiatry* 162:776–87.

Markus, H. R., and S. Kitayama. 1991. "Culture and the Self: Implications for Cognition, Emotion, and Motivation." *Psychological Review* 98:224–53.

Marshall, R. O., R. Spitzer, and M. R. Liebowitz. 1999. "Review and Critique of the New DSM-IV Diagnosis of Acute Stress Disorder." *American Journal of Psychiatry* 156:1677–85.

Martin, J. B. 1987. "Molecular Genetics: Applications to the Clinical Neurosciences." *Science* 238:765–72.

Marx, J. H., and S. L. Spray. 1972. "Psychotherapeutic 'Birds of a Feather': Social Class Status and Religio-cultural Value Homophily in the Mental Health Field." *Journal of Health and Social Behavior* 13:413–28.

Masson, J. M. 1984. *The Assault on Truth: Freud's Suppression of the Seduction Theory.* New York: Farrar, Straus, and Giroux.

Mastekaasa, A. 1992. "Marriage and Psychological Well-Being: Some Evidence on Selection into Marriage." *Journal of Marriage and the Family* 54:901–11.

Maxmen, J. 1985. *The New Psychiatrists.* New York: New American Library.

McCarthy, L. P., and J. P. Gerring. 1994. "Revising Psychiatry's Charter Document DSM-IV." *Written Communication* 11:147–92.

McGue, M., and D. J. Lykken. 1992. "Genetic Influence on Risk of Divorce." *Psychological Science* 3:368–73.

McGuffin, P., P. Asherson, M. Owen, and A. Farmer. 1994. "The Strength of the Genetic Effect: Is There Room for an Environmental Influence in the Aetiology of Schizophrenia?" *British Journal of Psychiatry* 164:593–99.

McHugh, P. R. 1992. "Psychiatric Misadventures." *American Scholar* (autumn):497–510.

———. 1999. "How Psychiatry Lost Its Way." *Commentary* (December):32–38.

McKeon, P., and R. Murray. 1987. "Familial Aspects of Obsessive-Compulsive Neurosis." *British Journal of Psychiatry* 151:528–34.

McLean, A. 1990. "Contradictions in the Social Production of Clinical Knowledge: The Case of Schizophrenia." *Social Science and Medicine* 30:969–85.

Mead, M. 1928. *Coming of Age in Samoa.* New York: Morrow.

Mechanic, D. 1978. *Medical Sociology,* 2d ed. New York: The Free Press.

———. 1995. "Sociological Dimensions of Illness Behavior." *Social Science and Medicine* 41:1207–16.

———. 1998a. "Cultural and Organizational Aspects of Application of the Americans with Disabilities Act to Persons with Psychiatric Disabilities." *The Milbank Quarterly* 76:5–23.

———. 1998b. "Emerging Trends in Mental Health Policy and Practice." *Health Affairs* 17:82–98.

———. 1999. *Mental Health and Social Policy,* 4th ed. Boston: Allyn and Bacon.

Mechanic, D., and D. D. McAlpine. 1999. "Mission Unfulfilled: Potholes on the Road to Mental Health Parity." *Health Affairs* 18:7–21.

Mechanic, D., and D. Rochefort. 1992. "A Policy of Inclusion for the Mentally Ill." *Health Affairs* 11:128–50.

Meltzer, H. Y., P. Cola, L. Way, P. A. Thompson, B. Bastani, M. A. Davies, and B. Snitz. 1993. "Cost Effectiveness of Clozapine in Neuroleptic-Resistant Schizophrenia." *American Journal of Psychiatry* 150:1630–38.

Menaghan, E. G. 1989. "Role Changes and Psychological Well-Being: Variations in Effects by Gender and Role Repertoire." *Social Forces* 67:693–714.

Menaghan, E. G., and M. A. Lieberman. 1986. "Changes in Depression Following Divorce: A Panel Study." *Journal of Marriage and the Family* 48:319–28.

Mendlewicz, J., and J. D. Rainer. 1977. "Adoption Study Supporting Genetic Transmission in Manic-Depressive Illness." *Nature* 360:268–329.

Merikangas, K. R. 1990. "The Genetic Epidemiology of Alcoholism." *Psychological Medicine* 20:11–22.

———. 1995. "Contribution of Genetic Epidemiologic Research to Psychiatry." *Psychopathology* 28:41–50.

Merikangas, K. R., and J. Angst. 1995. "Comorbidity and Social Phobia: Evidence from Clinical, Epidemiologic, and Genetic Studies." *European Archives of Psychiatry and Clinical Neurosciences* 244:297–303.

Merikangas, K. R., J. Angst, W. Eaton, et al. 1996. "Comorbidity and Boundaries of Affective Disorders with Anxiety Disorders and Substance Misuse: Results of an International Task Force." *British Journal of Psychiatry* 168:58–67.

Merikangas, K. R., B. A. Prusoff, and M. M. Weissman. 1988. "Parental Concordance for Affective Disorders: Psychopathology in Offspring." *Journal of Affective Disorders* 15:279–90.

Merikangas, K. R., N. J. Risch, and M. M. Weissman. 1994. "Comorbidity and Co-transmission of Alcoholism, Anxiety, and Depression." *Psychological Medicine* 24:69–80.

Merikangas, K. R., W. Wicki, and J. Angst. 1994. "Heterogeneity of Depression: Classification of Depressive Subtypes by Longitudinal Course." *British Journal of Psychiatry* 164:342–48.

Merton, R. K. 1938. "Social Structure and Anomie." *American Sociological Review* 3:672–82.

Messing, S. D. 1959. "Group Therapy and Social Status in the Zar Cult of Ethiopia." In *Culture and Mental Health*, ed. M. Opler, 319–32. New York: Macmillan.

Micale, M. S. 1995. *Approaching Hysteria: Disease and Its Interpretations*. Princeton, N.J.: Princeton University Press.

Michels, R., and P. M. Marzuk. 1993. "Progress in Psychiatry." *The New England Journal of Medicine* 329:552–60.

Miech, R. A., A. Caspi, T. E. Moffitt, B. R. Entner Wright, and P. A. Silva. 1999. "Low Socioeconomic Status and Mental Disorders: A Longitudinal Study of Selection and Causation during Young Adulthood." *American Journal of Sociology* 104:1096–1131.

Miller, J. R. 1998. *The Nurture Assumption*. New York: The Free Press.

Miller, W. R., and R. K. Hester. 1989. "Treating Alcohol Problems: Toward an Informed Eclecticism." In *Handbook of Alcoholism Treatment Approaches*, ed. R. K. Hester and W. R. Miller, 3–13. New York: Pergamon.

Millon, T. 1983. "The DSM-III: An Insider's Perspective." *American Psychologist* 38:804–14.

Mirowsky, J. 1985. "Depression and Marital Power: An Equity Model." *American Journal of Sociology* 91:557–92.

Mirowsky, J., and C. E. Ross. 1989a. "Psychiatric Diagnosis as Reified Measurement." *Journal of Health and Social Behavior* 30:11–26.

———. 1989b. *Social Causes of Psychological Distress*. New York: Aldine de Gruyter.

———. 1999. "Well-Being across the Life Course." In *A Handbook for the Study of Mental Health and Illness: Social Contexts, Theories, and Systems*, ed. A. V. Horwitz and T. L. Scheid, 328–47. New York: Cambridge University Press.

Mortensen, P. B., C. B. Pedersen, T. Westergaard, J. Wholfahrt, H. Ewald, O. Mors, P. K. Andersen, and M. Melbye. 1999. "Effects of Family History and Place and Season of Birth on the Risk of Schizophrenia." *New England Journal of Medicine* 340:603–8.

Mullan, M. J., and R. M. Murray. 1989. "The Impact of Molecular Genetics on Our Understanding of the Psychoses." *British Journal of Psychiatry* 154:591–95.

Mumford, D., N. Mohammed, J. Faiz-ul-mulk, and I. Baig. 1996. "Stress and Psychiatric Disorder in the Hindu Kush: A Community Survey of Mountain Villages in Chitral, Pakistan." *British Journal of Psychiatry* 168:299–307.

Murphy, J. M. 1976. "Psychiatric Labeling in Cross-Cultural Perspectives." *Science* 191:1019–28.

Murray, R. M. 1979. "A Reappraisal of American Psychiatry." *The Lancet*, 3 February, 255–58.

Myers, D. G., and E. Diener. 1995. "Who Is Happy?" *Psychological Science* 6:10–19.

Narrow, W. E., D. A. Regier, D. S. Rae, R. W. Manderscheid, and B. Z. Locke. 1993. "Use of Services by Persons with Mental and Addictive Disorders: Findings from the National Institute of Mental Health Epidemiologic Catchment Area Program." *Archives of General Psychiatry* 50:95–107.

Nathan, P. E. 1994. "DSM-IV: Empirical, Accessible, Not Yet Ideal." *Journal of Clinical Psychology* 50:103–11.

National Institute of Mental Health Psychopharmacology Service Center Collaborative Study Group. 1964. "Phenothiazine Treatment in Acute Schizophrenia." *Archives of General Psychiatry* 10:246–56.

National Institute of Mental Health. 1998. *Genetics and Mental Disorder: Report of the National Institute of Mental Health's Genetics Workgroup.* Rockville, Md.: National Institute of Mental Health.

Nelkin, D., and M. S. Lindee. 1995. *The DNA Mystique: The Gene as a Cultural Icon.* New York: W. H. Freeman.

Nelson-Gray, R. O. 1991. "DSM-IV: Empirical Guidelines from Psychometrics." *Journal of Abnormal Psychology* 100:308–15.

Nesse, R. M. 1987. "An Evolutionary Perspective on Panic Disorder and Agoraphobia." *Ethology and Sociobiology* 8:73S–83S.

New York Times. 1994. 19 April, C1.

———. 1999. "King Midas's Funeral: Happy Hour at a Tomb." 23 December, A18.

New York Times Magazine. 1997. "Best-Selling Prescription Drugs." 23 November, 17.

Nicholi, A. M. Jr. 1987. "Psychiatric Consultation in Professional Football." *New England Journal of Medicine* 316:1095–1100.

Noble, E. P., K. Blum, T. Ritchie, A. Montgomery, and P. J. Sheridan. 1991. "Allelic Association of the D2 Dopamine Receptor Gene with Receptor-Binding Characteristics in Alcoholism." *Archives of General Psychiatry* 48:648–54.

Nolan, J. L. Jr. 1998. *The Therapeutic State: Justifying Government at Century's End.* New York: New York University Press.

Nolen-Hoeksema, S. 1987. "Sex Differences in Unipolar Depression: Evidence and Theory." *Psychological Bulletin* 101:259–82.

Nuckolls, C. W. 1992. "Toward a Cultural History of the Personality Disorders." *Social Science and Medicine* 35:37–47.

O'Dea, T. F. 1957. *The Mormons.* Chicago: University of Chicago Press.

Ofshe, R., and E. Watters. 1994. *Making Monsters: False Memories, Psychotherapy, and Sexual Hysteria.* Berkeley: University of California Press.

Olfson, M., and H. A. Pincus. 1994a. "Outpatient Psychotherapy in the United States, I: Volume, Costs, and User Characteristics." *American Journal of Psychiatry* 151:1281–88.

———. 1994b. "Outpatient Psychotherapy in the United States, II: Patterns of Utilization." *American Journal of Psychiatry* 151:1289–94.

Olfson, M., M. Guardino, E. Struening, F. R. Schneier, F. Hellman, and D. F. Klein. 2000. "Barriers to the Treatment of Social Anxiety." *American Journal of Psychiatry* 157:521–27.

Olfson, M., S. C. Marcus, H. A. Pincus, J. M. Zito, J. W. Thompson, and D. A. Zarin. 1998. "Antidepressant Prescribing Practices of Outpatient Psychiatrists." *Archives of General Psychiatry* 55:310–16.

Olivardia, R., H. G. Pope Jr., and J. I. Hudson. 2000. "Muscle Dysmorphia in Male Weightlifters: A Case-Control Study." *American Journal of Psychiatry* 157:1291–96.

Omer, H., and R. Dar. 1992. "Changing Trends in Three Decades of Psychotherapy Research: The Flight from Theory into Pragmatics." *Journal of Consulting and Clinical Psychology* 60:88–93.

Orlinsky, D. E., K. Grawe, and B. K. Parks. 1994. "Process and Outcome in Psychotherapy—Noch Einmal." In *Handbook of Psychotherapy and Behavior Change,* 4th ed., ed. A. E. Bergin and S. L. Garfield, 270–378. New York: John Wiley.

Padgett, D. K., C. Patrick, B. J. Burns, and H. J. Schlesinger. 1994. "Ethnicity and the Use of Outpatient Mental Health Services in a National Insured Population." *American Journal of Public Health* 84:222–26.

Pardes, H., C. A. Kaufmann, H. A. Pincus, and A. West. 1989. "Genetics and Psychiatry: Past Discoveries, Current Dilemmas, and Future Directions." *American Journal of Psychiatry* 146:435–43.

Parsian, A., and C. R. Cloninger. 1991. "Genetics of High-Risk Populations." *Addiction & Recovery* 11:9–11.

Parsons, T. 1951. *The Social System.* New York: The Free Press.

Paykel, E. S., A. Tylee, A. Wright, R. G. Priest, S. Rix, and D. Hart. 1997. "The Defeat Depression Campaign: Psychiatry in the Public Arena." *American Journal of Psychiatry* 154:59–65.

Pearlin, L. I. 1989. "The Sociological Study of Stress." *Journal of Health and Social Behavior* 30:141–256.

———. 1999. "Stress and Mental Health: A Conceptual Overview." In *A Handbook for the Study of Mental Health: Social Contexts, Theories, and Systems,* ed. A. V. Horwitz and T. L. Scheid, 161–75. New York: Cambridge University Press.

Pearlin, L. I., M. A. Lieberman, E. G. Menaghan, and J. T. Mullan. 1981. "The Stress Process." *Journal of Health and Social Behavior* 22:337–56.

Peltonen, L. 1995. "All Out for Chromosome Six." *Nature* 378:665–66.

Penrose, L. S. 1934. "The Detection of Autosomal Linkage in Data which Consist of Pairs of Brothers and Sisters of Unspecified Parentage." *Eugenics* 6:133–38.

Pepper, H. P. 1945. "A Note on the Placebo." *American Journal of Pharmacy* 117:409–12.

Perls, F. 1964. *Ego Hunger and Aggression.* New York: Random House.

Persons, J. B. 1986. "The Advantages of Studying Psychological Phenomena Rather than Psychiatric Diagnoses." *American Psychologist* 41:1252–60.

———. 1991. "Psychotherapy Outcome Studies Do Not Accurately Represent Current Models of Psychotherapy: A Proposed Remedy." *American Psychologist* 46:99–106.

Persons, J. B., M. E. Thase, and P. Crits-Christoph. 1996. "The Role of Psychotherapy in the Treatment of Depression: Review of Two Practice Guidelines." *Archives of General Psychiatry* 53:283–90.

Pescosolido, B. A., J. Monahan, B. G. Link, A. Stueve, and S. Kikusawa. 1999. "The Public's View of the Competence, Dangerousness, and Need for Legal Coercion of Persons with Mental Health Problems." *American Journal of Public Health* 89:1339–45.

Pichot, P. J. 1997. "DSM-III and Its Reception: A European View." *American Journal of Psychiatry* 154:47–54.

Pickar, D., and J. K. Hsiao. 1995. "Clozapine Treatment of Schizophrenia." *Journal of the American Medical Association* 274:981–83.

Pincus, H. A., A. Frances, W. W. Davis, M. B. First, and T. A. Widiger. 1992. "DSM-IV and New Diagnostic Categories: Holding the Line on Proliferation." *American Journal of Psychiatry* 149:112–17.

Pincus, H. A., T.L. Tanielian, S. C. Marcus, M. Olfson, D. A. Zarin, J. Thompson, and J. M. Zito. 1998. "Prescribing Trends in Psychotropic Medications: Primary Care, Psychiatry, and Other Medical Specialties." *Journal of the American Medical Association* 279:526–31.

Pinker, S. 1997. *How the Mind Works.* New York: W. W. Norton.

Pipher, M. 1994. *Reviving Ophelia: Saving the Selves of Adolescent Girls.* New York: Ballantine.

Plomin, R., and D. Daniels. 1987. "Why Are Children in the Same Family so Different from One Another?" *Behavioral and Brain Sciences* 10:1–60.

Plomin, R., M. J. Owen, and P. McGuffin. 1994. "The Genetic Basis of Complex Human Behaviors." *Science* 264:1733–39.

Plomin, R., P. Lichtenstein, N. L. Pedersen, G. E. McClearn, and J. R. Nesselroade. 1990. "Genetic Influence on Life Events during the Last Half of the Life Span." *Psychology and Aging* 5:25–30.

Plunkett, R. J., and J. E. Gordon. 1960. *Epidemiology and Mental Illness.* New York: Basic Books.

Pollack, W. S. 1999. *Real Boys: Rescuing Our Sons from the Myths of Boyhood.* New York: Owl Books.

Pope, H. G. Jr., A. J. Gruber, B. Mangweth, B. Bureau, C. deCol, R. Jouvent, and J. I. Hudson. 2000. "Body Image Perception among Men in Three Countries." *American Journal of Psychiatry* 157:1297–1301.

Popper, K. 1959. *The Logic of Scientific Discovery.* London: Hutchinson.

Porter, T. M. 1995. *Trust in Numbers: The Pursuit of Objectivity In Science and Public Life.* Princeton, N.J.: Princeton University Press.

Prager, J. 1998. *Presenting the Past: Psychoanalysis and the Sociology of Misremembering.* Cambridge: Harvard University Press.

Prescott, C. A., and K. S. Kendler. 1999. "Genetic and Environmental Contributions to Alcohol Abuse and Dependence in a Population-Based Sample of Male Twins." *American Journal of Psychiatry* 156:34–40.

Price, J. S., and L. Sloman. 1987. "Depression as Yielding Behavior: An Animal Model Based on Schjelderup-Ebbe's Pecking Order." *Ethology and Sociobiology* 8:85S–98S.

Quitkin, F. M., J. G. Rabkin, J. Gerald, J. M. Davis, and D. F. Klein. 2000. "Validity of Clinical Trials of Antidepressants." *American Journal of Psychiatry* 157:327–37.

Rabkin, J. G., and E. L. Struening. 1976. "Life Events, Stress, and Illness." *Science* 194:1013–20.

Radloff, L. 1975. "Sex Differences in Depression: The Effects of Occupation and Marital Status." *Sex Roles* 1:249–65.

———. 1977. "The CES-D Scale: A Self-Report Depression Scale for Research in the General Population." *Applied Psychological Measurement* 3:249–65.

Raghunathan, A. 1999. "A Bold Rush to Sell Drugs to the Shy." *New York Times,* 18 May, C1.

Raleigh, M. J., and M. T. McGuire. 1984. "Social and Environmental Influences on Blood Serotonin Concentrations in Monkeys." *Archives of General Psychiatry* 41:405–10.

Rapoport, J. L. 1989. *The Boy Who Couldn't Stop Washing.* New York: E. P. Dutton.

Rasmussen, S. A., and M. T. Tsuang. 1986. "Clinical Characteristics and Family History in DSM-III Obsessive-Compulsive Disorder." *American Journal of Psychiatry* 143:317–22.

Read, Piers P. 1992. *Alive.* New York: Avon/Eos.

Redlich, F. C., and S. R. Kellert. 1978. "Trends in American Mental Health." *American Journal of Psychiatry* 135:22–28.

Regier, D. A., C. T. Kaelber, D. S. Rae, M. E. Farmer, B. Knauper, R. C. Kessler, and G. S. Norquist. 1998. "Limitations of Diagnostic Criteria and Assessment Instruments for Mental Disorders." *Archives of General Psychiatry* 55:109–15.

Regier, D., W. E. Narrow, D. S. Rae, R. W. Manderscheid, B. Z. Locke, and F. K. Goodwin. 1993. "The de Facto U.S. Mental and Addictive Disorders Service System: Epidemiologic Catchment Area Prospective 1-Year Prevalence Rates of Disorders and Services." *Archives of General Psychiatry* 50:85–94.

Reiss, D., R. Plomin, and E. M. Hetherington. 1991. "Genetics and Psychiatry: An Unheralded Window on the Environment." *American Journal of Psychiatry* 148: 283–91.

Rende, R. D., R. Plomin, D. Reiss, and E. M. Hetherington. 1993. "Genetic and Environmental Influences on Depressive Symptomatology in Adolescence: Individual Differences and Extreme Scores." *Journal of Child Psychology and Psychiatry* 34:1387–98.

Rice, G., C. Anderson, N. Risch, G. Ebers, et al. 1999. "Male Homosexuality: Absence of Linkage to Microsatellite Markers at Xq28." *Science* 284:665–67.

Richman, J. A. 1988. "Deviance from Sex-Linked Expressivity Norms and Psychological Distress." *Social Forces* 67:208–15.

Rieff, P. 1961. *Freud: The Mind of the Moralist.* Garden City, N.Y.: Doubleday Anchor.

———. 1966. *The Triumph of the Therapeutic: Uses of Faith after Freud.* New York: Harper & Row.

Risch, N. 1990. "Linkage Strategies for Genetically Complex Traits, II: The Power of Affected Relative Pairs." *American Journal of Human Genetics* 46:229–41.

———. 1991. "Genetic Linkage Studies in Psychiatry: Theoretical Aspects." In *Genetic Issues in Psychosocial Epidemiology,* ed. M. T. Tsuang, K. S. Kendler, and M. J. Lyons, 71–93. New Brunswick, N.J.: Rutgers University Press.

Risch, N., and K. R. Merikangas. 1993. "Linkage Studies of Psychiatric Disorders." *European Archives of Psychiatry and Clinical Neurosciences* 243:143–49.

Roazen, P. 1992. *Freud and His Followers.* 1975. New York: Da Capo Press.

Robins, L. N. 1985. "Epidemiology: Reflections on Testing the Validity of Psychiatric Instruments." *Archives of General Psychiatry* 42:918–24.

———. 1986. "The Development and Characteristics of the NIMH Diagnostic Interview Schedule." In *Community Surveys of Psychiatric Disorders,* ed. M. M. Weissman, J. K. Myers, and C. E. Ross, 403–28. New Brunswick, N.J.: Rutgers University Press.

Robins, L. N., and S. Guze. 1970. "Establishment of Diagnostic Validity in Psychiatric Illness: Its Application to Schizophrenia." *American Journal of Psychiatry* 126:983–87.

Robins, L. N., and J. E. Helzer. 1986. "Diagnosis and Clinical Assessment: The Current State of Psychiatric Diagnosis." *Annual Review of Psychology* 37:409–32.

Robins, L. N., J. E. Helzer, M. M. Weissman, H. Orvaschel, E. Gruenberg, J. D. Burke Jr., and D. A. Regier. 1984. "Lifetime Prevalence of Specific Psychiatric Disorders in Three Sites." *Archives of General Psychiatry* 41:949–56.

Robins, L. N., and D. A. Regier, eds. 1991. *Psychiatric Disorders in America: The Epidemiological Catchment Area Study.* New York: The Free Press.

Robinson, L. A., J. S. Berman, and R. A. Neimeyer. 1990. "Psychotherapy for the Treatment of Depression: A Comprehensive Review of Controlled Outcome Research." *Psychological Bulletin* 108:30–49.

Robinson, P. 1993. *Freud and His Critics.* Berkeley: University of California Press.

Roe, A., and B. Burks. 1945. *Adult Adjustment of Foster Children of Alcoholic and Psychotic Parentage and the Influence of the Foster Home.* New Haven, Conn.: Yale University Press.

Rogler, L. H. 1996. "Framing Research on Culture in Psychiatric Diagnosis: The Case of the DSM-IV." *Psychiatry* 59:145–55.

———. 1997. "Making Sense of Historical Changes in the Diagnostic and Statistical Manual of Mental Disorders: Five Propositions." *Journal of Health and Social Behavior* 38:9–20.

Rogler, L. H., and D. E. Cortes. 1993. "Help-Seeking Pathways: A Unifying Concept in Mental Health Care." *American Journal of Psychiatry* 150:554–61.

Rogler, L. H., D. E. Cortes, and R. G. Malgady. 1991. "Acculturation and Mental Health Status among Hispanics." *American Psychologist* 46:585–97.

Rogow, A. A. 1970. *The Psychiatrists*. New York: Putnam.

Rorty, R. 1989. *Contingency, Irony, and Solidarity*. Cambridge: Cambridge University Press.

Rose, R. J. 1991. "Twin Studies and Psychosocial Epidemiology." In *Genetic Issues in Psychosocial Epidemiology*, ed. M. T. Tsuang, K. S. Kendler, and M. J. Lyons, 12–32. New Brunswick, N.J.: Rutgers University Press.

Rose, R. J., M. Koskenvuo, J. Kaprio, S. Sarna, and H. Langinvainio. 1988. "Shared Genes, Shared Experiences, and Similarity of Personality: Data From 14,288 Adult Finnish Cotwins." *Journal of Personality and Social Psychology* 54:161–71.

Rosen, G. 1968. *Madness in Society*. New York: Harper.

Rosenfield, S. 1980. "Sex Differences in Depression: Do Women Always Have Higher Rates?" *Journal of Health and Social Behavior* 21:33–42.

———. 1983. "Sex Roles and Societal Reactions to Mental Illness." *Journal of Health and Social Behavior* 23:18–24.

———. 1989. "The Effects of Women's Employment: Personal Control and Sex Differences in Mental Health." *Journal of Health and Social Behavior* 30:77–91.

———. 1992. "The Costs of Sharing: Wives' Employment and Husbands' Mental Health." *Journal of Health and Social Behavior* 33:213–25.

———. 1999. "Gender and Mental Health: Do Women Have More Psychopathology, Men More, or Both the Same (and Why)?" In *A Handbook for the Study of Mental Health: Social Contexts, Theories, and Systems*, ed. A. V. Horwitz and T. L. Scheid, 349–60. New York: Cambridge University Press.

Rosenfield, S., and S. Neese-Todd. 1993. "Elements of a Psychosocial Rehabilitation Clubhouse Associated with a Satisfying Quality of Life." *Hospital and Community Psychiatry* 44:76–78.

Rosenhan, D. L. 1973. "On Being Sane in Insane Places." *Science* 179:250–58.

Rosenthal, D. 1970. *Genetic Theory and Abnormal Behavior*. New York: McGraw-Hill.

Rosenthal, D., P. H. Wender, S. S. Kety, J. Weiner, and F. Schulsinger. 1971. "The Adopted-Away Offspring of Schizophrenics." *American Journal of Psychiatry* 138:307–11.

Ross, C. A., S. Joshi, and R. Currie. 1990. "Dissociative Experiences in the General Population." *American Journal of Psychiatry* 147:1547–52.

Ross, C. E., J. Mirowsky, and K. Goldstein. 1990. "The Impact of the Family on Health: The Decade in Review." *Journal of Marriage and the Family* 52:1059–78.

Ross, C. E., J. R. Reynolds, and K. J. Geis. 2000. "The Contingent Meaning of Neighborhood Stability for Residents' Psychological Well-Being." *American Sociological Review* 65:581–98.

Rothman, D. J. 1971. *The Discovery of the Asylum: Social Order and Disorder in the New Republic*. Boston: Little, Brown.

Rowe, D.C. 1994. *The Limits of Family Influence: Genes, Experience, and Behavior*. New York: Guilford Press.

Rudorfer, M. V. 1996. "Ethnicity in the Pharmacologic Treatment Process." *Psychopharmacology Bulletin* 32, special issue:181–82.

Ryder, N. B. 1965. "The Cohort as a Concept in the Study of Social Change." *American Sociological Review* 30:843–61.

Sabshin, M. 1990. "Turning Points in Twentieth-Century American Psychiatry." *American Journal of Psychiatry* 147:1267–74.

Sartorius, N., A. Jablensky, and R. Shapiro. 1978. "Cross-Cultural Differences in the Short-Term Prognosis of Schizophrenic Psychoses." *Schizophrenia Bulletin* 4:102–13.

Sartorius, N., A. Jablensky, A. Korten, G. Ernberg, M. Anker, J. E. Cooper, and R. Day.

1986. "Early Manifestations and First-Contact Incidence of Schizophrenia in Different Cultures." *Psychological Medicine* 16:909–28.

Scarr, S., and K. McCartney. 1983. "How People Make Their Own Environments: A Theory of Genotype-Environment Effects." *Child Development* 54:424–35.

Schaffer, R. 1991. *America in the Great War: The Rise of the War Welfare State.* New York: Oxford University Press.

Schatzberg, A. F. 2000. "Pros and Cons of Prozac and Its Relatives." *American Journal of Psychiatry* 157:323–25.

Scheff, T. J. 1966. *Being Mentally Ill: A Sociological Theory.* Chicago: Aldine.

Scheffler, R. M., and A. B. Miller. 1989. "Demand Analysis of Mental Health Services Use among Ethnic Subpopulations." *Inquiry* 26:202–15.

Schneider, J. W. 1985. "Social Problems Theory: The Constructionist View." *Annual Review of Sociology* 11:209–29.

Schofield, William. 1964. *Psychotherapy: The Purchase of Friendship.* Englewood Cliffs:, N.J. Prentice-Hall.

Schou, M., N. Juel-Nielson, E. Stromgren, and H. Voldby. 1954. "The Treatment of Manic Psychoses by the Administration of Lithium Salts." *Journal of Neurology, Neurosurgery, and Psychiatry* 17:250–60.

Schreiber, F. R. 1973. *Sybil.* Chicago: Regnery.

Schwartz, S. 1991. "Women and Depression: A Durkheimian Perspective." *Social Science and Medicine* 32:127–40.

———. 1999. "Biological Approaches to Psychiatric Disorders." In *A Handbook for the Study of Mental Health: Social Contexts, Theories, and Systems,* ed. A. V. Horwitz and T. L. Scheid, 79–103. Cambridge: Cambridge University Press.

Scott, W. J. 1990. "PTSD in DSM-III: A Case in the Politics of Diagnosis and Disease." *Social Problems* 37:294–310.

Scull, A. T. 1979. *Museums of Madness: The Social Organization of Insanity in Nineteenth Century England.* New York: St. Martin's Press.

Scull, A. T., C. MacKenzie, and N. Herevey. 1996. *Masters of Bedlam: The Transformation of the Mad-Doctoring Trade.* Princeton, N.J.: Princeton University Press.

Searles, J. S. 1988. "The Role of Genetics in the Pathogenesis of Alcoholism." *Journal of Abnormal Psychology* 97:153–67.

Segall, M. H., W. J. Lonner, and J. W. Berry. 1998. "Cross-Cultural Psychology as a Scholarly Discipline: On the Flowering of Culture in Behavioral Research." *American Psychologist* 53:1101–10.

Segalowitz, S. J. 1999. "Why Twin Studies Really Don't Tell Us Much about Human Heritability." *Behavioral and Brain Sciences* 22:904–5.

Seligman, M.E.P. 1995. "The Effectiveness of Psychotherapy: The *Consumer Reports* Study." *American Psychologist* 50:965–74.

Sellin, T. 1938. *Culture Conflict and Crime.* New York: Social Science Research Council.

Selye, H. 1956. *The Stress of Life.* New York: McGraw-Hill.

Shadish, W. R. Jr., and R. B. Sweeney. 1991. "Mediators and Moderators in Meta-analysis." *Journal of Consulting and Clinical Psychology* 59:883–93.

Shapiro, D., and D. Shapiro. 1982. "Meta-analysis of Comparative Therapy Outcome Studies: A Replication and Refinement." *Psychological Bulletin* 92:581–604.

Shapiro, S., E. A. Skinner, M. Kramer, D. M. Steinwachs, and D. A. Regier. 1985. "Measuring Need for Mental Health Services in a General Population." *Medical Care* 23:1033–43.

Sharkey, J. 1999. "Mental Illness Hits the Money Trail." *New York Times,* 6 June, E5.

Shaw, C., and H. McKay. 1942. *Juvenile Delinquency in Urban Areas.* Chicago: University of Chicago Press.

Shea, M. T., I. Elkin, S. D. Imbr, S. M. Sotsky, et al. 1992. "Course of Depressive Symptoms over Follow-up: Findings from the NIMH Treatment of Depression Collaborative Research Program." *Archives of General Psychiatry* 49:782–87.

Shepherd, M. 1993. "The Placebo: From Specificity to the Non-specific and Back." *Psychological Medicine* 23:569–78.

Shilts, R. 1987. *And the Band Played On: Politics, People and the AIDS Epidemic.* New York: St. Martin's.

Shorter, E. 1992. *From Paralysis to Fatigue: A History of Psychosomatic Illness in the Modern Era.* New York: The Free Press.

———. 1994. *From the Mind into the Body: The Cultural Origins of Psychosomatic Symptoms.* New York: The Free Press.

———. 1997. *A History of Psychiatry: From the Era of the Asylum to the Age of Prozac.* New York: John Wiley & Sons.

Showalter, E. 1985. *The Female Malady: Women, Madness, and English Culture, 1830–1980.* New York: Pantheon.

———. 1997. *Hystories: Hysterical Epidemics and Modern Media.* New York: Columbia University Press.

Silventoinen, K., J. Kaprio, E. Lahelma, and M. Koskenvuo. 2000. "Relative Effect of Genetic and Environmental Factors on Body Height: Differences across Birth Cohorts among Finnish Men and Women." *American Journal of Public Health* 90:627–30.

Simon, R. W. 1995. "Gender, Multiple Roles, Role Meaning, and Mental Health." *Journal of Health and Social Behavior* 36:182–94.

———. 1997. "The Meanings Individuals Attach to Role Identities and Their Implications for Mental Health." *Journal of Health and Social Behavior* 38:256–74.

———. 1998. "Assessing Sex Differences in Vulnerability among Employed Parents: The Importance of Marital Status." *Journal of Health and Social Behavior* 39:38–54.

Simpson, R. 1996. "Neither Clear nor Present: The Social Construction of Safety and Danger." *Sociological Forum* 11:549–62.

Singer, S. 1985. *Human Genetics.* New York: W. H. Freeman.

Skodol, A. E. 2000. "Diagnosis and Classification of Mental Disorders." In *American Psychiatry after WWII: 1944–1994,* ed. R. W. Menninger and J. C. Nemiah, 430–57. Washington, D.C.: American Psychiatric Press.

Slater, L. 1998. *Prozac Diary.* New York: Random House.

Sloman, L., M. Konstantareas, and D. W. Dunham. 1979. "The Adaptive Role of Maladaptive Neurosis." *Biological Psychiatry* 14:961–71.

Smith, M. L., and G. V. Glass. 1977. "Meta-analysis of Psychotherapy Outcome Studies." *American Psychologist* 32:752–60.

Smith, M. L., G. V. Glass, and R. H. Miller. 1980. *The Benefits of Psychotherapy.* Baltimore, Md.: Johns Hopkins University Press.

Smith-Rosenberg, C. 1972. "The Hysterical Woman: Sex Roles and Role Conflict in 19th Century America." *Social Research* 39:652–78.

Smoller, J. W., and M. T. Tsuang. 1998. "Panic and Phobic Anxiety: Defining Phenotypes for Genetic Studies." *American Journal of Psychiatry* 155:1152–62.

Sonnenstuhl, W. J. 1996. *Working Sober: The Transformation of an Occupational Drinking Culture.* Ithaca: ILR Press.

Spector, M., and J. I. Kitsuse. 1977. *Constructing Social Problems*. Menlo Park, Calif.: Cummings.

Spitzer, R. L. 1991. "An Outsider-Insider's Views about Revising the DSMs." *Journal of Abnormal Psychology* 100:294–96.

———. 1999. "Harmful Dysfunction and the DSM Definition of Mental Disorders." *Journal of Abnormal Psychology* 108:430–32.

Spitzer, R. L., J. Cohen, J. Fleiss, and J. Endicott. 1967. "Quantification of Agreement in Psychiatric Diagnosis." *Archives of General Psychiatry* 17:83–87.

Spitzer, R. L., and J. Endicott. 1978. "Medical and Mental Disorder: Proposed Definition and Criteria." In *Critical Issues in Psychiatric Diagnosis*, ed. R. L. Spitzer and D. F. Klein. New York: Raven Press.

Spitzer, R. L., and J. L. Fleiss. 1974. "A Re-analysis of the Reliability of Psychiatric Diagnosis." *British Journal of Psychiatry* 125:341–47.

Spitzer, R. L., M. Sheehy, and J. Endicott. 1977. "DSM-III: Guiding Principles." In *Psychiatric Diagnosis*, ed. V. Rakoff, H. Stancer, and H. Kedward, 1–24. New York: Brunner/ Mazel.

Spitzer, R. L., and J. B. Williams. 1987. "Revising DSM-III: The Process and Major Issues." In *Diagnosis and Classification in Psychiatry: A Critical Appraisal of DSM-III*, ed. G. Tischler, 425–33. New York: Cambridge University Press.

Spitzer, R. L., J.B. Williams, K. Kroenke, M. Linzer, F. V. deGruy, S. R. Hahn, D. Brody, and J. G. Johnson. 1994. "Utility of a New Procedure for Diagnosing Mental Disorders in Primary Care: The PRIME-MD 1000 Study." *Journal of the American Medical Association* 272:1749–56.

Spitzer, R. L., J. B. Williams, and A. Skodal. 1980. "DSM-III: The Major Achievements and an Overview." *American Journal of Psychiatry* 137:151–64.

Srole, L., T. S. Langner, S. T. Michael, M. K. Opler, and T.A.C. Rennie. 1962. *Mental Health in the Metropolis: The Midtown Manhattan Study*. New York: McGraw-Hill.

Starr, P. 1982. *The Social Transformation of American Medicine*. New York: Basic Books.

Stavrakaki, C., and B. Vargo. 1986. "The Relationship of Anxiety and Depression: A Review of the Literature." *British Journal of Psychiatry* 149:7–16.

Stein, D. M., and M. J. Lambert. 1984. "On the Relationship between Therapist Experience and Psychotherapy Outcome." *Clinical Psychology Review* 4:127–42.

Stein, L. I., M. A. Test, and A. J. Marx. 1980. "Alternatives to Mental Hospital Treatment I: Conceptual Model Treatment Program and Clinical Evaluation." *Archives of General Psychiatry* 37:392–97.

Stein, M. B., K. L. Jang, and W. J. Livesley. 1999. "Heritability of Anxiety Sensitivity: A Twin Study." *American Journal of Psychiatry* 156:246–51.

Strupp, H. H. 1965. "Discussion." *International Journal of Psychiatry* 1:165–69.

Styron, W. 1992. *Darkness Visible: A Memoir of Madness*. New York: Vintage Books.

Sue, S. 1988. "Psychotherapeutic Services for Ethnic Minorities: Two Decades of Research Findings." *American Psychologist* 43:301–8.

Susser, E. S., and S. P. Lin. 1992. "Schizophrenia after Prenatal Exposure to the Dutch Hunger Winter of 1944–1945." *Archives of General Psychiatry* 49:983–88.

Swazey, J. P. 1974. *Chlorpromazine in Psychiatry*. Cambridge: MIT Press.

Swidler, A. 1986. "Culture in Action: Symbols and Strategies." *American Sociological Review* 51:273–86.

Swindle, R., K. Heller, B. Pescosolido, and S. Kikuzawa. 2000. "Responses to Nervous Breakdowns in America over a 40-Year Period." *American Psychologist* 55:740–49.

Szasz, T. S. 1961. *The Myth of Mental Illness.* New York: Hoeber-Harper.

Takeuchi, D. T., C. Chun, and H. Shen. 1996. "Stress Exposure and Cultural Expressions of Distress." Paper presented at annual meeting of the American Sociological Association, New York, August.

Takeuchi, D. T., E. Uehara, and G. Maramba. 1999. "Cultural Diversity and Mental Health Treatment." In *A Handbook for the Study of Mental Health: Social Contexts, Theories, and Systems,* ed. A. V. Horwitz and T. L. Scheid, 550–65. New York: Cambridge University Press.

Tausig, M., and R. Fenwick. 1999. "Recession and Well-Being." *Journal of Health and Social Behavior* 40:1–16.

Tavris, C. 1992. *The Mismeasure of Woman.* New York: Simon & Schuster.

Terr, L. C. 1994. *Unchained Memories: True Stories of Traumatic Memories Lost and Found.* New York: HarperCollins.

Thapar, A., and P. McGuffin. 1994. "A Twin Study of Depressive Symptoms in Childhood." *British Journal of Psychiatry* 165:259–65.

Thase, M. E. 1999. "How Should Efficacy Be Evaluated in Randomized Clinical Trials of Treatments for Depression?" *Journal of Clinical Psychiatry* 60, suppl. 4:23–31.

Thase, M. E., and David J. Kupfer. 1996. "Recent Developments in the Pharmacotherapy of Mood Disorders." *Journal of Consulting and Clinical Psychology* 64:646–59.

Thoits, P. A. 1983. "Dimensions of Life Events that Influence Psychological Distress: An Evaluation and Synthesis of the Literature." In *Psychosocial Stress: Perspectives on Structure, Theory, Life-Course, and Methods,* ed. H. Kaplan, 33–103. New York: Academic Press.

———. 1985. "Self-Labeling Processes in Mental Illness: The Role of Emotional Deviance." *American Journal of Sociology* 91:221–49.

———. 1999. "Sociological Approaches to Mental Illness?" In *A Handbook for the Study of Mental Health: Social Contexts, Theories, and Systems,* ed. A. V. Horwitz and T. L. Scheid, 121–38. New York: Cambridge University Press.

Thornhill, R., C. T. Palmer, and M. Wilson. 2000. *A Natural History of Rape: Biological Bases of Sexual Coercion.* Cambridge: MIT Press.

Thornton, A., and W. I. Rodgers. 1987. "The Influence of Individual and Historical Time on Marital Dissolution." *Demography* 24:1–22.

Time. 2000. "Cracking the Code!" July 3, cover.

Toby, J. 1998. "Medicalizing Temptation." *The Public Interest* 130:64–78.

Tomes, N. 1984. *A Generous Confidence: Thomas Story Kirkbride and the Art of Asylum-Keeping, 1840–1883.* Cambridge: Cambridge University Press.

———. 1990. "Historical Perspectives on Women and Mental Illness." In *Women, Health, and Medicine in America,* ed. R. D. Apple, 143–71. New York: Garland.

Torrey, E. F. 1998. *Out of the Shadows: Confronting America's Mental Illness Crisis,* 2d ed. New York: John Wiley.

Tsuang, M. T. 2000. "Genes, Environment, and Mental Health Wellness." *American Journal of Psychiatry* 157:489–91.

Tsuang, M. T., W. S. Stone, and S. V. Faraone. 2000. "Toward Reformulating the Diagnosis of Schizophrenia." *American Journal of Psychiatry* 157:1041–50.

Tucker, G. J. 1998. "Putting DSM-IV in Perspective." *American Journal of Psychiatry* 155:159–60.

Tucker, J. 1999. *The Therapeutic Corporation.* New York: Oxford University Press.

Turner, R. J. 1999. "Social Support and Coping." In *A Handbook for the Study of Mental Health: Social Contexts, Theories, and Systems,* ed. A. V. Horwitz and T. L. Scheid, 198–210. New York: Cambridge University Press.

Turner, R. J., and D. A. Lloyd. 1999. "The Stress Process and the Social Distribution of Depression." *Journal of Health and Social Behavior* 40:374–404.

Turner, R. J., and M. O. Wagenfeld. 1968. "Occupational Mobility and Schizophrenia: An Assessment of the Social Causation and Social Selection Hypotheses." *American Sociological Review* 32:104–13.

Turner, R. J., B. Wheaton, and D. A. Lloyd. 1995. "The Epidemiology of Stress." *American Sociological Review* 60:104–25.

Tyrer, P. 1985. "Neurosis Divisible." *The Lancet,* 23 March, 685–88.

Umberson, D. 1987. "Family Status and Health Behaviors: Social Control as a Dimension of Social Integration." *Journal of Health and Social Behavior* 28:306–19.

Umberson, D., K. Williams, and K. Anderson. 2000. "Violent Behavior: An Expression of Emotional Upset?" Paper presented at the August 2000 meetings of the American Sociological Association, Washington, D.C.

U.S. Department of Health and Human Services. 1999. *Mental Health: A Report of the Surgeon General.* Rockville, Md.: U.S. Department of Human Services, Substance Abuse and Mental Health Services Administration, Center for Mental Health Services, National Institutes of Health, National Institute of Mental Health.

Vaillant, G. E. 1984. "The Disadvantages of DSM-III Outweigh the Advantages." *American Journal of Psychiatry* 141:542–45.

Valenstein, E. S. 1998. *Blaming the Brain: The TRUTH About Drugs and Mental Health.* New York: The Free Press.

Vega, W. A., and R. G. Rumbaut. 1991. "Ethnic Minorities and Mental Health." *Annual Review of Sociology* 17:351–83.

Veroff, J., R. A. Kulka, and E. Douvan. 1981. *Mental Health in America: Patterns of Help-Seeking from 1957 to 1976.* New York: Basic Books.

von Knorring, A., R. Cloninger, M. Bohman, and S. Sigvardsson. 1983. "An Adoption Study of Depressive Disorders and Substance Abuse." *Archives of General Psychiatry* 40:943–50.

Wade, T. D., C. M. Bulik, M. Neale, and K. S. Kendler. 2000. "Anorexia Nervosa and Major Depression: Shared Genetic and Environmental Risk Factors." *American Journal of Psychiatry* 157:469–71.

Wahlbeck, K., M. Cheine, A. Essali, and C. Adams. 1999. "Evidence of Clozapine's Effectiveness in Schizophrenia: A Systematic Review and Meta-analysis of Randomized Trials." *American Journal of Psychiatry* 158:990–99.

Waite, L. J. 1995. "Does Marriage Matter?" *Demography* 32:483–501.

Waitzkin, H., and H. Magana. 1997. "The Black Box in Somatization: Unexplained Physical Symptoms, Culture, and Narratives of Trauma." *Social Science and Medicine* 45:811–25.

Wakefield, J. C. 1992a. "The Concept of Mental Disorder: On the Boundary between Biological Facts and Social Values." *American Psychologist* 47:373–88.

———. 1992b. "Disorder as Harmful Dysfunction: A Conceptual Critique of DSM-III-R's Definition of Mental Disorder." *Psychological Review* 99:232–47.

———. 1993. "Limits of Operationalization: A Critique of Spitzer and Endicott's (1978) Proposed Operational Criteria for Mental Disorder." *Journal of Abnormal Psychology* 102:160–72.

———. 1994. "Is the Concept of Mental Disorder Culturally Relative?" In *Controversial Issues in Mental Health*, ed. S. A. Kirk and S. D. Einbinder, 11–17. Boston: Allyn and Bacon.

———. 1996. "DSM-IV: Are We Making Diagnostic Progress?" *Contemporary Psychology* 41:646–52.

———. 1997a. "Diagnosing DSM-IV—Part I: DSM-IV and the Concept of Disorder." *Behavioral Research in Therapy* 35:633–49.

———. 1997b. "Normal Inability versus Pathological Disability: Why Ossorio's Definition of Mental Disorders Is Not Sufficient." *Clinical Psychology: Science and Practice* 4:249–58.

———. 1997c. "But Are They Psychiatric Disorders? Conceptual Validity of DIS Diagnostic Criteria and ECA Prevalence Estimates." Unpublished manuscript, Rutgers University.

———. 1999a. "Evolutionary versus Prototype Analyses of the Concept of Disorder." *Journal of Abnormal Psychology* 108:374–99.

———. 1999b. "The Measurement of Mental Disorder." In *A Handbook for the Study of Mental Health: Social Contexts, Theories, and Systems*, ed. A. V. Horwitz and T. L. Scheid, 29–57. New York: Cambridge University Press.

Walkup, J. 1986. "Order and Disorder in Freud's Vienna." *Social Research* 53:579–90.

Wallace, A.F.C. 1972. "Mental Illness, Biology, and Culture." In *Psychological Anthropology*, rev. ed., ed. F. Hsu, 363–402. Cambridge: Schenkman.

Wallerstein, R. S. 1986. *Forty-two Lives in Treatment: A Study of Psychoanalysis and Psychotherapy*. New York: Guilford.

Walsh, B. T., and M. J. Devlin. 1998. "Eating Disorders: Progress and Problems." *Science* 280:1387–90.

Walters, E. E., and K. S. Kendler. 1995. "Anorexia Nervosa and Anorexic-like Syndromes in a Population-Based Female Twin Sample." *American Journal of Psychiatry* 152:64–71.

Warner, L. A., R. C. Kessler, M. Hughes, J. C. Anthony, and C. B. Nelson. 1995. "Prevalence and Correlates of Drug Use and Dependence in the United States: Results from the National Comorbidity Survey." *Archives of General Psychiatry* 52:219–29.

Waxler, N. E. 1974. "Culture and Mental Illness: A Social Labeling Perspective." *Journal of Nervous and Mental Disease* 159:379–95.

———. 1979. "Is Outcome for Schizophrenia Better in Non-industrial Societies? The Case of Sri Lanka." *Journal of Nervous and Mental Disease* 167:144–58.

Weeks, D. E., and K. Lange. 1988. "The Affected-Pedigree-Member Method of Linkage Analysis." *American Journal of Human Genetics* 42:315–26.

Weissman, M. M., E. S. Gershon, K. K. Kidd, et al. 1984. "Psychiatric Disorders in the Relatives of Probands with Affective Disorders." *Archives of General Psychiatry* 41:13–21.

Weissman, M. M., and G. L. Klerman. 1977. "Sex Differences and the Epidemiology of Depression." *Archives of General Psychiatry* 34:98–111.

———. 1985. "Gender and Depression." *Trends in Neuroscience* 8:416–20.

Weissman, M. M., J. K. Myers, and C. E. Ross, eds. 1986. *Community Surveys of Psychiatric Disorders*. New Brunswick, N.J.: Rutgers University Press.

Weissman, M. M., and E. S. Paykel. 1974. *The Depressed Women: A Study of Social Relationships*. Chicago: University of Chicago Press.

Wender, P. H. 1987. *The Hyperactive Child, Adolescent and Adult: Attention Deficit Disorder Throughout the Lifespan*. New York: Oxford University Press.

Wender, P. H., S. S. Kety, D. Rosenthal, F. Schulsinger, J. Ortmann, and I. Lunde. 1986.

"Psychiatric Disorders in the Biological and Adoptive Families of Adopted Individuals with Affective Disorders." *Archives of General Psychiatry* 43:923–29.

Wender, P. H., D. Rosenthal, S. S. Kety, F. Schulsinger, and J. Welner. 1974. "Crossfostering: A Research Strategy for Clarifying the Role of Genetic and Experiential Factors in the Etiology of Schizophrenia." *Archives of General Psychiatry* 30:121–28.

Wheaton, B. 1990. "Life Transitions, Role Histories, and Mental Health." *American Sociological Review* 55:209–23.

———. 1999. "The Nature of Stressors." In *A Handbook for the Study of Mental Health: Social Contexts, Theories, and Systems*, ed. A. V. Horwitz and T. L. Scheid, 176–97. New York: Cambridge University Press.

White, H. R., and S. Hansell. 1997. "Alcohol, Health and Social Class." *ABMRF Journal* 7:93–107.

Whiting, J., and I. Child. 1953. *Child Training and Personality: A Cross-Cultural Study*. New York: Yale University Press.

Widiger, T. A., A. J. Frances, H. A. Pincus, and W. W. Davis. 1990. "DSM-IV Literature Reviews: Rationale, Process, and Limitations." *Journal of Psychopathology and Behavioral Assessment* 12:189–202.

Widiger, T. A., A. J. Frances, H. A. Pincus, W. W. Davis, and M. B. First. 1991. "Toward an Empirical Classification for the DSM-IV." *Journal of Abnormal Psychology* 100:280–88.

Widom, C. S., T. Ireland, and P. J. Glynn. 1995. "Alcohol Abuse in Abused and Neglected Children Followed-Up: Are They at Increased Risk?" *Journal of Studies on Alcohol* 56:207–17.

Williams, D. R., and M. Harris-Read. 1999. "Race and Mental Health: Emerging Patterns and Promising Approaches." In *A Handbook for the Study of Mental Health: Social Contexts, Theories, and Systems*, ed. A. V. Horwitz and T. L. Scheid, 295–314. New York: Cambridge University Press.

Wilson, D. R. 1997. "Evolutionary Epidemiology." *ASCAP* 10:12–27.

Wilson, E. O. 1998. *Consilience: The Unity of Knowledge*. New York: Alfred A. Knopf.

Wilson, M. 1993. "DSM-III and the Transformation of American Psychiatry: A History." *American Journal of Psychiatry* 150:399–410.

Wilson, G. T., and C. G. Fairburn. 1993. "Cognitive Treatments for Eating Disorders." *Journal of Consulting and Clinical Psychology* 61:261–69.

Wing, J. K. 1978. *Reasoning about Madness*. New York: Oxford University Press.

Wohl, R. 1979. *The Generation of 1914*. Cambridge: Harvard University Press.

WPA Dysthymia Working Group. 1995. "Dysthymia in Clinical Practice." *British Journal of Psychiatry* 166:174–83.

Wright, L. 1997. *Twins and What They Tell Us about Who We Are*. New York: John Wiley & Sons.

Wright, R. 1994. *The Moral Animal: Evolutionary Psychology and Everyday Life*. New York: Pantheon.

Wurtzel, E. 1997. *Prozac Nation: Young and Depressed in America*. New York: Riverhead Books.

Yap, P. M. 1965. "*Koro*—a Culture-Bound Depersonalization Syndrome." *British Journal of Psychiatry* 111:43–50.

Young, A. 1995. *The Harmony of Illusions: Inventing Post-traumatic Stress Disorder*. Princeton, N.J.: Princeton University Press.

Zarin, D. A., H. A. Pincus, B. D. Peterson, J. C. West, A. P. Suarez, S. C. Marcus, and

J. S. McIntyre. 1998. "Characterizing Psychiatry with Findings from the National Survey of Psychiatric Practice." *American Journal of Psychiatry* 155:397–404.

Zent, M. R. 1984. "Sex and Mental Disorder: A Reappraisal." *Sociological Focus* 17:121–36.

Zerubavel, E. 1997. *Social Mindscapes: An Invitation to Cognitive Sociology.* Cambridge: Harvard University Press.

Zetzel, E. 1965. "Discussion." *International Journal of Psychiatry* 1:144–50.

Zimmerman, M., W. McDermut, and J. I. Mattia. 2000. "Frequency of Anxiety Disorders in Psychiatric Outpatients with Major Depressive Disorder." *American Journal of Psychiatry* 157:1337–40.

Zito, J. M., D. J. Safer, S. dos Reis, J. F. Gardner, M. Boles, and F. Lynch. 2000. "Trends in the Prescribing of Psychotropic Medications to Preschoolers." *Journal of the American Medical Association* 283:1025–30.

Zubin, J. 1977. "But Is It Good for Science?" *The Clinical Psychologist* 31:1, 5–7.

from personal problems to discrete diagnoses, 72–74
and plethora of mental disorders, 79–80
role of clinicians in development of, 70–72
role of researchers in development of, 67–69
DSM-III-R, 79, 80
DSM-IV, 2–3, 21, 79
See also specific disorders
diagnostic classification (schemes), 218
future of, 226–27
interests served by, 105–6
limits of, 108–14
standards for evaluating the effectiveness of, 215
usefulness, 10–16
Diagnostic Interview Schedule (DIS), 85, 86, 89
diagnostic psychiatry, 2
vs. asylum psychiatry, 2
bedrock assumption, 107
classification of symptoms, 3
current status, 38
disease/medical model and, 3–4, 180, 191, 213
future of, 224–29
limitations of and problems with, 10, 20, 105, 107, 108, 111–13, 129
neglect of sociocultural factors, 13–15, 20, 57–58, 158, 221
with nonpsychotic conditions, 13–14, 109
medications and, 192, 193, 206
objectivity, 57–59
origins and emergence of, 64–67, 211
decline of dynamic psychiatry and, 54–55, 57–59, 82, 210–11
as scientific revolution, 56–57, 80–81
psychoses and, 109
social deviance and, 222–24
system of ordering, 111
therapeutic culture and, 41
and treatment implications, 113
See also *Diagnostic and Statistical Manual of Mental Disorders* (DSM), DSM-III

disease model of mental illness, 3–6, 180, 191, 213–15, 244n. 8
advocacy groups and, 156, 212–13
emergence and persistence of overly expansive model of, 16
limitations, 8–9
treatment and, 3–4
See also biological/biomedical models; diagnostic psychiatry
dissociative identity disorder. *See* multiple personality disorder (MPD)
divorce. *See* marital dissolution
dominance and dependence, 172–77
cultural meanings, 177–79
dominant reflex theory of disease, 119–20
dream interpretation, 42
drug abuse and dependence
prevalence, 87, 102–3, 166–67
See also alcohol abuse
drug treatments, 101, 113, 181, 205–6
disease model, diagnostic psychiatry, and, 66, 156, 183–84, 191–93, 206–7
DSM-III and, 78–79
evaluating, 187–89
research studies, 189–94, 241n. 3, 242n. 8, 242–43n. 14
and the future, 225
prevalence, 4
See also pharmaceutical companies
drug use, 26, 33, 34
Durkheim, Émile, 7, 161
dynamic psychiatry, 1–2, 5, 6, 53–54, 120
bridging of normal behavior and the abnormal, 41, 42, 50, 53–54, 70, 105
decline of, 54, 57–64
diagnosis in, 56
DSM-III and, 71–72
expansion of mental disorder in, 39–40, 53–54 (*see also* abnormal)
as general psychology, 41–43, 208–9
neglect of sociocultural factors, 47–48
rise of, 40–53
sociological aspects, 48–52, 54–55, 71, 209–10
changed medical culture, 58–61
cultural delegitimation, 62–64

dynamic psychiatry (*cont.*)
  subjectivity, imprecision, and untestability, 57–60, 64, 75
dynamic treatments, 47–54, 78, 196–98. *See also* psychotherapy(ies)
dysfunction, internal. *See* internal mechanisms, dysfunctional

eating disorders, 90, 124–26, 148
Edgerton, Robert B., 33
environmental factors, 136, 149–51, 238n. 6
Epidemiologic Catchment Area (ECA) study, 86–88, 95, 221
etiology. *See* mental disorder(s), causes
Eysenck, Hans J., 195–98

family history studies, 111–12
Feighner, John, 64–69, 85
Feighner criteria, 64–69, 72, 79, 113
Fitzgerald, F. Scott, 33
Food and Drug Administration (FDA), 78, 79, 188
Foucault, Michel, 7–8, 19
Frances, Allen, 79
Freud, Sigmund, 1, 40–46, 49, 53, 58, 60

"gay gene," 149
gender comparable roles, 176–77. *See also* dominance and dependence
gender differences in mental disorders, 119, 122, 125–26, 128–29
  social distress and, 173–74
generational effects on mental disorder, 164–65. *See also* genetic foundations of mental disorders
genetic factors, 238nn. 7, 8, 9, 239nn. 15, 16
  separation of environmental forces from, 136
  See also specific disorders
genetic foundations of mental disorders
  findings regarding, 142–46
  individual and population risk and, 152–54
  inter-individual and inter-group differences and, 151–52
  and minimization of environmental influences, 150–51
  what is inherited, 146–48

genetic inheritance, as environment specific, 149
genetic vulnerability, 147–49
genetics, 133, 134, 155–56
  as ideology, 154–55
genotype, 146–47
Griesinger, Wilhelm, 39
group therapies, 234n. 4
Gulf War Syndrome, 240n. 19

hallucinations, 25, 26
health insurance
  coverage of psychotherapy, 75
  See also managed care; reimbursement systems
Helzer, John, 71
Hemingway, Ernest, 33
homosexuality, 149
hysteria, 118–21
  changes in prevalence of, 118, 120
hysterical symptoms, 43, 44

identity, personal, 237n. 7
immigrants, 127
insurance. *See* health insurance
internal mechanisms, dysfunctional, 22–24, 28, 35, 89, 158, 223, 234n. 2
  causes of, 23–24
    vs. choosing not to function/conform, 23, 35, 93
    social factors as, 24, 29–31
    See also dynamic psychiatry
internalized feelings and disorders, 128–29
Interpretation of Dreams, The (Freud), 42

Jackson, S. W., 182, 203–4
Jews, attraction to dynamic psychiatry, 48–50, 63–64

Kadushin, C., 69–70
Kraepelin, Emil, 39, 68, 69
Kramer, Peter, 187
Kuhn, Thomas, 56–57, 64

labeling mental disorders, 116
Laing, R. D., 62, 63
Lamarckian inheritance, 164